On the Ancient History of the Silk Road

On the Ancient History of the Silk Road

Chuanming Rui
Shanghai Academy of Social Sciences, China

World Scientific

NEW JERSEY • LONDON • SINGAPORE • BEIJING • SHANGHAI • HONG KONG • TAIPEI • CHENNAI • TOKYO

Published by

World Scientific Publishing Co. Pte. Ltd.
5 Toh Tuck Link, Singapore 596224
USA office: 27 Warren Street, Suite 401-402, Hackensack, NJ 07601
UK office: 57 Shelton Street, Covent Garden, London WC2H 9HE

Library of Congress Cataloging-in-Publication Data
Names: Rui, Chuanming, author.
Title: On the Ancient history of the Silk Road / Chuanming Rui,
　　Shanghai Academy of Social Sciences, China.
Other titles: Si lu gu shi san lun. English.
Description: New Jersey : World Scientific, [2021] | Includes index.
Identifiers: LCCN 2020056882 | ISBN 9789811232961 (hardcover) |
　　ISBN 9789811234477 (paperback) | ISBN 9789811232978 (ebook) |
　　ISBN 9789811232985 (ebook other)
Subjects: LCSH: Silk Road--History. | Asia, Central--History. | China--Foreign relations--To 1644.
Classification: LCC DS329.4 .R852313 2021 | DDC 950--dc23
LC record available at https://lccn.loc.gov/2020056882

British Library Cataloguing-in-Publication Data
A catalogue record for this book is available from the British Library.

丝路古史散论
Originally published in English by Fudan University Press
Copyright © Fudan University Press 2017
Sponsored by Chinese Fund for the Humanities and Social Sciences

Copyright © 2021 by World Scientific Publishing Co. Pte. Ltd.

All rights reserved. This book, or parts thereof, may not be reproduced in any form or by any means, electronic or mechanical, including photocopying, recording or any information storage and retrieval system now known or to be invented, without written permission from the publisher.

For photocopying of material in this volume, please pay a copying fee through the Copyright Clearance Center, Inc., 222 Rosewood Drive, Danvers, MA 01923, USA. In this case permission to photocopy is not required from the publisher.

For any available supplementary material, please visit
https://www.worldscientific.com/worldscibooks/10.1142/12180#t=suppl

Desk Editors: George Vasu/Lixi Dong

Typeset by Stallion Press
Email: enquiries@stallionpress.com

About the Author

Chuanming Rui obtained his PhD in history from Fudan University. He is a researcher at Shanghai Academy of Social Sciences and a visiting professor at National Institute for Advanced Humanistic Studies, Fudan University. His main research fields include the history of Sino-foreign relations, the ancient history of Central Eurasia and the Silk Road. He has published some books in Chinese including *A Comparative Study on the Symbols of China and the West*; *A History of Cultural Intercourses between China and Central Asia*; *Studies on Ancient Turkic Inscriptions*; *Studies on Manicheism in the East and Studies on the Ancient Silk Road*. In addition, he has translated and published several English masterpieces into Chinese, such as *History of Civilizations of Central Asia Vol. 1*, edited by UNESCO, and *The Elementary Forms of the Religious Life* by Emile Durkheim.

Preface

Since this book takes *Silk Road* as the topic and title, I shall give this term a definition, at least a general one for this monograph.

At first, "Silk Road" was only a phrase used by scholars in a small sphere, and was not strictly defined. Later, in pace with the deepening and extensive academic research, this name was becoming more and more popular, and even frequently appeared in documents of the Chinese government and articles of the mass media in the mid-2010s. It is now a well-known term among the people because of its rich connotations in international economic construction and cultural communications. For everyone, including the scholar inventing this term, it is indeed an unexpected piece of matter.

The first appearance of the "Silk Road" should date back to the 19th century. Ferdinand von Richthofen, the famous German geographer, applied the new term "Silk Road" in his related writings. He had been to China and other regions of the Far East twice in the 60s and 70s of the 19th century. In the second investigation, he spent four years traveling over a dozen provinces in China. Since then, a monograph about China was written by Richthofen. Several decades later, a masterpiece with a total of five volumes was published completely and titled *China* when Mr. Richthofen had already passed away.[1]

In ancient China, especially in the eras before the Tang Dynasty, external communications with other parts of Eurasia were mainly carried out through land ways, which started from northwestern China. And, the main product exported by the Chinese was quality silk. Hence, Richthofen called these long terrestrial passages the "Silk Road", which corresponded to the word "Seidenstrasse" in German, his native language.

The "Silk Road" defined by Richthofen roughly comprises the thoroughfares located in the areas northwest of China proper. It starts from the Weishui 渭水 river basin, goes through the *Western Regions* 西域, the present Xinjiang Province, and crosses "Central Asia" in a narrow sense, namely, Kyrgyzstan, Uzbekistan and Tajikistan. Therefrom, many roads lead toward South Asia, Aral Sea, Caspian Sea, Persia and so on. Finally, the "Silk Road" arrived at Syria. Of course, via some waterways in the Mediterranean, one could continue his travel from Syria and reach Istanbul in Turkey or Rome in Italy.

Later, in the wake of the "Silk Road" becoming more famous among the public and its significance manifesting more obviously, the definition of it became more perfect, and involved roads of wider scope. Generally speaking, it may be classified into "two major categories and three primary routes". That is to say, the two major categories consist of the "Terrestrial Silk Road" and "Maritime Silk Road"; the three primary routes consist of the "Steppe Silk Road", "Oasis Silk Road" and "Maritime Silk Road". The "three primary routes" are included in the "two major categories".

A brief description of the "three primary routes" is given as follows. The so-called "Steppe Silk Road" usually refers to the roads starting from the north of Yellow River valley, accessing the Mongolian Plateau, passing through the Siberian steppe, reaching the northern shores of the Aral Sea, Caspian Sea and Black Sea, and even the farther regions of Eastern Europe. Because these roads mainly pass through the steppes in which the nomads lived for thousands of years, they are together called the "Steppe Silk Road". The "Oasis Silk Road" refers to the roads starting from North China, passing through the western region of the Yellow River and Tarim Basin, crossing Central Asia, leading to West Asia, Asia Minor or South Asia. Most of these roads go across the oases in the deserts, so they are named the "Oasis Silk Road". As for the "Maritime Silk Road", their beginning points are distributed along the coastal areas of China, and passing through Southeast Asia, Sri Lanka and India, these sea routes reach the Red Sea, the Mediterranean and the east coast of Africa. They are called the "Maritime Silk Road" because of all the routes going through the oceans.

Recently, a new expression of the Silk Road has been that of "Three Major Silk Roads". That is to say, the Silk Roads are divided into three categories. One of them is the "Northwestern Silk Road"; it is a name for the terrestrial routes starting from northwestern China. The second one is the "Maritime Silk Road", which may differentiate into two routes, namely, "South Route" leading to Southeast Asia, West Asia and North Africa and "East Route" leading to Korea and Japan. The third one is the "Southwestern Silk Road", which starts from southwestern China, passes through Sichuan and Yunnan Provinces, and connects Myanmar, India and Central Asia.

Despite the different viewpoints on the definition of "Silk Road", we may find easily that the so-called "Silk Road" is in fact a wide traffic network spreading all over the Asia, Europe and Africa of the ancient world instead of one or some thoroughfares. In other words, such traffic networks will certainly exist in any region as long as humans inhabit that place. Exactly for this reason, it is impossible that the ancient people transported only silks through these traffic networks. Perhaps the proportion of silk was very low in some people's commodities, leading to no silk deals in many regions. In spite of this fact, all these roads on lands and waters are still called the "Silk Road"; even those having been named the "Ceramic Road", "Rhubarb Road" and "Musk Road" could be included in the "Silk Road" in a broad sense.

Therefore, today's "Silk Road" is no longer a simple concept of roads or traffic, nor is it a concept of sole silk trading. In fact the term "Silk Road" signifies a comprehensive communication of economy, culture, politics, military and even population between ancient China and foreign countries. For this reason, we may think the ancient history of the "Silk Road" is roughly equivalent to the "history of communication between China and foreign countries" in ancient times.

The aim of bringing about the above conclusion is to emphasize that all contents of Sino-foreign exchanges which will be discussed in this book may be regarded as the ancient history of the "Silk Road". My specialized field deals with the "history of ancient Sino-foreign relations", "history of ancient Central Asia" and more. Obviously, these topics are inextricably linked to the "Silk Road". In my nearly hundred papers, many of them have dealt with the material exchanges between ancient China and foreign countries, such as the relationship between foreign fine horses and Chinese political and social development, as well as the features and effects of the silk export. In addition, some papers discussed the interactions between the nomads of Central Eurasia and the rulers of China, such as the analysis of the reasons, methods and functions for the "intermarriage" policy, and discussion of the role played by the Turks in world history. Furthermore, I studied the Sogdians on the Silk Road, probing into their enormous influence on Chinese economy, culture, religion, politics and even military affairs. Finally, I discussed more about the issue of religious and cultural communication on the Silk Road, focusing on the Manichaeism of the East.

Over dozens of years, I have studied some topics, in a scope not too small, such as the communication of material and spiritual civilizations on the Silk Road, the "Western Foreigner" 西胡 and the "Northern Foreigner" 北胡, geographical research on the "Silk Road", the spreading of ancient foreign religions and the Sino-foreign exchanges involving economic, cultural and military aspects. In this book, though the content basically touches upon the topics mentioned above, it should not be regarded as a systematic study on the ancient history of the "Silk Road" after all. In other words, this book only pays attention to some important issues of the "Silk Road", but is not a comprehensive study on it.

In spite of this shortage, there are still many new opinions and original ideas in this book. Some of them have been accepted by many scholars already, or have offered enlightenment to the academic world. What I want to emphasize is that this book is not a collection of my papers, but a redescription of the important topics on the ancient Silk Road which I have studied. In order to help the common readers understand the content better, I give certain number of explanations and brief introductions in some places. If both the scholars and the common readers could obtain benefit from the reading of this book, I will be very satisfied.

This book, which is not very large and nor excellent, is offered to the readers who are keen to explore the ancient history of the Silk Road. Good luck to all readers.

Chuanming Rui
January 2020

Contents

About the Author	v
Preface	vii
Part I The Silk Road and the Nomads	**1**
Chapter 1 Foreign Fine Horses and the Sino-Foreign Intercourses	**3**
1. The Steeds of Rulers in Ancient Times	3
2. The Horse Cultures Derived from Foreign Countries	23
Chapter 2 The Purpose and Effect of Silk Exportation	**39**
1. The Main Purposes of Chinese Silk Exportation	40
2. The Influence of Silk Export on the World	57
Chapter 3 Intermarriage as a Political Weapon Among the Powers	**69**
1. Intermarriage Aimed at Alleviating the Hostility from Other Powers	71
2. Intermarriage Aimed at Ingratiating and Rewarding the External Tribes	76
3. Intermarriage Aimed at Sowing Discord among Tribes Abroad	80
4. Intermarriage Aimed at Competing with Chinese Adversary by the Aid of External Forces	84
5. A Brief Comment on the Pros and Cons of Intermarriage	91

Chapter 4   餛飩 Huntun and 渾脫 Huntuo Derive from the Nomads — **99**
1. Wonton 餛飩 is a Kind of Foreign Food — 99
2. Huntuo 渾脫 is the Invention of the Nomads — 101
3. Huntuo Hat 渾脫帽 and Huntuo Dance 渾脫舞 — 106

Chapter 5   On the Etymon of Taohuashi 桃花石 — **111**
1. Different Perspectives Relevant to this Topic — 112
2. 大漢 Dahan Has the Most Lasting Reputation and the Greatest Impact Among the Barbarians — 116
3. The Pronunciation of Dahan and Tabγač — 120
4. A Speculation about the Etymon of 大家 Dajia and 宅家 Zhaijia — 122

Chapter 6   The *Prehistoric* Habitations of the Turks and Their Migration — **127**
1. Historical Facts Revealed by Legends of the Turkic Origin — 128
2. The Name "阿史那" Manifests Its Origin of Caspian Sea — 130
3. The Asena Turks were Expert in Smelting of Iron — 133
4. The Asena's Institutions were Similar to that of the Khazars — 135
5. The Asena's Official Titles were Similar to that of the Khazars — 138
6. The Asena's Customs were Similar to those of the Peoples in the Caspian Region — 141
7. Other Elements in the Culture of the Asena Turks — 144
8. The Possible Routes of Migration of the Asena Turks — 146

Part II   The Sogdians, the Special Role on the Silk Road — **149**

Chapter 7   On the Distinction Between 粟特 Sute and 粟弋 Suyi — **151**
1. The Geographic Environment and Political History of Soghd — 151
2. An Investigation on 粟弋 Suyi — 165

Chapter 8   The Economic and Cultural Activities of the Sogdians in China — **179**
1. 酒家胡 Jiujiahu in Inland China — 179
2. The Spread of Exotic Music and Dance in Inland China — 189

Chapter 9	**The Influence and Domination of the Sogdians on the Nomads**	**205**
1.	The Sogdians and the Turk Khanate	205
2.	The Sogdians and the Uighur Khanate	214
Chapter 10	**Military and Political Advantages of the Sogdians: Taking the Five Dynasties as an Example**	**225**
1.	The Sogdians were Valorous and Adept at Fighting	225
2.	The Sogdians were Good at Politics	233
3.	The Reasons for Thriving of the Sogdian Military and Political Officials	241
Chapter 11	**On the Meaning and Origin of 曳落河 Yeluohe and 柘羯 Zhejie**	**245**
1.	Various Opinions about 曳落河 Yeluohe and 柘羯 Zhejie	245
2.	The Basic Features of *Yeluohe* and *Zhejie*	248
3.	The Institution of Slave Army in the Ottoman Empire	254
4.	The Possible Common Origin of Yeluohe-Zhejie and Solak-Spahi	258

Part III	**Silk Road and the Spread of Religious Ideas**	**261**
Chapter 12	**The Symbol Swastika in China**	**263**
1.	The Date When the Swastika Becomes a Chinese Character	263
2.	Swastika in Ancient China	266
3.	The Relations between Chinese Character 卍 and Indian Cultures	269
4.	A Discussion on 室利靺蹉 Shilimocuo and 塞縛悉底迦 Saifuxidijia	272
5.	The Meaning of Swastika in Ancient China	274
6.	A Brief Conclusion	280
Chapter 13	**Discussion on the Relations between 饕餮 Taotie and Greedy Demon**	**281**
1.	The Related Records in Chinese Ancient Literatures	281
2.	The Main Viewpoints and Conflicting Opinions of Modern Times	284
3.	Āz or Greedy Demon in the West Asia	289
4.	On the Relationship Between Taotie 饕餮 and Greedy Demon	295

Chapter 14	On the Origin of the Title Mani	**305**
1.	The *Maṇi Buddha* in Buddhist Sutras	306
2.	The Meaning of "Maṇi" in Buddhist Sutras	307
3.	Manichean Ideas about the "Maṇi" or Pearl	313
4.	Analysis and Deduction	317

Chapter 15	Origins and Variations of the Belief in "Killing Someone in Order to Save Him"	**323**
1.	The Belief in "Killing Someone in Order to Save Him" in Ancient China	324
2.	Teachings Forbidding Killing in Manicheism	333
3.	The Manichean Concept of Light Elements	337
4.	A Brief Conclusion	347

Chapter 16	A Speculation on the Possible Manichean Influence on Wuzetian and Baijuyi	**351**
1.	About the Religious Ideas of Wuzetian 武則天	351
2.	The Poem on Manicheism Said to be Written by Baijuyi 白居易	365

Index of Chinese Literatures	379
Index	387

Part I

The Silk Road and the Nomads

The Japanese scholar Shiratori Kurakichi 白鳥庫吉 used to come up with a penetrating conclusion to epitomize the relations between ancient China and inhabitants in Central Eurasia: "Rivalries between the South and the North; Intercourses between the East and the West." It has been accepted almost by the whole academic circle. What this conclusion mainly emphasizes is that the northern nomads often intruded with force into the farming areas in the south, while the residents of the East and the West interacted peacefully in most cases. Obviously, during those ages, the nomads living in the North of China and Central Eurasia were the protagonists of the historical process, and were called 北胡 *beihu* (the Northern Foreigners or the Northern Barbarians) by the Chinese.

In ancient China, the so-called 胡 *Hu* was a proper name used to refer to the non-Han nationality people living both outside and inside China. That is to say, geographically, the *Hu* originate from the external countries or frontier regions. As far as blood is concerned, the *Hu* did not have any blood relationship with the Han people. In terms of the culture, the *Hu* were very backward in civilization. More concretely, the *Hu* could be divided into 西胡 *xihu* (the Western Foreigner), 北胡 *beihu* (the Northern Foreigner) and 東胡 *donghu* (the Eastern Foreigner), depending on their relative locations with China proper. The *Beihu*, the nomads who lived in Central Eurasia and the north of China, had great influences on the politics and militaries of the Chinese dynasties. I will cite several examples here to discuss briefly some important events that occurred on the Silk Road, and show the enormous impact of the nomads who established close relations with Chinese governments.

Chapter 1

Foreign Fine Horses and the Sino-Foreign Intercourses

1. The Steeds of Rulers in Ancient Times

According to an ancient geographical concept, the area of ancient *China* 中國 was far less than that of present *China*. Generally speaking, *China* was defined only by the jurisdiction of one or some relatively powerful regimes which were centered in Chinese mainland. Therefore, in terms of the origin of fine horses, their places of production are almost always thought of as "external countries", even if these regions are actually provinces of present China, such as Inner Mongolia, Xinjiang 新疆 and Qinghai 青海.

The famous horses in historical records, especially the horses associated with emperors, were almost all from the "external countries". *Shiyiji* 拾遺記 (*Supplementary Notes*) was written in the Eastern Jin Dynasty 東晉 (317–420), which says King Mu of Zhou 周穆王 (the 11th–10th century BC) possessed eight swift horses. The first one of them was named 絕地 Juedi: while it ran, it was like a bolt of lightning, and the four hooves did not even touch the ground. The second one was called 翻羽 Fanyu: it ran very fast and even surpassed the birds. The third one's name was 奔霄 Benxiao: it could travel thousands of miles overnight. The fourth one was called 超影 Chaoying: it could keep up with the movement of the sun. The fifth one was named 逾輝 Yuhui: its fur was sleek just like the light. The sixth one was called 超光 Chaoguang: its speed was not inferior to light, and ten shadows would emerge while it was running. The seventh one was called 騰霧 Tengwu: it ran so fast that it made the rider feel as if he were flying in the clouds. The eighth one was named 挾翼 Jiayi: it had wings on its flanks. King Mu of Zhou traveled for long distances by a carriage, which was driven by these eight horses in turn.[1]

It seems that these eight horse names recorded by *Shiyiji* hardly showed their "foreign colors". However, similar records in an earlier book *Mutianzizhuan* 穆天子傳 (*Tale of King Mu, Son of Heaven*) reveal obviously that they all originated from regions outside. *Mutianzizhuan* gives names for these eight horses as 赤驥 Chiji, 盜驪 Daoli, 白義 Baiyi, 踰輪 Yulun, 山子 Shanzi, 渠黃 Quhuang, 華騮 Hualiu and 綠耳 Lüer, respectively. We can find that most of these names are actually transliterated from the Turkic languages, if we make some inquiries. Here are several instances.[2]

The first item I am going to discuss is the appellation *Daoli* 盜驪. There are different names for this steed in various antiquarian works, such as 駣騋, 桃騋 and 駣騄.[3] Though the forms of them are different, they are pronounced as the same "taoli", which is similar to "daoli" 盜驪. Evidently, all of them should be the transliterated names from a certain foreign word. Some claim that 驪 li means black, and 盜驪 daoli means the black horse with a slender neck, as if the Chinese characters of this name contain the meanings related to horse. In fact, however, this is a wrong opinion. When a comprehensive comparison of these different names is made, we will certainly arrive at the conclusion of *transliteration*.

---

[1] Cf. *Shiyiji* 拾遺記 (*Supplementary Notes*) fasc. 3, collated and annotated by Qi Zhiping 齊志平, Zhonghua Book Company 中華書局, 1981, p. 60. The Chinese text is as follows: "王馭八龍之駿: 一名絕地, 足不踐土; 二名翻羽, 行越飛禽; 三名奔霄, 夜行萬里; 四名超影, 逐日而行; 五名踰輝, 毛色炳耀; 六名超光, 一形十影; 七名騰霧, 乘雲而奔; 八名挾翼, 身有肉翅。遞而駕焉, 按轡徐行, 以匝天地之域。"

[2] A study on the foreign origin of fine horses of Chinese emperors is in my paper "Original Names of Horses in the Possession of Zhoumuwang and Tangtaizong" (周穆王唐太宗駿馬名號考), *Jinan History* 暨南史學, No. 1, Jinan University Press 暨南大學出版社, 2002, pp. 19–29.

[3] The original Chinese text is in *Guangyashuzheng* 廣雅疏證: "《史記·秦本紀》'造父得驥溫驪', 徐廣云: '溫, 一作盜.' 《索隱》云: '鄒誕生本作駣, 音陶.' 則盜驪即此駣。... 《玉篇》作桃; 《御覽》引《廣雅》, 亦作 '桃'; 《集韻》云: '駣, 獸名, 似馬.'" See Wangniansun 王念孫, *Guangyashuzheng*, fasc. 10b, Commercial Press 商務印書館, 1935, in *Congshujichengchubian* 叢書集成初編, p. 1486.

In ancient Turkic dialects, the words toruğ, doruğ, doru, etc., all mean horses with chestnut and auburn colors. For example, in a sentence of *The Kül Tigin Inscription*, "Thirdly, he mounted Yigän Silig Beg's dressed bay horse and attacked"[4] (the 33rd line of the east side), the "bay horse" is quite rightly the English translation of the Turkic word toruğ, and it is the same as doruğ or doru existing in other Turkic dialects today. Undoubtedly, their pronunciation is quite close to that of Daoli 盜驪, so it is reasonable to think that 盜驪 may be a transliteration of the horse name in Turkic dialects.

On the contrary, the same conclusion could be drawn from a principle taking account both of pronunciation and meaning. Husanxing 胡三省 explains the sentence "the horse ridden by Yaoxiang is named Limeigua 襄所乘駿馬曰䯁眉騧" of *Zizhitongjian* 資治通鑒, and thinks that 䯁 li means yellowish black color. So, the words 驪 and 䯁 are similar both in the pronunciation and meaning. Therefore, the designation Daoli 盜驪 indicates the meaning of yellowish black, namely, chestnut, auburn and bay. Apparently, Daoli 盜驪, one of the eight fine horses owned by King Mu of the Zhou, was of the foreign origin.

The second instance is 白義 Baiyi, also one of the swift horses in the possession of King Mu of Zhou. It is called 白犧 Baixi in 列子 *Liehtzu*, a Taoist text attributed to Lieyukou 列御寇, and 奔霄 Benxiao in *Shiyiji* 拾遺記. Though the word Benxiao seems to suggest a meaning of "running (thousands of miles) overnight", it is still a transliteration after a phonetic comparison of it with *Baiyi* and *Baixi*. Besides, Baiyi 白義 will show more clearly its foreign origin when comparing it with the appellation of fine horses obtained by Emperor Wu of Han 漢武帝 (r. 141–87 BC) from the Western Regions.

According to *Shiji* (史記, *The Records of the Grand Historian*), after the expedition of Dawan 大宛 (approximately Fergana nowadays), Emperor Wu of the Han obtained some swift horses called 蒲梢 Pushao. *Hanshu* 漢書 (*History of the Former Han*) has a similar record: After opening up of communication with Fergana and Parthia, "After that, treasures like pearls, tortoiseshell, rhinoceros horn, and peacock feathers filled his harem, and horses like Pushao, Dragon-pattern, Fisheye, and Blood Sweat horses filled the Imperial Palace; herds of elephants, lions,

---

[4] Talāt Tekin, *A Grammar Orkhon Turkic*, Indiana University Press, 1968, p. 269.

bulldogs, and ostriches are fed in the enclosure."⁵ The designation 蒲梢 Pushao in *History of the Former Han* is also written as 蒲騷 Pusao or 蒲捎 Pushao in other literatures. Thus, we are sure the horse name Pushao 蒲梢 is a transliterated one.

Generally speaking, the pronunciations of all these Chinese names, such as 白義 Baiyi, 白犧 Baixi, 奔霄 Benxiao, 蒲梢 Pushao, 蒲騷 Pusao and 蒲捎 Pushao, could be attributed to an approximate pronunciation of the Turkic words *bo:z at* or *bo:z yunt*, both of them meaning grey or dark grey horse. Among the nomads of ancient Central Eurasia, light colored horses were reserved for high-ranking personages. For example, in the Oghuz epics, the great Khan Bayindir, "the axis of Turkestan", rode a *boz* horse. In the Alexander romances of the early Anatolian literature, the immortal Khidr also rode a *boz* horse.⁶ So, it is possible that 白義 Baiyi or 蒲梢 Pushao was a kind of fine horse dedicated to Chinese Emperors by tribal chiefs in Central Eurasia.

Third, we will talk about the 華騮 Hualiu of King Mu of Zhou. In his annotation for *Mutianzizhuan*, Guopu 郭璞 (276–324) of the Jin Dynasty explained that the color of 華騮 hualiu is yellow and reddish, and is really the so-called 棗騮 Zaoliu. That means Hualiu should be a horse with yellow and red fur. Interestingly, the ancient Turks are familiar with a kind of horse, which is called kula:; its pronunciation is similar to Chinese characters hualiu 華騮. Besides, the color of the kula: is said to be yellow or yellowish brown, bay and umber. Anyhow, its fur is similar to yellow, brown and tan, which is closed to the color of 華騮 Hualiu depicted in Chinese literature.

Another piece of evidence showing the foreign origin of Hualiu is that this kind of horse has always been regarded as a rare and noble mount. Zangi, a medieval scholar, mentioned the horse qula or kula, which is fawn colored, and also has auspicious black spots, black back-lines, mane and tail. The kula named by the Turks is considered a solar horse and has been represented as a royal mount in many Ottoman paintings. Besides,

---

⁵Cf. *Hanshu* 漢書 (*History of the Former Han*), fasc. 96b, Zhonghua Book Companyk 中華書局, 1962, p. 3928. The Chinese text is as follows: "聞天馬、蒲陶則通大宛、安息。自是之後，名珠、文甲、通犀、翠羽之珍盈於後宮，蒲梢、龍文、魚目、汗血之馬充於黃門，鉅象、師子、猛犬、大雀之群食於外囿。"
⁶Cf. Emil Esin, "The Horse in Turkic Art", *Central Asiatic Journal*, Vol. 10, No. 3–4, 1965, pp. 176–177.

In Başkurdistan, semi-wild fawn horses with black lines on the spine are considered the issue of the aquatic stallions of the Volga.[7]

George Vernadsky relates that an Ossetian scholar had told him that some good breed horses of the Alans survived in the Eisk region on the east coast of the Azov Sea until the Russian Revolution of 1917. Among these elite horses, the most valued are the roan ones, which are called *xalas* (pronounced as *khalas*) in Ossetian dialect, literally of "hoar-frost" color. They have a black stripe along the back; the mane and the tail likewise are black. This Ossetian scholar once owned a horse like this. He described the horse as "tall, lean, and swift like the tempest".[8] Obviously, the xalas mentioned by this Ossetian scholar is actually the fine horse kula:, kula or qula designated by the Turks.

From here, we see that the elite horse Hualiu of King Mu of the Zhou should be Foreign Horse 胡馬 kula:, xalas, etc., deriving from Central Eurasia. In addition to the above-mentioned cases, other horses of King Mu of the Zhou also quite clearly originated from foreign countries. For example, the 踰輪 Yulun is likely to be a transliterated name of the Turkic yegren, for the latter means bay horse or chestnut horse. Again, 渠黃 Quhuang may be the transliteration of the Turkic kuba:, which means dark yellow and dark brown, and is often referred to the coat colors of horse, cattle and other animals. All these points of evidence distinctly indicate that the eight horses driven by King Mu of the Zhou during his Western Tour were all good breed horses from external countries. Thus, we could speculate that more than 3000 years ago, the elite breeding horses originating from foreign regions played an important role in the social life, traffic and even military activities of the Chinese regimes.

In addition to the 八駿 *Bajun* (The Eight Steeds) owned by King Mu of Zhou 周穆王, the 昭陵六駿 *Zhaolingliujun* (The Six Steeds of Zhao Mausoleum) of Taizong of the Tang 唐太宗 (r. 626–649) are also famous in Chinese history. All of these six horses surely had foreign origins. One of them was 颯露紫 Saluzi, which was the most favorite horse of Taizong. *Cefuyuangui* 冊府元龜 (*Outstanding models from the storehouse literature*) gives a detailed description about the merits of 颯露紫 Saluzi: "The Emperor owned a horse named 馺露紫霜 Saluzishuang. Whenever he fights with the enemy, he rides on it. The horse runs fast and leaps nimbly,

---

[7] Emil Esin, "The Horse in Turkic Art", *Central Asiatic Journal*, Vol. 10, No. 3–4, 1965, p. 191.
[8] George Vernadsky, *The Origins of Russia*, Oxford University Press, 1959, p. 19.

thus helps the Emperor to smash the enemy and win the victory. On one occasion the Emperor attacks the army of Wangshichong 王世充 (?–621) at 蓋馬坊 Gaimafang for a long time. The horse is shot by an arrow, and jumps up on an old embankment. Qiuxinggong 丘行恭 pulls out the arrow, but the horse dies soon. The Emperor greatly mourned for the horse and set a stone statue for it."[9] This passage depicts vividly this gallant steed, and also reveals a valuable fact, namely, that the horse name Saluzi 颯露紫 is probably a transliteration, because the other Chinese name of it, *Saluzishuang* 馺露紫霜, pronounces the same as the former.

The pronunciation of the characters 颯 and 馺 is exactly the same in medieval Chinese, while the 露 is pronounced as *luo'*. As we know, there was a famous horse in ancient Central Eurasia, with a name is similar to 颯露紫. It is said that in the Caspian region there was a fine horse resembling the horse *xalas*, which was called *saurag* in the Alan dialect, and meant "black spine (horse)". These horses were so distinguished that even the tribes or their chiefs took it as their own names. As an example, an Alanic chieftain of the late fourth century who joined the Goths in the latter's drive to the Balkans was called Safrac. This is apparently the Latin transliteration of the Alanic word saurag (literally "black back"), the name of a breed of horses somewhat resembling the *xalas* (*chalyi*) horses.[10]

Allen says that the most valued breed of Kabardian horse is called *shaulokh* in Circassian, and there is a breed of Arabian horses called *shalua* in Arabic. The Circassian term derives from the Alanic, and the Arabic possibly from the Circassian. In his book, Allen gives an example of how highly prized the shaulokh horses were. For such a horse, David Soslan, the Ossetian consort of Queen Thamar of Georgia, paid a village and a castle.[11] Apparently, the horse saurag was so excellent that it was just like the 汗血馬 hanxuema (*Blood Sweat Horse*) in the palace of Wudi of the Han 漢武帝.

On the one hand, saurag was a very precious and famous horse in ancient Central Eurasia; on the other hand, its pronunciation is similar to

---

[9] Cf. *Cefuyuangui* 冊府元龜 (*Outstanding models from the storehouse literature*, photo reprint, Zhonghua Book Company 中華書局, 1960), fasc. 42, p. 477. The Chinese text is as follows: "初, 帝有駿馬, 名馺露紫霜, 每臨陣多乘之, 騰躍摧鋒, 所向皆捷。嘗討王世充于隋蓋馬坊, 酣戰移景, 此馬為流矢所中, 騰上古堤, 右庫直丘行恭拔箭, 而後馬死。至是追念不已, 刻石立其像焉。"

[10] Cf. George Vernadsky, *The Origins of Russia*, Oxford, 1959, p. 19.

[11] Cf. W.E.D. Allen, *A History of the Georgian People*, London, 1932, pp. 332–333.

that of *salu* 飒露, so we have a good reason to regard saurag as the pronouncing origin for 飒露紫 salu purple, one of the 昭陵六骏 (*Six Steeds of Zhao Mausoleum*). As for the character 紫 zi (purple) in the Chinese name, it probably refers to the color of the horse fur. Since saurag means "black spine", the coat of it may be mainly brunet. Thus, the Chinese translation 紫 (purple) is rather suitable.

Another instance is 特勒骠 Telebiao, which is also one of the Six Steeds of the Zhao Mausoleum owned by Taizong of the Tang. The inscriptions on the existing stone tablet for the six horses have been seriously eroded, so it is difficult to identify now. So, we have to cite the horse names and the words according to 六骏图讃辩 *Liujuntuzanbian* (*Remark and Analysis on the Six Steeds*) written by Zhangchao 張玿 (1625–1694?) in the Qing Dynasty. In this writing, the horse name is 特勒骠 telebiao, instead of the prevalent name 特勤骠 teqinbiao.

The reason for 特勒 tele being changed into 特勤 teqin is a misunderstanding; that is to say, in ancient books, the official title 特勤 teqin of the Turks is often miswritten as 特勒 tele, thus some scholars changed almost all 特勒 tele into 特勤 teqin. Apparently, this is a wrong idea and an inappropriate practice. The correct name of the fine horse here ought to be 特勒, for the following reason. As a general rule for elite horse designation, the name is either in accordance with its coat color or the tribe it came from. So, it is not uncommon that the name of the horse is exactly the same as that of its place of origin or its tribe. For example, almost all the 蕃馬 fanma (the foreign horses) of the Tang Dynasty were named after the tribes breeding them. Some records say the following: "The 拔曳固馬 bayegu horse is similar to the 骨利幹馬 guligan horse. Many of them have the coat with black spots, just like leopard." "The 延陀馬 yantuo horse resembles the 同羅馬 tongluo horse. Both of them are originated from 駱馬 luo horse and 驄馬 cong horse." "The 僕固馬 pugu horse is smaller than the 拔曳固馬 bayegu horse, and is similar to the 同羅馬 tongluo horse." "The 突厥馬 tujue horse is distinguished in martial arts. It has a moderate and sturdy stature, running fast and distant, so is the best mount for fighting and hunting." "The 契丹馬 qidan horse is skilled in jumping. Its body is smaller than the tujue horse, so could run nimbly in forest." "The 奚馬 xi horse has a good physique superior to that of qidan horse. The other aspects are the same as qidan horse."[12]

---

[12] See *Tanghuiyao* 唐会要 (*Important Documents of the Tang*), Shanghai Classics Publishing House 上海古籍出版社, 1991), fasc. 72, pp. 1546–1549.

特勒 Tele was also a famous nomadic tribe in the ancient Mongolian plateau or more extensive area. 回紇傳 *Huihezhuan* (*The Biography of the Uighurs*) of 舊唐書 *Jiutangshu* (*Old History of the Tang*) says the following: "The ancestry of the Uighurs is the descendant of the 匈奴 Xiongnu (The Huns). It is known as 鐵勒 Tiele during the Later Wei 後魏 period (386–534). It has a small population, but a strong fighting force. This tribe allies with 高車 Gaoche and is subject to 突厥 Tujue (the Turks). It is renamed 特勒 Tele recently."[13] Hence, we know that the Tele tribe was named the Tiele 鐵勒. According to the *Tiele Biography* of *Suishu* 隋書 (*History of the Sui*), the Tiele was a tribal confederation consisting of various tribes. They were distributed in vast regions of Central Eurasia, and inhabited along the endless valleys and waters. At least forty tribes belonged to this Tiele confederation, such as 僕骨 Pugu, 同羅 Tongluo, 韋紇 Weihe, 拔也古 Bayegu and 薛延陀 Xueyantuo. They extended from the Mongolian Plateau westward to the so-called Western Sea, which might refer to the present Black Sea.[14]

Since the influence of the Tiele or Tele tribes during the Sui and Tang Dynasties was very great, it is reasonable to think that the name "Tele Horse 特勒馬" did exist. Although *Tanghuiyao* does not directly mention "Tele horse", the above-mentioned bayegu horse 拔曳固馬, tongluo horse 同羅馬, pugu horse 僕固馬, yantuo horse 延陀馬, etc., could be called Tele Horse 特勒馬 altogether. Furthermore, even if the Tele Horse 特勒馬 was not named after the tribal title, it is completely possible that it was named after its breeding place. *Tanghuiyao* mentions a place for horse-raising, namely, Wutele *Mountain* 烏特勒山, which was a good pasture, for several kinds of fine horses had gathered there. This Wutele Mountain 烏特勒山 was also called Tele Mountain 特勒山 in other paragraphs. *Tanghuiyao* describes the Wutele or Tele Mountain as follows: "The 回紇馬 Huihe Horse is similar to 僕骨馬 Pugu horse, both of them are settled on the north of Wutele Mountain." "The 俱羅勒馬 Juluole horse is similar to Huihe horse, they are in the north of the Tele Mountain."

---

[13] Cf. *Jiutangshu* 舊唐書, fasc. 195, Zhonghua Book Company 中華書局, 1975, p. 5195.
[14] Cf. *Suishu* 隋書, fasc. 84, Zhonghua Book Company 中華書局, 1973, pp. 1879–1880. A lot of studies have been given to the tens of tribes belonging to Tiele; the views, however, are greatly different. In my paper "A New Study on Tribes of *Tiele*" 鐵勒部落新考 (in *Gansuminzuyanjiu* 甘肅民族研究, 1991, No. 1–2), I point out some mistakes on the tribal names in *Sui Shu* published by Zhonghua Book Company in 1973, and give a new study on 15 very disputable names. It may be a reference for readers.

"The 契苾馬 Qibi horse and the 突厥馬 Tujue horse in south of the Desert belong to same kind. It migrated from Liangzhou 涼州 to the Tele Mountain."[15]

These pieces of evidence show clearly that one of the Six Steeds 六駿 of the Emperor Taizong of the Tang was more likely to be 特勒驃 telebiao rather than 特勤驃 teqinbiao. Undoubtedly, such horses originated from foreign countries.

Though the 八駿 Bajun of King Mu of Zhou and the 六駿 Liujun of the Emperor Taizong of the Tang are very famous in the history, once they are compared with the 汗血馬 Hanxuema (*The Blood Sweat Horse*) of Wudi 武帝 of the Han, they are considerably inferior in terms of the prestige and influence.

The "Blood Sweat Horse 汗血馬" is a title for a kind of good breeding horse, which had been known in classical records for more than 2000 years ago. *Shenyijing* 神異經 (*Miraculous Stories*) depicts this horse as follows: In the southwestern region of Dawan 大宛, there was a kind of fine horse. Its physique was big and tall, with a long mane and tail, as well as strong feet. It could run 1000 *li* 里 in a day, and sweat bloody at noon. The rider had to wrap his head, waist and underbelly to avoid suffering disease, while the natives did not wrap.[16] It was said that this kind of valuable horse that ran a 1000 *li* a day and sweat blood could breed only in Dawan. So, this horse was regarded as extremely precious by the Chinese, especially their rulers.

Wudi of the Han 漢武帝 reigned from 141 to 87 BC. Because the former emperors Wendi 文帝 (r. 180–157 BC) and Jingdi 景帝 (r. 157–141 BC) peacefully constructed for a long period, when emperor Wudi succeeded to throne, the economic strength of the empire was greatly enhanced already. By means of the so-called 鑿空 zaokong (opening the way), namely, a diplomatic expedition led by Zhangqian 張騫 (c.164–113 BC), Wudi associated with many states in the Western Regions 西域,

---

[15] *Tanghuiyao* 唐會要, fasc. 72, pp. 1547–1548.
[16] This paragraph is recorded in *Shenyijing* 神異經 (*Miraculous Stories*) written by Dongfangshuo 東方朔 of the Han Dynasty, and was extracted later by *Yiwenleiju* 藝文類聚 (*Collection of Literature Arranged by Categories*) written in the Tang Dynasty. Cf. *Yiwenleiju*, fasc. 93, punctuated and proofread by Wangshaoying 汪紹楹, Shanghai Classics Publishing House 上海古籍出版社, 1982, p. 1615. The Chinese text is as follows: "西南大宛宛丘, 有良馬, 其大二丈, 鬣至膝, 尾委於地, 蹄如升, 腕可握。日行千里, 至日中而汗血。乘者當以綿絮纏頭、腰、小腹, 以避風病, 其國人不纏也。"

suppressing the Xiongnu 匈奴 to a great extent. His prestige thus spread far away to foreign countries. During those years, the external communication was very frequently more than a dozen or at least five or six diplomatic corps being sent to foreign regions every year. At the same time, many missions of foreign states came to China for return visits or paying tributes to the imperial court. So, the Emperor was very proud of this flourishing scene of 萬國來朝 wanguolaichao (all nations coming to pay tribute).

A certain man having visited Dawan along with a mission told Wudi that a kind of good breed horse was produced there. They were strong and ran swiftly, and most of them existed in the city Ershi 貳師 of Dawan. At first, the envoys wanted to take some horses back at a high price, in order to dedicate them to the Emperor. Unexpectedly, the natives determinedly refused, and even hid the horses to prevent repeatable enquiring by the Chinese.

These words aroused the strong desire of Wudi. He decided to get the Blood Sweat Horses by any means. He believed that as an exalted Chinese emperor, it was by no means a problem for him to gain some fine horses from a barbaric state. Moreover, he did not attempt to get these horses without paying. On the contrary, he intended to buy them at a premium. Thus, he appointed Cheling 車令 as a leader of the official mission visiting Dawan. A lot of money and treasure was carried with them which included a horse statue of pure gold.

When the Dawan government learned about this message, their king discussed it with some high officials. Some people thought it was better to accept the request of the Chinese, because the payment for the horse was so great that they would not suffer losses at all. Besides, if they refused this trade, the Chinese might be very angry, the expeditionary force could be sent, and it would endanger the Dawan regime. Others, however, disagreed with this view. They thought it is extremely far from China to Dawan, and there were countless mountains and waters between the two countries, which were difficult to cross. If the Chinese army went along the northern roads, the fierce nomadic Huns would obstruct them. If they went along the southern roads, the vast desert lacking waters and plants would certainly be a dangerous barrier for them. Some time ago, hundreds of Chinese envoys tried to cross this region, but more than half of them died because of hunger and thirst. Therefore, if a large number of Chinese troops came, they would find it very difficult to succeed. So, the conclusion was that it was unnecessary to worry about the results of refusing to sell horses. At last, the king accepted the latter opinion, namely, refusing to sell the Blood Sweat Horses.

The natives of Dawan not only refused selling the steeds but also abused the Chinese envoys. They boasted that their people were so rich that they did not need the money and treasure of the Chinese at all and their attempt of buying horses was just a delusion. These provocative words and behavior outraged the ambassadors from China. They threw down the golden horse and broke it, and vowed to "destroy the foolish barbarians", departing hatefully. Obviously, this conflict was provoked by the Dawan officials. But, instead of self-examination, they took a more irrational action. They fabricated an excuse of "Chinese insulting us", and demanded that the cavalry stationed along the eastern border of their own country assault the Chinese mission, loot their possessions and even kill all of them. Fortunately, a few persons had fled this country. They returned to China and reported this robbery to the Emperor.

When Wudi learnt the news, he was greatly enraged. He decided immediately to organize an expeditionary army, intending to teach Dawan a good lesson, punishing it severely. One of his important purposes was of course seizing the Blood Sweat Horses by force. Yaodinghan 姚定漢 who once visited Dawan suggested that the military strength of Dawan was actually very weak, so it was enough to annihilate the enemy using 3000 soldiers with strong bows and arrows. The Emperor firmly believed these words, because previously a troop of only seven hundreds cavalrymen had taken the kingdom of Loulan 樓蘭 and captured their king. He thought this expedition was very easy, just like a breeze. For this reason, the Emperor appointed Liguangli 李廣利 as the leader of this expedition army. Liguangli was the elder brother of Lifuren 李夫人, who was one of the wives loved by the Emperor, and bore a son for him. Apparently, this expedition was regarded by Wudi as a great achievement which could be gained easily, so he gave the honorable title "General Ershi 貳師將軍" to Liguangli. It meant that Liguangli would be the great General conquering the city Ershi 貳師 of Dawan and capturing the Blood Sweat Horses.

Liguangli formed an expeditionary force of less strength in 104 BC. He did not pay special attention to the military power of Dawan, so mobilized only 6000 cavalrymen of some feudatory states in the Western Regions, and recruited tens of thousands of young loafers in northwestern

China. This seemingly mighty troop was actually a weak one, and was not better than a motley crew.

Sure enough, the Western Expeditionary Force led by General Ershi, far from wining the expected victory, suffered a lot of obstruction, and even the army provisions became a serious problem that was difficult to solve. The reason for this situation is as follows. Originally, Liguangli believed that when his expeditionary army passed through the countries of the Western Regions, the native people would certainly be willing to provide logistics services. But, the reality was very disappointing, for all these natives were worried about being harassed and plundered by Chinese soldiers, so they shut gates of their cities, and refused to supply food and water for the troops coming from the emperor of Han. The Chinese servicemen were hungry, thirsty and annoyed. Correspondingly, they had to attack these cities and fortresses. Unfortunately, this action aroused more panic and rage among the natives, because it seemed to verify the rumor circulating earlier, which said that the "Chinese Emperor will annex states of the Western Regions." As a natural result, the native folks resisted the Chinese troop more firmly.

In this way, a very sad and vicious circle was formed. On the one hand, the Chinese army intensified the military pressure on the countries of the Western Regions because of their failure to obtain the necessary logistical supplies from them. On the other hand, the more martial pressure these states suffered, the fiercer the resistance they displayed, which resulted in more serious lack of manpower and material resources of the expeditionary troop. Thus, when the General Ershi arrived at the city Yucheng 郁成 on the eastern border of Dawan, there were only a few thousand soldiers available. And, this exhausted army lost a lot again while attacking the city of Yucheng.

At that time, Liguangli no longer had the confidence to carry out the expedition further. He dispiritedly ordered his troops to withdraw. This former domineering expeditionary force now returned eastward dejectedly with the remnants of a routed army. Two years later, they arrived at Dunhuang 敦煌, an important town on the northwestern border of China. The number of their martial members was only one tenth or two tenths as compared with the previous figure. Liguangli wrote a report in Dunhuang and submitted it to the Emperor in the capital. In the report, he said that because of the long distance between China and Dawan, it was very difficult for the logistics of the expeditionary army. Thus, the Chinese soldiers suffered the serious torment of hunger and thirst, and a lot of them died in succession. Then, this general requested the Emperor to allow a postponement of a new expedition, so that his army could obtain the necessary rest and replenishment.

Thus, a "glorious victory" expected by the Wudi two years earlier became a miserable defeat. He felt a great humiliation, but lacked better measures to improve the situation at that time. He had to work off his anger by blaming General Liguangli, accusing him of "disobeying the imperial order" due to the failure of the expedition. As a punishment, Liguangli and his army were not allowed to enter Yumen Pass 玉門關 to return home until they conquered Dawan and gained the Blood Sweat Horse. Anyone daring to enter Yumen Pass would be put to death immediately. Liguangli was forced to obey this order, and temporarily remained in Dunhuang together with his servicemen.

At the same time, the war against the Xiongnu 匈奴 in the north was not successful either. A troop of more than 20000 men led by Zhaoponu 趙破奴 was annihilated completely when it marched deep into the Xiongnu territory. Therefore, many courtiers suggested that the Emperor should refrain from dispatching an expeditionary army again to Dawan in order to strike the Xiongnu with all strength. But, Wudi disagreed with them. He claimed that if the great Han regime could not master the little state of Dawan, it would certainly be despised by the countries farther away, such as Daxia 大夏. Besides, the nearer countries, such as Wusun 烏孫 and Luntai 輪台, might also attempt to revolt. In this way, the great Han Empire would be ridiculed by other countries, on the one hand, and on the other hand, the valued Blood Sweat Horse would never reach the imperial court. Obviously, the real reason for insisting on the second expedition by the Emperor lay in the so-called "reputation" of his regime and coveting the Blood Sweat Horse.

Then, Wudi punished some high officials who objected to the second expedition to Dawan, such as Dengguang 鄧光. At the same time, he recruited soldiers, mobilized manpower and collected material resources on a large scale. They prepared for the second expedition actively. The Emperor provided amnesty to many prisoners and allowed them to serve in the army; he recruited vagrants and knights from the frontier regions. There were a total of 60000 soldiers, 100000 cattle and 30000 horses, as well as tens of thousands of donkeys and camels, which were used to transport foods, clothes, weapons, etc. This time, Wudi carefully and fully prepared for the expedition to ensure that the Chinese won the war. The troops were equipped with a lot of water workers in order to cut off the water source of the enemy during war, as the water resource in Dawan was in rather short supply. The Emperor also appointed two persons as the officials managing horses, so as to pick the finest horses in Dawan. At the same time, there were 180000 border guards stationed in Jiuquan 酒泉 and Zhangye 張掖; those officials serving the prison sentence were also dispatched to provide equipment and transport foods for the expeditionary forces. Such "national mobilization" caused serious turmoil all over the country. People were filled with a lot of hate.

In the third year of the Taichu 太初 reign (102 BC), General Ershi carried on the expedition to Dawan once again. This time, the Chinese force was so strong that none of the states of the Western Regions along the marching lines dared to resist again. Instead, most of them opened the gates of their cities to "greet" these uninvited guests, and strove as much as possible to provide foods and drinks for the soldiers. The regime of Luntai 輪台, however, still refused to yield to the conquerors. Unfortunately, their capital fell after a few days of fierce battle, and a terrible massacre of the city was undertaken by the expeditionary force.

In order to facilitate the march and easily obtain provisions, Liguangli partitioned his troops into several divisions advancing in different courses. He personally commanded a division of 30000 fighters and arrived at the eastern border of Dawan earlier than others. The army of Dawan was defeated by the powerful archers of the Chinese, so they had to retreat to the city of Yucheng 郁成城, intending to entrench it. However, Liguangli no longer wanted to waste time in attacking the city; instead, his troop bypassed the city of Yucheng and directly raided the capital Guishan 貴山. As soon as they reached the city of Guishan, Liguangli gave an order to cut off the city's water supplying sources outside of the capital, thereby seriously disturbing the defenders. Then, he surrounded the city with heavy troops, attacking day and night, for as many as more than 40 days.

Later, the circumstance became increasingly worse. The water was lacking, the outer walls were broken and General Jianmi 煎靡 was captured. The inner city of the capital was also in great danger. Therefore, the Dawan nobles rushed to discuss this situation, trying to find some devices to solve the problem. At last, they decided to sacrifice King Wugua 毋寡 of Dawan as a scapegoat. They killed the King, and sent messengers with the King's head to General Ershi Liguangli, requesting an interview and seeking peace. They conveyed the words of those nobles and high officials as follows:

Initially, only because of the arbitrariness of the King, the natives of Dawan hid the Blood Sweat Horses, raided and killed the Chinese envoys, and robbed their belongings. They operated under the orders of the King. Actually, the King committed monstrous acts. Now, they had executed the King, and offered an apology to the great emperor of the Han. As reparation, General Ershi may extract the best among their horses as their tribute to Chinese Emperor. Besides, they would do their best to supply provisions for the Chinese troops. Their sole requisition was that the Chinese forces end the military action and begin peaceful coexistence with the Dawan regime. If this requisition could not be accepted by General Ershi, the only way for Dawan would be to kill all these precious horses and begin a desperate fight with the Chinese. The result of the latter was not distinct yet, because the reinforcements from Kangju 康居 would arrive soon, the perfect defeat of Dawan was not necessary.

These words showed both the stick and the carrot so that Liguangli did not dare refuse categorically. After repeatedly weighing the pros and cons, he decided to accept Dawan's request of suing for peace. As a result, Liguangli gained dozens of the best Blood Sweat Horses and more than 3000 secondary swift horses. Moreover, he suggested that Meicai 昧蔡, an aristocrat of the pro-China group, inherit the throne. This new king signed a covenant with the Han government, confirming that Dawan was a vassal of the Great Han Empire. When all these affairs were finished, General Ershi Liguangli triumphantly returned eastward together with his troops.

Evidently, Wudi had indeed got the so-called "precious horse" at last, but at a stupendous price. The fact was that in a period of four years, the Emperor mobilized hundreds of thousands of people all over the country, squandered vast amounts of wealth, waged two expeditions and caused a loss of 50000 injuries and deaths, whereas what he achieved was only thirty Blood Sweat Horses and a titular vassal, a small country far away from China. At that time, through many military operations including the expeditions to Dawan, the Emperor of the Han exhausted almost all wealth accumulated by his forefathers over a long period, bringing about national trepidation. The loss was surely greater than the gain. However, as the Emperor of a powerful regime, he did not realize immediately that his wrong actions caused grave suffering to the country and its people. He was very proud of his "expeditionary achievements", thinking that the Blood Sweat Horses were a sign of his "great exploits". So, he granted higher posts to many servicemen who participated in the expeditions, and rewarded them a lot of money and treasure. Two of them were given the title of Marquis, three of them were promoted to 九卿 jiuqing (Nine Chamberlains) and more than 100 people were rewarded an official salary of 120000 kilograms of rice per year.[17]

In addition, Wudi smugly wrote a poem for his fine horse 蒲梢 Pushao originating from Dawan. It said the following: "The Heavenly Horse comes here from the farthest West country. It passes across ten thousand *li* 里 in order to submit to my virtue. I conquer the foreign state by means my authority. When my troops transited the desert, all countries over the world will be obedient to me."[18] This poem shows clearly that the main reason for the self-satisfaction of Wudi was not in fact the excellence of the valued horse originating from Dawan, but the symbolic meaning of the eastern emperor possessing the western fine horse, that is to say, Wudi obtained this precious "heavenly horse" because of his own *Virtue*. The obtaining of the steed represents that all the foreign states submit to the great Han Empire or the Emperor of the Han. In other words, the Emperor's real purpose for seeking for the good breed horse at all costs was to gain his personal prestige or to display the so-called "political significance". Thus, when the minister Jian 汲黯 persuaded the Emperor not to compose a poem for the horse, he was very unhappy.

In later times, there were various reviews and critiques on the two military expeditions to Dawan launched by Emperor Wudi; some eulogized his operations, while some criticized them severely. I will not give a definite judgment here, but just list two facts. First, considering the long-standing benefits, these expeditions were really an active contribution to the communication between China and foreign regions, resulting in the importation of the Blood Sweat Horses from Dawan. Second, in the short term, these wars indeed brought about a tremendous disaster to the Chinese populace and the society. Just for this reason, a dozen years later, the Emperor Wudi issued an edict of self-criticism to repent for his former sins.

By this token, the influence of Wudi's Blood Sweat Horses 汗血馬 on the Chinese regime, whether positive or negative, is much greater than

---

[17] For these stories of the expeditions to Dawan led by General Liguangli, one might refer to *The Account of Dawan* in *Shiji* 史記, fasc. 123, pp. 3174–3178; and *The Biography of Liguangli* in *Hanshu* 漢書, fasc. 61, pp. 2699–2702.

[18] Cf. *Shiji* 史記, fasc. 24, p. 1178. The Chinese text is: "天馬來兮從西極, 經萬里兮歸有德。承威靈兮降外國, 涉流沙兮四夷服。"

that of the Eight Steeds 八駿 owned by King Mu of Zhou and the Six Steeds 六駿 owned by Taizong of the Tang. However, after a brief observation for the measure of introducing foreign horses adopted by King Wuling of Zhao 趙武靈王, we have to admit that his operation exerts an even greater influence on Chinese civilization than that of Wudi of the Han.

King Wuling was the monarch of Zhao Kingdom, one of the seven powerful regimes in the period of the "Warring States" about 2500 years ago. These seven powers were named 齊 Qi, 楚 Chu, 燕 Yan, 韓 Han, 趙 Zhao, 魏 Wei and 秦 Qin. They allied or fought with some others in different phases, forming a fierce and complex struggle that lasted hundreds of years. The domain of the kingdom of Zhao consisted of the northern and middle parts of present Shanxi Province, as well as the western and southern parts of Hebei Province. Among these seven states, the kingdom of Zhao was not the most powerful in terms both of territory or strength. Just after a very aggressive reformation carried out by King Wuling, this country quickly rose in a short period. This famous reformation was designated as 胡服騎射 hufuqishe in Chinese historic records, which means introducing fine horses of the nomads, dressing the same as the nomads and learning from their equestrian skill and archery. As for the specific process of this great reformation having a far-reaching impact on China, a detailed description is given in *Shiji*.[19]

One day in the spring of the 19th year of King Wuling's reign (307 BC), he discussed the political affairs with his courtiers. The King was quite worried about his country because the current international situation was very unfavorable to the kingdom. Though the former kings had adopted many measures to consolidate the national defense, such as construction of the Great Wall and an expedition against Linhu 林胡 (a nomadic tribe), the outcome was not satisfactory at all. At that time, the nomadic foreigners in the region of Zhongshan 中山 became a serious danger for the kingdom of Zhao. The kingdom of Yan 燕 outside the north border was coveting the Zhao regime. Besides, the eastern neighbor was the ambitious Donghu 东胡 (the Tungus). Finally, in the western regions, there were foreign nomads Linhu 林胡 and Loufan 樓煩, as well as the kingdoms of the Qin 秦 and Han 韓, all of them awaiting a good opportunity to conquer the kingdom of Zhao. King Wuling of Zhao said that

---

[19] Cf. *Shiji* 史記, fasc. 43, pp. 1805–1811.

they must do something to get rid of such a plight. He then offered a proposal of strengthening the national power. That is to say, their army must abandon the traditional fighting way of war chariots, and change over to cavalryman, namely, one horse carrying one rider. Furthermore, they must wear the straitjacket like those of the foreign nomads, for the purpose of convenient riding. The most important thing, of course, was the excellent equestrian skill and archery. So, they must learn from the "barbaric" foreigner, their fierce neighbor.

Sadly, however, all the people present except Louhuan 樓緩 refused to accept the proposal of King Wuling on the grounds that they could not change the etiquette formulated by the ancestors. The king was very dispirited. He immediately summoned Feiyi 肥義, the prime minister, and tried to obtain his support and asked him for a solution. After learning the whole story, Feiyi seriously advised the king with an ancient maxim that if the monarch was hesitant about the major affairs, he will accomplish nothing eventually. He stated further that since King Wuling considered this matter for a long time, and clearly comprehended the advantages of hufuqishe 胡服騎射, it was unnecessary to hesitate any more. Generally speaking, the insights of rich wisdom were not understood by everyone; the great achievements are not created by ordinary persons. All these deeds and achievements of the divine kings and sages in the past ages have fully proved this truth. Therefore, the king must insist on his own ideas decisively, practicing the so-called hufuqishe determinedly, never being irresolute and never being afraid of irresponsible remarks by ordinary persons.

When King Wuling heard these words, he completely understood at once. He set himself as an example, first dressed in the nomadic costume, and then began to formulate the training scheme of riding skill and archery for his troops. He knew exactly that the real enhancement of the national military strength could not depend only on a single king and a few supporters; as many people as possible, especially the high officials and nobles, must join them actively. Thus, the king immediately sent an aide to visit his uncle, Prince Cheng 公子成, a prestigious senior member of the royal family, and tried to persuade this prince to accept the king's reform scheme, and work together with him. But, Prince Cheng still firmly insisted on his initial opinion, namely, "the reformation of hufuqishe 胡服騎射 changes the classic teaching, alters the traditional morality, and violates the Chinese manners and customs", so this reformation was unacceptable. Thus, king Wuling decided to persuade Prince Cheng personally. His words were reasonable and invigorating:

"Originally the clothing is designed to be convenient for person's action and work; the etiquette is established to facilitate the implementation of various affairs. The ancient sages formulate etiquettes according to different circumstances, its aim is to benefit the people and strengthen the country. The custom of the barbarians in Nanyue 南越 (the Southern Yue) includes haircutting, tattooing and baring arms, etc., while the consuetude of Dawu 大吴 (the Great Wu) consists of dyeing black teeth and rough clothes. Although their dressing styles are different, the purposes of benefiting the people and strengthening the country are exactly alike. Therefore, there is no need to pursue unitary costume form. It is quite natural that all over the world countless things are protean, and a lot of circumstances are different, thus the sages will never compel the people to wear clothes in same style."

"Now what you emphasize is the traditions and customs practiced for generations, whereas what I want to emphasize is how to formulate new rules for adapting to the new environment. Making a comprehensive view of the current world, we will find that our country is surrounded by many strong opponents. There are kingdoms Yan 燕 and Donghu 東胡 in the east, and kingdoms Qin 秦, Han 韓 as well as the nomadic power Loufan 樓煩 in the west. Therefore, we will not be able to protect our people and territory from being ravaged by them, if we do not possess a powerful and efficient cavalry. It was indeed because of the overly weak army, our ancestors were trampled often by the foreign barbarians. We must not give up the effort of guarding the country just for a reason of being afraid of being accused of violating the classical teaching. At least I will never do like this!"

Prince Cheng was greatly moved by these words. He felt incredibly ashamed of his recent statements and actions. Then, he apologized to the king sincerely, and confessed that his previous opinion was wrong. He accepted the nomadic costume, swift horse, and bow and arrows bestowed by King Wuling on the spot, and went to the palace on the subsequent day dressed in this clothing.

After the king's repeated explanations and persuasions on the importance of changing costume, most of the courtiers who dissented and hesitated began to alter their opinions gradually. They understood the far-reaching significance of the so-called hufuqishe more or less, or were forced to obey the order from the monarch; in any case, all of them wore the hufu 胡服 (foreign costume) and practiced the riding and archery. It is indeed an everlasting truth that "people follow the example of their superiors." While the king and his officials were promoting the movement of changing costume actively, the ordinary folks all over the country imitated their actions one after another. Within the borders of the kingdom of Zhao, there were many foreign residents familiar with the nomadic lifestyle, so the *hufuqishe* was quickly popularized in this country. Not long after, the military strength of their troops was increased greatly.

King Wuling of Zhao was practical and realistic; he did not stick to so-called 古訓 guxun (classical teaching), and offered the far-sighted proposal of *hufuqishe*. All these ideas and operations helped this regime to rapidly gain fruitful results. In the next year, after the reformation of *changing costume*, King Wuling of Zhao personally led an army of numerous members and invaded the kingdom of Zhongshan 中山, advancing on the city of Ningjia 寧葭 (northwest of the city of Shijiazhuang 石家莊, present Hebei Province). Soon afterward, he expanded westward, occupied vast areas formerly belonging to the foreign nomads and arrived at the city of Yuzhong 榆中 (northwest of the county of Dongsheng 東勝, present Inner Mongolia). Under such a strong pressure, the ruler of the Linhu 林胡 regime was forced to present a tribute of fine horses, showing a submitting desire.

In addition, in the 21st year of King Wuling's reign (305 BC), he attacked the kingdom of Zhongshan 中山 once again. Under the command of the king, his troops successively captured Danqiu 丹丘, Shuangyang 爽陽, Hongzhisai 鴻之塞, Haocheng 鄗城, Shiyi 石邑, Fenglong 封龍, Dongyuan 東垣, etc. The kingdom of Zhongshan was compelled to cede four cities to the kingdom of Zhao in order to sue for peace. In the 23rd year, the 25th year and the 26th year of King Wuling's reign, the kingdom of Zhao launched several wars against the kingdom of Zhongshan, thereby expanding its territory to the kingdom of Yan 燕 and the region of Dai 代 to the north, and the Yunzhong 雲中 and Jiuyuan 九原 to the west. Later, in the 3rd year of King Huiwen 惠文王 (296 BC), who was the son of King Wuling, the kingdom of Zhao destroyed the kingdom of Zhongshan, and banished its king to the region of Fushi 膚施. In brief, since the reformation of *hufuqishe* had been practiced, the kingdom of Zhao achieved brilliant military victories in a short period of ten years. It destroyed the kingdom of Zhongshan 中山, defeated the powers of Linhu 林胡, Loufan 樓煩, and erected the counties of Yunzhong 雲中, Yanmen 雁門 and Dai 代. An extensive territory occupied by this kingdom included the present western part of Hebei 河北 Province, the northern part of Shanxi 山西 Province and the Hetao 河套 region (the great band of the Yellow River). As a result of the reformation, the kingdom of Zhao evolved into a powerful regime. The implementation of *hufuqishe* played an important role in this outstanding achievement.

The kingdom of Zhao developed rapidly and became one of the powerful hegemons in a short period because of the reformation of *hufuqishe*. Other kingdoms of the Warring States were inspired greatly by this undoubted fact, so they followed the example one after another.

Not long afterward, the *huma* 胡馬 (the foreign horses) and its corresponding cultures spread all over China. As a result, the military strength of those kingdoms was enhanced enormously. Furthermore, some new elements relating to the horse appeared in the social culture of China some years later.

2. The Horse Cultures Derived from Foreign Countries

In terms of the horse cultures introduced from foreign countries, the 胡服 hufu (the foreign costume) and 騎射 qishe (the equestrian skill and archery) mentioned above are exactly the typical examples, especially the former. Generally speaking, the 胡服 hufu in Chinese refers to the costumes worn by the inhabitants of the vast steppes in Central Eurasia. The dresses of this style are very convenient for riding and shooting with arrows. These clothes are skintight, and fit for nimble motions, which were invented by the nomads, who are excellent riders. Many persons think the earliest people riding horses were the Scythians. In the long nomadic history, the Scythians created a rich culture related to the horse, which not only exerted enormous influence over the people in Central Eurasia but also reformed the civilizations of the regions adjacent to Central Eurasia. The so-called *hufu* 胡服 is one of the typical instances.

When a person rides, he has to separate his two legs on either side of the horse. So, the first feature of the "foreign costume" was that one part of this costume was the trouser, consisting of a pair of legs. In Chinese classics, this costume is called 絝 or 袴 ku, corresponding to 褲 ku in modern Chinese, referring to "trouser".

Another feature of the Scythian costume was reflected in the shoes and boots made of leather. The leather boot was usually wrapped around the calf; some high boots could reach the knee, and wrap the whole trouser leg inside. This attire was also designed for the convenience of riding, namely, for the ease of leaping up and down. At first, the *hufu* (foreign costume) and the *qishe* (equestrian skill and archery) were introduced into China as military skills, hence the leather boots became one of the special decorations of the servicemen. A description about it is given in *Suishu*: "Only the costume for riders is outfitted with the boots, namely the foreign shoes. The boots are convenient for motions, and is now a component of the military uniform of China."[20]

The Scythians usually wore a coat on the upper body. The coat was tied around the waist with a girdle instead of buttons. The coat was rather loose, but its sleeves were very narrow and the cuffs fastened at the wrists. The coat was often adorned with some slivers of gold or copper. Besides, a pointed cap was also a component of their attire in many tribes.

Although the trousers and leather boots are quite simple and common costumes in modern China, this type of dress was not introduced into the kingdom of Zhao until the end of the fourth century BC, and then were gradually popularized all over China. The so-called *hufu* in Chinese classical books might be similar to the Scythian attire, but is not entirely the same. At least the crown of the *hufu* adopted by King Wuling of the Zhao was not as pointed as that of the Scythian cap, but was decorated with a marten tail.

It is said that King Wuling adorned his costume with a golden marten on the crown, and inserted the marten tail to show his noble status. Later, when the kingdom of Qin 秦 destroyed the Zhao regime, the king of Qin gave the crown of the former king of Zhao to his servant in order to insult King Wuling. As the son and successor of King Wuling, King Huiwen 惠文王 (r. 298–266 BC) wore a crown like that of his father. Thereby, this kind of crown was called *zhaohuiwenguan* 趙惠文冠 (the crown of the king Huiwen of the Zhao). A number of years later, this coronet gradually transformed into a type of costume for military officials, and is also named 武冠 wuguan (the military coronet), 大冠 daguan (the grand coronet), 武弁大冠 wubiandaguan (the grand coronet for military official) and so on. In addition to the marten tail, the ornaments of the military coronet include other materials, such as the blue ribbon of silk and the feathers of the bird 鶡 he, which is a fierce pheasant. It is said that once two pheasants fight with each other, they will not stop until one dies. Thus, the decoration of the *he*'s feathers symbolized the gallantry of the wearer.

---

[20] Cf. *Suishu*, fasc. 12, p. 276.

The girdle of the "foreign costume" is called 具帶 judai in Chinese. The exquisite ones are decorated with gold.[21] In the 6th year (174 BC) of 前元 qianyuan reign of Wendi, the emperor sent a letter to Modu 冒頓, the monarch of the Xiongnu, to express his friendship. At the same time, a lot of gifts were presented to Maodun, including various dresses, fine silks and delicate ornaments used for foreign costumes.[22] About these gifts, Mengkang 孟康 noted that the belt decorated with gold (具帶 judai) was the grand girdle around the waist. Zhangyan 張晏 said that it was called 郭落帶 guoluodai by the 鮮卑 Xianbei tribe, the name for a propitious animal, which the foreigner 東胡 Donghu were particularly fond of. And, Yanshigu 顏師古 (581–645) thought the 犀毗 xipi was the hook on the foreign girdle. According to the historical records, "the girdle decorating with gold" mentioned here was introduced into China as early as the 4th century, namely, the period after King Wuling's reformation.

The *hufu* 胡服 introduced by King Wuling was designated 上褶下袴 *shangxixiaku*, meaning that a short coat was worn on the upper part, and trousers were worn on the lower part. Zhangshoujie 張守節 stated the sentence "reformation and wearing the foreign costume 革政而胡服" in *Shiji*, and thought that the "foreign costume" in the period of Warring States was exactly the fashionable clothes coming from the Western Regions in the Tang Dynasty. Liuxi 劉熙 said in his *Shiming* 釋名 (*Explanation of Terms*) that the word 褶 xi meant coat; and the 大褶 daxi (big coat) flowed down to the knee. Yanshigu 顏師古 stated in a note that 褶 xi was the outermost coat of all cloths. Its shape resembled a robe, with a short body and loose sleeves. These words showed clearly that even the "big coat" 大褶 can only cover the knee; other coats may be shorter.

Before the introduction of *hufu*, there was a kind of 襦袴 ruku in China, but it was only underwear with a pair of short fork tubes. This underwear had to be covered by a lower garment (裳 chang), thereby

---

[21] This girdle is written as 貝帶 beidai in *Hanshu*, and is explained by Yanshigu 顏師古 as "the belt adorned with the oceanic shells" 海貝飾帶. But, Wangguowei 王國維 signifies his dissent. He thinks this girdle originated from the inland where the nomads lived, which is arid and short of water. So, the oceanic shellfish is difficult to find there. Besides, since it is adorned with gold, it is almost impossible to decorate it again with the shells. Therefore, the so-called 貝帶 should be corrected as 具帶. Cf. Wangguowei 王國維, *A Study on the Foreign Costume* 胡服考, in his *Guantangjilin* 觀堂集林, Zhonghua Book Company 中華書局, 1959, p. 1572.

[22] Cf. *Hanshu*, fasc. 94a, p. 3758.

greatly hindering the free movement of the legs. Because the traditional clothes were detrimental for riding, King Wuling of Zhao adopted the foreign costume as the attire of his people. On the upper body, they wore a short coat, and on the lower body, they wore trousers with two legs. Their soldiers became much more nimble in battle.

Soon after the *hufu* was introduced in the kingdom of Zhao, it also became popular in other countries. The *Zhushujinian* 竹書紀年 (*Bamboo Annals*) records that in the 17th year of King Xiang of the Wei 魏襄王, the king ordered both the civil officials and military men to wear the foreign costume, which was called 貉服 haofu, namely, 胡服 hufu.[23] The 17th year of King Xiang of Wei 魏襄王 is equal to the 24th year of King Wuling of Zhao 趙武靈王, namely, 302 BC. It means that from the earliest introduction of *hufu* into the country of Zhao to the introduction into the kingdom of Wei, there is only a short gap of five years in between.

Zhanguoce 戰國策 (*Stratagems of the Warring States*) gives a story as follows. Tiandan 田單, an official of the kingdom of Qi 齊, was going to attack the nomads in the north, but Luzhongzi 魯仲子 predicted that he could not be victorious. As expected, after a battle enduring three months, his army did not make any progress. At the same time, a nursery rhyme ridiculing them circulated in the battlefield and its neighboring regions. It said, even though the soldiers of Qi possess grand coronets and long swords, they could not defeat the foreign nomads.[24] Tiandan was very worried by it and then went to Luzhongzi for advice. Luzhongzi analyzed the real reasons for different results of Tiandan's military operations. Formerly, Tiandan had vanquished a strong hostile force with only a small number of warriors, because they were falling into a dangerous situation and had to risk their life to fight. And since then, the equipage of the troops was improved greatly; "girdles decorated with gold" were worn by the soldiers. As a result of the good conditions, they became being

---

[23] Cf. *Zhushujinian* 竹書紀年 (*Bamboo Annals*), "The Biography of Wei", in Fangshiming & Wangxiuling 方诗铭、王修龄, *A Collection and Research on Bamboo Annals of the Ancient Edition* 古本竹書紀年輯證, Shanghai Classics Publishing House 上海古籍出版社, 1981, p. 154. The Chinese text is as follows: "魏襄王十七年, 邯鄲命吏大夫奴遷于九原, 又命將軍、大夫、適子、戍吏皆貉服。"

[24] Cf. *Zhanguoce* 戰國策 (*Stratagems of the Warring States*), punctuated by Shanghai Classics Publishing House 上海古籍出版社, 1985, p. 467. The Chinese text is as follows: "大冠若箕, 修劍拄頤, 攻狄不能, 下壘枯丘。"

mortally afraid of death, and thus, it was impossible to win a victory once again.

Here, both the nursery rhyme and the words of Lu Zhongzi mentioned the attire of Tiandan's army, such as "grand coronet" and "girdle decorated with gold", which were actually the components of the *hufu* (foreign costume). Only about thirty years after the reformation of King Wuling, Tiandan of the Qi led an expedition to the northern nomadic lands, and at that time, the *hufu* had already become the military costume of the Qi. This fact indicates that many Chinese regimes were zealous in introducing the horse and costume from foreign countries.

A book 鶡冠子 *heguanzi* is listed in *Yiwenzhi* 藝文志 (*Treatise of Literature*) of *Hanshu* 漢書, and an explanation is given as follows: "The people of the Chu 楚 inhabit in the remote mountains. Their coronets are ornamented with feathers of the bird 鶡 he."[25] Initially, the "coronet ornamented with feathers of the *he*" was a part of the *hufu* of King Wuling; a period later, so-called *hufu* began to be popular in the Kingdom Chu.

Down to the period of the Qin 秦 and Han 漢 Dynasties, a lot of warriors, high-ranking officials and members of the royal family wore the foreign costumes (*hufu*). *Shiji* 史記 mentioned that during the reign of Huidi of the Han 漢惠帝 (195–188 BC), the court gentlemen 郎 and palace attendants 侍中 wore a 淡拔冠 danba coronet and 具帶 judai (girdle). The so-called *danba coronet* is a coronet adorned with feathers of the bird of prey, namely, the crown worn by King Wuling after his introduction of the foreign costume. It is similar to the 鶡冠 "coronet he". In addition, *Shiji* also recorded that after the king of Qin conquered the Zhao kingdom, he granted palace attendants the "danba coronets" as a reward. Obviously, in the Qin 秦 Dynasty, the *hufu* (foreign costume) was already prevalent in the palace.

Hanshu 漢書 tells us that a portrait of the ancient warrior Chengqing 成慶 or Jingke 荊軻 was painted on the palace gate of Liuqu 劉去, the great-grandson of the Emperor Jingdi 景帝 (157–141 BC). This warrior wore the attire of a short coat, big trousers and a long sword. Prince Guangchuan 廣川王 of Liuqu was fond of this costume, so he wore outfits with a long sword of 7.5 *chi* 尺, and wore clothes just the same as that

---

[25] See *Hanshu*, fasc. 30, p. 1730. The Chinese text is as follows: "楚人，居深山，以鶡為冠。" On the contrary, Yanshigu 顏師古 thinks "the coronet is consisted of feathers of the bird *he* 以鶡鳥羽為冠."

of the portrait.[26] *Hanshu* recorded elsewhere that Prince Changyi 昌邑, a grandson of Emperor Wudi 武帝 (142–87 BC), "wears short coat, big trouser and coronet Huiwen."[27] Apparently, all of these coats, trousers and coronets were typical *hufu* (*foreign costume*). Therefore, the *hufu* was possibly rather fashionable and popular in China in the 2nd and the 1st centuries BC.

After the Western Jin 晉 Dynasty, during a long period, northern China was dominated by the nomads originating from foreign countries. Those tribes called 五胡 wuhu (the five foreign tribes), such as 匈奴 Xiongnu, 鮮卑 Xianbei and so on, were almost all the famous riding people who had pastured in the steppes of Central Eurasia for thousands of years. As for the 羯胡 Jiehu, though they may stem from the resident people in the Syr Darya Valley,[28] they possessed a more advanced horse culture because of their long-standing livelihood in Central Asia. All of these foreigners or barbarians (胡人 huren) promoted the developing of "foreignization" (胡化 huhua) and "Horse Cultures" in China.

In the Southern and Northern Dynasties, a great number of foreigners or barbarians poured into China. They brought about a popularizing of *hufu* (the foreign costume) in China. A scholar in the Song 宋 was sure that since the period of the Northern Qi (北齊 beiqi, 550–577), the foreign attires had been seen almost all over China. For example, Shenkuo 沈括 (1031–1095) mentioned the *hufu* in his *Mengxibitan* 夢溪筆談 (*Brush Talks from Dream Brook*). He mentioned his personally experiences and the historical literature records.

"Officials living in the Central Plains of China all modeled their costumes on those of the ethnic groups living in the north and west ever since the Northern Qi Dynasty (ca. 550–77). Tight sleeves, short coats, boots and belts with pendent rings were what they wore. Tight sleeves are convenient for riding on a horse and shooting arrows while short coats and

---

[26] Cf. *Hanshu*, fasc. 53, p. 2486.

[27] Cf. *Hanshu*, fasc. 63, p. 2767.

[28] The surname of the royal family of the regime 後趙 (Hou Zhao, The Later Zhao) was 石 (*shi*), stemming from Jiehu (羯胡). The feature of their appearance was a long nose and sunken eyes. Many indications showed that they originated from the kingdom Shi (石) in Sogdiana, that is to say, they were the Sogdians belonging to Eastern Iran. Yao weiyuan (姚薇元) offered this viewpoint earlier, cf. his *A Research on the surnames of the foreigners in Northern Dynasties* 北朝胡姓考, Science Publishing House 科學出版社, 1958, pp. 355–358.

boots are suitable for walking on the grassland. The ethnic groups are fond of luxuriant green grass and they often sit, lie, and even sleep on the grassland. When I was dispatched as an envoy to the state of Liao in the north, I saw this with my own eyes. What is more, I even saw their royal court set up in the thick grass. On the day when I visited their court, it had just rained. My clothes and trousers all got wet after I walked through the grass. On the contrary, the local people did not get wet at all. Hung to the pendent rings attached to their belts were small objects such as knives, swords, bows and arrows, handkerchiefs, pockets containing calculating objects and flints. Later, those small objects were removed, but the pendent rings were kept intact, which were used to hang small objects just like the belts that fixed the saddle on the horseback. The upper part of the pendent rings was called *daikua*, which was a piece of ornamental object hung to the belt. The emperor must wear a belt with thirteen ornamental objects made of gold and jade. It still remained so during Wude period of the reign of Emperor Gaozu (618–626) and Zhenguan period of the reign of Emperor Taizong (627–649). After Kaiyuan period of the reign of Emperor Xuanzong (713–741), garments and belts turned to be a bit loose while most other old dressing styles remained unchanged. The clasp was still used to fasten belts. The styles of the costumes of present day dynasty have partly inherited the tradition and partly undergone necessary changes. Our ethical culture is much more mature than ever before."[29]

However, these *hufu* introduced to China in successive dynasties were not necessarily related to the importing of *huma* (the foreign horses) directly; they may have evolved gradually due to the mutual imparting. Especially in the Sui and the Tang, a large number of 胡人 (the foreigners or barbarians) were actually 西胡 Xihu (the Western Foreigner), namely, the Sogdians coming from Sogdiana in Central Asia. Most of the Sogdians were the residents of the oases, who engaged in agriculture and

---

[29] Cf. Shenkuo 沈括, *Mengxi Bitan* 夢溪筆談 (*Brush Talks from Dream Brook*), fasc. 1, tr. by Wanghong 王宏 and Zhaozheng 趙崢, Sichuan People's Publishing House, 2008, pp. 14–17. The Chinese text is as follows: "中國衣冠, 北齊以來乃全非古制。窄袖, 緋綠短衣, 長靿靴, 有蹀躞帶, 皆胡服也。窄袖利於馳射, 短衣、長靿皆便於涉草。胡人樂茂草, 常寢處其間。予使北時, 皆見之, 雖王庭亦在深薦中。予至胡庭日, 新雨過, 涉草, 衣袴皆濡, 唯胡人皆無所沾。帶衣所垂蹀躞, 蓋欲佩帶弓劍、帉帨、算囊、刀礪之類。自後雖去蹀躞, 而猶存其環, 環所以銜蹀躞, 如馬之鞦根, 即今之帶銙也。天子必以三環為節, 唐武德、貞觀時猶耳。開元之後, 雖仍舊俗而稍褒博矣, 然帶鉤尚穿帶本為孔。本朝加順折, 茂人文也。"

commerce. Although their costumes also had the features of narrow sleeves and binding waists, they were different more or less from those created by the ancient nomads. Anyway, their costumes were more suitable for movement, particularly horse riding, than the traditional ones of China. As a result, the *hufu* invented by 北胡 Beihu (the Northern Foreigner) and 西胡 Xihu (the Western Foreigner) was gradually accepted by the people all over China; thereby, the former *foreign costume* became the present *national quintessence*.

In addition to the *hufu*, some athletics and cultural activities relating to the horse were also introduced from foreign countries. For example, polo is a game which was introduced along with the excellent equestrian skill of the foreigners. This game is called 打毬 daqiu (play the ball) or 擊鞠 jiju (hit the ball) in Chinese. Extensive venues and many horses were required for this game, so it was a quite extravagant one. In early stages, it could only circulate within the upper society, especially royal members. The palaces with good conditions were the best polo fields.

It is said that polo is derived from Persia. Later, it spread westward to Asia Minor and eastward to Central Asia, including present Xinjiang 新疆 of China. From Central Asia, the game of polo continued to spread eastward, and was introduced into inland China at last. Duhuan 杜環 of the Tang Dynasty wrote in his *Jingxingji* 經行記 (*Record of Travels*) that in the country Fergana there was a forest named 波羅 *boluo*, and a ball field was in the forest. The "ball field" here may refer to polo field because of the similarity of pronunciation of *boluo* and *polo*. Polo is a game played between two teams. The players must ride on horses and use wooden hammers with long handles to hit a ball. That is to say, players of the polo game must be skilled in riding. As we know, Fergana is the ancient country Dawan 大宛, which is famous for producing elite horse, namely, the Blood Sweat Horses 汗血馬. Therefore, it is reasonable that the game of polo had been prevalent in Fergana, the country possessing a long-standing horse cultural tradition.

Polo was quite common already in the Tang Dynasty, especially circulating among the upper classes. Emperor Taizong 太宗 had once been attracted by this game. *Fengshiwenjianji* 封氏聞見記 (*Records of the Hearsays by Mr. Feng*) relates a story: "The emperor Taizong once ascended the city gate tower Anfu 安福, and said to his courtier, 'I was told that the western foreigners playing polo very well, so asks them to demonstrate it, and learn to play it. I watched the matches and enjoyed them much. Yesterday, while I was resting in Shengxian Lou 升仙樓

(the Pavilion Shenxian), the foreigners playing polo in the street invited me to admire their matches. Apparently, the foreigners thought I was fond of polo, so played it purposely. Thus, I understand that the monarch must be very cautious about all his activities. I have already burnt the ball in order to admonish myself'."[30]

Although Emperor Taizong was once attracted by polo, he could abstain from polo, because he was indeed a famous "sagacious monarch" after all. His descendants, however, were quite different from him; they seemed to be addicted to polo. For example, a story in *Fengshiwenjianji* depicts the remarkable skills of Prince Linzi 臨淄王, the future emperor Xuanzong 玄宗 (r. 712–756), in both polo playing and horse riding. During the reign of Jingyun 景雲 (710–712), a Tibetan diplomatic corps was sent to the Tang regime. The emperor entertained them by showing them a game of polo. The Tibetan ambassador suggested playing a match between his polo team and that of the Tang. After several sets, the Tibetan team won all the matches. Then, the emperor ordered Prince Linzi 臨淄 and three other noblemen to compose a team and play against the Tibetan team consisting of ten members. In the match, Prince Linzi spurred the horse swiftly and hit the ball nimbly; finally, these four officials won the game. The emperor was very joyful, and bestowed a lot of things on them. After Prince Linzi succeeded the throne, he often personally played the polo or frequently admired these matches with his attendants and officials.[31]

From the quotation above, we know that Xuanzong was an excellent player of polo before he succeeded to the throne, and he was fond of this sport all his life. The polo game had been prevalent in China during the reign of Xuanzong, and continued to circulate for a long time. In the reign of Daizong 代宗 (r. 763–779), this game was restricted to a certain extent because of its excessive cost. In the year 765 or 766, Liugang 劉剛 offered a suggestion to the imperial administration and said that the sport

---

[30] Cf. *Fengshiwenjianji* 封氏聞見記 (*Records of the Hearsays by Mr. Feng*), fasc. 6, p. 58.
[31] Cf. *Fengshiwenjianji*, fasc. 6, pp. 53–54. The Chinese text is as follows: "景雲中, 吐蕃遣使迎金城公主, 中宗於梨園亭子賜觀打毬。吐蕃贊咄奏言:'臣部曲有善毬者, 請與漢敵。'上令仗令內試之, 決數都, 吐蕃皆勝。時玄宗為臨淄王, 中宗又令與嗣虢王邕、駙馬楊慎交、武延秀等四人敵吐蕃十人。玄宗東西驅突, 風回電激, 所向無前, 吐蕃功不獲施。... 中宗甚悅, 賜強明絹數百段。學士沈佺期、武平一等皆獻詩。開元、天寶中, 玄宗數禦樓觀打毬為事, 能者左縈右拂, 盤旋宛轉, 殊可觀。然馬或奔逸, 時致傷斃。"

polo would damage both the person's health and the horse's body, so it was unnecessary to adopt such a dangerous game instead of many other good amusements. The minister approved of this suggestion, and took measures of restriction. Finally, because polo was a common game of the army, it was not absolutely forbidden, but frequent playing was impermissible.

Obviously, at that time, polo was only slightly restrained instead of being prohibited. In the later period of the Tang, the rulers appeared to indulge in this game even more. According to *Xintangshu*, as soon as emperor Muzong 穆宗 (r. 820–824) was enthroned in 820 AD, he played polo with his household troops and hunted in the suburbs.[32] The following year, in lunar February, he played polo in Palace Linde 麟德殿. In 822 AD, in lunar November, he became sick as a result of playing polo, and never recovered from the illness, and died two years later. Jiutangshu said, "In the day *gengchen* 庚辰, the emperor plays polo with his attendants in the palace. One of the attendants suddenly fells down from the horse, just like been struck by some object. The emperor is extremely scared, stopping the playing immediately. As a result, he could stand on the feet no more, becomes grievous dizzy, and has to always lie on the bed."[33]

Emperor Jingzong 敬宗 (r. 824–826), the successor and son of Muzong, was also very fond of polo, and his skill could even be superior to that of his father. According to Xintangshu, in his first month on the throne, Jingzong played polo at least three times.[34]

In addition, emperor Xuanzong of Tang 唐宣宗 (r. 846–859) was also an expert in polo. *A Collection Narrating the Tang* (*Tang Yulin* 唐語林) recorded that "Xunzong was adept at both of shooting and polo. His horse ran swiftly and nimbly, it did not equip any other adornments except for the snaffle. While he was playing he brandished mallet quickly, could hit the ball continuously for hundreds times, and the horse ran rapidly too, just like lightning. All the master hands among the troops admired the emperor's excellent skill."[35]

---

[32] Cf. *Xintangshu* 新唐書, fasc. 8, p. 222.
[33] Cf. *Jiutangshu* 舊唐書, fasc. 16, p. 501.
[34] Cf. *Xintangshu* 新唐書, fasc. 8, p. 227.
[35] Cf. *Tangyulin* 唐語林 (*A Collection Narrating the Tang*), fasc. 7, in Zhouxunchu 周勛初, *Tangyulinjiaozheng* 唐語林校證 (*A Correction and Study on A Collection Narrating the Tang*), Zhonghua Book Company 中華書局, 1987, pp. 633–634,

Again, Emperor Xizong 僖宗 (r. 873–888) was also a past master at polo. He even boasted that he was so skillful that he would certainly win the championship in the whole country. *Zizhitongjian* recorded that this emperor was good at riding and shooting, especially playing polo. He once said, "If I join the imperial examination for polo playing, I am sure I will be the champion."[36] Apparently, he was full of confidence and conceit.

Most of the emperors and members of the upper classes of the Tang were fond of polo. They build many polo fields in the palaces or official mansions. For instance, there was a polo field in the north of the imperial palace. Another was located in the south of Pond Longshou 龍首池, while the Pond was within the Palace Daming 大明宮. During the reign of Wenzong 文宗 (r. 826–840), Pond Longshou was filled and converted into a polo field. In addition, all the three palaces of the emperor, empress and empress dowager, as well as the mansions of sixteen princes, possessed polo fields. In the era of Xuanzong 玄宗, Yangshen 楊慎 resided in Block Jinggong 靖恭坊, and his polo field was built in the west of the block. In the era of Dezong 德宗 (r. 779–804), Minister Lisheng 李晟 built a polo field in his own house located in Block Yongchong 永崇坊. And, in the period of Wenzong 文宗, the imperial secretary Wangyuanzhong 王源中 built a polo field in his residence in Block Taiping 太平坊.

Since polo was a hobby of the rulers, it naturally became a fashionable game of the youth in towns, especially in the capital Changan 長安. In a poem written by Likuo 李廓 of the Tang, the recreations of the young men in Changan are vividly depicted. Its content is roughly as follows: It is a very common scene that several young companions sauntered round the city; they ride the swift horses, play polo, wear the special costumes for polo; sometimes they depart for spring scenery early in the morning, and being tipsy while return to home in the evening; they often kill their time in the whorehouse overnight, singing and dancing continuously.[37] In addition to the emperors, the dignitaries, the servicemen and the youths, even the literati and the maids in palaces are fond of polo playing. For

---

[36] Cf. *Zizhitongjian* 資治通鑑, fasc. 253, p. 8221.
[37] Cf. *Quantangshi* 全唐詩 (*The General Anthology of Tang Poetry*), fasc. 24, p. 328, Zhonghua Book Company 中華書局, 1960. The Chinese text is as follows: "追逐輕薄伴，閒遊不著緋。長攏出獵馬，數換打毬衣。曉日尋花去，春風帶酒歸。青樓無晝夜，歌舞歇時稀。"

example, in a poem written by a poetess named Mrs. Huarui 花蕊夫人, the affair of the palace maids learning to play polo is mentioned.

Polo was played in the Tang Dynasty, and was still prevalent in the Song 宋, Yuan 元 and Ming 明 Dynasties thereafter. *Dongjingmenghualu* related that since the imperial family crossed southward over the Yangtze River in the final phase of the Northern Song, the servicemen played polo in the Palace Baojinlou 寶津樓 on the 3rd day of lunar March every year. Polo was one of the various amusements offered to the sovereigns. Small-scale polo was played by menfolk, while large-scale polo was played by eunuchs. The players wore jade girdles and red boots, and rode ponies. Everybody mastered the riding skill, ran swiftly and postured gracefully.[38]

The traditional customs of the Liao 遼 (907–1125) still existed in the Jin 金 Dynasty (1115–1234). Every year on the fifth day of lunar May, the ceremony of heaven worship was held on a polo field, and polo matches would be held there after the ceremony. A detailed description of polo playing is given in *Jinshi* 金史. "When the polo is playing, everybody rides his conventional horse, and holds the mallet with a long handle, which is a few *chi* 尺 in length. The end of the mallet is the shape of the crescent moon. The players are divided into two teams, to compete for hitting one ball. In the southern end of the polo field two pillars are set, and a board is mounted between them. A hole is dug in the lower part of the board as the goal, on the back of the goal a net is covered. The one hitting the ball into the net is the winner. It is also said that two goals are set on the opposite sides of the field. Both of the two teams try to hit the ball into the opposite goal; if they done, they are the winner. The ball is small, just like a fist. It is made by hollowing tough wood and painting red. All the players are agile."[39]

Until the earlier period of the Ming Dynasty, polo still circulated in the palaces. During the era of Yongle 永樂 (1402–1424), an official Wangfu 王紱 wrote a poem titled "On the Double Fifth Festival, Attended the Imperial Banquet and Watched the Riding and Polo." He depicted polo

---

[38] Cf. *Dongjingmenghualu* 東京夢華錄 (*The Records of the Former Eastern Capital*), in Yiyongwen 伊永文, *Dongjingmenghualujianzhu* 東京夢華錄箋注 (Comments on *The Records of the Former Eastern Capital*), Zhonghua Book Company 中華書局, 2006, pp. 689–690.

[39] Cf. *Jinshi* 金史 (*History of the Jin*), fasc. 35, Zhonghua Book Company 中華書局, 1975, p. 827.

playing by the palace security guards, and said that the polo field was built in the eastern garden, and so on.

Another famous cultural item introduced to inland China along with the *huma* 胡馬 (the foreign horses) is the "horse dance" 馬舞. That is to say, a tamed horse is able to coordinate its motions with music and rhythm, and dances lightly and gracefully, just like a human dancer.

During the era of the Three Kingdoms, Caozhi 曹植, the younger brother of the emperor of the kingdom of Wei 魏, acquired a fine horse from Dawan 大宛. Later on, he dedicated the horse to Emperor Wendi 文帝 (r. 220–226). In his report submitted to Emperor Caozhi, he depicted this good horse. He said that it was an extraordinary horse from Dawan, with purple fur. He taught the horse to genuflect to persons, and was successful at last. In addition, it could dance in harmony with the drum's rhythm. Obviously, genuflecting to humans and being on the beat with the music were the basic features of the "horse dance". Thus, we know that at least in the end of the Later Han and the era of the Three Kingdoms, the "horse dance" had already appeared in inland China. And, the inventors of the "horse dance" were quite probably the residents in Central Asian, for the horse mentioned by Caozhi came from Dawan. Furthermore, the "horse dance" prevailed most in the period of Emperor Xuanzong of the Tang (r. 712–756), and those dancing horses were almost all from Central Asia.

A story about the "horse dance" in the period of Emperor Zhongzong 中宗 is recorded in *Jinglongwenguanji* 景龍文館記 (*Records of Jinglong Library*). The emperor held a banquet to entertain the Tibetan ambassadors, and a wonderful act of horse dance was performed. These dancing horses were dressed in multicolored silk; the saddle and other adornments were also decorated with gold and silver. As soon as the music was sounded, all the horses danced to the tune, being in great harmony. After a while, the musicians gave wine to the horses; surprisingly, these horses were able to hold the cups to their mouths for drinking. Then, the horses repeatedly lay down and stood up again staying in tune with the music beat. This performance amazed the Tibetan envoys.

However, it seems that the size of the "horse dance" of Zhongzong was far less than that in the era of Xuanzong. A description is given in *Xintangshu* about the dancing horse in the period of Xuanzong. Xuanzong arranged a hundred horses to perform the "horse dance". They were divided into two groups on the right and left, and stood on beds carried by some strong men, gracefully dancing to the music. The dozen musicians were all handsome youths, dressed in yellow coats and adorned jade belts, standing on both sides. Every year, on the emperor's birthday, these dancing horses performed under the Qinzhenglou 勤政樓. After the "horse dance" was finished, the emperor held a luxurious banquet to entertain his courtiers in Qinzhenglou. On this day, even before dawn, the honor guards of the palace and other officials had already begun to prepare for the celebration. A variety of music was offered by the dozens of musicians, and among the numerous acts, there were also many acrobatics and amusements originating from foreign countries. Horses, elephants as well as rhinoceroses were led to the spot, dancing and saluting the guests. Hundreds of palace servants in colored silk costumes beat the big drums, and played various musical compositions. This celebration of the emperor's birthday was held every year, becoming a convention.[40] In the above description, the "horse dance" is called "foreign acrobatic", which shows clearly that the "horse dance" was indeed a kind of foreign culture.

Another book *Minghuangzalu* 明皇雜錄 depicts the dancing horses more vividly and concretely. It said, "The emperor Xuanzong once gave the order to train horses for dancing. There are altogether four hundreds horses in the palace. They are divided into several groups, and are named respectively. At that time, some fine breed horses are often dedicated to Chinese emperor by foreign countries. After careful teaching, these horses all master the knack of dancing. Then they wore embroidered cloths, adorned the manes with gold, silver, pearls and jade. The dance music is titled *qingbeiyue* 傾盃樂 (*Drinking Wine Music*). When the horses dance, their heads and tails move nimbly in tune with the music. Three layers of plank are constructed for the horse dance; a person rides on the horse and climbs up the top layer, dancing and rotating at lightning speed. Or some strong men bear a bed, on which the horse dances gracefully. A few musicians stand around, all of them are handsome, and wear light-yellow dresses decorated with jade belts. Every year on the birthday of the emperor, these horses dance under the Qinzhenglou 勤政樓. Since the emperor Xuanzong has taken refuge in the region of Shu 蜀 (present

---

[40] Cf. *Xintangshu*, fasc. 22, p. 477. The Chinese text is as follows: "玄宗又嘗以馬百匹，盛飾分左右，施三重榻，舞《傾盃》數十曲，壯士舉榻，馬不動。樂工少年姿秀者十數人，衣黃衫，文玉帶，立左右。每千秋節，舞於勤政樓下，後賜宴設酺，亦會勤政樓。其日未明，金吾引駕騎，北衙四軍陳仗，列旗幟，被金甲，短後繡袍。太常卿引雅樂，每部數十人，間以胡夷之技。內閑廄使引戲馬，五坊使引象、犀，入場拜舞。宮人數百衣錦繡衣，出帷中，擊雷鼓，奏《小破陣樂》，歲以為常。"

Sichuan Province), all these dancing horses are scattered among the people."[41]

Amazingly, though the dancing horses suffered greatly from the "An-Shi Rebellion" 安史之亂, they had not forgotten the dancing skill after many years, and were still able to adjust their footsteps to the rhythm of the music. A story about this phenomenon is also given in *Minghuangzalu*: Before his rebellion, Anlushan 安祿山 (703–757) often admired the horse dance together with the emperor and other courtiers, and enjoyed it very much. So, he got a few dancing horses in his own headquarters in Fanyang 范陽. Later, these horses were transferred to General Tianchengsi 田承嗣 (705–779), who did not know their specialty, and so placed them together with other common warhorses. One day, a celebration was held among his servicemen. While the music was played, a horse danced immediately. The soldiers thought it was mad and struck it heavily. But, the horse misunderstood the behavior, and felt that it was punishment for its inferior dance, so it danced more seriously. Finally, this dancing horse was killed by the beating. Some people knew it was a dancing horse, but dared not to tell the truth to General Tian, fearing his cruelty.

These dancing horses mentioned in *Minghuangzalu* were fine breed horses originating in foreign regions, which indicates that the horses in Central Asia were apt to be trained in dancing. Luguimeng 陸龜蒙 (?–881), a poet of the Tang, showed clearly in his poem "The Dancing Horses" that all those dancing horses of Emperor Xuanzong came from Central Asia. It said, "All the 400 Longsun 龍孫 (the fine horses) come from Yueku 月窟 (Central Asia). Their graceful steps are in harmony with the music. While the dance finishes, they seem to ask rewards from the emperor, all turn their heads toward the monarch's palace, but dare not to whinny."[42]

In Tang poetry, the so-called Yueku 月窟 (literally *the Moon Cavern*) is unrelated to the moon or something like that, but is a general term for the lands in the far west. That is to say, it refers to the present

---

[41] Cf. *Minghuangzalu* 明皇雜錄 (*A Miscellaneous Record of the Emperor Ming*), in *Tangwudaibijixiaoshuodaguan* 唐五代筆記小說大觀 (*A Collection of the Notes and Novels in the Tang and the Five Dynasties*), Shanghai Classics Publishing House 上海古籍出版社, 2000, p. 972.

[42] Cf. *Quantangshi*, fasc. 629, p. 7225. The Chinese text is as follows: "月窟龍孫四百蹄, 驕驤輕步應金鞞。曲終似要君王寵, 回望紅樓不敢嘶。"

Xinjiang 新疆 of China, or some countries in Central Asia, such as Kazakhstan, Kyrgyzstan, Uzbekistan, Tajikistan and Turkmenistan. In addition, it is also used to refer to farther countries, such as Persia of West Asia and India of South Asia.[43] Besides, the so-called Longsun 龍孫 (literally *grandson of the dragon*) is also unconnected with the dragon and its descendant; it is only a nickname for fine horses. Thus, the expression "dragon's grandsons coming from the moon cavern" in the poem can be understood perfectly as "elite horses coming from Central Asia".

Throughout the thousands of years, the influence of foreign horses on China has been far more than the military and cultural aspects mentioned above. What is particularly pointed out here is that in some periods, the horses coming from foreign countries have had a major impact on Chinese economy. We will discuss this in the next chapter, and deal with the topic of silk exportation.

---

[43] Cf. Fangshiming 方詩銘, *nishangyuyichuanziyuegongdexinjie* 《霓裳羽衣》傳自月宮的新解 ("A new Explanation on the Viewpoint of the Dance Music nishangyuyi Originating from the Moon"), in *Journal of Chinese Literature and History* 中華文史論叢, Vol. 48, 1991, pp. 53–56.

Chapter 2

The Purpose and Effect of Silk Exportation

It is well known that the main highways of the ancient world are designated as "silk roads", because most of the commodities circulating through them were silks, which were produced in China abundantly. Thus, when the subject of the Silk Road is discussed, the problems of silk and silk trade are inevitably concerned.

Generally speaking, modern scholars tend to regard the silk exportation from China, which began at least in the first millennium BC, as a trade or commerce, as if the Chinese governments of various periods exported large amounts of silk only for their economic benefits. Of course, in terms of the contemporary situation, this concept is not incorrect, but in ancient ages, silk exportation probably had nothing to do with economy. In fact, in most cases, the silk export of ancient Chinese regimes was not aimed at trade, but out of political, diplomatic or military considerations, at least the period from the Han to Tang Dynasties. Some discussions on this topic will be given as follows.[1]

---

[1] On the problems of silk exportation of ancient China, one may refer to Ruichuanming 芮傳明, "Lungudaisichoushuchuzhifeimaoyixing 論古代絲綢輸出之非貿易性" (*On the Non-trade Feature of Silk Exportation in Ancient China*), in *Shilin* 史林 (*Historical Review*), No. 3, 1996.

1. The Main Purposes of Chinese Silk Exportation

According to historical records, most of the silks in vast quantity exported from China were first obtained by the nomadic people inhabiting in the adjacent regions north of China; then, all these silks or a part was transported to other countries. So, through an investigation on the silk deals between Chinese regimes and the nomadic tribes neighboring China, especially those bordering north of or west of China, the outline of silk exportation in various periods might manifest, and is helpful to draw a more reliable conclusion.

The ancient Chinese regimes exported silks for several purposes, generally speaking, with the main ones listed as follows:

(1) The Chinese rulers exported silks for the purpose of obtaining the support of foreign forces.

Since a very early period, it was not uncommon that a number of strong powers fight with each other to struggle for the hegemony of China. In the period from the Han 漢 to the Tang 唐 Dynasties, the political situation of the northern part of China was particularly confusing. Every ruler who intended to seek hegemony would leave no stone unturned in strengthening his power; one policy they frequently adopted was using the nomadic forces outside China. Of course, as an exchange condition, the Chinese rulers had to export a great amount of silks. A typical example was seen in the relationships between the regimes of the Northern Zhou 北周 (557–581), Northern Qi 北齊 (550–577) and Turkic Khanate.

In the fifth decade of the sixth century, the Ashina 阿史那 clan of the Turkic tribe 突厥 established its political power in the Altai regions, and was soon thriving and prospering. Not long after, these Turks conquered many tribes, and finally founded a powerful nomadic khanate with vast territories including the Mongolian Plateau and parts of Central Eurasia. *Zhoushu* 周書 gave a description of this extensive khanate: "(The Turks) destroy the Hephthalites 嚈噠 in the west, defeat the Khitans 契丹 in the east, annex the Kirghiz 契骨 in the north, and conquer all the countries beyond the Chinese borders. Its territory starts from west of the Liao Sea 遼海, extends westward to West Sea; its south border starts from the north of the Desert and extends northward to the North Sea. There are ten thousand *li* 里 between the east and west, and five or six thousand *li* between the south and north. All of these regions belong to the Turks."[2] This is a vivid portrayal of the heyday of the Turkic Khanate; at that time, the supreme ruler of the Khanate was Mahān Qaghan 木杆可汗 (553–572), whose name is Sijin 俟斤.

Another paragraph of *Zhoushu* states the following: "After Sijin's death, his younger brother Taspar Qaghan 他鉢可汗 (572–578) becomes the successor. Since the reign of Sijin, the Turks have become more and more wealthy and powerful, thus intend to encroach China. Then the imperial court of the Zhou makes intermarriage with them, and affords one hundred thousand bolts of colored silks annually. All of the Turks in capital enjoy lavish hospitalities; the Turks who wear the silk and eat the meat usually as many as thousands. At the same time, being afraid of being plundered by the Turks, the government of Qi 齊 also gives a great deal of silk and wealth to the Turks, even empties its own state treasury."[3]

Apparently, a 100000 bolts of silk exportation per year was really a heavy finance burden for the Northern Zhou 北周 regime, while nearly the whole treasury of the Northern Qi 北齊 given to the Turks was surely a larger wealth than that of the former. In light of this, in this period, the quantity of silk transported from China into the nomadic lands was extremely great. No wonder Taspar Qaghan arrogantly claimed, "As long as my two sons in the south observe filial piety, we are no worry about silk and money."[4] Here, the so-called "two sons" was actually a disparaging term referring to the Northern Zhou 北周 and the Northern Qi 北齊.

At first glance, that the two Chinese regimes spared no expense to afford a large amount of silk to the Turks seems just for the purpose of establishing friendship with them or reducing their hostilities. But, the truth is that the two Chinese regimes were not only eager for friendship of the Turks but also for their hostility toward the other Chinese opponent. Both the two governments presented silk and other things to the Turks, and strove for intermarriage with the Turks on the condition that the Turks must help the giver attack his rivalrous regime. Therefore, in certain cases, the true or main purpose of the "intermarriage with the Barbarians" or silk exporting by the Chinese governments was "taking advantage of the military forces abroad to fight against the domestic rivals."

---

[2] Cf. *Zhoushu* 周書, fasc. 50, Zhonghua Book Company 中華書局, 1971, p. 909.
[3] *Ibid.*, p. 911.
[4] *Ibid.*

As earlier as the sixth decade of the sixth century, two regimes located in the east and west of the Northern China, respectively, started their struggle for a "Turkic ally". At that time, Mahān Qaghan 木杆可汗 reigned, and naturally played the leading role in this fierce "fight for intermarriage". Zhoushu says the following:

> The Northern Zhou went to war with the Northern Qi frequently, mobilizing troops almost every year. So, it often allied with the Turks, and took them as the external military assistance. In the reign of Emperor Gongdi 恭帝 of the Western Wei 西魏 (535–556), Mugān Qaghan was going to marry off his daughter to Yuwentai 宇文泰,[5] but the latter died before the contract was signed. Soon after, Mahān Qaghan promised to marry off another daughter to Emperor Wudi 武帝 of the Northern Zhou, the son of Yuwentai. However, the emperor of the Northern Qi also immediately sent missions to the Turks for intermarriage. Mugān Qaghan intended to tear up the former contract, because the dowry given by the Qi government was much more than that of the Zhou. Then, the emperor of the Northern Zhou dispatched the Liangzhou governor 凉州刺史 Yangjian 楊荐 and the earl Wangqing 王慶 as envoys to the Turks to seek an alliance again. Owing to their analysis and debate, Mugān Qaghan finally refused the request of the Qi and promised to have intermarriage with the Zhou. Furthermore, the Turks were going to attack the Qi eastward with a strong army.[6]

As soon as the marriage with the Zhou was confirmed, the Turkic ruler Mahān Qaghan immediately planned to conquer the Northern Qi jointly with the Northern Zhou. This fact distinctly shows that the main aim of the vast exportation of silk by the Zhou was to take advantage of the Turkic forces to seize hegemony of China.

For this political situation of that period, a thorough analysis was given in an edict issued by Emperor Wendi 文帝 (r. 581–604) of the Sui 隋 Dynasty: "Earlier, when the Wei 魏 regime is declining, disasters happen one after another, the Zhou and the Qi confront against each other, leading to fragmentation of China. The barbarian Turks collude respectively with both of the two powers. What the Zhou worries about is that

---
[5] He was then the highest and most powerful official of the Western Wei regime, and also the father of the emperors of the Northern Zhou Dynasty established slightly later.
[6] Cf. *Zhoushu* 周書, fasc. 50, p. 911.

the Qi of the East would establish deep friendship with the Turks; while the Qi also fears that the Zhou would become a real ally of the Turks. Both the two Chinese regimes believe that their safety or danger depends on the position of the Turks. So, they compete with each other for pleasing the Turks, exhausting resources of folks to satisfy their requirements, and empting wealth of the state treasury to entertain the barbarians living in deserts. The people all over China suffer greatly."[7] Evidently, such measures taken by the two Chinese regimes did not aim at the economic benefits at all, but at a pure consideration of political struggle within China.

Another example is recorded in *Zizhitongjian* 資治通鑑, which tells a story of "silk exporting for political purposes". At the end of the Sui Dynasty, Liyuan 李淵, the founder of the Tang Dynasty, launched an armed uprising in Taiyuan 太原; he gave a large quantity of silk to the Turks aiming at utilizing their armies. A detail description of this process is as follows:

> Liuwenjing 劉文靜 persuaded Liyuan to ally with the Turks, in order to take advantage of the Turkic forces to strengthen his power and promote his fame. Liyuan followed the advice, and personally wrote a letter with humble words to Shadpit Qaghan 始畢可汗, and then sent a mission to the Turks with a generous gift. The letter said, "I would like to lead a righteous army, support emperor of the Sui, and have intermarriage with the Turks, just like the doings in the reign of Kaihuang 開皇 (581–600). If you are willing to march southward with me together, please do not harass the people of our country. If you intend to have intermarriage with us, you can get a great deal of silks and wealth without any laboring. You can choose freely at your will."
>
> After reading the letter, Shadpit Qaghan said to his ministers, "I quite know the emperor of the Sui; if we uphold him now, he will surely soon kill Prince Tang 唐公 and attack me. So as long as Prince Tang claims to be emperor himself, I will certainly support him with strong forces at any time." Then, the Qaghan ordered his officials to write a letter in reply according to the words he had just said. The diplomats of the Tang came back in seven days; all civil and military officials were overjoyed, and urged Liyuan to accept the suggestion of the Turk Qaghan.[8]

---

[7] Cf. *Suishu* 隋書, fasc. 84, Zhonghua Book Company 中華書局, 1973. p. 1866.
[8] Cf. *Zizhitongjian* 資治通鑑, fasc. 184, pp. 5737–5738.

Not long afterward, a deal of silk and horse was carried out between the Tang and the Turks:

> The Turk Khanate sent their Great General Kangshaoli 康鞘利 and others to Liyuan with a thousand horses for trading, and promised to dispatch troops to accompany Liyuan's march southward. As for the members of the army, the Turks could meet any requirements. On the day of Dingyou 丁酉, Liyuan received Kangshaoli and other envoys. He accepted the letter of the Turk Qaghan with great respect, and presented generous gifts to these emissaries. However, he only bought half of the horses brought by Kangshaoli, which were the good ones selected from all horses. His subordinates said that they were willing to buy the other horses with their private money. But, Liyuan explained, "These barbarians are rich of horses, and are greedy for money. So if we always buy all of their horses they will bring them here continuously; thus you probably can't afford it. The reason why I buy less is to hint my poverty and that I am not in urgent need of horses. I will pay for these horses I bought, you need not spend your own money."[9]

Finally, Liyuan obtains military aid from the Turks on the condition of vast silks and wealth, as stated in *Zizhitongjian*:

> Liuwenjing 劉文靜 was dispatched to the Turks, requesting Shadpit Qaghan to send reinforcements, and contracted with the Turks. The treaty stated the following: "After the forces of the Tang and the Turks capture Chang'an, the capital, all the people and lands will belong to Prince Tang, while all the gold, jade, silk and other wealth will be owned by the Turks." Shadpit Qaghan was very joyful. On the day of Bingyin 丙寅, Shadpit Qaghan sent first his minister Jishi Tegin 級失特勤 to the military camp of Liyuan, telling him that the Turkic Army had already set out.[10]

According to these records cited above, at least three facts are distinctly shown. First, the purpose of allying with the Turks by Liyuan was merely utilizing the foreign forces to fight for the hegemony of China. Although Liyuan took "supporting emperor of the Sui" as an excuse, the

---

[9] See *ibid.*, p. 5740.
[10] See *ibid.*, p. 5742.

words "Prince Tang becomes emperor himself" of Shadpit Qaghan were the real inner intention of Liyuan!

Second, the Turks came to the Tang's territory with a lot of horses; though they claimed that they aimed at "reciprocal trade 互市", the true fact was apparently that they intended to ask for remuneration for their military aid. Elsewise, it was unnecessary to designate the high official Kangshaoli as an envoy holding the state letter. Of course, Liyuan clearly saw their real purpose, so he gave the Turks a great deal of gifts, and bought half of their horses at a price not low; at that time, people usually paid for horses with silks. We do not know the specific price of the horses, but it was surely very high. Since Liyuan worried that the Turk horses would be sent here continuously, it was quite possible that this trade of horse and silk was not a fair one.

Third, the words of the contract "all the people and lands will belong to Prince Tang, while all the gold, jade, silk and other wealth will be owned by the Turks" revealed more distinctly that exporting silks had completely become the payment for external mercenaries.

It is conceivable that in order to encourage the Turks to actively support the Tang power for capturing the hegemony of China, Liyuan paid a huge amount of silk and other wealth. Though a part of silk was exported in the name of *buying horses*, the essence of bribing for political motive can never be covered up.

(2) Exporting silk for the sake of peace and friendship in border regions.

Generally speaking, almost all the serious security threats suffered by Chinese regimes in history came from the north. The nomads inhabiting Central Eurasia were good at riding and shooting. They were brave and fierce, and were always the strong opponents of the Chinese in the South, the latter being mainly farmers with poorer military skills. Thus, the subject discussed repeatedly by the Chinese politicians was usually, "What is the best policy of pacifying borderlands". Although there are various opinions and views, in the end most people were inclined to agree with appeasement, namely, the so-called Jimi 羈縻 policy, which means roughly that the Chinese government controlled the barbarians around China by political or military forces on the one hand, and pacified them with vast economic profits on the other hand. A paragraph in *Cefuyuangui* 冊府元龜 analyses this policy more thoroughly.

It says that since the earlier times, the barbarians have harassed Chinese borderlands frequently. They can neither be civilized by education, nor be killed out by armies. Thus, it is very difficult to completely capture and annihilate them even by means of repeated expeditions. For this reason, the ancient sages and forerunners have to adopt the policy of pacifying. Emperor Gaozu 高祖 (r. 206–195 BC) of the Han Dynasty had intermarriage with the Xiongnu, and gave them a large amount of silks and foods. As a result, the peace was achieved, and the barbarians submitted to China. After that, the Queen of Gaozu (r. 187–180 BC), Emperor Wendi 文帝 (r. 180–157 BC) and their successors all took this policy. Therefore, Huhanye 呼韓邪 (?–31 BC), the Chanyu 單于 of the Xiongnu, claimed to surrender to the Han regime. Emperor Daowudi 道武帝 (r. 386–409) of the Northern Wei 北魏 (386–534) also agreed with this policy, believing it to be a good tactic suitable for the contemporary situation. This was actually the meaning of "rise to the occasion" as stated in the *Book of Changes* 易經.[11]

The so-called *Jimi Policy* 羈縻之策 was probably nothing but *pacifying*; and the content of *pacifying* was mainly intermarriage as well as exportation of a great quantity of silk and wealth. Therefore, it was surely that along with the implementation of the *Jimi Policy*, in the long term, a huge amount of silk was exported continuously from China to the barbarians surrounding China.

As early as the beginning of the Han Dynasty, Gaozu 高祖 accepted the recommendation offered by Loujing 婁敬 or Liujing 劉敬, adopting the policy of intermarriage 和親之策, marrying his biological daughter to the supreme ruler of Xiongnu 匈奴 (the Huns), Modu Chanyu 冒頓單于 and presenting a great deal of silk and other belongings to the Xiongnu annually. This measure mitigated the Huns' harassment on the northern borders of China.

---

[11] Cf. *Cefuyuangui* 冊府元龜, fasc. 978, Zhonghua Book Company 中華書局, 1960. p. 11486, The Chinese text is as follows: "戎狄之國, 世為邊患。禮義不能革其貪, 干戈不能絕其類。故上自虞夏商周, 固不程督, 雖有窮兵追擊, 而亦亡失略等。所謂 '獸聚鳥散, 從之如搏景' 者也。是以聖人用權變之道, 遠禦不絕而已。漢高始納奉春之計, 建和親之議, 歲用絮繒酒食奉之。非惟解兵息民, 亦欲漸而臣之, 為羈縻長久之策耳。高後、文帝, 至於宣、元, 皆用是道, 故得呼韓朝于北闕之下。及魏道武讀漢史, 至欲以魯元妻匈奴, 為之掩卷太息, 於是以諸女皆厘降於賓附之國。此乃深識從權濟時之略也。《易》曰：'惟幾也, 故能成天下之務。' 其是之謂乎？"

The recommendation offered by Loujing was seemingly rather reasonable; it said that the Han regime was founded not long ago, and both the soldiers and general public was disgusted with endless fights and wars, so it was impractical to conquer the Xiongnu with military forces. On the contrary, the Xiongnu were so barbaric and uncivil that the Chinese could not persuade them to accept peace by means of some arguments. Therefore, the best way was transforming the descendants of the Xiongnu into the subjects of the Han. That is to say, the emperor of the Han may marry his daughter to the Chanyu 單于 of the Xiongnu at present, and give him generous gifts. Chanyu will be certainly overjoyed at this abundant wealth, and dote on the Chinese princess, his wife. Naturally, their son, the grandson of the emperor, will surely be the successor of Chanyu in the future. Thereby, the Xiongnu will become subjects of the Han Dynasty without any war, because it was impossible and inconceivable that the grandson would attack against his grandfather.[12]

The intermarriage policy suggested by Loujing 婁敬 seemed to be rather wishful thinking, because all these suppositions would not necessarily occur, such as the Chinese princess becoming the Queen of Xiongnu and giving birth to a son, as well as the son succeeding his father in the future. Nevertheless, owing to the weaker military strength of China at that time, the Chinese could hardly defeat the Xiongnu in a short period, so it was a better way to pacifying the Xiongnu by affording a vast quantity of belongings and wealth.

Exactly because it was a policy with certain rationality, Emperor Gaozu accepted the recommendation of Loujing, and many of the succeeding monarchs of China emulated him too. In the period of the Former Han (206 BC–8 AD), the sovereigns such as Huidi 惠帝 (r. 194–188 BC), Queen Lü 呂后 (r. 187–180), Wendi 文帝 (r. 180–157 BC) and Xuandi 宣帝 (r. 74–49 BC) had intermarriage with the Xiongnu. Apparently,

---

[12] Cf. *Hanshu* 漢書, fasc. 43, p. 2122. The Chinese text is as follows: "高帝罷平城歸, 韓王信亡入胡。當是時, 冒頓單于兵強, 控弦四十萬騎, 數苦北邊。上患之, 問敬。敬曰: '天下初定, 士卒罷於兵革, 未可以武服也。冒頓殺父代立, 妻群母, 以力為威, 未可以仁義說也。獨可以計久遠子孫為臣耳, 然陛下恐不能為。'上曰: '誠可, 何為不能! 顧為奈何?' 敬曰: '陛下誠能以適長公主妻單于, 厚奉遺之, 彼知漢女送厚, 蠻夷必慕, 以為閼氏, 生子必為太子, 代單于。何者? 貪漢重幣。陛下以歲時漢所餘彼所鮮數問遺, 使辯士風諭以禮節。冒頓在, 固為子婿; 死, 外孫為單于。豈曾聞外孫敢與大父亢禮哉? 可毋戰以漸臣也。'"

China's governments exported innumerable silks to the nomads for the purpose of *pacifying borders* 安邊.

Even Emperor Wudi 武帝 (r. 140–87 BC), who was economically and militarily strong, still treated the Xiongnu kindly and generously at the beginning of his reign. In order to gain the goodwill of the Xiongnu, Wudi intentionally paid for the commodities of the Huns at a high price in the border markets: "At the beginning of his reign emperor Wudi holds the commitment of intermarriage with the Xiongnu, generously pays for them in border markets. So the Huns, from Chanyu 單于 to general public, all are friendly with Chinese, and frequented under the Great Wall of China."[13]

In fact, the so-called *border market* or *reciprocal trade* 互市 could be a mart setting in the border area for deals between Chinese and foreign persons. These deals there could be quite fair. However, under certain circumstances, these places became the organs for seeking frontier peace by vast wealth.

According to the true opinion of ancient politicians, the border market or reciprocal trade did not aim at real trade or bargain, but was only one of the measures to pacify the uncivilized people outside, namely, a so-called *tactic of conciliating the barbarians* 和戎之術。 A representative statement was given in *Cefuyuangui* 冊府元龜: "When the virtuous sovereigns rule the barbarians surrounding China, they adopt the policies of winning over and controlling through conciliation and pacifying. Its purpose is to keep peace in the border regions, and let the Chinese rest and recuperate. The carrying out of reciprocal trade means doubtlessly conciliation and pacifying. This policy is firstly adopted in the beginning of the Han Dynasty. Since then the fair places are selected, the regulations on the markets are observed. The Chinese trade with these barbarians, teach them faithfulness; and they comply with the rules always. This is exactly one of the tactics of conciliating the barbarians."[14] Thus, it can be seen that in ancient China probably few cases of silk deals could be called real "trade" in terms both the form and essence.

Emperor Wudi 武帝 believed that the Xiongnu were declining while the Han regime was growing stronger and enough to compel them to submit. In 107 BC, he sent Yangxin 楊信 as an envoy to Xiongnu and declared that if the Xiongnu wanted to intermarry with the Han, the son

---

[13] Cf. *Hanshu* 漢書, fasc. 94, p. 3765.
[14] Cf. *Cefuyuangui* 冊府元龜, fasc. 999, p. 11725.

of their Chanyu 單于 must be treated as a hostage staying in China. However, Chanyu refused this demand, and said, "This not the original contract. According to the original one, emperors of the Han should marry their daughters to our chiefs often, and give us silks and belongings. In return the Huns will harass Chinese borders no longer. But now you try to breach the contract, and make my crown prince as a hostage; it is absolutely unacceptable!"

In addition, in the year 89 BC, Hulugu Chanyu 狐鹿姑單于 (r. 96–85 BC) sent diplomats to the Han, and brought with them a letter to the emperor, which stated, "There are the Great Han in the South while the strong Hu 強胡 (the strong barbarians) in the North. So-called Hu 胡 is actually the beloved son of the heavenly god, so we distain to argue on little things. Now we willing to set up trade markets with the Han, and marry your princesses. You should give us annually ten thousand shi 石[15] of wine, 5000 hu 斛[16] of grain as well as ten thousand bolts of various silks; as for other belongings and wealth, may be the same quantity as before. If you do in such way, we will not plunder Chinese in the border regions anymore."[17]

Apparently, a historical truth was given in these paragraphs, that is to say, there was an implicit rule between Chinese rulers and the Xiongnu, at least in the period prior to the reign of Wudi. This so-called *implicit rule* was probably as follows: The Chinese government will supply the Huns with silks and other belongings annually, while the latter will constrain themselves from intruding into Chinese borders and harassing the people. In other words, the Han regime exported a great deal of silks in exchange for the Xiongnu no longer "plundering and harassing" them. It was conceivable that in order to pacify the barbarians and keep the peace of border regions, countless silks were exported by Chinese regimes during the long period.

Of course, for the sake of a peaceful existence in the frontier areas, Chinese rulers not only passively satisfied the material desires of the barbarians but sometimes also adopted certain active measures, such as the tactics of "using barbarous people to subjugate their own races"

---

[15] Shi 石, a unit of weight of ancient China. Generally, it equals 120 jin 斤, namely, 60 kilograms. So, "ten thousand shi 石" here equals 600 tons.
[16] Hu 斛, a unit of measure for grain in ancient China. Generally, it equals 100 sheng 升, and the sheng is a liter. So, "5000斛 of grain" here equals half a million liters of grain.
[17] Cf. *Hanshu* 漢書, fasc. 94, pp. 3773 and 3780.

以夷制夷 or "befriend the distant enemy while attacking those nearby" 遠交近攻. Namely, they often took advantage of the divergences among foreign tribes and provoked them into fighting with each other, so as to eliminate or mitigate the pressure suffered by China. However, these measures also required a huge amount of resources, a majority of them being silk. A typical example is in the story of Zhangqian's mission to the Western Regions during the reign of Wudi 武帝.

Wudi of the Han dispatched Zhangqian as an envoy to the states in the Western regions in 139 BC. Initially, this mission aimed at allying with the Great Yueshi 大月氏, the old enemy of the Xiongnu, persuading them to attack the Huns together with the Chinese. Besides, Zhangqian also attempted to establish friendly relations with other countries in Central Asia, so as to strengthen the forces against the Xiongnu. Obviously, the cost for allying with them was a great amount of money and belongings; only these things could cater to their pleasure. For example, among the people of the state of Dawan 大宛, China was known for its richness; thus, the officials of Dawan welcomed Zhangqian warmly, and endeavored to display their friendship. Zhangqian promised the king that the Chinese government would give him abundant wealth provided he allied with the Han. Moreover, Zhangqian suggested to Wudi that he could generously bribe the king of Wusun 烏孫, and have intermarriage with him so as to "cut off the right arm of Xiongnu", for the Wusun King was very greedy for the wealth of China. Soon after, Zhangqian was sent as the first ambassador to Wusun, and the gifts of gold, silk, etc., presented to the king by Wudi were worth a million.[18]

After the ruling family of the Han officially intermarried with Wusun 烏孫, much more silks and other things were exported abroad than before. For instance, in the reign of Yuanfeng 元封 (110–105 BC), Wudi designated the daughter of Liujian 劉建 as a princess to marry the king of Wusun. This princess was named Xijun 細君, and her father was the feudal prince of Jiandu 江都, of course a member of the imperial family.

---

[18] About the details, may cf. *Hanshu* 漢書, such as "大宛聞漢之饒財, 欲通不得, 見騫, 喜, 問欲何之。騫曰: '為漢使月氏而為匈奴所閉道, 今亡, 唯王使人道送我。誠得之, 反漢, 漢之賂遺王財物不可勝言。' 大宛以為然, 遣騫, 為發驛道, 抵康居。" and "'蠻夷戀故地, 又貪漢物, 誠以此時厚賂烏孫, 招以東居故地, 漢遣公主為夫人, 結昆弟, 其勢宜聽, 則是斷匈奴右臂也。既連烏孫, 自其西大夏之屬皆可招來而為外臣。' 天子以為然, 拜騫為中郎將, 將三百人, 馬各二匹, 牛羊以萬數, 齎金幣帛直數千鉅萬。" Cf. *Hanshu* 漢書, fasc. 61, pp. 2688 and 2692.

She brought a great dowry to Wusun, which included various clothes, vehicles, jewels and other valuable objects; besides, several hundreds of people accompanied her in her entourage. However, Princess Xijun was very depressed and sad, because her husband, the king of Wusun was an old man, and she was lonely in a strange country much far from her hometown. Wudi pitied her when he heard about this, so he annually sent special emissaries to the princess with a huge amount of silks and other belongings as gifts.[19] From here, we see that a great deal of silk and wealth was required for merely one intermarriage with the barbarians; hence, the total sum of exporting silk throughout the history was certainly great.

Chinese rulers often carried out the tactic of "using barbarous people to subjugate their own races". What they wanted most was that the barbarian regime menacing Chinese borders caused internal splits, and one of these groups sought support from China. If it really happened like that, the peripheral defending line would be indeed established, and a large quantity of wealth would be paid by the Chinese government. This wealth, including a great many silks of course, was used for encouraging and rewarding the *loyal* barbarians.

For example, during the reign of Xuandi 宣帝 (r. 74–49 BC), Chanyu Huhanye 呼韓邪 failed in the internal struggle of the Xiongnu. He immediately paid his respects to the emperor of the Han, submitted himself to the rule of the Han and requested the political and military support. In the beginning of 51 BC, Huhanye came to Palace in Ganquan 甘泉宮, and Emperor Xuandi ceremoniously received him; he was given more honor than the princes. As for the gifts, they were knives, swords, bows, arrows, vehicles, horses, gold, clothes and so on. Besides, 8000 bolts of various silks and 6000 *jin* 斤 of cotton were also included in the rewards. In the year 49 BC, Huhanye came to the imperial court once again to pay his respects to the Chinese emperor. He again gained generous rewards. In addition to the gifts, which were the same as before, he also got 110 sets of dresses, 9000 bolts of silks and 8000 *jin* of cotton. Huhanye went to

---

[19] Cf. the Chinese text in *Hanshu* 漢書: "烏孫以馬千匹聘。漢元封中,遣江都王建女細君為公主,以妻焉。賜乘輿服御物,為備官屬宦官侍御數百人,贈送甚盛。烏孫昆莫以為右夫人。匈奴亦遣女妻昆莫,昆莫以為左夫人。公主至其國,自治宮室居,歲時一再與昆莫會,置酒飲食,以幣帛賜王左右貴人。昆莫年老,語言不通,公主悲愁,自為作歌曰:'吾家嫁我兮天一方,遠託異國兮烏孫王。穹廬為室兮旃為牆,以肉為食兮酪為漿。居常土思兮心內傷,願為黃鵠兮歸故鄉。'天子聞而憐之,間歲遣使者持帷帳錦繡給遺焉。" See *Hanshu* 漢書, fasc. 96B, p. 3903.

China once again in 33 BC and gained more gifts; the number of clothes and silks doubled that given by the former emperor.

Besides, Fujulei Jodi-Chanyu 復株累若鞮單于 (r. 31–20 BC), the son of Huhanye, went to pay his respects to the emperor of the Han in lunar January of the fourth year of Heping 河平 (25 BC), and obtained very generous gifts including 20000 bolts of silk and 20000 *jin* of cotton. In the reign of Emperor Aidi 哀帝 (r. 7–2 BC), the Former Han regime was declining, and its political and economic circumstances were deteriorating. Nevertheless, the government still gave Uchjulu Jodi-Chanyu 烏珠留若鞮單于 (r. 8 BC–13 AD) a great deal of silk when he visited China in 1 BC. The quantity of gifts was even more than before, including 30000 bolts of colored silks and 30000 *jin* of cotton.[20]

Obviously, those Huns who were loyal to China were favored and trusted deeply by the monarchs of the Han, and could of course get generous rewards. As compared with these riches and wealth, the demand of "10000 bolts of miscellaneous silks" claimed earlier by Hulugu Chanyu 狐鹿姑單于 does not appear to be greedy at all. It is evident that all these exporting silks and goods had nothing to do with *trade*.

(3) Exporting silks aimed at showing off the *greatness* to foreign countries

Nearly all Chinese emperors held a strong desire to display their "greatness" or other "excellent qualities", pretending to be a "wise leader", enough to rule the whole world. Therefore, they often satisfied their own vanity at the cost of vast wealth. In ancient China, a large quantity of silks was transported abroad exactly under thus circumstance. A typical example is that of Emperor Yangdi 煬帝 (r. 604–617) of the Sui Dynasty who gave a vast amount of silk and money to the Turks and other barbarian states to burnish his reputation.

Suishu 隋書 states the following: "Soon after Gaozu 高祖 dies, Yangdi 煬帝 commits adultery with the wives of his father. As soon as the funeral of the late emperor finishes, Yangdi leaves the capital immediately and makes an inspection journey to distant areas. At that time the peace has kept for many years, and the government possesses powerful military force and strong economic strength. Hence Yangdi wants to set up great achievements just like that done by emperors Shihuang 始皇 of the

---

[20] Cf. *Hanshu* 漢書, fasc. 94B, pp. 3798–3799, 3803, 3808, 3817.

Qin 秦 and Wudi 武帝 of the Han 漢 whom he has admired for long time. Then Yangdi constructs luxury palaces and other buildings on a large scale, at a cost of innumerable resources. Besides, he dispatches many messengers to foreign countries far away, invites them visiting China. Those who come and pay respects to Chinese emperor would get generous rewards, while the states did not obey will suffer attacking from the Sui."[21]

Obviously, Yangdi only superficially emulated the emperors of ancient times but did not understand the teaching of "winning people by virtue", whereby at the end he lost both the popular feeling and state wealth. A paragraph in *Suishu* vividly describes the absurd practice done by Emperor Yangdi:

Peiju 裴矩, one of the high officials of the Sui, designed this farce of "all barbarians coming to pay respects" 四夷來朝. He sent delegates to the king of Gaochang 高昌 and the governor of Yiwu 伊吾, inducing them to come to visit the emperor by promising vast wealth. When Yangdi arrived at the western border regions, the king of Gaochang and dozens of chiefs of other western states all prostrated themselves before the emperor. At the scene, numerous Chinese wore ornate costumes, played music, burned incense and sang joyfully. Besides, there were a lot of male and female *spectators* dressed up beautifully, extending tens of *li* 里. Yangdi was very delighted with this scene, and thought that it displayed the prosperity of China. In the winter, Yangdi went to the east capital Luoyang 洛陽, and accepted the suggestion offered by Peiju to approve the enacting of plays on a large scale in the whole city, because many rulers, officials and merchants of foreign countries had come to Luoyang. There were many actors and actresses in the central area of the city, showing their multitudinous skills; the spectators wearing silk and jewelry numbered hundreds of thousands. The Chinese officials and populace were compelled to act as audiences. Moreover, Yangdi ordered all shops to supply free delicious foods and wine for barbarians coming there, entertaining them cordially. Therefore, all these foreigners sighed with emotion that "China is really a paradise on the earth!" This grand banquet lasted a month.[22]

---

[21] Cf. *Suishu* 隋書, fasc. 4, p. 94.
[22] Cf. *Suishu* 隋書, fasc. 67, pp. 1580–1581. The Chinese text is as follows: "(裴) 矩遣使說高昌王麴伯雅及伊吾吐屯設等, 啗以厚利, 導使入朝。及帝西巡, 次燕支山, 高昌王、伊吾設等, 及西番胡二十七國, 謁於道左。皆令佩金玉, 被錦罽, 焚香奏樂, 歌舞

Undoubtedly, any foreigner will praise China for its *prosperity* when he sees such a grand scene, and any guest will surely believe China was really a country like paradise when he fully enjoys free feasts every day. Unfortunately, all these gorgeous scenes and good reputation were obtained at the cost of countless state resources. Regardless of other consumption, the quantity of squandered silk alone was great, for instance, the silk for bribing the chiefs of dozens of western states, the silk clothes worn by a crowd of tens of *li*, the silk dresses of hundreds of thousand spectators in the eastern capital and the silk for various decorations; the quantity of all these silks was surely astonishing. In order to carry out the political exercises of the Chinese emperor, a huge amount of silk was exported or wasted, and what he received was only some hollow praise coming from the barbarians.

Another example similarly revealed that Yangdi exported a large amount of silk for his own vanity; it was shown in the events associated with the emperor and Qimin Qaghan 啟民可汗. The latter was previously the younger brother of Išbara Qaghan 沙鉢略可汗 (r. 578–587 AD) of the Eastern Turk Khanate, and was given the title Qimin 啟民 by the Chinese emperor after he submitted himself to the Sui. Qimin Qaghan played a role of being absolutely loyal to the Chinese regime, and his words and actions demonstrated this distinctly. He once presented a report to Emperor Wendi 文帝 (r. 581–604), guaranteeing that he was willing "to be a servant herding livestock for the Sui regime forever."

When Emperor Yangdi 煬帝 took a tour to Yulin 榆林 of the western border areas in 607 AD, Qimin Qaghan showed his loyalty to the Sui regime once again; he even requested the Chinese emperor to allow the Turks to change their costumes into those of the Chinese. He said the following: "Now I am no longer the former Turk Qaghan of the remote area, but the obedient subject of Your Majesty. I humbly beg Your Majesty to show mercy, promise our Turks dressing as same as people of the great country China. Now I and all of my people implore Your Majesty to agree with this request."

喧噪。復令武威、張掖士女盛飾縱觀，騎乘填咽，周亙數十里，以示中國之盛。帝見而大悅。... 其冬，帝至東都，矩以蠻夷朝貢者多，諷帝令都下大戲。征四方奇技異藝，陳於端門街，衣錦綺、珥金翠者，以十數萬。又勒百官及民士女坐棚閣而縱觀焉。皆被服鮮麗，終月乃罷。又令三市店肆皆設帷帳，盛列酒食，遣掌番率蠻夷與民貿易，所至之處，悉令邀延就坐，醉飽而散。蠻夷嗟嘆，謂中國為神仙。"

As the chief of a powerful nomadic khanate, Qimin Qaghan bowed to Yangdi in such a way that his behavior satisfied the vanity of the emperor. Therefore, when Qimin Qaghan went to offer good horses, Yangdi at first rewarded him with 12000 bolts of silk; then he gave 200000 silks to Qimin Qaghan and his ministers, and held a grand banquet to entertain the Turks.

Thereafter, Emperor Yangdi continued his tours among the frontier regions, and even went northward to the residence of Qimin Qaghan. The Qaghan celebrated Yangdi's birthday with great respect, the emperor rejoiced greatly, and wrote a poem to show off his *achievements* and *prestige*. He was very proud of the fact that the Turks yielded to the Sui, and bragged that the emperor of the Han was inferior to himself. Thus, the gifts he gave to the Turks increased more and more, and accordingly, a vast amount of silk circulated to foreign countries continuously.[23]

Here, what we see is only a deal exchanging Chinese silk for the flattery of the foreigners; there was no any real "trade" at all. This example might be thought as not a typical one, for Yangdi was a fatuous monarch. However, what was done by the famous Emperor Wudi 武帝 of the Han manifested clearly in almost all autocratic rulers intending to exchange a great deal of wealth for their own "prestige", regardless of poverty.

For instance, *Biography of Zhangqian* 張騫傳 of *Hanshu* 漢書 says that after Zhangqian's mission to the Western Regions, the Han regime frequently communicated with many states in Central Eurasia, and hence more and more foreign diplomats, merchants and religious personages came to China. In order to show off the prosperity, richness and power of China, as well as the "greatness" of the monarch, Emperor Wudi spent much money and silk on these foreigners, just like the doings of Yangdi of the Sui.

On the orders of Wudi, the government often gave generous rewards to the foreign visitors to display the affluence of China. With fighting contests, various performances and many monstrous acts and exhibits on the streets and squares, all foreign guests were to be treated to these entertainments. Furthermore, they were guided to visit state treasuries and warehouses, so as to understand about the richness of China. Since then,

---

[23] For the story about Qimin Qaghan, cf. *History of the Sui* 隋書, fasc. 84, *Biography of the Turks*, pp. 1873–1875. And, the Chinese text of the poem written by Yangdi is as follows: "鹿塞鴻旗駐，龍庭翠輦回。氈帳望風舉，穹廬向日開。呼韓頓顙至，屠耆接踵來。索辮擎膻肉，韋韝獻酒杯。何如漢天子，空上單于台。"

the foreign missions and traders visited China more frequently, and many kinds of magic, acrobatics and plays were introduced into China from other countries of the world, too.[24]

In fact almost every autocratic monarch had the ambition of "dominating the world", though the degrees of their desires might be different. Thus, as long as suitable conditions appeared, such as strong economic strength and active aid of foreign states, the ruler probably could not help trying to exchange the state wealth for his own "prestige". Therefore, it was quite possible that both the "fatuous monarch" and the "wise monarch" exported innumerable silk and other wealth to foreign countries, aiming at the yielding of the barbarians and praise from the foreigners. In this process of exchange, there was no "trade" in true meaning.

The three kinds of phenomena listed above were only the main forms of the non-trade silk exportation in ancient China. Numerous other cases were surely not real "trade" either, for example, the gifts given to the noble hostages and envoys of foreign states,[25] congratulatory gifts for intermarriages with foreign states,[26] courtesy presents on the death of foreign rulers[27] and a great deal of rewards to foreign general public who

---

[24] Cf. *Hanshu* 漢書, fasc. 61, p. 2697. The Chinese text is as follows: "是時，上方數巡狩海上，乃悉從外國客，大都多人則過之，散財帛賞賜，厚具饒給之，以覽視漢富厚焉。大角氐，出奇戲諸怪物，多聚觀者，行賞賜，酒池肉林，令外國客遍觀各倉庫府藏之積，欲以見漢廣大，傾駭之。及加其眩者之工，而角氐奇戲歲增變，其益興，自此始。而外國使更來更去。"

[25] In 50 AD, the Southern Chanyu 南單于 of the Xiongnu sent his son to China as a hostage. In addition to the clothes, gold, vehicles, foods, etc., the gifts rewarded by Emperor Guangwudi 光武帝 included also 10000 bolts of silk and 10000 *jin* of cotton. Besides, the subordinates of this noble hostage got 10000 bolts of silk, too. Similar gifts were given to the Huns annually. Cf. *Houhanshu* 後漢書, fasc. 89, *Biography of the Southern Huns* 南匈奴傳, Zhonghua Book Company 中華書局, 1965.

[26] In order to commend the "Loyalty" of Chuluo Qaghan 處羅可汗 of the Western Turk Khanate, Yangdi 煬帝 married off Princess Xinyi 信義公主 to him; a portion of the congratulatory gifts included 1000 sets of silk costumes and 10000 bolts of silk. Cf. *Suishu* 隋書, fasc. 84, *Biography of the Western Turks* 西突厥傳.

[27] The Southern Chanyu 南單于 Huhanye 呼韓邪 died in 56 AD. The imperial court of the Han dispatched a mission to condole him, and rewarded the Xiongnu 4000 bolts of silk and other belongings. Thenceforth, as long as their Chanyu died, the Huns could receive a gift the same as this. Cf. *Houhan* 後漢書, fasc. 89, *Biography of the Southern Huns* 南匈奴傳.

had already yielded to China.²⁸ Sometimes, the Chinese government had to pay a large amount of silk as the ransom to return the people being taken away by certain foreign forces.²⁹

According to the historical records, the accounts of silk export during the Han and the Tang Dynasties were nearly all for the so-called "non-trade exportation", while those cases of real silk trade were very rare in records. Thus, we have to admit that the silk exportation during the period of the Han and the Tang did not mainly aim for trade or commercial profits.

2. The Influence of Silk Export on the World

In ancient China, especially during the period of the Han and the Tang, silk exporting had direct or indirect magnificent influences on politics and society throughout the world. Two instances are given as follows.

First, in the latter part of the sixth century, violent political struggles and even military conflicts occurred among the Turks, Persians and Byzantines. These countries were located, respectively, in Central Eurasia, West Asia and Asia Minor. The inducement of these events was silk.

Išbara Qaghan 沙鉢略可汗 of the Turks died in 587 AD; Emperor Wendi 文帝 of the Sui dispatched a special envoy to condole him, and rewarded the Turks 5000 bolts of silk. Cf. *Suishu* 隋書, fasc. 84, *Biography of the Turks* 突厥傳.

Šadpït Qaghan 始畢可汗 of the Turks died in 619 AD; Emperor Gaozu 高祖 of the Tang ordered all his officials of the capital go to the Turk embassy to condole him, and rewarded the Turks 30000 bolts of silk. Cf. *Xintangshu* 新唐書, fasc. 215 A, *Biography of the Turks A* 突厥傳上.

²⁸ At the beginning of his reign, Emperor Taizong 太宗 of the Tang ended the Eastern Turk Khanate. Then, government of the Tang granted generous money and belongings to the numerable Turks surrendering to China. The governor of Liangzhou 涼州 Lidaliang 李大亮 said in his report to the emperor that in recent years countless Turks went to China for refuge. The government rewarded five bolts of silk and one garment to everyone yielding to the Tang, and all of their chiefs were appointed as high officials. So, this measure spent state many resources. Cf. *Zhenguanzhengyao* 貞觀政要 (*A Digest on the Governance of Zhenguan*), fasc. 9.

²⁹ For example, *Zizhitongjian* 資治通鑑 (fasc. 193) recorded that in the late period of the Sui many Chinese were captured by the Turks. After the collapse of the Eastern Turk Khanate, the Chinese emperor paid ransom for them in silk and gold, and hence 80000 persons were set free. The sum of the ransom is not known, but it could up to million or half a million bolts of silk, because so many people were waiting to be ransomed.

In the fifth decade of the sixth century, the Turks' ruling family was the Ashina 阿史那 clan and the base area was located south of the Altai Mountains. Later, they overthrew their suzerain Rouran 柔然, and established a vast and powerful nomadic khanate in Central Eurasia. Generally speaking, the direct descendants of the regime's founder Bumïn Qaghan 土門可汗 dominated the eastern portion of the khanate, its main territory being the Mongolian Plateau, while Bumïn's younger brother Istami Qaghan 室點密可汗 and his direct descendants controlled the present Xinjiang 新疆 province as well as steppe regions west of the Altai Mountains.

In the earlier period of his reign, Istami Qaghan led ten grand chiefs and their tribe members, summing up to 100000, to conquer wide territories in the Western Regions. In 554–555 AD, one of the powerful states in the Western Regions was conquered by him. It was the Gaochang 高昌 Kingdom, equivalent to present Turpan Basin. In two or three years thereafter, Istami Qaghan successively put the states surrounding Tarim Basin under the control of Turkic forces. Then, he began to strike the Hephthalites 嚈噠, the mightiest rival of the Turks in the Western Regions.

Not long after, Istami Qaghan defeated the Hephthalites successfully by virtue of the international situation at that time. In 531 AD, Khosrow I succeeded the throne as the new king of the Sasanian Kingdom in West Asia. Soon after his ascent to the throne, Khosrow carried out administrative reforms and military reforms, centralized his government and organized a strong army, especially the cavalry. Hence, this Persian regime became quite powerful. In order to make great achievements, Khosrow first targeted his eastern neighbor the Hephthalite state, which had struggled with the Persians for many years.

In 562, Khosrow signed a Fifty-Year Peace Treaty with Justinian, the emperor of Byzantine Empire. With this stable peace agreement with the Byzantines in the west, Khosrow began to focus his attention on the eastern Hephthalites, and allied with the Turk khanate which had just risen in Central Eurasia. The two regimes had intermarriage first, and Istami Qaghan promised to marry his daughter off to Khosrow. Then, they reached an agreement that they would launch a joint attack on the Hephthalites, and share the whole territory of the Hephthalites after their state was smashed.

On the one hand, Istami Qaghan led the Turkic troops, going all the way south and captured the Hephthalite territory north of the Amu Darya. Then, he went southward across this river, advancing into the core area of the Hephthalites. As a result, the main force of the Hephthalites was defeated, and the capital Balkh, which was located on the south bank of the upstream of Amu Darya, was captured. On the other hand, the Persian army led by their king Khosrow won great victories. Their main target was the region south of the Amu Darya; so, a vast tract of the Hephthalite territory fell into their hands. According to the agreement between the two states, the money and belongings they seized would belong to each party, but the lands taken from the Hephthalites should be distributed by the way previously set by them. Thus, the Turks occupied the Hephthalite territory north of the Amu Darya, while the Persians got the lands south of the river, including the former capital Balkh of the Hephthalites.

The base camp of the Turkic expeditionary force was located in the Fergana Basin of the middle reaches of the Syr Darya. After the war with the Hephthalites, a little before 558 AD, Khosrow went to Fergana in the north and married the daughter of Istami. The two powers had intermarriage with each other, celebrated victories joyfully.

Now, the former territory of the Hephthalites was divided up between the Turks and the Persians, the two countries bound by the Amu Darya. Then, the Turks expanded further westward by their victorious prestige. In the period of 562–567 AD, the Turks swept away the remnants of the Hephthalites north of the river Amu, and went on a cleanup of the Avars or so-called "pseudo Avar" (the Ogors), who were a nomadic tribe defeated already by the Turks before. Finally, the Avars were forced to flee westward and seek the refuge of the Byzantine influence. That time was seemingly the greatest prosperous period of the Turk Khanate.

However, the new situation caused new problems, because after collapse of the Hephthalite regime, the Turk Khanate and the Sasanian Empire become two directly adjacent countries. Thereby, conflicts of interests between them increased, and the main inducement was silk.

The Turks conveniently got great deal of silk from China and sold it to the merchants and other persons farther west to make huge profits. For this purpose, the Turks were eager to expand the silk market within the Sasanian Empire, even demanding that they sell silk directly to the people farther west of the Sasanian Empire.

Istami Qaghan sent a mission to the Persians. Its leader was named Maniakh, a Sogdian merchant who had communicated frequently with officials of the Turk Khanate. The Persians were very reluctant to let the Turks possess the huge profits of the silk trade alone, and even tried to dominate the intermediary trade of silk between China and the western world. So, they refused to accept Maniakh's request under various pretexts. Finally, the Persians did a very unintelligent thing, which had serious consequences.

A certain person called Katulphs, who had been an official of the Hephthalite government, surrendered to the Sasanian regime later. He suggested to the Persians that they should belittle the silk of the Turks in public, and burn them off, so as to show that there was no market for their silks in Persia, and force the Turks to abandon the intention of silk trading in Persian regions. The Persian rulers accepted this suggestion, and burned the silk. Facing the protest and condemnation of the Persian public, the Turkic mission returned home immediately.

In order to maintain friendly relations between the Turk Khanate and the Sasanian Empire, Istami Qaghan did not retaliate against the Persians, but dispatched a mission once again and tried to persuade the Persian government to open the silk market. This time, however, the Persians did something even more horrifying. They put poison in the food of the Turkic mission, causing the death of most members; they spread rumors that the Turks died of environmental inadaptability. Thus, the relationship between the Turks and the Persians deteriorated sharply, and they could not be friends and allies anymore.

Istami Qaghan did not take fierce hostile action against the Persians immediately, but adopted another strategy to get back at them. That is to say, he decided to change his ally from the Sasanian Empire to the Byzantine Empire. The latter was the western neighboring country of the former, and once had military conflicts with it. Therefore, on the one hand, the new alliance made the Persians reduce the pressure on the Turks in the east, and on the other hand, it was favorable for opening a direct silk trade channel from the oriental regions to the Byzantine Empire and other western countries. Not long after, a diplomatic mission of the Turks was dispatched to the Byzantine Empire; the chief of this mission was still the experienced trader and diplomatist Maniakh, the Sogdian.

These Turks went westward along the so-called *Steppe Silk Road*. The travel route was roughly as follows: It started from the regions of present Issyk-Kul or Fergana, where the main base ground of the Turks was located. It continued westward along the river Syr Darya, arrived at the north shore of the Aral Sea; then, it led west to the north shore of the Caspian Sea and crossed Volga River at its low reaches; after crossing over the Caucasus mountain range and passing its southern slope, it went into the Byzantine Empire in Asia Minor in the end. This regime is also called the "Eastern Roman Empire" by historians.

The Turks carried with them a large quantity of fine silk as a gift to the Byzantine rulers and commodity for sale. They were entertained warmly by the Romans and replied to many questions asked by the Roman Emperor about the Turks. Maniakh conveyed the attitude of Istami Qaghan that the Turks were willing to conclude a peace treaty with Byzantium and form a friendly alliance to oppose against the common enemies. The Romans accepted this suggestion unhesitatingly. They promised to do their best to resist the rivals of the Turks, and welcomed the Turks selling silk freely in their country. Apparently, the tactics of "change of alliances" was greatly successful.

At that time, the reigning Byzantine emperor was Justin II (520–578 AD), who attached great importance to the friendly relationship between the Romans and the Turks. He soon dispatched a mission to pay a return visit, advancing eastward together with the Turkic mission. The Roman mission was a high-level delegation, for its leader Zemarchus was the Praefect of the eastern cities of the Byzantine Empire. Zemarchus, Maniakh and other diplomats of the Roman and Turk regimes left Byzantium for the Turk Khanate in August 569 AD.

They made the journey along the Steppe Silk Road; after a long trudge for many days, they arrived at the territories of the Sogdians controlled by the Turks. As soon as the Romans dismounted from their horses, certain Turks presented them with some iron, which seemed to be offered for sale. Besides, some others showed off their performances and announced themselves as the witches to clean away the evil spirits in their bodies. These conjurors put all the baggage of the Romans in the middle, then begin ringing bells and beating drums over the baggage, while some others ran round it, burning incense, chanting spells and raging about like maniacs. In the end, they made Zemarchus and his companions pass through the fire stack, performing an act of purification.

After this rite of exorcism, the Romans were guided to a certain mountain called Ectag or the Golden Mountain, which was the residence of the Turk Qaghan. Zemarchus and his fellows were immediately summoned to an interview with Istami Qaghan in a grand and luxurious tent. Zemarchus presented the national credentials to the Qaghan and make a polite speech. He emphasized that the Romans were always eager to establish a friendly alliance with the Turks. Istami replied in a similar manner.

Then, the Turks graciously entertained the Byzantine ambassadors over the next three days, displaying their luxurious living and delicious diet, and at the same time showing off their "close relations" with the Romans, so as to warn against the Persians. Later, Istami Qaghan requested Zemarchus and his twenty followers to accompany him to conquer the Persians. Obviously, the true reason for this request made by the Qaghan was not for enhancing military strength but to give a clear signal to the Persians that the Turks and the Byzantines would jointly attack the Persians.

Thus, Zemarchus and his subordinates went with Istami to fight against the Persians. When they pitched a camp at a place called Talas, an ambassador from the Persians came to meet Istami. When they met, the Turkic Qaghan accorded to the Romans much more honorable treatment while heaping great reproaches on the Persians. The Persian envoy vehemently refuted the charge of the Qaghan. In this case, they broke up. The Turks continued to actively prepare to oppose the Persians. This result was exactly what Istami Qaghan hoped for, because this incident could provide a good excuse for conquering Persia.

In order to further strengthen the friendship with Byzantium, Istami Qaghan sent another mission, which went westward along with the Roman mission led by Zemarchus. The chief of the Turk mission was Tagma, who was an official with the title Tarkhan. The former chief Maniakh of the Turk mission had died, but his son became one of the members of the present mission, and his rank was only next to that of Tagma Tarkhan.

On their way to Byzantium, many other tribes also joined them one after another, because they were eager to establish friendly relations with the powerful Romans, developing economic and political communications. Thus, this diplomatic corps grew into a large team.[30]

Afterward, there were frequent communications between the two regimes. As far as we know, the missions dispatched by Byzantium, in addition to that of Zemarchus, included those led by Anankhast, Eutychius, Herodian, Paul and Valentin. Some among them had been emissary twice to the Turk Khanate, such as Valentin. As for the Turks, on the one hand, they directly sent many diplomatic corps to Byzantium, and

---

[30] The details about the intercourses between the Turks and the Byzantines were recorded by Byzantine historian Menander, cf. Henry Yule, *Cathay and the Way Thither*, Vol. 1, revised by Henri Cordier, Munshiram Manoharlal Publishers, 1916, pp. 205–212.

on the other hand, a lot of Turk diplomats and traders often went to Byzantium with the Roman missions returning to their homelands. Besides, many other nomadic tribes in Central Eurasia also sent missions to the West for trading or diplomacy. Thus, the Steppe Silk Road crossing Central Eurasia and running along the northern shores of Aral Sea and Caspian Sea was flourishing at that time.

In the second year of his reign, the Byzantine Emperor Tiberius (r. 574–582 AD) dispatched a mission to the Turks, with its chief being an imperial guard officer, named Valentin. More than one hundred Turks, who were former Turkic diplomats staying in Byzantium, returned home eastward along with these Roman ambassadors. After a long water and land journey, the first high-ranking chief receiving Valentin was Turxanthus, the son of Istami Qaghan, the late supreme ruler of the Western Turk Khanate. Shortly after Istami's death, the western territories of the Turkic Khanate were dominated by two sons of the late Qaghan, one being Turxanthus, the other Tardu.

The purposes of this Byzantine mission focused on two aspects: to inform the Turks of Tiberius' succession on the one hand, and to reaffirm the alliance between Byzantium and the Turk Khanate on the other hand. Valentin emphasized particularly the promise of Istami Qaghan that the Turks would have the same enemies and friends as Byzantium. Apparently, the Romans demanded the Turks cooperate firmly with them to oppose the Persians.

Later, Valentin and his fellows attended the funeral of Istami Qaghan. According to Turkic custom, all participants must hold the rite of *Cutting Face*, that is to say, they have to cut their own faces by knives and bleed them, so as to express their condolences to the dead. Taking the overall interests into account, Valentin ordered all his fellows to "cut face" like the Turks, though it was a *barbarian* custom unsuitable for the Romans. A few days later, the Romans attended a ceremony of "burying alive" of this funeral. Four prisoners of war from foreign tribes and several horses favored by Istami Qaghan were killed in front of his mausoleum as sacrifices. When the funeral ceremonies ended, at Turxanthus' disposal, Valentin and other Romans went east to meet another high-ranking chief Tardu, who was also the son of Istami Qaghan.

Istami Qaghan died in 576 AD; within thirty years thereafter, the western Turk Khanate was controlled mainly by his son Tardu Qaghan. The king of Sasanian Persia Khosrow died in 579, and his son Hormizd IV succeeded to the throne. This king had a nickname, "son of Turkic woman", because his mother was the daughter of Istami Qaghan, and married the Persian king Khosrow when the Turk Khanate allied with the Sassanid Empire. Thus, in terms of the kinship, the Persian King Hormizd and the Turk qaghan Tardu were "nephew and uncle", and should have been close and friendly. In fact, however, the state relationship between Persia and the Turk Khanate was far from being so; in the years of 588–589 AD, a fierce war broke out between the two powers.

Persia suffered attacks from three strong forces at the same time. The Turk troops invaded Persia from the east, claiming to number 300000 members, but probably 100000 at most. Their commander appeared to not be an indigenous Turk, but a senior general of the Sogdians, named Schaba. Therefore, it was quite possible that there was only a small portion of Turks in this army, and most of them might be the warriors in Sogdian regions, who were controlled by the Turkic suzerain. In any case, this army advanced very smoothly at the beginning. After crossing the Amu Darya, they immediately occupied the Badakhshan area, a large region in the northeastern part of present Afghanistan, taking the upper reaches of the Amu Darya as the northern boundary and the Hindu Kush Mountains as the southern boundary. Then, they advanced further westward and captured Herat in the northwestern part of present Afghanistan.

At the same time, the Byzantine troops invaded the western frontiers of Persia through the desert in Syria. Another force cooperating with Byzantium was its loyal ally, the Khazars. The Khazars inhabited in the regions of Southern Russia and the Caspian Sea, living in semi-nomadic life and could be subsumed under the Turkic race. Their chieftain led the army personally, exerting pressure on the northern borders of Persia from the Caucasus Mountains. Astoundingly, they captured Derbent, a strategic fortress on the western coast of Caspian Sea, and plundered with no mercy. Relying on the precipitous terrain of the Caucasus, Derbent had been an important fortress since ancient times, and was taken by the Persians as a firm citadel to deter the invasion of the northern barbarians. So, the fall of Derbent was really a tremendous shock and great failure for the Persian Empire.

In the ensuing years, there are many wars among the Turks, the Persians and the Byzantines. Any them won or lost in various battles, the details of which will not be given here. Nevertheless, the "strategic partnership" between the Western Turk Khanate and the Byzantium lasted decades; at least until the end of the sixth century, the two powers still kept up friendly relations. In 598 AD, envoys of the Turks arrived at

Byzantium and presented to Emperor Maurice (r. 582–602 AD) a letter from the Turk Qaghan. In the letter, the Qaghan claimed himself to be "Great Chieftain of Seven Clans and Lord of Seven Regimes", displaying a rather proud attitude. He said that in the half a century since the foundation of the Turk Khanate, the Turks gained great achievements in the West, seeming to inform the Romans, his ally, of this situation. This letter was written by Tardu Qaghan, whose father was the late Istami Qaghan, a powerful monarch who enjoyed a high reputation.

In ancient times, the silk exportation of China impacted the world greatly. The second instance of this phenomenon is as follows. It is so-called "silk–horse trade" 絹馬交易 between the Tang Dynasty and the Uighur Khanate. This term was invented initially by a Japanese Scholar Matsuda Hisao 松田壽男 (1903–1983). It means that the Chinese governments exchanged their silks for horses of the nomads in Central Eurasia, thus forming trade relations.

However, after concretely analyzing various cases of silk and horse exchange, we can find that most of them cannot be regarded as "trade" in the sense of modern economics, because there were often great disparities of price between the two commodities of silk and horse. In other words, with respect to the economic profits, they were not fair trade at all. Here, we will take the "silk–horse trade" after *An-Shi Rebellion* 安史之亂 in the Tang Dynasty as an example, to analyze its influences.

Anlushan 安祿山 rebelled in 755 AD; soon after, half the territory of the Tang regime fell into the hands of the rebel forces, and Emperor Xuanzong 玄宗 had to flee to Sichuan for refuge. Then, his son Suzong 肅宗 succeeded him, defeated the rebels with the aid of the nomadic Uighurs, finally recovered two capitals, Chang'an 長安 and Luoyang 洛陽, and quelled the rebellion. Both the rulers of China and the Uighurs thought that the "revival" of the Tang regime should be attributed to the success to the Uighurs; thus it was natural that a huge quantity of reward was given to these nomads, with a majority of the "reward" being silk.

On the contrary, after the fierce war, China, especially its northern portion, suffered seriously, with war supplies being scarce, and horses too. For example, before the war, the government of the Tang possessed more than 300000 battle steeds, but when Emperor Suzong 肅宗 succeeded the throne, there were only tens of thousands left. Since China needed a large number of war steeds at that time, the nomadic Uighurs provided rich resources of horses; accordingly, a huge amount of silk was exported to the *barbarian territory* from China.

As time went by, more and more Chinese silk was transported abroad. One of the main reasons was that more and more horses were imported into China, while the other factor was the rising prices of the horses. For instance, in the reign of Taizong 太宗 (r. 626–649 AD), the price of a horse was one bolt of silk, while more than one hundred years later, after the period of the *An-Shi Rebellion* (755–763 AD), the price of a horse had risen up to ten or even forty bolts. The Tang government had to tolerate such an unfair deal, because the Uighur army was the "great benefactor" of the Tang regime; the so-called "payment for the horse" was in fact the "prize for military aid". In other words, the deal of silk and horse was not a real "trade".

A record is given in the *Xintangshu* 新唐書: "At that time emperor Daizong 代宗 (r. 762–779 AD) treats the Uighurs generously because of their great contribution of recovering the two capitals. He intermarries with the Uighur Qaghan, and pays more than million bolts of silk annually for 100 thousand horses they presenting to China. Hence the Chinese financial resource is exhausted so that the government fails to pay all arrears for the horse."[31] Obviously, these silks were far more than those given to the Turks by the Beizhou 北周 regime, the latter being only 100000 bolts of silk per year.

Another paragraph in *Zizhitongjian* 資治通鑑 reveals more clearly the helplessness and predicament of the Tang government. It says the following: "since the reigning of emperor Suzong 肅宗 (r. 756–762 AD), the Uighurs demand reciprocal trade every year. One horse is sold for forty bolts of silk. The sum of horses is often up to tens of thousands, but most of the horses are inferior. The imperial court suffers it much, hardly ever buy out all the horses they bring here. The Uighur ambassadors and their trader frequent the Ministry of Foreign Affairs. Later, in 773, emperor Daizong 代宗 intends to please the Uighurs, orders the officials to buy out all horses of the Uighurs in Capital. In the autumn, when these Uighurs return home, they load the rewards and horse payment obtained from China with more than thousand carriages."[32]

In order to *requite the great favor*, or rather as compelled by the powerful force of the Uighurs, Chinese emperors exchanged a huge amount of silk for many inferior horses. It was a very unfair deal, causing the Tang regime to suffer a heavy loss and seriously impacting the national welfare

---

[31] Cf. *Xintangshu* 新唐書, fasc. 51, p. 1348.
[32] Cf. *Zizhitongjian* 資治通鑑, fasc. 224, p. 7221.

and people's livelihood. A poem written by the famous poet Baijuyi 白居易 vividly reveals this social phenomenon.

The title of this poem is *Yinshandao* 陰山道 (*The Road in Yin Mountains*). Yin Mountains are located in the North of China, rich in waters and grasslands; it was good land for nomadic life. Thus, various nomadic peoples have lived there since early times, and the name "Yinshan 陰山 (Yin Mountains)" was also used to designate almost all regions where the nomads lived. Apparently, the so-called "Yinshan" in this poem meant the whole country of the Uighurs, while the "road" meant the traffic roads from China to Uighur country.

The poem says that there are abundant waters and lush plants in the Yin Mountains, but when the Uighurs drive horses to China, all the grasses along the roads are eaten up, and the fountains and streams are dried up, many horses are ill or die because of being hungry and thirsty. The Uighurs exchange one horse for fifty bolts of Chinese silk; a deal like this never ends. The Chinese textile women work indefatigably day and night to product more silk, but they are not able to weave enough superior silk to satisfy the Uighurs. When the Uighur Qaghan complains about the inferior silk, the Chinese emperor has to pay for horses with the fine silk in the national treasury. The Uighur Qaghan obtains the payment of horses and a wealthy reward cheerily. The barbarians are so greedy that next year they bring China twice as many horses as before. For such barbarians, the Chinese rulers can do nothing but nail-biting.[33]

In the poem, the verse "養無所用去非宜 yangwusuoyongqufeiyi" meant that if Chinese accepted these horses and herded them here, they were too many to be used, and if they refused to buy them, it was unsuitable. Here, the "non-trade feature" of silk was distinctly visible. Besides, the verse "縑絲不足女工苦 jiansibuzunügongku", "內出金帛酬馬值 neichujinbochoumazhi", "縑漸好馬漸多 jianjianhaomajianduo" and so on revealed vividly that because of this "silk trade" the ordinary

---

[33] Cf. *Quantangshi* 全唐詩, fasc. 427, p. 4705. The Chinese text is as follows: "陰山道, 陰山道, 紇邏敦肥水泉好。每至戎人送馬時, 道旁千里無纖草。草盡泉枯馬病羸, 飛龍但印骨與皮。五十匹縑易一匹, 縑去馬來了無日。養無所用去非宜, 每歲死傷十六七。縑絲不足女工苦, 疏織短截充匹數。藕絲蛛網三丈餘, 回紇訴稱無用處。咸安公主號可敦, 遠為可汗頻奏論。元和二年下新敕, 內出金帛酬馬值。仍詔江淮馬價縑, 從此不令疏短織。合羅將軍呼萬歲, 捧授金銀與縑采。誰知黠虜啟貪心, 明年馬來多一倍。縑漸好, 馬漸多, 陰山虜, 奈爾何!"

Chinese suffered greatly and the Chinese government fell into a financial predicament. Therefore, though the "silk–horse trade" between China and the Uighur Khanate had positive significance if we view it from a holistic and long-term perspective, it caused a tremendous negative impact on the Tang regime and its people at that time.

Chapter 3

Intermarriage as a Political Weapon Among the Powers

Generally speaking, the term 和親 heqin (Intermarriage) in Chinese history refers to the alliances formed between powerful families or regimes by means of marriages; its purpose is political or economic interests. Most of the intermarriage cases in history are those between Chinese regimes and foreign barbarian powers. The so-called *Barbarians* (huren 胡人) are mainly the "北胡 beihu" (Northern Barbarians). *Cefuyuangui* 册府元龜 gives a brief comment on the intermarriage cases in history:

The Barbarians had been the scourge in the Chinese border areas since earlier times. The Chinese civilization could not dispel their greed, nor could war cause their people to perish. In ancient times, though the Chinese armies once pursued and attacked them fiercely, they ran away swiftly just like beasts and birds. So, the ancient sages had to conciliate these barbarians and control them with adaptability in tactics. Initially, Emperor Gaozu of the Han accepted the advice proposed by Fengchun 奉春, intermarried with the barbarian Xiongnu and gave them large quantities of silk and food annually. His purpose was not only to avoid warfare and pacify the people but also to gradually control these foreign barbarians. Intermarriage had become a long-term national policy. Since then, the Queen of Gaozu 高后, Emperor Wendi 文帝 as well as Emperors Xuandi 宣帝 and Yuandi 元帝 all followed this policy; thus, the ruler of the Xiongnu Huhanye Chanyu 呼韓邪單于 had to submit to the Han at last. When Emperor Dauwu (道武) of the Northern Wei read the sentence "(the Emperor) will marry his only daughter to the Huns" in *History of the Han*, he could not help sighing. Then, he married off his daughters to the rulers of China's vassal states. Apparently, he understood deeply the tactics of adjusting to changing circumstances. The saying "the flexibility is the foundation of all successes" in *The Book of Changes* is just what it means.[1]

This passage expresses the following meaning: Chinese regimes had been unable to deal with the barbarians on the boundary since ancient times. These barbarians could neither be civilized by education nor annihilated by killing, so the only way was to bribe them with massive wealth, in exchange for temporary peace. In the reign of the first emperor of the Han Dynasty, the nomads Xiongnu were growing strong, so the Chinese emperor was forced to accept Loujing's suggestion, of marrying off his daughter to the ruler of Xiongnu, and gave them large number of silks and other belongings annually. This tactic was called *Intermarriage* 和親. After that, many emperors carried out the same policy, and achieved better results. Thus, the *Intermarriage Tactic* was regarded as a good policy for governing states.

The saying "Intermarriage can realize peace and control the barbarians" played a great influence on the later generations, and even most of the modern scholars are in favor of this policy, thinking it was advantageous for alleviating conflict among Chinese and foreigners, and for giving the populace a more comfortable life. However, the reasons for intermarriages in history were not so simple, and the results and impacts were not always harmless. I will give a brief analysis on this topic in this chapter, showing more vividly the relationship between ancient China and its neighboring barbarians.[2]

---

[1] The Chinese text is as follows: "戎狄之國世為邊患, 禮義不能革其貪, 干戈不能絕其類. 故上自虞夏商周, 固不程督, 雖有窮兵追擊, 而亦亡失略等, 所謂獸聚鳥散, 從之如搏景者也. 是以聖人用權變之道, 遠禦不絕而已. 漢高始納奉春之計, 建和親之議, 歲用絮繒酒食奉之, 非惟解兵息民, 亦欲漸而臣之, 為羈縻長久之策耳. 高后、文帝, 至於宣、元, 皆用是道, 故得呼韓朝于北闕之下. 及魏道武讀漢史, 至 '欲以魯元妻匈奴', 為之掩卷太息, 於是以諸女皆釐降於賓附之國. 此乃深識從權濟時之略焉. 《易》曰 '惟幾也, 故能成天下之務', 其是之謂乎!" cf. *Cefuyuangui* 冊府元龜, fasc. 978, p. 11486a.

[2] About this subject, may refer to my article "On the Pros and Cons of Intermarriages in Ancient China" 古代和親利弊論, in *Shilin* 史林, No. 2, 1997.

1. Intermarriage Aimed at Alleviating the Hostility from Other Powers

According to the existing historical records, the first intermarriage began in the reign of Emperor Gaozu 高祖 of the Han. Regardless of whether this is a fact, we will start with this example.

During the last ten years of the third century BC, the Qin 秦 regime was destroyed and the Han 漢 Dynasty was established. At that time, both the Chinese society and economy were seriously broken, and the military force was also greatly weakened. At that time, the Xiongnu, a nomadic tribe in the Mongolian plateau, was rising and flourishing; under the command of their Chanyu 單于 Modu 冒頓, they conquered vast regions in Central Eurasia, and attempted to invade southward into China.

In the autumn of 201 BC, the Xiongnu attacked the fortress Mayi 馬邑; the general of this fortress surrendered, and the Huns troops advanced further southwards, reaching Jinyang 晉陽. In the next winter, Gaozu led the expedition personally and ventured deep into the enemy territory, but fell into a trap, and was surrounded by the Huns in Baideng Mountain 白登山 of Pingcheng 平城.³ Fortunately, his official Chenping 陳平 succeeded in persuading Chanyu's wife to accept the suggestion of withdrawing troops. She received a large number of jewels from Chenping as a bribe, and thereby demanded that her husband, Chanyu of the Xiongnu, let the Chinese army run away. After being surrounded for seven days, Emperor Gaozu and his expeditionary force escaped from the death trap at last.⁴

It was exactly this situation of the powerful Xiongnu frequently invading China that caused Loujing 婁敬 to offer this tactic of *Intermarriage*. He suggested that Gaozu should marry off his biological daughter to Modu Chanyu, the ruler of Xiongnu, and present them with a lot of goods, foods and money annually. As for its effects, Loujing estimated the following very optimistically: If the Chinese emperor did so, the barbarians would be very happy, and surely let the Chinese princess be the queen; thus, her son will naturally be the successor of the Xiongnu monarch. Therefore, the present ruler of the Huns would be the son-in-law of the Chinese emperor, while their future ruler will be the grandson of the Chinese emperor. The grandson would not dare be hostile to his

---
³Cf. *Shiji* 史記, fasc. 110, p. 2894.
⁴Cf. *Shiji* 史記, fasc. 56, pp. 2057–2058.

grandfather. Thus, China can dominate the barbarians without any military actions.[5]

Obviously, though the prospect depicted by Loujing was very rosy, it still included many uncertainties. For example, after the Chinese princess marries Xiongnu Chanyu, she may not necessarily be the queen, and might not give birth to a son; furthermore, her son may not necessarily be the successor of the Xiongnu monarch. Even if her son became the sovereign, it was not necessarily for him to keep peace with China for a long time.

So many uncertainties displayed that the so-called *benefits* pointed out by Loujing perhaps were only his own wishful thinking or self-comfort. In fact, the Chinese princess was only a hostage to ensure that a large amount of wealth was transported from China into Xiongnu continuously. Besides, the Huns could enhance their political status among the barbarians by means of the affinity with China. When Loujing offered the *Intermarriage Policy*, he was worried about his suggestion being refused; later, the emperor married off to the Chanyu only a princess of the royal family instead of his biological daughter. Both facts clearly showed that this *intermarriage* was only an expedient measure adopted by the Chinese monarch, or a humiliating measure.

Let us check over the actual effect of this intermarriage. In the winter of 198 BC, a princess of the royal family rather than the emperor's own daughter was sent to Xiongnu for intermarriage. The leader of the diplomatic corps was Loujing. Modu Chanyu 冒頓單于 gained a great quantity of silk, wine, rice and other foods, and became the *brother* of Gaozu of the Han. Thus, the Huns slightly alleviated the intrusions into Chinese boundary regions, but they still supported the rebels of China. The Chinese northern frontiers had not achieved complete peace.

A few years later, Emperor Gaozu died in 195 BC. His son succeeded the throne as Huidi 惠帝, but the real ruler was his mother, Queen Lü 呂后. Queen Lü, however, suffered from extreme provocation and insult by the Xiongnu ruler. Modu Chanyu sent a letter to Queen Lü, saying that he was now a bachelor, while the Chinese ruler was also a widow, so it was very suitable for them to marry. Though Queen Lü was very angry and unpleasant, she finally replied to Chanyu in a humble attitude. She said that she was becoming old and weak, her hair was falling and the teeth dropping, and it was even difficult to walk. Therefore, she was not a

---

[5] Cf. *Hanshu* 漢書, fasc. 43, p. 2122.

good consort for Chanyu, and Chanyu should select a young and beautiful girl as a wife. Besides, she presented some royal vehicles and horses to Chanyu as a gift, paying homage to this monarch.[6] As a result of this incident, a princess of the royal family was sent to marry Modu Chanyu in the spring of 192 BC. Apparently, the so-called *intermarriage* at that time was just an expedient policy of enduring humiliation. The Xiongnu only slightly reduced the military pressure on the Chinese border regions, and did not become a real *brother* or *son-in-law* of the Chinese emperors.

In the following ten years, the northern borders of China were relatively peaceful, but since the year 183 BC, the bordering intrusions of the Huns became frequent. In September of 183 BC, Chinese government had to dispatch troops to the north to resist the Xiongnu; in the next lunar June, the Huns invaded the territory of Didao 狄道, and attacked the city of Heyang 河阳; in lunar December of 181 BC, they intruded into Didao again, plundering and taking away more than 2000 Chinese people.

Possibly, this situation forced Emperor Wendi 文帝 to intermarry again with Xiongnu immediately after his succession (180 BC). Unfortunately, one of the Xiongnu princes invaded into the regions south of the Yellow River not long after this intermarriage, plundering and killing many Chinese. Wendi condemned Xiongnu for the perfidious act, and ordered Prime Minister Guanying 灌嬰 to lead a cavalry army of 80000 members to attack them and drive them off the Chinese border. The next year, the Xiongnu Chanyu sent a letter to Wendi, saying he agrees with the suggestion of intermarriage previously offered by the Han government; at the same time, he announced that the Huns had already conquered all states in the Western Regions 西域. Apparently, he tried to threaten the Chinese with military power. After a serious discussion, the Han government decided to make peace with the Xiongnu by means of so-called *Intermarriage*, rather than resisting them by military action. Thus, a daughter of a royal family was sent to marry to the Xiongnu ruler; she was also titled as *princess*.[7]

However, the Chinese did not get real peace, for the Huns still frequently intruded into Chinese northern borders. Wendi was forced to greatly increase the border guard troops, which resulted in insufficient local food supply.[8] In the winter of 166 BC, Laoshang Chanyu 老上單于

---

[6] Cf. *Hanshu* 漢書, fasc. 94a, pp. 3754–3755.
[7] Cf. *Shiji* 史記, fasc. 110, pp. 2895–2896.
[8] Cf. *Shiji* 史記, fasc. 30, p. 1419.

invaded China with a powerful army of 140000 people, attacking the cities of Chaona 朝那 and Xiaoguan 蕭關, and killing the governor of Beidi 北地; their military scouts arrived at the farther regions. Wendi was very angry and attempted to personally lead a punitive expedition against Xiongnu. More than a month later, the Huns were driven out of China by the government's army.[9] Since then, the northern frontiers were frequently attacked by the Xiongnu, and the Han government suffered greatly because of the arduous military confrontations.

In lunar June of 162 BC, the imperial family intermarried with the Xiongnu once again, but this *intermarriage* was another humiliating treaty of surrender. According to *Zizhitongjian* 資治通鑒, the Huns frequently intruded into Chinese boundary areas, plundering and killing many inhabitants and livestock; the regions of Yunzhong 雲中 and Liaodong 遼東 suffered particularly. Thus, the Chinese emperor sent emissaries to Xiongnu, demanding them to stop intrusions; the Huns agreed with the suggestion of intermarriage again.[10]

Wendi said in the imperial edict that Xiongnu had intruded into Chinese frontiers for many years, killing numerous Chinese. The warfare occurred often, and the both Chinese and Xiongnu were not able to live peacefully. In order to relieve the misery of the populace, he dispatched messengers to Xiongnu many times, persuading their Chanyu to recover friendship with the Han Dynasty. Therefore, the Xiongnu ruler intermarried with the Grand Han, becoming the brother of the Chinese emperor. Henceforth, a new relationship between the Han and Xiongnu started.[11]

Obviously, this intermarriage was also the result of ceaseless invasions by the Huns. The sentence "numerous Chinese messengers are often seen on the roads leading to the Huns" in the imperial edict shows indeed the frequent communication between the Han and Xiongnu on the one hand but also hints that the Han rulers were very anxious to conclude a peace treaty with the Huns on the other hand. In this respect, China was evidently at a disadvantage.

The next year, Laoshang Chanyu 老上單于 died, and his son succeeded to the throne and was titled as Junchen Chanyu 軍臣單于; Wendi arranged for a princess to marry him too. However, soon after this intermarriage, Junchen Chanyu invaded the regions of Shangqun 上郡

---

[9] Cf. *Zizhitongjian* 資治通鑑, fasc. 15, pp. 497–498.
[10] Cf. *Zizhitongjian*, fasc. 15, p. 504.
[11] Cf. *Hanshu*, fasc. 4, p. 129.

and Yunzhong 雲中, killing many people. The Chinese government had to send a large number of soldiers to the northern borders, even mobilizing an elite army to guard the capital. The seriousness of the situation could be seen from these events.

In 156 BC, Emperor Jingdi 景帝 dispatched Qingzhai 青翟 to Xiongnu to discuss intermarriage affairs. In the next autumn, the two powers talked about the intermarriage. In 152 BC, a Chinese princess was sent to marry the Xiongnu sovereign. In 148 BC, however, their friendly relations were broken off by the Huns' invasion of China. In lunar June of 144 BC, the Xiongnu invaded Shangqun 上郡 on a large scale; in 142 BC, they plundered the Yanmen 雁門 region again. Generally speaking, during the fifteen years of Jingdi's reign, China kept a relationship of intermarriage with the Xiongnu; there are some trading, presenting of gifts and marriages between them. The Huns eased the degree of intrusion, but did not maintain a completely peaceful relationship with China.

At the beginning of his reign, Wudi 武帝 also adopted the same policy as his ancestors, "strictly perform the intermarriage contracts, and pay high price for their commodities." The Xiongnu, however, still frequently intruded into Chinese borders. What he said to his officials in 134 BC exactly reflected this situation: "I have sent young girls to marry Xiongnu's Chanyu, gave them a lot of money and silk. But they are arrogant than before, harass our borders constantly. It is quite unfortunate."[12] From this fact, we know that if the Chinese rulers begged for peace, it would encourage the enemy to be more unbridled.

As the historical facts show above, we know that the so-called *Intermarriage Policy*, which started from Gaozu 高祖 of the Han and was carried forward by Huidi 惠帝, Queen of Gaozu, Wendi 文帝 and Jingdi 景帝 successively, was actually expediency when China faced an enemy far more powerful than itself. As a result, the Chinese government got only a short reprieve and slightly moderated intrusion by the barbarians along the northern borders, while the cost was the loss of a great amount of gold, silver, silk, foods and other commodities, as well as the reduction in international status. Besides, this policy might have induced a stronger desire for wealth, causing the barbarians to strengthen the threat of force to China.

---

[12] Cf. *Hanshu* 漢書, fasc. 6, p. 162.

These monarchs of the Han Dynasty reduced their military operations because of the intermarriage policy, thereby gaining enough time and money to develop the domestic economy and society. However, this policy also had a negative impact on China; what Jiayi 賈誼 told Emperor Wendi clearly shows this influence:

"Now the Xiongnu ravage our country ceaselessly, cause our people suffering greatly, and the Chinese government is forced to pay them large amount of gold and silk annually. The barbarians conquer us just like the powerful lords, while our rulers pay tribute to them just like the weak subjects. It is like a man being suspended with the head downward, it cannot go on like this anymore … At present, in the western and northern boundary regions, even the high officials have to go to battle in person, and all people could not be rest normally except the children. Every scout and guard work day after night; all generals and soldiers sleep with the armors … Your Majesty, as an emperor of the grand Han, you cannot just be a seigneur of the barbarians, low status and suffer greatly. It is time to end this situation!"[13]

As a politician and scholar contemporary with the heyday of the *Intermarriage Policy*, Jiayi surely mastered enough facts and evidence to prove his views. By this token, there were both advantages and disadvantages in these so-called *Intermarriages* with the Xiongnu rulers in the earlier period of the Han Dynasty. It is not quite proper that some scholars of the later generations give excessive praise to this intermarriage policy.

2. Intermarriage Aimed at Ingratiating and Rewarding the External Tribes

In the case of the enemy being strong while China was weak, the Chinese government was forced to intermarry with the barbarians. Hence, once this situation changed, the Chinese would probably refuse intermarriage, or deliberately increase its difficulty. Since the succession of Emperor Wudi 武帝, such cases often appeared in the relationship between the Han and Xiongnu. At that time, the Chinese economy was substantially improved, food and wealth increased so greatly that grain was rotting due to accumulation, and money was too great to be counted. As a result, the

---

[13] Cf. *Hanshu* 漢書, fasc. 48, pp. 2240–2241.

attitude of Chinese politicians to the barbarians was very different from that of the past.

It was exactly the fact that intermarriage could not prevent the Xiongu's intrusion that caused Wudi to accept the suggestion offered by Wanghui 王恢 to set up ambushes in Mayi 馬邑 in 134 BC, attempting to assault the Xiongnu. Although this operation was unsuccessful because of the message being leaked in advance, it was undoubted that the Chinese government began to alter its attitude and measure toward intermarriage.

For example, Wudi refused the suggestion of Jian 汲黯 to have intermarriage with the Xiongnu and stop fighting with them, because he had won several victories against the Xiongnu.[14] After the Chinese troops led by Weiqing 衛青 and Huoqubing 霍去病 defeated the Xiongnu army and killed 100000 people, the Xiongnu yielded and asked for intermarriage. Though Doctor Dishan 狄山 fully analyzed the benefits of intermarriage, Wudi only sent him to a frontier stronghold to see if the Xiongnu were really in compliance with the peace contract. Unfortunately, a month later Dishan was beheaded by the barbarians who invaded China.[15]

After suffering heavy military strikes, the Xiongnu adopted the suggestion of Zhaoxin 趙信, asking for intermarriage once again. The Emperor of the Han demanded the Xiongnu "to be a vassal state, and pay tribute to the Han punctually", so this intermarriage failed.

In 107 BC, as an envoy, Yangxin 楊信 was dispatched to the Xiongnu. He claimed that the intermarriage must be conditional on the fact of Chanyu's son being a hostage in China. Chanyu thought this proposal was contrary to previous treaties, and refused to accept it.[16] All these facts indicate that when the general situation changed, the intermarriage policy of China also underwent tremendous changes.

However, this does not mean the Chinese government no longer used *Intermarriage* as a diplomatic weapon; they just altered the purpose of this tactic. In 33 BC, Chanyu Huhanye 呼韓邪 paid respects in person to the Chinese emperor, and requested intermarriage. Yuandi 元帝 promised Chanyu that he would become a *son-in-law* of the emperor, and marry a beautiful court lady. This girl was known as Wangzhaojun 王昭君.

Strictly speaking, this was not at all the so-called *Intermarriage* like the one at the beginning of the Han Dynasty. At first, Wangzhaojun was

---

[14] Cf. *Hanshu* 漢書, fasc. 50, pp. 2319–2320.
[15] Cf. *Shiji* 史記, fasc. 122, p. 3141.
[16] Cf. *Hanshu* 漢書, fasc. 94A, pp. 3771, 3773.

only an ordinary folk girl; later, she was selected as one of the spare wives of the emperor, but failed to become a real concubine for many years. Thus, she volunteered to marry the Xiongnu ruler. Yuandi presented Wangzhaojun as a gift to Huhanye, to reward his loyalty.

Wangzhaujun was neither a daughter of the emperor nor even a member of the imperial family, but merely one of the many spare concubines neglected by the emperor. Thus, this intermarriage seemed to be a drama, or just a joke.[17] Nevertheless, Huhanye Chanyu still behaved pleasantly. He said to the Chinese emperor gratefully, "We will be sure to guard the Chinese borders where from the west of Shanggu 上谷 to Dunhuang 敦煌, we will do so forever." The real reason for his saying and doing was that the general situation had already changed into a *weak Xiongnu and powerful China*.

Huhanye was the son of Xulüquanqu 虛閭權渠 Chanyu, but his succession was taken away by the Right Prince Tuqitang 屠耆堂 after the death of his father in 60 BC. Huhanye was forced to seek refuge from his father-in-law, who occupied the eastern territories. Subsequently, Huhanye was chosen as the Chanyu by people of the eastern regions, and fought with Tuqitang frequently; the latter ruled the western regions.

Although Huhanye defeated Tuqitang and forced him to commit suicide, he was at a great disadvantage in battles with the other four Xiongnu chiefs. Among his people, it was said that "ten thousand persons are killed, and eight or nine of ten livestock loses. People are so hungry that they even eat the dead human flesh."[18] Shortly after, the Left Prince Hutuwus 呼屠吾斯 claimed himself as Zhizhi 郅支 Chanyu. He defeated Huhanye and captured his headquarters. So, Huhanye Chanyu had to go southward together with all his people, seeking shelter in Chinese boundary areas. He sent his son and younger brother to pay respects to the Chinese emperor at first; later, he paid the emperor homage in person

---

[17]According to official history, the fact of this intermarriage is as follows: Wangzhaujun's homeplace is in present Hubei 湖北 province. During the reign of Yuandi, she was selected as one of the spare concubines, but she never became the emperor's sexual partner. When Huhanyu came to China, Yuandi presented him with five palace ladies. When the emperor found Wangzhaojun to be very beautiful and gentle, he was extremely surprised and repentant. But, it is too late to keep her in China. In order to show his trustworthiness, Yuandi had to let Wangzhaojun marry the Xiongnu Chanyu at last. Cf. *Houhanshu* 漢書, fasc. 89, p. 2941.

[18]Cf. *Hanshu* 漢書, fasc. 8, p. 266.

several times. In 33 BC, Huhanye came to China once again. At that time, Zhizhi Chanyu had already been killed by generals Ganyanshou 甘延壽 and Chentang 陳湯 three years earlier.

It is conceivable that Huhanye was very joyful for his formidable opponent Zhizhi's death on the one hand, but was also afraid of suffering the same fate on the other hand. Thus, he handled the relations with China very carefully and even humiliatingly. His request of "being son-in-law of the Chinese emperor", his promise of "guarding the Chinese borders from the west of Shanggu to Dunhuang forever" and that he gave the honorable title "Queen to Pacify the Barbarians" (寧胡閼氏) to Wangzhaojun were all intended to please the Chinese emperor and the Han government.

Under such a situation, it was unnecessary for the Chinese rulers to humbly ask for Intermarriage with Xiongnu or other powerful foreign states just as their ancestors had done. Therefore, Wangzhaojun, who married Huhanye Chanyu, was in fact only a palace lady. This marriage was claimed to be intermarriage for the sake of winning over the Xiongnu Chanyu. Besides, this marriage could expand Huhanye's political impact, urging him serve the Chinese government better.

During the Han and Tang period, there were many other intermarriages with the character of encouragement and reward just like that of Wangzhaojun. For instance, Loulan 樓蘭 was a small country in the Western Regions. Its new king Angui 安歸 obeyed Xiongnu, refused to pay respects to the Han regime and often killed Chinese envoys on their journey. But, his younger brother Weituqi 尉屠耆 surrendered to the Han and exposed all the doings of Angui. Thus, in 77 BC, Fujiezi 傅介子 was dispatched to Loulan, looking for a chance to murder King Angui. Soon after, at a banquet, Fujiezi killed Angui while he was drunk.

The Chinese emperor immediately claimed Weituqi as the new king of Loulan, and changed the state title into Shanshan 鄯善. A palace lady was given to Weituqi as his wife. When she went to Shanshan to intermarry with the king, many high officials led by the prime minister came to see her off.[19] The ceremony was quite grand, though its real purpose was fostering a pro-China regime. This marriage was similar to that of Wangzhaojun and Huhanye. It was only a reward for Weituqi's loyalty, and had little impact on the relations between these two governments.

Another example is as follows. After his succession, Emperor Yangdi 煬帝 of the Sui 隋 Dynasty was eager to show off his power to foreign

---

[19] Cf. *Hanshu* 漢書, fasc. 96A, p. 3878.

countries. He adopted the suggestion offered by Peiju 裴矩, seduced western rulers to China with a lot of money on the one hand, and conquered the nomadic tribe of Tuyuhun 吐谷渾 on the other hand, for the sake of terrorizing other countries. Being forced by these measures, Quboya 麴伯雅, the king of Gaochang 高昌, sent delegates to pay tribute to China in 608 AD. Yangdi of the Sui was delighted and satisfied, and rewarded the envoys with a lot of things. The next year, Quboya personally came to China, and followed Yangdi in conquering Korea. He stayed in China for two or three years.

All these doings distinctly showed that Quboya was exactly a *loyal official* to Yangdi. So, the emperor assigned a girl of the imperial family to marry him, Princess Huarong 華容. After he returned home, Quboya ordered all his people to change their own traditional dress and adornment into that of the Chinese style. Apparently, he expressed his loyalty to the *Great Sui* regime in this way.[20]

The above examples indicate that even under the situation of Chinese regimes being powerful and the foreign countries being weak, Chinese rulers would still intermarry with them. However, the scale and grade of such intermarriages might be lesser. Generally speaking, the Chinese only aimed at rewarding loyal subjects in foreign countries. Besides, the impact of these intermarriages on the international situation would not be great.

3. Intermarriage Aimed at Sowing Discord among Tribes Abroad

The ancient Chinese regimes often had conflicts of interest with foreign states, especially thriving barbarian powers. Sometimes, the Chinese rulers adopted a relatively negative compromise policy to ensure temporary peace; sometimes they took the active strategy, attempting not only to keep borders' tranquility but also to expand Chinese powers further outside its territory. Reviewing the whole history, whether the Chinese governments were defensive or offensive, the *Intermarriage* seems to have always been an important means. Here, I will discuss *Intermarriage* which was used as an aggressive weapon.

A typical example is the intermarriage of Wudi of the Han and the nomadic tribe Wusun 烏孫. This suggestion was offered by Zhangqian 張騫.

---

[20] Cf. *Suishu* 隋書, fasc. 83, pp. 1847–1848.

After his diplomatic visit to the Western Regions, Zhangqian learned that the Wusun were originally a small country located between Dunhuang 敦煌 and the Qilian mountains 祁連山, just like the former Darouzhi 大月支/大月氏. Later, they suffered from the invasion of the Xiongnu, and were forced to flee to the Yili River 伊犁河 valley, west of the Xiongnu. Consequently, the Wusun were very hostile to Xiongnu, and often had military conflicts. Zhangqian proposed that China can attract the Wusun to return to their homeland by means of intermarriage and a lot of wealth, urging them to fight against Xiongnu, namely, "cutting off the right arm of the Xiongnu". Wudi accepted this idea and immediately appointed Zhangqian as a general, leading three hundred members, carrying 10000 livestock and tens of millions in gold, silver and silk with them, to visit Wusun and its neighboring countries.[21]

At first, the king of Wusun Kunmo 昆莫 refused to accept the proposal of opposing the Xiongnu together with the Han, because he did not know whether the Chinese army was powerful enough to defeat Xiongnu; besides, there was a strong pro-Xiongnu force inside his country. It is not until Xiongnu was about to send troops to punish it for its pro-China activities that Wusun agreed to ally with China. Kunmo hurriedly sent envoys to the Han, asking for the intermarriage. At last, Wudi married off Princess Xijun 細君, the daughter of the Prince of Jiangdu 江都, Liujian 刘建, to Kunmo. A lot of money and belongings, as well as several hundreds of eunuchs and servants were presented to Xijun and Kunmo.[22]

Apparently, the purpose of this costly and distant intermarriage was to "befriend the distant enemy while attacking those nearby 遠交近攻" or "using barbarous people to subjugate their own races 以夷制夷." The common strike target of the Han and Wusun was the Xiongnu. However, the result was not quite perfect. In fact, when the Wusun intermarried with China, they intermarried with Xiongnu at the same time. Kunmo married Xijun as the *Right Wife* and married the daughter of Xiongnu Chanyu as his *Left Wife*. Therefore, Wusun did not make a real alliance with China from the beginning.

After the death of Princess Xijun, Princess Jieyou 解憂, the granddaughter of the Prince of Chu 楚 Liuwu 劉戊, married the King of Wusun Cenzou 岑陬. During the reigns of Zhaodi 昭帝 and Xundi 宣帝, both Princess Jieyou and King Cenzou wrote to the Chinese emperors,

---

[21] Cf. *Hanshu* 漢書, fasc. 61, p. 2692.
[22] Cf. *Hanshu* 漢書, fasc. 96b, pp. 3901–3910.

pleading China to send troops to support Wusun to resist against the Xiongnu invasion. Then, the Han government dispatched powerful troops of 150000, led by five generals and divided into several groups, to attack the Xiongnu. In 71 BC, they won a great victory.

This was the biggest military operation striking against the Xiongnu in the decades since China intermarried with the Wusun. After this war, Xiongnu suffered a gradual decline because of the great loss of its populace, livestock and belongings, while the Chinese strength also suffered severe damage. As for the Wusun, they sent only an army of 50000, but they plundered much in the war, with a mere part of the booty being up to 700000 livestock. Therefore, the truth was that the Han protected Wusun rather than a Han–Wusun alliance defeating Xiongnu together. This result was quite different from that of the intermarriage during the reign of Emperor Wudi.

When the king of Wusun asked for intermarriage once again in 64 BC, the foreign minister Xiaowangzhi 蕭望之 refused this demand and said the following: "Wusun is very far from China, so it is difficult for China to control Wusun's events and situations. It is unsuitable to promise the intermarriage." Later, he points out the following: "Wusun often hesitates to choose its position, thereby is not easy to ally with. Formerly our Princess stays in Wusun for more than forty years, but has not been trusted by the king, and the Chinese borders have not been peaceful. This has been proved by the facts."

Xiaowangzhi was a foreign minister, so these words were surely justified. Thus, it was not difficult to judge the proportion of pros and cons in these intermarriages aimed at "sowing discord among tribes abroad". If we take into account the great amount of silk and other property exported for decades, the benefits received by the Chinese from this kind of intermarriage may be less.

In the history of the Sui, there are several examples of the intermarriage aimed at dividing and disintegrating hostile powers. For instance, Tuli 突利 was a minor Qaghan dominating the northern part of the Turk Khanate. When he asked for intermarriage with the Sui, Emperor Wendi 文帝 of the Sui offered the terms in exchanged for the intermarriage, namely, in turn, Tuli Qaghan must kill Dayi 大義 Princess, who was an imperial family member of the former dynasty, and had successively married three Turk Qaghans and was very hostile to the present regime.

After Dayi Princess's death, the rulers of the Sui provoked conflict among the Turks once again. They drove a wedge between the Prime

Qaghan Dulan 都藍 and the minor Qaghan Tuli, causing these two cousins to suspect each other. They deliberately gave Tuli Qaghan special treatment, let Anyi 安義 Princess marry him, and often sent envoys to Tuli Qaghan. As expected, Dulan Qaghan was very indignant because even as a Prime Qaghan, he got worse treatment than the Minor Qaghan Tuli. Henceforth, Dulan Qaghan no longer paid respects to China and often harassed the Chinese borders.[23]

Thereafter, the Sui government dispatched troops in succession to strike the Turks of Dulan Qaghan invading Chinese borders. Besides, in order to foster a pro-China regime of the Turks, the Sui government sent troops to protect Tuli Qaghan who was disastrously defeated by Dulan, and settled his tribe in a vast area south of the Yellow River. Wendi of the Sui gave Tuli a glorious title of Qimin Qaghan 啟民可汗.

Although Qimin Qaghan thankfully said that his people "will pasture livestock for the Great Sui forever", expressing his determination in *guarding the Chinese borders*, his opponents were in fact defeated mainly by the Chinese army. In other words, the Sui government spent much for Qimin Qaghan. Besides, Yangdi 煬帝, the son of Wendi, was greatly vainglorious, so he rewarded Qimin a lot of wealth for his humility and obedience. The intermarriage with Qimin Qaghan did not seem to bring much benefit for the Chinese regime.

At the first, Chuluo 處羅 Qaghan of the West Turk Khanate agreed to be a subject of China, just like Qimin Qaghan, and he sent friendly ambassadors to the Sui. However, Chuluo Qaghan did not warmly welcome Yangdi at an appointed site when the emperor journeyed westwards in 610. Yangdi was so furious that he attempted to kill the Qaghan. He adopted the proposal offered by Peiju 裴矩, demanding that another Qaghan Shekui 射匱 destroy Chuluo and his army. As a reward, a Chinese princess would marry Shekui Qaghan, and the Chinese emperor will support him to be the Prime Qaghan of the Turk Khanate. Finally, Yangdi successfully carried out this plot. The *Intermarriage*, however, played a disgraced role here; it was just helpful to satisfy the vainglory of a silly monarch.

Many other examples of intermarriage are no longer listed in detail. In short, those intermarriages aimed at disintegrating the hostile powers abroad were not as effective as expected; moreover, if it was not operated properly, intermarriage might induce damage to the Chinese themselves.

---

[23] Cf. *Suishu* 隋書, fasc. 84, pp. 1871–1872.

4. Intermarriage Aimed at Competing with Chinese Adversary by the Aid of External Forces

When the Chinese political situation was unstable or many warlords struggled with each other for the dominance of China, intermarriages between China and foreign countries would become more frequent. Especially, when there were powerful nomadic regimes in the neighboring regions of China, the Chinese warlords would certainly attempt to ally with them for the sake of increasing their own strength and winning in the battle for hegemony. During the centuries when the Turks and Uighurs flourished in Central Eurasia, the Chinese regimes intermarried with them many times. The purpose of these intermarriages, of course, was "drawing support from the external forces." If the Chinese rulers handled this matter properly, they might benefit more; if they were eager for quick success, it tended to bring endless trouble.

Before the Tang regime was established, Liyuan 李淵 actively proposed intermarriage with the Turks. In the spring of 617, the Turk cavalry of tens of thousands invaded Taiyuan 太原, the important base area of Liyuan's territory. At that time, Liyuan's army was so weak that the barbarians could come and go freely. But, the Turks suspected the Tang troops had ambushes, so withdrew overnight.

Owing to the fact that the Turks did not know the actual situation of the Tang regime, Liyuan personally wrote a letter to Turk Qaghan, humbly asking for the military support of the Turks to compete for the dominant power of China. He said the following: "I will lead all of my troops to pacify whole China, assist the new emperor of the Sui, and intermarry with the Turks, just as did in the reign of emperor Wendi 文帝. Is not it a good thing? Though the present emperor cannot quite satisfy you, his great-grandfather Wendi was very kind to you. If you follow me and do not harass the common people, all the war booty including money, silk and girls can be rewarded to you. If you are not willing to go deeply into China because of the distant way, you may also stay here, intermarry with us, and wait for a large amount of wealth without mobilizing any troop. Anyway, you may choose the most proper thing to do."[24]

---

[24] Cf. Wendaya 温大雅, Datangchuanyeqijuzhu 大唐創業起居注 (*Records of the Tang Dynastic Founder's Daily Activities*), punctuated and proofread by Lijiping 李季平 and Lixihou 李錫厚, Shanghai Classics Publishing House 上海古籍出版社, 1983, pp. 8–9.

Here, Liyuan falsely claimed that he was going to assist the new emperor of the Sui. In fact, he attempted to realize his own political ambition with the help of external military forces. Subsequent events show that the Turks were only willing to support Liyuan as the Chinese emperor instead of the puppet monarch of the Sui Dynasty because they believed that Liyuan will keep his promise, rewarding the Turks with a lot of wealth. Finally, Liyuan actually accepted the Turks' offer.

Liyuan's trusted follower Liuwenjing 劉文靜 brokered this agreement. Liuwenjing promised Shadpit Qaghan 始畢可汗, "we will take the capital with your army together. The people and lands should belong to Prince of Tang (Liyuan), while the money, silk, gold and jewels belong to Qaghan."[25] Shadpit Qaghan was very delighted, and immediately sent soldiers and horses to come to do "trade". Though Liyuan dared not accept all these soldiers and horses, thereby limiting the Turks' trample to a certain extent, his purpose of capturing the throne by means of external army was fully uncovered.

There is no detailed description on the intermarriage between Liyuan and Turk Qaghan in the historic records. *The Biography of Imperial Family* 宗室傳 of *Jiutangshu* 舊唐書 says that in 617 and 618, Lichen 李琛, the Prince of Xiangwu 襄武, and the minister of Rituals Ministry Zhengyuanshu 鄭元璹 were dispatched to the Turks. They gave some actresses who sang and danced to the Qaghan, attempting to intermarry with him. Similar stories are recorded in *Tanghuiyao* 唐會要 and *Cefuyuangui* 册府元龜, see Chapters 94 and 98, respectively.

According to these descriptions, the so-called *Intermarriage* between Liyuan and Shadpit Qaghan was seemingly only with several common girls instead of imperial princesses. However, the actual situation at that time was that Liyuan was eager to ask for the aid of the Turks, so he handled such important affairs irresponsibly. Besides, if Shadpit Qaghan married only one or few Chinese actresses, it would have been impossible that he would send envoys in summer of 618 to Tang for discussing the intermarriage.[26] Therefore, possibly, for the sake of protecting the reputation of the founder of the Tang, later historians deliberately deleted the details of the intermarriage between Liyuan and the *barbarian* ruler.

The intermarriages between the Tang and the Uighurs start since the year of 755 when the rebellion of Anlushan 安祿山 and Shisiming

---

[25] Cf. *Jiutangshu* 舊唐書, fasc. 57, p. 2292.
[26] Cf. *Tanghuiyao* 唐會要, fasc. 94, p. 2000.

史思明 broke out. Both Anlushan and Shisiming were so-called 胡人 (huren, the Barbarians or Foreigners), as their parents were Sogdians and Turks. Soon after his rebellion, Anlushan captured the two capitals of the Tang, namely, the East Capital Luoyang 洛陽 and the West Capital Changan 長安. Emperor Xuanzong 玄宗 was forced to flee to Shu 蜀, the present Sichuan Province, a mountainous basin southwestern of China. The Tang regime was in a very dangerous position.

After the succession in the summer of 756, Suzong 肅宗 tried to quell the rebellion with the help of barbarian military forces. He designated Lichengcai 李承寀, a son of the late Prince of Bin 邠 Lishouli 李守禮, as the Prince of Dunhuang 敦煌. Later, Lichengcai was sent to the Uighur Khanate as an envoy together with general Shiginfshen 石定審. A daughter of the Uighur Qaghan married Lichengcai, and gained an honorable title *Bilga Princess*. This was the first intermarriage of the Tang Dynasty with the Uighurs.

At the same time, Gelei 葛勒 Qaghan of the Uighurs asked for intermarriage with the Tang Dynasty. Suzong attached great importance to this matter, and immediately granted his youngest daughter as the Ningguo 寧國 Princess, and sent her to marry Gelei Qaghan in lunar July of 758. It seemed to be the first time in Chinese history that a real daughter of the emperor married the ruler of the barbarians. It fully displayed the fact that at that time the Tang regime was very eager to ally with the powerful nomadic khanate. The Uighurs did not disappoint China. In lunar August of the same year, the Qaghan presented five hundred horses to the Chinese government, and ordered a troop of cavalry of 3000 led by his prince and prime minister to assist the emperor in suppressing the rebels.[27]

Gelei Qaghan died in lunar April of 759, and thereby Ningguo Princess came back to China. Another girl Liwan 李琬, the daughter of the Prince of Rong 榮, remained behind in Uighur country. As a concubine accompanying Ningguo Princess, she had gone there the previous year. Now, she was titled *Minor Ningguo Princess* 小寧國公主 and was going to marry to the new Qaghan. Later, this Minor Ningguo Princess married in succession two Uighur Qaghans, Yingwu 英武 Qaghan and Yingyi 英義 Qaghan, and had two sons. She does not die until 791, living in Uighur country for more than 30 years.

---

[27] Cf. *Jiutangshu* 舊唐書, fasc. 195, pp. 5200–5201.

In the twilight years of Minor Ningguo Princess, Uighur Qaghan Kutlug 骨咄祿 asked many times to marry another Chinese princess, but Dezong 德宗 refused this proposal, because this Qaghan once insulted him. On the contrary, Prime Minister Limi 李泌 insisted that they should consider the overall situation to intermarry with the Uighurs. Finally, in 787, Dezong agreed with Limi's suggestion and let his eighth daughter, titled Xianan 咸安 Princess, marry the Uighur Qaghan.

In lunar October of the following year, Uighur Qaghan dispatched a big diplomatic mission of more than 1000 members led by their Prime Minister to China to escort the princess to the wedding. The Qaghan achieved what he wished for, and submitted a letter to the Chinese emperor, expressing his friendship: "we were formerly the brothers, but now I am your son-in-law, similar to your son. If your country is invaded by the Western Barbarians, I will lead my troops to destroy them."[28] The so-called *Western Barbarians* 西戎 here referred to the Tibetans and other tribes west of China. In light of this, Dezong promised this intermarriage, though the purpose was not asking for direct military support of the Uighurs, but was apparently to take advantage of their strong military powers indirectly. In other words, this intermarriage was not a voluntary and active *Good Neighborly* behavior.

Xianan Princess married in succession several Qaghans, namely, Tianqin 天親 Qaghan, his son Zhongzhen 忠貞 Qaghan, his grandson Fengcheng 奉誠 Qaghan and the former Prime Minister Huaixin 懷信 Qaghan. After her death, though the Uighurs asked for intermarriages many times, the Tang government did not make any promise until the year 821, when the tenth (or fourth, fifth) younger sister of Muzong 穆宗 was designated as Taihe 太和 Princess, to marry Chongde 崇德 Qaghan of the Uighurs. Three years later, Chongde Qaghan died and Taihe Princess continued to live during the reigns of the Qaghans of Zhaoli 昭禮, Zhangxin 彰信, Kesa 盧馺 and Wujie 烏介. According to the customs of the nomads, Taihe Princess could marry them successively.

Since the period of Suzong, the Tang Dynasty intermarried with the Uighurs frequently. At first, the Tang government obviously aimed to take advantage of the powerful military forces of the Uighurs to recover the lands captured by the rebels of Anlushan and others. Later, the Tang government was forced to intermarry with the Uighurs and pay them a lot of wealth, of course, and had to trade with the Uighurs in silk and horses on

---

[28] Cf. *Xintangshu* 新唐書, fasc. 217A, p. 6124.

a large scale, because they had to reward the Uighurs for their great merit of recovering the two capitals. On the contrary, they were afraid that the Uighurs would harass the Chinese when the government was unable to satisfy their desires.

It is possible that in the earlier period, there were more advantages and less disadvantages in intermarriage, while in the later period intermarriage lost more than it gained. The words in the imperial edict to Taihe Princess by Wuzong in 842 clearly display those facts: "You, my aunt, have married to the Qaghan in distant country for more than twenty years. Your life is hard, suffer greatly … For the purpose of seeking for peace, the former emperors let you marry to the barbarian. We believe the Uighurs can certainly drive away our enemies, protect the Chinese from war disaster. But now the Uighurs act unreasonably, they recklessly plunder the people living along the Chinese borders, including the barbarians seeking shelter there …"[29] Apparently, there were no benefits any longer in intermarriage with the Uighurs.

Some intermarriages at the end of the Northern Dynasties aimed at more political and military interests. For example, the Chinese regimes of Eastern Wei 东魏, Western Wei 西魏, Northern Qi 北齊 and Northern Zhou 北周 competed to draw in the nomadic powers of the Rouran 柔然 and Turk 突厥, intermarrying with them, presenting them with a lot of money and scheming against each other. Their purposes were the same: to take advantage of the military forces of these barbarians, defeat their adversaries and dominate the whole of China by themselves in the end.

In lunar April of 533, Xiaowudi 孝武帝, the last monarch of the Northern Wei 北魏, ordered Langya 琅琊 Princess, the oldest daughter of Prince of Fanyang 范陽 Yuanhai 元海, to marry Anagui 阿那瓌, the ruler of Rouran 柔然. However, before this intermarriage was done, the regime Northern Wei was already split into Eastern Wei and Western Wei; emperor Xiaowudi fled westward and sought asylum in the territory of Yuwentai 宇文泰. Then, Eastern Wei and Western Wei waged a fierce struggle for intermarriage with Rouran.

Emperor Wendi 文帝 of the Western Wei 西魏 let Huazheng 化政 Princess, daughter of Yuanyi 元翌, marry Anagui's younger brother Tahan 塔寒, and he himself married the daughter of Anagui. At the same time, a large amount of money and silk was given to these barbarians.

---

[29] Cf. Lideyu 李德裕, *Huichangyipinji* 會昌一品集, fasc. 5, pp. 32–33, in *Preliminary Edition of Series Integration* 叢書集成初編, The Commercial Press 商務印書館, 1935.

Then, Rouran supported the Western Wei to strike against the Eastern Wei. Anagui detained Yuanzheng 元整, the envoy of Eastern Wei, even murdering him soon after. Again, in the year 538, Rouran plundered in succession Youzhou 幽州, Sizhou 肆州 and other regions of the Eastern Wei. As a result, the relations between Rouran and Eastern Wei became very tense. At this time, the powerful minister Gaohuan 高歡 of the Eastern Wei proposed the conciliatory policy to seek Rouran's friendship. Through some hard work, the two powers resumed their peaceful communications in 540.

It happened that the daughter of Anagui died of sickness; she was married to Emperor Wendi of the Western Wei earlier. The Eastern Wei immediately sent a mission to Rouran, attempting to foment discord. The envoys rumored that the daughter of Anagui was murdered by Wendi and his officials, and Huazheng Princess who was married to Anagui was not of the true imperial blood. Furthermore, they boasted that the emperors of the Eastern Wei originated from the real royal family of the Wei. If the Rouran intermarried with the Eastern Wei, they will certainly get a true imperial Princess, and will also get powerful military support from the Eastern Wei, thereby taking revenge for the crimes done by the Western Wei.

Anagui was persuaded, and so established friendly relations with the Eastern Wei and proposed marriage of his son Anluochen 庵罗辰 to Eastern Wei. In lunar June of 541, Anle 安樂 Princess, the younger sister of the Prince of Changshan 常山 Yuanzhi 元騭, married Anluochen. A grand ceremony was held, and many gifts were given to the Rouran. In the following year, Linhe 鄰和 Princess, the granddaughter of Anagui, married Gaozhan 高湛, the ninth son of Gaohuan 高歡. Later, Gaozhan succeeded the throne, becoming Emperor Wuchendi 武成帝 of the Northern Qi 北齊. In 546, the beloved daughter of Anagui married Gaohuan. From the point of view of intermarriage, the Eastern Wei seemed be more successful because, according to the historic records, the Rouran did not harass the borders of Eastern Wei until this regime collapsed. Of course, the Eastern Wei paid considerable economic price for these intermarriages.[30]

---

[30] For the intermarriages among Rouran, Western Wei and Eastern Wei, see *The Biography of Rouran* 蠕蠕傳 in *History of the Northern Dynasties* 北史, fasc. 98; *Biography of Yangjian* 楊荐傳 and *Biography of Wangqing* 王慶傳 in *History of the Zhou* 周書, fasc. 33, and so on.

The Gao 高 family and the Yuwen 宇文 family established regimes of the Northern Qi 北齊 and the Northern Zhou 北周, respectively. The two regimes were inherited from the Eastern Wei and Western Wei, respectively. Just like their predecessors, Northern Qi and Northern Zhou also fiercely struggled for the sake of intermarrying with the barbarians, but now the object was the Turks instead of the Rouran. This was because the Turks had already replaced the Rouran, becoming the overlords of the Mongolian Plateau.

At the end of the Western Wei, Mahān Qaghan 木杆可汗 of the Turks promised to marry off his daughter to the powerful Prime Minister Yuwentai 宇文泰 of the Western Wei. But, Yuwentai died soon after, thus there was no time for their wedding. After the Northern Zhou was formally established by Yuwentai's son, its rulers were increasingly eager to intermarry with the Turks for the purpose of taking advantage of the military forces of the barbarians. Then, Mahān Qaghan let his other daughter marry Emperor Wudi 武帝 Yuwenyong (宇文邕). However, their opponent Northern Qi 北齊 also dispatched envoys to the Turks to propose marriage and promised a more generous gift. In the face of the temptation of great benefits, Mahān Qaghan tried to tear up the marriage contract with Northern Zhou.

When Wudi of the Northern Zhou learnt the news, he immediately dispatched capable officials to the Turks, such as Yangjian 楊荐, Wangqing (王慶) and others. They demanded that Qaghan keep his word on the one hand, and promised to give much more money and silk to the Turks on the other hand. After many twists and turns, Mahān Qaghan finally decided to intermarry with the Northern Zhou. In 568, Emperor Wudi held the wedding with Mahān Qaghan's daughter, who was generally called as *Ashina Queen* 阿史那皇后. Later, the Northern Zhou regime married off the Qianjin 千金 Princess, the daughter of Prince of Zhao 趙, to the Turk Qaghan in 579. In order to intermarry with the Turks, the Northern Zhou spent countless material and financial resources. The reward was that as an ally the Turks often assisted Northern Zhou to attack Northern Qi. However, they did not care about the suffering of the common people.

When the Chinese powers struggled for hegemony, they spent a lot of money and even humiliatingly begged for intermarriage with powerful barbarians, to take advantage of their military forces. Such intermarriages were at most beneficial to the rulers themselves; as for the whole country and its people, the negative results were very obvious.

Emperor Wendi 文帝 of the Sui Dynasty listed some facts about the intermarriages among the Northern Zhou, Northern Qi and Turks in an edict, revealing the maladies of such intermarriages on the whole:

"Formerly, when the Wei regime is declining, disasters followed one after another. The Zhou and Qi rival against each other, split off China. The barbarians Turk communicate with both regimes. Thus, the Zhou is afraid that the Qi establishes a better relation with the Turks; while the Qi also fears that the Zhou becomes a firm ally of the Turks. Therefore, both of the two Chinese regimes leave the safety of their countries to the Turks to decide. They exhaust the resources of their people to supply the barbarians and abandon all the wealth in the treasury to the deserts. The whole China is greatly harassed by them. Besides, these barbarians plunder Chinese borders and kill our people frequently. They are still harming our country to this day."[31]

5. A Brief Comment on the Pros and Cons of Intermarriage

Summarizing the above discussion, we could give a brief comment on the pros and cons of Intermarriage in ancient China as follows:

(1) In terms of the motives for intermarriage, it is almost unexceptional that any party in any era did it with deep utilitarianism. They were so eager for quick success that they did not even take into account the long-term benefits at all. The emperors of the Han, such as Gaozu 高祖 and his successors, promised to intermarry with the barbarians obviously because they had no alternative. The nomadic Xiongnu were very powerful, while the newly established Han regime was rather weak; the latter was forced to give much silk and property to Xiongnu in the form of Intermarriage, in exchange for a temporary peace. The fact that Lühou 呂后, the Queen of Gaozu, had to endure the great insult given by Modu Chanyu 冒頓單于 clearly displays that such intermarriages were only the weaker party's acts of begging for peace.

---

[31] Cf. *Suishu* 隋書, fasc. 84, p. 1866.

Of course, the initiative of intermarriages was not rare, with examples such as the intermarriage with Wusun 烏孫 in the reign of Wudi of the Han. This intermarriage aimed at making an alliance with Wusun, "cutting off the right arm of the Xiongnu", carrying out the strategy of so-called "befriend the distant enemy while attacking those nearby".

In the Sui Dynasty, the tactic of disintegrating the Turks was thought to be rather successful and was known in contemporary and later generations. And, an important means of the disintegrating tactic was intermarriage, such as the marriages with Tuli Qaghan 突利可汗 and Shekui Qaghan 射匱可汗 of the Turks. The exchange condition for intermarriage proposed by the Sui rulers was that the marrying object must destroy certain factions within their own regime, or kill certain important personages of their own state. In other words, such intermarriage was in fact a terrible murdering transaction.

In the struggle for the hegemony of China, the Eastern Wei 東魏-Western Wei 西魏 and the Northern Qi 北齊-Northern Zhou 北周 were two pair of irreconcilable rivals. Their urgent matters were either avoiding being defeated by the opponent or devising a way to destroy the enemy. Thus, their major policies were formulated almost around this theme. Intermarriages with the powerful nomads Rouran and Turk were also carried out according to this principle.

If someone begged for support from the barbarian military forces by means of intermarriage, to fight for China's hegemony, he would be accused of being a *traitor*. Liyuan 李淵 sought military support from the Turks by means of so-called intermarriage. Though he claimed this action aimed to assist the Sui regime, Liyuan privately admitted that it was in fact a pretext for capturing supremacy of China. As for the result of intermarriage with the Uighurs in the reign of Emperor Suzong 肅宗, the Uighur Qaghan indeed provided powerful cavalry and recovered the two capitals of the Tang, but this intermarriage was also very utilitarian. The subsequent facts show that its sequel was quite serious.

For the Chinese regimes, intermarriage was often a measure of expediency, while for the foreign tribes, the intermarriage was purely a transaction. First of all, what they cared about most was money and belongings. Formerly, it was mainly because of the temptation of money and silk that the Xiongnu agreed to intermarry with the Han. According to the concept of the Xiongnu, the condition of intermarriage was just "the Han sends princesses often, and gives a lot of silk and foods to Xiongnu."

Besides, China was a traditional civilized power, with a high reputation among the barbarians. Thus, the barbarian tribes were quite willing to take advantage of the intermarriage with Chinese regime to increase their influence and power on other countries, or they could at least protect themselves from the harm of other powers. For example, as mentioned above, exactly because of the support of Chinese forces, the Wusun avoided being destroyed by the Xiongnu.

Generally speaking, both the Chinese regimes and the foreign tribes regarded the intermarriage as a political and diplomatic tactic solving the current pressing problems. Therefore, their motives were all very selfish and even short-sighted. Thereby, it was natural to result in considerable negative effect.

(2) As far as the economic consequences of the intermarriage were concerned, the Chinese governments certainly had serious losses. Intermarriage meant friendly exchange; the main mode of *Friendly Exchange* in ancient China was always embodied as that the barbarians paying tributes to China, and the Chinese rulers rewarding them and opening trade markets for them. In most cases, however, neither the *paying of tribute* nor the *rewarding* and *reciprocal market* was a real trade in the modern sense. The reason was that such exchanges were far from equal in the economic value. The Chinese monarchs either rewarded the foreign guests a great amount of belongings to show their generosity, or were forced to transport silk and money to the powerful barbarians in exchange for temporary border peace. Naturally, if they attempted to take advantage of foreign military forces, they had to pay in more *gifts*.

Emperor Gaozu of the Han adopted the proposal offered by Loujing 婁敬, and intermarried with Modu Chanyu of the Xiongnu. Thereafter, the Han government presented "the Xiongnu a great quantity of various silks, wines and foods, etc. annually." Nobody knows the exact number of these properties given by the Han monarchs. But, the demand in a letter sent to Wudi 武帝 by Hulugu Chanyu 狐鹿姑單于 may be a reference: "What I demand are 10000 *shi* 石 of mellow wine, 5000 *hu* 斛 of rice and 10000 bolts 匹 of sundry silks annually" (see *Biography of the Xiongnu* 匈奴傳 in *Hanshu* 漢書). From Emperor Gaozu 高祖 to Huidi 惠帝, Wendi 文帝 and Jingdi 景帝, the Han Dynasty intermarried with the Xiongnu for about seventy years. It can be supposed that during this period, the whole amount of money and silks given by China to the barbarians was extremely great. Even Emperor Wudi 武帝 still ordered his officials "to obey the intermarriage contract and to pay rich reward for Xiongnu's commodities."

During the reigns of Xuandi 宣帝, Yuandi 元帝 and Chengdi 成帝 of the Han, Huhanye 呼韓邪 Chanyu and his successor Fujulei Jodi 復株纍若鞮 intermarried with China and they received more property than their predecessors. Huhanye married Wangzhaojun 王昭君. When he came to pay tribute to the Chinese emperor in 51 BC, he was rewarded with 8000 bolts of fine silk and 3000 kilograms of raw silk, as well as other belongings. He came to China once again in 49 BC, and got 9000 bolts of fine silk and 4000 kilograms of raw silk. What he was rewarded in 33 BC was double that of 49 BC. In 25 BC, his son Fujulei Jodi paid tribute to Chengdi 成帝 and he was rewarded 20000 bolts of fine silk and 20000 kilograms of raw silk. Furthermore, in 1 BC, the Chanyu Uchjulu Jodi 烏株留若鞮 gained 30000 bolts of fine silk, 30000 kilograms of raw silk and other belongings.[32] Obviously, the properties transported from China to the barbarian nomads increased year by year because of the intermarriages.

The Northern Qi and Northern Zhou confronted each other in Northern China. Both these regimes were desperate to intermarry with the Turks, so as to strengthen their military forces. Thus, the economic prices they paid for this purpose were far more than what the Han Dynasty paid to the Xiongnu. After intermarrying with the Turks, the Northern Zhou not only supplied "them 100 thousand bolts of silks annually" but also entertained the Turks living in the capital, supplying them silk dresses and delicious foods. Such *Distinguished Guests* often numbered as many as a thousand. The Northern Qi tried to bribe the Turks as much as possible too, thereby leading to the emptying of the treasury.

Later, a historic record describing this situation said, "The Zhou and Qi compete to intermarry with the Turks, exhaust their treasury to please them." No wonder the Taspar Qaghan 他鉢可汗 once proudly claimed, "As long as my two sons in the South are filial, I am never worried about the lack of wealth."[33] Here, the "two sons" meant the regimes Northern Qi

---

[32] All these data are recorded in *Biography A of the Xiongnu* 匈奴傳 in *Hanshu* 漢書, fasc. 90.
[33] About these words, cf. *Biography of the Turks* 突厥傳 in *Zhoushu* 周書, fasc. 50 and *Biography of the Turks* 突厥傳 in *Suishu* 隋書, fasc. 84, etc.

and Northern Zhou. Evidently, at that time, the Qi and Zhou were very despised by the Turks, though they gave them countless money and belongings.

The intermarriages of the Tang and the Uighurs started after the rebellion of Anlushan 安禄山 and Shisiming 史思明. At first, the purpose of the Tang was to recover the capitals and wide territories occupied by the rebels with the help of the Uighur forces. At the end, although its wish came true, an era of massive outflow of money and silk began too. Mainly in the form of the *Silk–Horse Trade* 絹馬交易, a great deal of Chinese wealth flowed to the Uighurs. As this topic has been discussed in previous chapters, I will not say more here. In short, in a period of one hundred years, the Tang government was forced to buy the Uighur horses at a high price. The main reason was that the Uighurs once set up a great achievement of regaining lost territory, and intermarried with the Tang in the long term. In particular, their powerful strength made the Tang rulers dare not easily refuse their request. This so-called *Trade* lasting a century was probably one of the major reasons for the decline of the Tang.

(3) The biggest and most direct victims of the *Intermarriage Policy* were the women. Although many of the girls marrying the barbarians were not truly the emperor's biological daughters, most of them were members of the imperial family, having the honorable title *Princess*, and their political status was far higher than that of the common people. However, once she was designated as the object of the Intermarriage, she completely lost her liberty. She had to stay away far from her hometown and parents and suffer from homesickness. Besides, according to the barbarian customs, if her husband died, she was forced to marry the inherited ruler. Thus, it was not uncommon for a Chinese Princess to marry several rulers of the barbarian tribes. In this case, these *Princesses* were like commodities, and could be sold at all times and places but were irresistible to all. The *Love* enjoyed by common folk had nothing to do with them. In short, they were in fact merely *Things* instead of *Humans*, and were used by the male rulers in exchange for political interests.

When Loujing 婁敬 suggested that Emperor Gaozu marry off his daughter Luyuan Princess 魯元公主 to the ruler of Xiongnu, Queen Lühou 呂后 strongly disagreed, claiming that she absolutely refused to *discard* her only daughter to the Xiongnu (cf. *Biography of Liujing*

劉敬傳 in *Hanshu* 漢書). At that time, Xiongnu frequently invaded China, and the Han's security was seriously threatened. Even in such a dangerous situation, the capable politician Lühou still refused to marry off her daughter to Xiongnu, which sufficiently indicates that such *Intermarriage* was really an extremely painful thing. The fact that Lühou used the word *discard* instead of *marry* vividly reflects that the Princess of Intermarriage was actually merely a victim.

Emperor Wudi 武帝 of the Han let Xijun 細君 marry the ageing Kunmo 昆莫, king of the Wusun 烏孫. But, the princess and the king inhabited different places, only meeting once every year. Even when they met, they hardly talked, because they did not know each other's parent language. So, the Princess Xijun was very lonely and sad. Soon after, Kunmo asked Xijun to remarry his grandson Cenzou 岑陬. Though this demand was refused by the Princess, Wudi ordered her to accept this proposal, stating, "in order to ally with Wusun to destroy the Xiongnu, you must follow their customs" (see *Biography of The Western Regions* 西域傳 in *Hanshu* 漢書, fasc. 96). Obviously, in such a case, both the mind and body of this princess would be greatly hurt.

Some believed that Wangzhaojun 王昭君 actively requested to marry the Xiongnu Chanyu because she could not stand the loneliness of the inner palace. Others thought that she sacrificed her personal interests for the benefit of the whole country. Whatever the reason, either statement suggests that for her personally, this intermarriage was not happy, even very painful. After the death of Huhanye 呼韓邪, Wangzhaojun requested to return home, but was refused by Emperor Chengdi 成帝, and was ordered to continue to stay in the barbarian country, and to marry the son of Huhanye (cf. *Biography of the Southern Xiongnu* 南匈奴傳 in *Houhanshu* 后漢書, fasc. 89).

Ningguo Princess 寧國公主, the youngest daughter of Emperor Suzong 肅宗 of the Tang, was sent to marry Qaghan of the Uighur. Suzong saw her off in person. Before she left, the princess cried, "I intermarry with the Uighur Qaghan for the sake of the whole country, even if die I will not regret it." These words seemed to be quite impassioned, but implied that the princess had suffered great pain and harm from the intermarriage.

The Qaghan died in the following year, and Ningguo Princess was almost forced to be buried alive with him. Later, the Minor Ningguo Princess 小寧國公主 married two Qaghans in succession. Xianan Princess 咸安公主 married four Uighur Qaghans successively in

20 years, and died in 808. Roughly, she lived less than 40 years. Her short life was probably related to her severe mental and physical distress.

Taihe Princess 太和公主, the daughter of Emperor Xianzong 憲宗, married Chongde Qaghan 崇德可汗 of the Uighurs during the reign of Muzong 穆宗. A few years later, Chongde Qaghan died and his younger brother Zhaoli Qaghan 昭禮可汗 succeeded to the throne. Eight years later, in 832, Zhaoli Qaghan was murdered, and his nephew Zhangxin Qaghan 彰信可汗 succeeded him as Qaghan. Seven years later, there was civil war and unrest in the Uighur Khanate. Zhangxin Qaghan committed suicide, and Esa Qaghan 廅馺可汗 became the new ruler.

It was quite possible that in these turbulent days, Taihe Princess had to marry all these Qaghans in succession. The mental torture she suffered is conceivable. Not long after, the Uighurs were defeated by the Kirghiz 黠戛斯, and thus Taihe Princess was captured by the Kirghiz. Then, Wujie Qaghan 烏介可汗, the new ruler supported by thirteen tribes, robbed her back again. Undergoing a lot of sufferings, Taihe Princess did not return to her homeland China until 843.

The truth about the so-called *Intermarriage* was probably that the male rulers resided comfortably in palaces or mansions, while those weak girls are shouldered the important responsibility of the safety of the whole regime. They were forced to stay away from home and marry the barbarian chiefs of the distant countries. They sacrificed their personal happiness in exchange for their monarch's *Political Achievements*. Such *Intermarriage* was not worthy of praise at all.

(4) From a long-term perspective, the intermarriages had certain positive significance. The main achievement was promoting cultural communications between the Chinese regimes and the outlying districts or foreign countries. The intermarriage with Tibet 吐蕃 in the reign of Taizong of the Tang was a typical instance.

In 641, Wencheng Princess 文成公主 married the ruler of Tibet, Songzän Gambo 松赞干布. Songzän Gambo was greatly honored that his wife was a princess of the Great Tang, and thus he listened very much to the Princess, including in customs and so on. For instance, the Princess disliked the Tibetan custom of coloring the face red 赭面; Songzän Gambo immediately ordered a suspension of this practice. In addition, this Tibetan monarch took off his leather clothes and put on silk dresses, just like the Chinese. He demanded that the children of tribal chiefs study

Chinese literature and read Chinese classical works. A number of Chinese scholars were invited to write official documents.[34] Therefore, the Chinese culture gradually spread to remote areas, even foreign countries. Correspondingly, the foreign or *barbarian* cultures of the nomads and other nations were also more or less introduced into China. All these were conductive to the communication and development of civilization in every part of the world.

As mentioned above, a large quantity of silk and property of China was exported to distant regions along with the intermarriages. Particularly, silk was the traditional specialty of China and was quite needed by almost all people of the world. The nomads around the Chinese regimes were eager to act as intermediaries, reselling Chinese silk to more remote areas and making great profits. Therefore, for thousands of years, Chinese silks were exported not only to the surrounding regions of China but also to more distant districts. It greatly facilitated the economic interaction between China and these regions.

In ancient times, the cases of intermarriages of Chinese governments and other foreign countries were not very many, but the marriages between ordinary Chinese and foreigners or barbarians were far more numerous. Thereby, various kinds of blood fusions resulted from these marriages. Marriages and blood fusions among different nations favored communication and the spread of civilization, as well as strengthening the feelings and unity among all ethnic groups. This was the long-term positive effect of *Intermarriage*.

---

[34] Cf. *Jiutangshu* 舊唐書, fasc. 196A, p. 5222.

Chapter 4

餛飩 Huntun and 渾脫 Huntuo Derive from the Nomads

In ancient times, those who communicated most frequently with Chinese were the nomads living in the north or northwest of China, who were generally called 夷 yi, 狄 di and 胡 hu by the Chinese. Although these barbarians were often underestimated by the highly civilized Chinese, they actually made considerable contributions to world civilization. Here, I am going to briefly discuss several kinds of material cultures originating from the so-called *Barbarians*.

1. Wonton 餛飩 is a Kind of Foreign Food

A common food in modern China is called *huntun* 餛飩 or *yuntun* 雲吞, namely, the wonton. This is a kind of food made of flour. Its preparation method is roughly as follows: mix the flour with pure water, then roll out the dough into thin pieces of 10 cm square, and wrap delicious stuffing of meat, vegetables and shrimp in the pieces. Finally, cook them thoroughly in the soup, and it is done. The preparation method of the wonton is similar to that of the dumpling, which is very popular in the north of China. But the wonton's sheet is square instead of round, and the wonton is eaten with a delicious soup.

It seems that there is little difference between the wonton of ancient times and that of modern ages. For example, Gaolian 高濂 of the Ming Dynasty depicted the wonton as follows:

"Putting a little salt in some fine flour, and combining the flour with small amount of water. Then frequently kneading it and forming dough. Cutting the dough into many pieces and rolling them out into thin sheets respectively. These thin sheets are used to wrap various stuffing. As for the stuffing, it could be meat paste, mixing with scallion, ginger, bamboo shoots and others. Naturally, the stuffing of flesh of shrimp, crab and fishes are more delicious. When the wonton is cooking, the soup must be tasty and thick; some thin bamboos should be put in soup, to stir the boiling soup from time to time. Thus, the wonton will not break and become slippery."[1]

Obviously, the cooking methods of the wonton both in the past and present are similar, and it is one of the daily delicious foods. Then, what about the origin of this kind of food? Let us check first its various names in Chinese ancient literatures. For example, Likuangai 李匡乂 of the Tang Dynasty said that because this food has a plump and round appearance, its pronunciation is the same as 渾沌 huntun, which means plump, round and without clear outline. In addition, a character component of food "食" is added to show its food feature, thereby it is written as 餛飩 *huntun*.[2]

Simaguang 司馬光 of the Song Dynasty pointed out that in the book *Boya* 博雅 a certain food was named 膃肫 huntun, which can also be called 餫肫 huntun or 餛肫 huntun. Fangyizhi 方以智 of the Ming Dynasty listed more names for this delicious food in his *Tongya* 通雅, such as 餫飩 huntun, 渾沌 huntun, 鶻突 hutu, 餶飿 guduo, 骨董 gudong, 榾柮 guduo, 糊塗 hutu and so on.[3] Evidently, there is no resemblance between the meanings of all these names except their approximate pronunciations. Furthermore, some names are literally meaningless. Therefore, it is certain that these names are translated from a foreign

---

[1] Cf. Gaolian 高濂, *Eight Chapters of Life Nourishing* 遵生八箋, proofread and punctuated by Wangdachun 王大淳, Bashu Publishing House 巴蜀書社, 1992, p. 822. The Chinese text is as follows "白麵一片, 鹽三錢, 和如落索麵。更頻入水搜和爲餅劑, 少頃操百遍, 摘爲小塊, 擀開, 綠豆粉爲餴, 四邊要薄, 入餡其皮堅。膘脂不可搭在精肉, 用葱白先以油炒熱, 則不羶氣。花椒、姜末、杏仁、砂仁、醬, 調和得所, 更宜筍菜、炸過萊菔之類, 或蝦肉、蟹肉、藤花、諸魚肉, 尤妙。下鍋煮時, 先用湯攪動, 置竹篠在湯內, 沸, 頻頻灑水, 令湯常如魚津樣滾, 則不破, 其皮堅而滑。"
[2] Cf. Likuangai 李匡乂, *Zixiaji* 資暇集, fasc. B, in *Sikuquanshu* 四庫全書, Taibei: The Commercial Press, 1986, pp. 850–162. The Chinese text is as follows: "餛飩, 以其象渾沌之形, 不能直書渾沌而食, 避之, 從食可矣。"
[3] Cf. Fangyizhi 方以智, *Tongya* 通雅, fasc. 39, in *Sikuquanshu* 四庫全書, pp. 857–748.

language other than Chinese. Namely, the delicious food wonton is originally from regions outside China.

Another piece of evidence also proves that the wonton originates from foreign countries. Chengdachang 程大昌 of the Song Dynasty cites a folk legend that the wonton is an innovative food invented by two barbarian tribes whose surnames are 渾 Hun and 屯 Tun. Chengdachang did not believe the wonton was the invention of the barbarians for the reason that the Chinese characters 餛 or 飩 have existed since very early times. But, his opinion was not so persuasive. On the contrary, this hearsay was in line with the thinking habits of the ancients, as they often named the imported goods after Chinese characters with a similar pronunciation, and even made up stories to explain it. Here, the surnames 渾 Hun and 屯 Tun are clearly used to match the pronunciation of 餛飩 wonton. So, the Chinese word 餛飩 is surely a transliteration name.

Now, we believe that the delicious food wonton was originally introduced from so-called *barbarian regions*. As for the reasons to take such a name, I am going to discuss it below in greater detail. Before that, let us first take a look at another object called 渾脫 huntuo, which was also introduced from foreign countries, and its origin is closely related to that of the wonton.

2. Huntuo 渾脫 is the Invention of the Nomads

Huntuo, or some words taking it as the root, may be different things, but it is certain that *huntuo* does not originate from the Chinese language. Chenshiyuan 陳士元 of the Ming Dynasty wrote in his *Interpretation of the Foreign Words in Historical Records* 諸史夷語解義 that the meaning of *huntuo* 渾脫 in Chinese was bag. Yeziqi 葉子奇, a contemporary of Chenshiyuan, described *huntuo* in more detail in his *Caomuzi* 草木子: "After killing a calf, the northerners make a hole in its spine, then take away all the flesh and bones inside the body, leave a complete skin. The tanned leather pouch can hold milk, wine and other liquids. It is called *huntuo* 渾脫."[4] It can be seen that the so-called *huntuo* is a leather pouch for holding liquids. Besides, the word *northerners* here actually refers to

---

[4] Cf. Yeziqi 葉子奇, *Caomuzi* 草木子, fasc. 4B, proofread and punctuated by Wudongkun 吳東昆, in *A Collection of the Notes and Novels in the Ming Dynasty* 明代筆記小說大觀, Shanghai Classics Publishing House 上海古籍出版社, 2005, p. 77.

the nomads or barbarians north of China proper. Obviously, *huntuo* originated from nomads outside China.

As a container for holding liquids, huntuo 渾脫 appeared much earlier than the Ming Dynasty, at least; it had already been recorded in literatures of the Tang and Song Dynasties. For example, Zhoumi 周密 of the Song Dynasty mentioned huntuo in his *Guixinzashi* 癸辛雜識, and pointed out that huntuo was one of the necessary supplies in desert life:

> There are thousands of miles of desert on the way to Uighur Khanate, where are no grass, tree and water springs, but the sand and dust obscure the sky. It takes a month to get through this desert. When people travel through this road, they often make large dough mixing with salt, and put it in the mouth of the camel and horse. Then they bind up livestock's mouth to prevent the dough from being eaten quickly, thereby these animals are able to sustain life for a longer period. As for the persons themselves, everyone carries some pastries and hang between his waist a pot of water, or they store water in the huntuo 渾脫 made of cowhide or sheepskin. Every day they only eat small amount of cake and drink very little water. Sometimes they lose their way and exhaust the water, they have to drink urine of the livestock, or juice extracted from their dung. So even the Uighurs themselves think this road is very difficult to pass, just like the road to heaven. At present many Uighurs take China, especially south of China, as their home, because they are not willing to return to their hard hometown.[5]

In addition, a poem written by Zhangyu 張昱 of the Yuan Dynasty talks about using the huntuo 渾脫 to store horse-milk wine: The tribal chief of the foreign country stored the fine horse-milk wine 馬湩/馬乳酒 in huntuo, and sent envoys to offer it to the Chinese emperor.[6] Here, the *madong* 馬湩 is a special product of the nomads, a wine made from horse milk, namely, *kumyss*. Evidently, the container used to store wine or water must be sealed well, otherwise the beverage cannot be stored for a long

---

[5] Cf. Zhoumi, *Guixinzashi* 癸辛雜識, proofread and punctuated by Wanggenlin 王根林, in 宋代筆記小說大觀 *A Collection of the Notes and Novels in the Song Dynasty*, Shanghai Classics Publishing House, 2001, pp. 5784–5785.

[6] Cf. Zhangyu 張昱, *Kexianlaorenji* 可閒老人集, fasc. 2, in *Sikuquanshu* 四庫全書, pp. 1222–1544. The Chinese text is as follows: "相官馬湩盛渾脫, 騎士題封抱送來。傳與內廚供上用, 有時直到御前開。"

time. Besides, such huntuo does not seem to be very large, otherwise it would be too bulky to hold by hand.

However, another huntuo must be as big as possible, because it was used to store water for extinguishing fires. The *Summary of the Military Affairs* 武經總要 written in the Northern Song mentions siege implements, saying that if the enemy guarding the city tried to set fire to the attack implements, the attackers should immediately extinguish the fire, and one of the fire extinguishers was a *huntuo of water* 渾脫水袋, namely, the leather bag storing water.[7] Since such a water bag aimed to extinguish fires, its capacity would certainly be as large as possible.

Summary of the Military Affairs describes such huntuo in detail: "The water bag is made of various animal skins, such as that of horse, cow etc. Its capacity is about 100000 ml. The end of a long bamboo of few meters is bound to the bag mouth, all joints of the bamboo are opened. When the combat vehicle is burning several warriors immediately hold this water bag to extinguish the fire. Each combat vehicle equipped with two water bags."[8] Apparently, this extinguishing-fire bag was big enough to contain water of around 100 kg, and needed several persons to operate it. The storing-wine huntuo and extinguishing-fire huntuo were very different in terms of size.

Another application of the huntuo in military matters was the vehicle for crossing rivers. When *Tondian* 通典 of the Tang mentioned the equipment used to cross waters by the army, it said, "besides, they also use the afloat bags. They blow the huntuo of sheep hide very full, tie the mouth of the bag, then bind huntuo under their arms and swim across the river."[9]

Sushi 蘇軾 of the Song Dynasty also mentioned the same matter: "I have heard that in the regions north of the Yellow River, people often make huntuo of sheep hide. They are so numerous that up to thousands. When the army meets rivers on the march and lack of ships, they have to

---

[7] Cf. Zhenggongliang 曾公亮 and others, *Summary of the Military Affairs* 武經總要, fasc. 10, in *Sikuquanshu* 四庫全書, pp. 726–366. The Chinese text is as follows: "緒棚, 接緒頭車。架木爲棚, 故曰緒棚。其高下如頭車, 棚上及兩旁皆設皮芭, 以禦矢石。若頭車進, 則益設之, 隨其遠近。若敵人以火焚車及棚, 則施設泥漿、麻搭、渾脫水袋以救之。"

[8] Cf. Wujingzongyao 武經總要, fasc. 12, in *Sikuquanshu* 四庫全書, pp. 726–408.

[9] Cf. Duyou 杜佑, *Encyclopaedic History of Institutions* 通典, fasc. 160, Zhejiang Classics Publishing House 浙江古籍出版社, 2000, p. 849.

use the huntuo 渾脫. However, it is apt to get worm-eaten."[10] *History of the Yuan* mentions the engagement situation of the Song and Yuan regimes, saying the following: "the guarders of Xuzhou 敘州 of the Song block the ferries of Yangtze River, thus the army of the Yuan could not cross the River. However, the Yuan's soldiers collected all the cowhides in their camp, and make them into huntuo and skin raft. By help of these vehicles, troops of the Yuan defeat their opponents, capture the ferries and built floating bridges for transporting army."[11]

As a vehicle for crossing water, the huntuo 渾脫 was not only used for military purposes but also as a civil appliance. Wangyande 王延德 of the Song Dynasty was dispatched as an envoy to Gaochang 高昌 State. He described the huntuo along the Yellow River. He started his journey from Xiazhou 夏州, passing through Huangyangping 黃羊平, a region abound with Mongolian gazelle. They went through the waterless desert, the regions of the Douluoluo 都囉囉 tribe and the Maonüwaizi 茅女喎子 tribe. The latter lived along the Yellow River. The local residents often made bags with sheep hides, filling them with air, thus forming floating vehicles for crossing the waters.[12]

Besides, Lixinheng 李心衡 of the Qing Dynasty said that the residents living along the Yellow River of Gansu and Qinghai Provinces were accustomed to using the huntuo: "There are many huntuo in the region of Xining 西寧 in Gansu 甘肅 Province, where is near the Yellow River. It is made of sheep hide, gouging out flesh and bone. Thus, the bag can float on the water and carry person to cross river. The verses of Likaixian 李開先 says, the huntuo can carry people across river in a short time without the need for any ship. It can be seen that the single huntuo is rather small and convenient. However, a huntuo can only carry one person, and his trousers would get wet. So the better vehicle is the skin

---

[10] Cf. Sushi 蘇軾, *Luanchengji* 欒城集, fasc. 41, in *Sikuquanshu* 四庫全書, pp. 1112–1474.
[11] Cf. *Yuanshi* 元史, fasc. 154, Zhonghua Book Company 中華書局, 1976, p. 3641.
[12] Cf. *The Record of Wangyande's Mission to Gaochang State* 王延德使高昌記, *in Collected Works of Wangguowei* 王國維遺書, Book XIII, Shanghai Classics Publishing House 上海古籍出版社, 1983, p. 4. The Chinese text is as follows: "初自夏州, 歷玉亭鎮。次歷黃羊平, 其地平而產黃羊。渡沙磧, 無水, 行人皆載水。凡二日, 至都囉囉族。漢使過者, 遺以財貨, 謂之打當。次歷茅女喎子族。族臨黃河, 以羊皮爲囊, 吹氣實之, 浮於水。或以橐駝牽木筏而渡。"

ship produced in Jinchuan 金川. Its fabrication process is simple and has wide range of applications."[13]

Now, we know that there were at least two kinds of huntuo, one being a skin bag to store liquid, such as water, wine or other beverages. Its volume depended on its purposes, such as drinking or fire-extinguishing. Another kind of huntuo was a sealed skin container filled with air. It could float on the water and carry persons or goods across the river. The latter's appearance of round, bulging and floating on the water was naturally reminiscent of the food huntun 餛飩 mentioned above. In fact, there is a close relationship between huntuo 渾脫 and huntun 餛飩. The names given to them by the ancients reveal this fact.

For instance, Yuqingyuan 余慶遠 of the Qing Dynasty mentioned vehicles for crossing water in regions of Yunnan. He directly called them huntun 餛飩: "Huntun 餛飩, namely leather bags recorded in *History of the Yuan* 元史. Bind three feet of the sheep hide and blow air into the hide through one foot. After the bag being full with air, tie the last foot up, then the huntun can carry man to cross the river. This is originally the Mongolian means for crossing water. The emperor Shizu 始祖 of the Yuan starts using these leather bags to carry soldiers crossing the river, and calls them as Pihuntun 皮餛飩, namely *wonton of skin*. The barbarians imitate this method and are still using it."[14] As already point out above, 餛飩 huntun was originally a Chinese translation of certain foreign languages, and apparently 餛飩 huntun and 渾脫 huntuo come from the same etymon. As for this source, we may briefly discuss it as follows.

The verb *kutur* is a word in northwestern dialects of ancient Turkic, and means "to pour out" or "to empty". It seems to be the earlier form for *kotor* of the Xakani dialect. Xakani is closely related to ancient Turkic and Uighur. Besides, the word *koṭar* of Osmanli, a southwestern dialect of ancient Turkic, also means "to empty" and "to dish up".[15]

---

[13] Cf. Lixinheng 李心衡, *Miscellanea of Jinchuan* 金川瑣記, fasc. 2, in *Preliminary Edition of Series Integration* 叢書集成初編, Book 96, Taibei: Xinwenfeng Publishing Company 新文豐出版公司, 1985, p. 279.

[14] Cf. Yuqingyuan 余慶遠, *A Record of Views and News in Weixi* 維西見聞紀, in *New Edition of Series Integration* 叢書集成新編, Book 94, Taibei: Xinwenfeng Publishing Company 新文豐出版公司, 1985, p. 565.

[15] Cf. Sir Gerard Clauson, *An Etymological Dictionary of Pre-Thirteenth-Century Turkish*, Oxford, 1972, p. 605.

From a phonetic point of view, the words *kutur, kotor* and *koṭar* are similar to 渾脫 *huntuo*, and the latter can be regarded as the transliteration of the former. In terms of the background of the times, since at least as early as the Tang Dynasty, the leather bags for crossing water were found, so it is reasonable to think the Chinese word 渾脫 *huntuo* derives from the ancient Turkic prevailing in Central Eurasia. As far as the meaning of this word is concerned, the etymon of 渾脫 can also be traced back to ancient Turkic because the above citations clearly show that the essential meaning of 渾脫 is "to empty (the viscera of cattle and sheep)". Zhengsuonan 鄭所南 of the Song Dynasty talked about various brutalities of the Mongolians. One of them was "to peel off the skin of a criminal" and was called 渾脫 *huntuo*.[16] So, this actually proves that the so-called 渾脫 *huntuo* means "hollow leather bag".

Therefore, we have quite a good reason to speculate that the leather bags named by the ancient Chinese as 渾脫, whether used to store liquids or filled with air, were invented by the nomads abroad. As for the name, it probably originates from the ancient Turkic *kutur, kotor* and *koṭar* because of their common feature of *hollow leather bag*. In addition, the food 餛飩 *huntun* made of flour was also an invention of the nomads. It floated in a soup, was round and bellying, just like the appearance of 渾脫 for crossing the river, thereby the homonym 餛飩 *huntun* and 餶飿 *guduo* became their names.

3. Huntuo Hat 渾脫帽 and Huntuo Dance 渾脫舞

The two other things originating from the barbarian culture 胡文化 were called 渾脫帽 *huntuo hat* and 渾脫舞 *huntuo dance*. They are obviously related to the *huntuo* 渾脫. *Xintangshu* 新唐書 said that the *huntuo hat* was invented by a high official Zhangsunwuji 長孫無忌: "Defender-in-chief 太尉 Zhangsunwuji creates the huntuo hat with black wool. Many other persons imitate him to make such hat, and name it as *Zhaogong huntuo* 趙公渾脫."[17] Zhangzhuo 張鷟 of the Tang gave the same description in his *Chaoyeqianzai* 朝野僉載: "Zhangsunwuji 長孫無忌

---

[16] Cf. Zhengsixiao 鄭思肖, *Xinshi, by Zhengsuonan of the Song* 宋鄭所南先生《心史》, fasc. B, in *Sikuquanshu Chunmu Congshu* 四庫全書存目叢書, Book 21, Qilu Publishing House 齊魯書社, 1997, pp. 21–140.

[17] Cf. *Xintangshu* 新唐書, fasc. 34, p. 878.

is crowned Duke of the Zhao 趙 regions. He creates the huntuo hat with black wool. People all over the country admire him."[18] Here, the *huntuo hat* was depicted as a kind of felt hat made of black wool.

In addition, it seemed that a certain kind of dance was also named *huntuo* because of having something to do with such a hat. Zizhitongjian 資治通鑑 records that Emperor Zhongzong 中宗 of the Tang used to play with the ministers, asking them to sing and dance. Among these shows, the dance performed by Zongjinqing 宗晉卿 was called *Huntuo* 渾脫. In his comment on this item, Husanxing 胡三省 wrote, "Zhangsunwuji 長孫無忌 invents the huntuo felt hat with black wool, many people copy such hat and name it as Zhaogong Huntuo 趙公渾脫. Later, it turned into a dance."[19]

Since the hat was hollow and made of the fur, it was reasonable to call it *huntuo* 渾脫. However, it was unconvincing to ascribe it to the invention of Zhangsunwuji, and it was possibly wrong to think the huntuo dance originated from the huntuo hat. This is because according to other documentation, the so-called the Huntuo Dance was obviously a foreign culture introduced into China by the barbarians.

For instance, during the reign of Emperor Zhongzong 中宗, Lüyuantai 呂元泰 offered proposals to the emperor. He said the following: "Now the people organize many huntuo teams, riding on the fine horses and wearing the barbarian dresses. They are called Sumuzhe 蘇穆遮. There are many flags and drums, just like the military arrays; they run and fight, so symbolizes war; they dress in fine silk clothes, thereby waste a lot of money; they collect taxes on the poor, thus damage the foundation of the regime. The barbarian adornment is not the noble culture; the huntuo is not honorable name. How can our civilized dynasty imitate the savage customs?"[20] Here, all the shows of wearing barbarian clothes, playing barbarian music and performing the huntuo dance were evidently referred to as "savage customs". Therefore, it is doubtless that

---

[18] Cf. Zhangzhuo 張鷟, *Chaoyeqianzai* 朝野僉載 (Draft Notes from the Court and the Country), fasc. 1, proofread and punctuated by Henghe 恆鶴, in *A Collection of the Notes and Novels in the Tang and the Five Dynasties* 唐五代筆記小說大觀, Shanghai Classics Publishing House 上海古籍出版社, 2000, p. 12.
[19] Cf. *Zizhitongjian* 資治通鑑, fasc. 209, Zhonghua Book Company 中華書局, 1956, pp. 6632–6633.
[20] Cf. *Xintangshu* 新唐書, fasc. 118, p. 4277.

both the *huntuo hat* and *huntuo dance* originated from the nomads or barbarians outside of China.

Although it is incorrect to ascribe the huntuo hat to Zhangsunwuji's invention, it may be true that the *huntuo dance* is a kind of dance wearing the huntuo hat. As for the features of the huntuo hat, we may refer to following information. Chenyang 陳暘 of the Song said in his *Book of the Music* 樂書 *Yueshu*, "When perform the *hare huntuo dance*, the actor clothes in silk dress of four colors, tying silver belt and wearing hare hat."[21]

History of the Song 宋史 depicts it in greater detail: "Each kind of team dance is divided into ten types, being named respectively. The kid team consists of 72 members. The first type is called Zhezhi 柘枝 team. Its members clothe in silk dress of five colors, wearing barbarian hat 胡帽, tying silver belt. … The seventh type is called hare huntuo team. Its members clothe in red silk dress of four colors, tying silver belt and wearing hare hat."[22] Obviously, this huntuo dance 渾脫舞 is called *hare huntuo dance* 玉兔渾脫舞 because all the dancers wear hare hats having the characteristics of hares.

Duananjie 段安節 of the Tang described various musical instruments, acrobatics and dances, including the flute, drum, mask plays, swallowing knives, spitting fire and sheep-head huntuo 羊頭渾脫.[23] Therefore, the distinction of hare huntuo dance 玉兔渾脫舞 and sheep-head huntuo dance 羊頭渾脫舞 is possibly that some dancers wore hare-head-shaped hats, and others wore sheep-head-shaped hats. Since the etymon of *huntuo* probably means *hollow leather bag*, such a huntuo hat might not only keep the shape of beast but would also be large and deep enough to cover the dancer's whole head, just like a hood. Such a costume is very peculiar, hence is apt to arouse people's interest. Naturally, this *huntuo dance* was classified as a foreign music and dance, just like Sumuzhe 蘇幕遮 and mask dance. The name *huntuo* still implied the close relation with *hollow leather bag*.

---

[21] Cf. Chenyang 陳暘, *Yueshu* 樂書, fasc. 184, in *Sikuquanshu* 四庫全書, pp. 211–829.
[22] Cf. *Songshi* 宋史, fasc. 142, Zhonghua Book Company 中華書局, 1975, p. 3350.
[23] Cf. Duananjie 段安節, *Yuefuzalu* 樂府雜錄 (*Miscellanea on the Ministry of Music*), in *Sikuquanshu* 四庫全書, pp. 839–991. The Chinese text is as follows: "樂有笛、拍板、答鼓, 即腰鼓也, 兩杖鼓。戲有代面。… 即有踏搖娘、羊頭渾脫、九頭獅子、弄白馬、益錢, 以至尋橦、跳丸、吐火、吞刀、旋盤、觔斗, 悉屬此部。"

Huntuo 渾脫, wonton 餛飩, huntuo hat 渾脫帽 and huntuo dance 渾脫舞 all originated from the ancient nomads. After they were introduced into China, the Chinese diet, military equipment, culture and entertainment changed a lot. This case plainly displays the great contribution to the world civilization offered by the Silk Road.

Chapter 5
On the Etymon of Taohuashi 桃花石

Changchunzhenren 長春真人 (Ever-Spring Immortal; his true name is Qiuchuji 丘處機), the Leader of Chinese Taoism, went to Sogdiana in 1227 upon the request of Genghis Khan, the Great Qaghan of the Mongolian empire. He passed through the city of Almalik located in the present Huocheng 霍城 of the Xinjiang Autonomous Region, and described this region in his travel notes: "Their farmers use channel to irrigate lands. The natives contain water in bottle and put it on the top of head, carrying home. When they see the Chinese apparatus for fetching water, they praise, 'Everything is wonderful in *Taohuashi* 桃花石!' So-called *Taohuashi* refers to the Chinese."[1] At that time, these regions were typical *Western Regions* 西域, hence the Chinese regime and its people were named *Taohuashi* 桃花石 by the foreigners. Then, why was China or Chinese called *Taohuashi* 桃花石?

In order to analyze the relations between Taohuashi and China, we have to trace back to some other similar names which were far earlier than the Mongolian ages. The spreading and modifying of these names have a close relationship with frequent communication between the Chinese and the foreigners or *Barbarians*. The discussion of these names is given as follows.

---

[1] Cf. Lizhichang 李志常, *A Record on the Westward Journey of Changchunzhenren* 長春真人西遊記, fasc. A, in *New Edition of Series Integration* 叢書集成新編, Book 97, Xinwenfeng Publishing Company 新文豐出版公司, 1985, p. 417.

1. Different Perspectives Relevant to this Topic

In the first half of the 7th century, the Byzantine historian Theophylactus Simocatta mentioned an oriental powerful regime in his work *History*, which mainly involved the events occurring in the reign of Emperor Maurice (582–602). It said that this great country was named Taugast, and its monarch was called Taissan, meaning *Son of the Heaven*. The throne was hereditary; the emperor had supreme authority and could not be offended. This country was abundant in products, and its people were very rich.

There was a large river in the center of Taugast. Previously, this river once divided the country into two regimes. Recently, the regime in black clothes destroyed the regime in red clothes, thus unifying the whole country. Its capital was also known as Taugast, and was said to be built by Alexander the Great when he conquered the East. Its people kept a frequent commercial relation with the Indians, so some claimed they were a branch of the Indians. They resided in the north, and were fair skinned. Taugast produced silkworms; the silk was spun out from these silkworms. There were various kinds of silkworms in Taugast; the people of Taugast were famous for raising silkworms.[2]

At the end of the 6th century the author told the reader that Taugast was divided into two regimes by a big river, and was unified in recent years. Obviously, this description was consistent with the fact that the Sui 隋 destroyed the Chen 陳 regime south of the Yangtze River and unified China in the late six century. In addition, China really had frequent exchanges with India and abundantly raised silkworms. Therefore, this *Taugast* mentioned by Simmocatta was doubtlessly China.

Besides, there were numerous words of *Tabγač* or words with *Tabγač* as the main body in ancient Turkic inscriptions of the first half of the 8th century.[3] For instance, "As mourners and lamenters there came from

---

[2] This description is cited from Henry Yule, *Cathay and the Way Thither*, Vol. I, pp. 29–32; in H. Cordier, 4 vols, London, 1915.

[3] The Turks of the Asena/Ashina 阿史那 clan flourished in the middle of the 6th century. They immediately established a powerful nomadic khanate in Central Eurasia, and had close intercourses with many Chinese regimes, such as the Northern Zhou 北周, the Northern Qi 北齊, the Sui 隋 and the Tang 唐. A hundred years later, they perished in the period of Emperors Taizong 太宗 and Gaozong 高宗 of the Tang, but revived in the Mongolian plateau thirty years later, establishing the so-called "The Second Turkic Khanate." The tombstones for several leaders of this khanate were erected in the first half

the east, from where the sun rises, the representatives of the people of the Bükli plain, the Tabɣač, the Tibetan, the Avar, the Byzantium, the Kirghiz, the Üč-Quriqan, the Otuz-Tatar, Qitan and the Tatabi ... This many peoples came and mourned and lamented" (*Kül Tegin Inscription*, East, line 4). Again, the Oguz kagan says, "You, Tabɣač, attack them from the south, and you, Qitan, attack them from the east, and I shall attack them from the north. Let the Turkish Sir people not make any progress at all in their land. Let us extinguish them completely, if possible" (*Tonyukuk Inscription*, South I, line 4).[4] As for other phrases with *Tabɣač* as qualifiers and modifiers, the following are mentioned throughout the texts of these inscriptions: *kagan of Tabɣač*, *people of Tabɣač* and *ranks of Tabɣač*.

According to the context of the inscriptions, *Tabɣač* distinctly referred to the Chinese regime or the main ethnic group of China, namely, the Chinese or the Hans 漢人. The pronunciation of *Tabɣač* was similar to that of *Taugast* mentioned by the Byzantine historian Simocatta, so both Tabɣač and Taugast quite probably meant the same country or nation, namely, China or Chinese.

In some later literatures, there were also a number of other names with similar pronunciations referring to China or its people. For example, a designation *Tabghāj* was found on the coins of Karakhanids of Central Asia. This regime existed from the 10th to 13th centuries, with Kashgar as the capital. In its heyday, its territory included the Junggar Basin and most of Tarim Basin's surrounding regions, as well as a vast area of Central Asia that reached the Balkhash Lake to the north, the Amu Darya to the south and the Aral Sea to the west.

Scholars have found that many Great Qaghan/Khan, vice-Qaghan and even feudal lords of Karakhanid adopted *Tabghāj Khan* as their title, and cast it on the coin, such as *Sulaiman Tabghāj Khan* and *Tabghāj Bugra Khan*. This is an honorary title to display one's noble origin and historical tradition. And, *Tabghāj* is exactly the name for *China* or *Chinese*.[5]

---

of the 8th century and are located on the banks of the Orkhon River. These inscriptions were written in Old Turkic and are abbreviated as Tonyukuk Inscription, Kül Tegin Inscription and Bilgä Kagan Inscription.

[4] Cf. Talāt Tekin, *A Grammar of Orkhon Turkic*, Bloomington: Indiana University Press, 1968, pp. 264, 284.

[5] For the Karakhanid coins and its title *Tabghāj*, cf. Jiangqixiang 蔣其祥, *The Karakhanid Coins in Xinjiang* 新疆黑汗朝錢幣, Xinjiang People's Publishing House 新疆人民出版社, 1990, pp. 31–115.

Furthermore, the Muslim historian Al-Biruni of the 11st century mentioned the title *Tamghaj* in his works. Abu al-Fida of the 14th century wrote the word *Timghaj* in his works. Besides, there are some other names with similar pronunciations in literatures of the Middle Ages, such as *Histoire des Mongols* written by d' Ohsson in the 19th century, *Biography of Jalal al-Din* (*Sirat al-Sultan Jalal al-Din Mangubirni*) written by al-Nasawi in the 13rd century and the famous Persian epic *The Book of Kings* (*Shahnameh*) written by Ferdowsi in the 10th century. Although the pronunciations of these names are different slightly, all of them doubtlessly refer to China or Chinese people.

Of course, as mentioned above, there was also a homophone word in ancient Chinese literature, namely, 桃花石 (taohuashi, literally *peach blossom stone*), and *taohuashi* also means China or Chinese people. Then, what is the common etymon to these names? They come from different languages, but with similar pronunciations and the same meaning. There are various opinions on this topic in academic circles.

At first, the French scholar Deguignes believed that it was a homophone of *Dawei* 大魏 (Grand Wei), which was an honorary title for the regime of the Northern Wei 北魏 established in the North of China by the Xianbei 鮮卑 tribe in the 4th–6th century. However, this view was soon rejected by others. Later, German scholar Hirth and Japanese scholar Kuwabara Jitsuzo 桑原騭藏 supposed that this name stemmed from the powerful dynasty Tang of the 7th–9th century, putting forward the statement of "*Tangjia* 唐家". But, the Achilles Heel of this opinion was the fact that the name *Taugast* appears in European literature as early as the sixth century; thus, it was not related to the Tang Dynasty. Afterward, Japanese scholar Shiratori Kurakichi 白鳥庫吉 and French scholar Pelliot claimed that this name originated from *Tuoba* 拓跋, a name for the imperial family of the Northern Wei 北魏 Dynasty. Although this view was popular home and abroad, there were still some people who questioned it.

The Chinese official Hongjun 洪鈞 of the late Qing Dynasty claimed in his *Criticism and Addendum on the Translations of the Yuan History* 元史譯文證補 that the *Tamgadj* in d' Osson's *Mongol History* and *Taohuashi* 桃花石 in *A Record on the Westward Journey of Changchunzhenren* 長春真人西遊記 all stemmed from *Daheshi* 大賀氏, one of the tribes of the Khitan 契丹.[6] Cenzhongmian 岑仲勉 said in his

---

[6] Cf. Hongjun 洪鈞, *Yuanshiyiwenzhengbu* 元史譯文證補, fasc. 22A, in *Preliminary Edition of Series Integration* 叢書集成初編, Book 3, Shanghai Commercial Press, 1936,

paper *An Explanation on Taohuashi* that the etymon of Taohuashi is Dunhuang 敦煌, a place name of the northwestern region of China. Thirteen years later, he rejected his former opinion, and thought that the etymon of *Taohuashi* should be traced back to Taiyue 太岳, Taitao 太檮 and Jiaohuo 焦穫 of remote ages.⁷

It seems that the viewpoints of Hongjun 洪鈞 and Cenzhongmian 岑仲勉 had little impact on the academic circle, while more people agreed with the statements of Tianzi 天子 and Dahan 大汗. Liangyuandong 梁園東 said in his paper *Taohuashi is Tianzi, Taohuashihan is Tiankehan* 桃花石爲天子,桃花石汗爲天可汗說⁸ that *Tabyač* is a variant of the Turkic word *Tangri*, the latter meaning heaven, while the former meant governor of the heaven, namely, Tianzi 天子 (emperor). That is to say, the designation of the Chinese emperor was used to name China. My teacher, Mr. Zhangxun 章巽 put forward the statement of *Dahan* 大汗 (Great Qaghan). He believes that the nomads abroad called Chinese emperors Qaghan, and added a respectful adjective 大 (*da*, Great), written as 大汗 (Dahan, Great Qaghan). Gradually, *Dahan* 大汗 became a special name for China or Chinese people.⁹

Obviously, as far as pronunciation is concerned, this opinion is superior to other views. However, it seems that another supposition would be more reasonable than this one, that is to say, the etymon of 桃花石 *Taohuashi* is 大漢 *dahan* rather than 大汗. Zhangxinglang 張星烺 put forward this idea as early as the 1930s, but he did not demonstrate it, thereby having little influence on scholars.¹⁰

---

p. 253. The Chinese text is as follows: "多桑書,字音如曰'唐喀氏',義不可解。其所謂'唐',必非唐宋之'唐'。及注《西遊記》,有謂漢人爲桃花石一語,循是以求,乃悟即契丹語之'大賀氏'也。蒙古稱中國爲契丹,今俄羅斯人尚然。... 是知契丹盛時,仍沿大賀氏之舊稱,故鄰國亦以氏稱之。"

⁷Later, this paper was collected in Cenzhongmian 岑仲勉, *Tujuejishi* 突厥集史 (*A Comprehensive History of the Turks*), Zhonghua Book Company 中華書局, 1958, pp. 1046–1059.

⁸Cf. *Bianzhenggonglun* 邊政公論 (*Studies on the Borderlands*), Vol. III, No. 4, April, 1944.

⁹Cf. Zhangxun 章巽, *Taohuashi and the Uighur Khanate* 桃花石和回紇國, in *Zhonghuawenshiluncong* 中華文史論叢 (*Journal of Chinese Literature and History*), Vol. II, 1983.

¹⁰Cf. Zhangxinglang 張星烺, *Zhongxijiaotongshiliaohuibian* 中西交通史料彙編 (*A Compilation of Historical Materials on the Intercourses between China and the Occident*), proofread by Zhujieqin 朱傑勤, Zhonghua Book Company 中華書局, 1977, Book 1, p. 90.

116   On the Ancient History of the Silk Road

I will discuss this topic here. What I need to point out is that though we find the word *Tabγač* only in the Turkic inscriptions of the 8th century, its primary formation must have been much earlier, because the Turks established the powerful Khanate in Central Eurasia as early as the middle of the 6th century. Thus, I will take *Tabγač* as the representative of all similar terms in the following discussion.

2. 大漢 Dahan Has the Most Lasting Reputation and the Greatest Impact Among the Barbarians

The various viewpoints listed above seem to follow a common principle, namely, searching for the representational title of the Chinese Dynasty, nation and place as much as one could, taking it as the etymon of *Tabγač*. Therefore, the statements of 大魏 *Dawei*, 拓跋 *Tuoba*, 唐家 *Tangjia*, 大賀氏 *Daheshi* and 敦煌 *Dunhuang* have been put forward successively. Among these names, those being less influential were not recognized much by the public, such as *Daheshi* and *Dunhuang*. On the contrary, the designation of a powerful dynasty has been always apt to be adopted by scholars, though the fact proves that it can never be the etymon of *Tabγač*. For example, Hanrulin 韓儒林 and Cenzhongmian 岑仲勉 still translated the *Tabγač* into 唐家 *tangjia* in their translations of the Turkic Inscriptions.[11]

Since the Etymon of a name or title depends on whether the influence of the name is great enough, the designation 大漢 Dahan is fully qualified as a representational name for China. First, after establishment of the first centralism empire Qin 秦, the Han 漢 Dynasty lasted for the longest time among all Chinese regimes, starting from the end of the 3rd century BC and ending at the early period of the 3rd century AD. That is to say, during

---

He wrote in the note, "I think the word *Taugast* was probably a homophone of 大漢 dahan. In modern Japanese 大漢 is pronounced as Daigan."

[11] For instance, in the Chinese translation of Kül Tegin Inscription, south, lines 4 and 5, Hanrulin 韓儒林 translates *Tabγač* into the Chinese word 唐家 (in *Journal of the National Beiping Institute* 國立北平研究院院務匯報, Vol. VI, No. 6, August, 1935). Cenzhongmian 岑仲勉 also translates *Tabγač* in the same way. Cf. his translations of the Turkic Inscriptions, in Cenzhongmian, *A Comprehensive History of the Turks* 突厥集史, Book II, Zhonghua Book Company 中華書局, 1958.

a long period of at least more than 400 years, the foreigners always regarded *China* as *Han* 漢.

Second, as far as the degree of prosperity is concerned, the Han Dynasty was comparable to the Tang Dynasty. People of the Han had frequent intercourses with nomads abroad, just like people did in the Tang Dynasty. Emperor Wudi 武帝 of the Former Han dispatched Zhangqian 張騫 to visit the Western regions, opening up large-scale foreign exchanges. In the Later Han era, Banchao 班超 and others ran the Western Region again. Besides, for several centuries, the Han regime waged many wars with the Xiongnu while often intermarrying and peacefully communicating with them. All these activities were very helpful to spread the reputation and name of *Han* to distant regions. I believe that even after the Tang Dynasty, the foreigners probably named China as "Han 漢" instead of "Tang 唐" or other designation. Because the earliest large-scale communications of the nomads with Chinese occurred in the Han Dynasty, the initial impression was the most profound one.

Third, 大漢 *Dahan* (Great Han) is an honorable and noble designation, one that both the Chinese and the foreigners were willing to use. On the contrary, other names, such as Tuoba 拓跋, were originally only tribe names, and later were even discarded by the royal family of the Northern Wei 北魏, replacing it with 元 Yuan. Therefore, in the mind of most foreigners, "漢 Han" was possibly more suitable for representing China than other designations.

The name "大漢 Dahan" frequently appeared in Chinese ancient literatures. The people of the Han era often self-proclaimed as Dahan, and were very proud of this designation. Particularly, when Chinese officials dealt with foreigners, they were especially proud of this title. For instance, in 65 AD, Zhengzhong 鄭眾 was sent as an envoy to Xiongnu 匈奴. He was abused by the Xiongnu Chanyu 單于 because of refusing to kowtow to the Chanyu.

Later, Emperor Mingdi 明帝 wanted to dispatch him to Xiongnu again, and he told the emperor, "I went there before, suffered a lot because I refused to prostrate myself before him. If I go there again, I will certainly be abused again. I am really unwilling to bow to such a barbarian together with Dahan's scepter. If your Majesty forced me to be the envoy, probably cause the prestige of Dahan 大漢 to be damaged."[12] This is one of the important reasons listed by Zhengzhong for refusing to be an envoy to

---

[12] Cf. *History of the Later Han* 後漢書, fasc. 36, p. 1225.

Xiongnu. He repeatedly emphasized the name "Dahan", evidently trying to inspire the emperor's sense of honor, thereby canceling the mission of sending him to Xiongnu. Obviously, at that time, Dahan was an honorific title of China used by Chinese officials.

In the first year of the reign of Emperor Hedi 和帝 (89 AD), Douxian 竇憲 and others made an expedition to Mobei 漠北 (North of the Desert), utterly defeating the Xiongnu in Jiluo Mountain 稽落山, and forcing hundreds of thousands of Xiongnu people to surrender to China. Then, Douxian climbed up to the top of Yanran Mountain 燕然山, where being 3000 *li* 里 away from Chinese frontiers, he erected a monument to show off this brilliant victory. The inscription states that this great victory not only gave vent to the hatred of the Xiongnu, but also opened up territory and enhanced prestige of *Dahan* 大漢."[13] Here, the "大漢 Dahan" was evidently the laudatory title the Chinese used for themselves. It seems that the Chinese historians were used to taking Dahan as a laudatory title of their regime, as the following paragraph shows: "Liangfeng 梁諷 is going on an expedition to attack Xiongnu, stations his army in bordering area and fully displays great strength and prestige of the Dahan, forcing the Xiongnu to be very afraid, thus come to surrender successively" (cf. *Donghanguanji* 東漢觀記, *Record of History of the Later Han*, fasc. 19, *Biography of Liangfeng*).

On the contrary, this designation seemed to also be recognized by the nomads or other barbarians outside. For example, Chanyu 單于 of the Xiongnu gave a letter to Emperor Wudi in 89 AD, saying the following: "There is *Dahan* in the South while the *Powerful Xiongnu* 強胡 in the North. Xiongnu is the favorite son of the God, and not to stick at trifles. Now I am willing to establish friendship with Your Majesty, marry your daughter. If you give us ten thousand *shi* 石 of wine, five thousand *hu* 斛 of rice, ten thousand bolts of silk and other commodities annually, I will not intrude your borders anymore."[14]

This letter was very arrogant in tone, and it was actually blackmailing property by force. Therefore, Chanyu called China as *Dahan*, just taking it as an ordinary name rather than an honorific title. Obviously, at least as early as the era of the Former Han, *Dahan* was only an ordinary name

---

[13] Cf. *History of the Later Han* 後漢書, fasc. 23, p. 815. The Chinese text is as follows: "… 遂逾涿邪，跨安侯，乘燕然，躡冒頓之區落，焚老上之龍庭。上以攄高、文之宿憤，光祖宗之玄靈，下以安固後嗣，恢拓境宇，振大漢之天聲。"

[14] Cf. *History of the Former Han* 漢書, fasc. 94A, p. 3780.

referring to China by the nomads. Just for this reason, after the Han regime perished, *Dahan* possibly still was regarded as the name of China; this tradition may have been kept for a considerable period, especially among the barbarians abroad.

In fact, after the Han Dynasty, the designation *Dahan* not only continued to exist, it was getting more and more popular among the Xiongnu. The main reason was that in the first half period of the 4th century, the descendants of Xiongnu established a regime in North China, which was named 漢 Han.

The founder of this regime was Liuyuan 劉淵. His ancestor was Modu Chanyu 冒頓單于, the powerful leader of the earlier Xiongnu. Emperor Gaozu 高祖 of the Han intermarried with Modu Chanyu, and they became brothers. Thus, the descendants of Modu Chanyu took Liu 劉 as their surname. Apparently, even though the Xiongnu and the Han regimes were hostile to each other for several hundred years, the descendants of Xiongnu were still proud of the Han. Doubtlessly, the designation Han was deeply rooted in the minds of the foreign people.

In 304 AD, Liuyuan 劉淵 proclaimed himself to be *King of the Han* 漢王, and determined Yuanxi 元熙 as the reign title. In the imperial edict, he distinctly declared that he inherited the royal family of the Han Dynasty, worshiped emperors of the Han, regarded them as his own ancestors and adopted the administrative system of the Han Dynasty. In addition, this Han regime often called itself *Dahan* 大漢 and *Huanghan* 皇漢; it is well known that the Chinese character 皇 *huang* also means 大 *da*, namely, great. Thus, it was unexpected that the laudatory title *Dahan* of the Han Dynasty was fostered and enhanced continuously by its *old enemy* Xiongnu after the Han regime's demise.

According to *Annal of Liucong* 劉聰載記 of *History of the Jin* 晉書, Chenyuanda 陳元達 said to Liucong, the son of Liuyuan 劉淵, that because the rulers of the Jin 晉 treated the people badly, they were exterminated by the God, while the Huanghan 皇漢 were blessed by the God, so the people wanted it revive the country. Here, the so-called 皇漢 Huanghan evidently referred to the Han regime established by Liuyuan 劉淵. In the same *Annal*, Kangxiang 康相 advised Liucong that he should be more careful of the regimes located in the east and north, instead of the countries located in the west and south, for the formers were more dangerous. In his saying, he repeatedly calls his own regime 大漢 *Dahan* or 皇漢 *Huanghan*. Besides, many other officials of this Xiongnu regime also frequently mentioned these names.

Briefly, although the *Han* 漢 regime in the period of Sixteen Countries lasted only for 25 years (304–329), it played a huge role in spreading the reputation of 大漢, especially among the nomads in Central Eurasia. Almost all scholars agree with the viewpoint that there is a close relation between the formation of *Tabγač* and the nomads of Central Eurasia. So, the most influential Chinese regime before the late 6th century is most likely the origin of the name *Tabγač*. Undoubtedly, the name 大漢 *Dahan*, which has the most influence of the nomads, should be the most probably origin of *Tabγač* and other similar names.

3. The Pronunciation of Dahan and Tabγač

As mentioned above, Mr. Zhangxun 章巽 offered a view that 大汗 Dahan might be the etymon of Tabγač. He compared the ancient pronunciations of 大汗 and 拓跋 with that of Tabγač, and convincingly concluded that 大汗 is closer to the pronunciations of all non-Chinese names than 拓跋. As we know, according to ancient Chinese, the pronunciations of 大漢 and 大汗 are almost completely the same, while in modern Chinese, their pronunciations are identical. That is to say, as far as pronunciation is concerned, 大漢 and 大汗 have the same qualification to be the etymon of Tabγač and some other names.

Then, we are going to discuss further this problem: How does the designation "大漢" transform into Tabγač and other homophones?

Chinese regimes frequent had military conflicts and peaceful intercourses with the nomads of Central Eurasia, so the designation 大漢 *Dahan*, the representational name for Chinese Dynasty, was first known among these nomads; then, it spread to more distant areas, such as Western Asia and Asia Minor. It is inevitable that after a long period of time and remote transmission, there are slight deviations in the pronunciation of this name. Therefore, the name appearing in the nearest region to China and at the earliest time should be the correct one. For this reason, one can suppose that the name *Tabγač* used by the ancient Turks was a standard translation name, because they established a powerful khanate as early as the middle of the 6th century, and recorded this name in their ruler's monuments of the 8th century.

Of course, the existing name *Tabγač* was only the name for China given by the Turks, corresponding to the Chinese characters 大漢 dahan. The Xiongnu, who were hundreds of years ahead of the Turks, possibly also had a similar pronouncing name to refer to 大漢. Unfortunately, it was not handed down. According to some historical literatures, the Tujue 突厥 were a branch of the Xiongnu 匈奴, and the former were the Turks who established a powerful khanate in the 6th century. Whether they belonged to the same race or not, both the tribes were undoubtedly nomads living in the same regions of Central Eurasia for a long period. Thus, it is logical that they had similar cultures and used the same name for China.

In the era of the Byzantine historian Simocatta, the Turks dominated Central Eurasia and had frequent contact with Chinese regimes in the east, such as the Northern Zhou 北周, the Northern Qi 北齊 and the Sui 隋. The Turks also communicated with Persia and Byzantium in the west, and had complicated relationships of war and peace among them. In the second half of the 6th century, direct official contact was established between the Turks and Byzantines, and missions of the two regimes frequently visited each other.[15] Against such a background, the scholars and common people found it easy to learn about China from these Turks. Quite possibly, the name *Taugast* given by Simocatta derives also from the Turkic traders, travelers, diplomatic envoys, etc. Exactly for this reason, the pronunciation of *Taugast* is closer to *Tabyač* than other names given by the Muslim historians of later generations.

Initially, how did the Chinese word 大漢 *Dahan* evolve into the ancient Turkic term *Tabyač*? Many modern scholars believe that the letter *č* in *Tabyač* is an abbreviation of *či*, and the latter is a suffix of the noun in Altaic languages. After the *či* was added to the end of a noun, this word would mean "one who specializes in this kind of work". Thus, *Tabyač* means *Administrator of the Heaven*, namely, sovereign or 天子 (Tianzi, Son of the Heaven). Although the Turkic suffix -*č* may have the function of turning a noun into a word meaning "a person who specializes in certain work", for example, turning *paint* into *painter*, *sculpture* into *sculptor*, etc., it is not the case for *Tabyač*, I think.

First, it is just a supposition that the suffix -*č* is the abbreviation of -*či*. It is not a final conclusion. Second, also more importantly, there is another noun suffix -*č* in ancient Turkic, which turns the noun into a word with the meaning of *respectable* and *beloved*. For instance, there is a sentence in

---

[15] Another contemporary Byzantine historian Menander gave a detailed description on the intercourses between the Turk Khanate and Byzantium. Cf. C. Müller, *Fragmenta Historicorm Graecorum*, Paris, 1851, Unveranderer Nachdruck, Frankfurt, 1975, Vol. IV, *Menandri Protectoris Fragmenta*.

the 4th line of the right side of the Ongin Inscription, a Turkic monument erected in 732–734, located on the banks of Ongin River of Mongolia; it says, "My beloved wise father, I held your funeral and celebrated your obsequies." Here, the reason for the meaning of "beloved father" is that in the Turkic text, a suffix -č is added to the *ata* (father), turning this word into atač.[16]

In view of such a grammar of ancient Turkic, I believe the name *Tabyač* is the same case. That is to say, this name originated from the barbarians' honorific title for China: *Tabya* corresponds to 大漢 *Dahan*; after the suffix -č is added to it, the *Tabyač* means "respected Dahan" (Great Han Dynasty). In the letters exchanged between emperors of the Han and rulers of the Xiongnu, we find many greeting words, such as "I, emperor of the Han send my cordial regards to you, the great Chanyu of Xiongnu, and wish you good health" and "I, the great Chanyu of Xiongnu give Your Majesty the warmest greeting. My very best wishes to your health" (cf. *Biography of Xiongnu* 匈奴傳 in *History of the Former Han* 漢書).

By this token, it is quite reasonable that the Xiongnu called the Han Dynasty or other Chinese regimes "Respectable Dahan". Furthermore, in ancient times, the so-called barbarians were usually in great awe of Chinese regimes, thus it was natural that they referred to China with great respect. As time goes by, *Tabyač* gradually became a proper name used by foreign people to call China.

The designation *Tabyač* derives from 大漢 Dahan; it circulated among many tribes and nations beyond China. When it spread back to Chinese again, it was misread as the pronunciation of 桃花石 Taohuashi. Therefore, nobody knows where it comes from anymore.

4. A Speculation about the Etymon of 大家 Dajia and 宅家 Zhaijia

Since the Sui and Tang Dynasties, the Chinese emperors appeared to be often called 大家 *dajia*. For example, *Qingsuogaoyi* 青瑣高議 recorded that the powerful minister Yangsu 楊素 did not follow the will of Emperor

---

[16] About the grammar and illustrative sentences of this noun suffix -č, cf. Talat Tekin, *A Grammar of Orkhon Turkic*, pp. 104, 256, 259, Bloomington: Indiana University Press, 1968.

Wendi 文帝, falsifying the decree after his death, to make Yangdi 煬帝 the new emperor. When he returned home, he said to his kinsfolks, "I have already promoted that kid, make him the 大家 dajia. I am not sure if he is qualified for the throne?"[17] Apparently, the emperor was also called 大家 dajia.

Jiutangshu 舊唐書 recorded that the Tibetans sent Lunmisa 論彌薩 as an envoy to the Tang to seek peace. Empress Wuzetian 武則天 entertained them with Chinese music. The Tibetan envoys enjoyed it greatly, and Lunmisa thanked the empress and said, "Ever since we come to China, we have been warmly entertained, and listen to the wonderful music I had never heard before. We are very poor and lowly, being difficult to repay your great grace, so I can only sincerely wish 大家 (Your Majesty) long live."[18] From this paragraph, we can see that the name 大家 was not only a designation for Chinese emperors but also a very honorific and formal title for them.

A Collection Narrating the Tang 唐語林 recorded a story: One day Xuanzong 玄宗 of the Tang played polo with others; Prince of Rong 榮王 fell off his horse and fainted. Thus, Huangfanchuo 黃幡綽 advised Xuanzong, "大家 dajia are not young anymore and your health is related to the safety of the whole country, if the horse runs too fast to control and cause Your Majesty to fell off, all people will fall into despair! So Your Majesty should enjoy the sight of others' polo playing, just like in the face of delicious food, the desires of the mouth and eyes would be satisfied."[19] This instance also proves that the appellation 大家 is the same as *Your Majesty*.

However, there was still a slight difference between *Dajia* and *Your Majesty*, because the latter could not be used by the emperor to refer to himself, while the former can. *Jiuwudaishi* 舊五代史 (*Old History of the Five Dynasties*) recorded a story about Emperor Taizu 太祖 of the Liang 梁 regime. At the end of the Tang Dynasty, Zhaozong 昭宗 summoned Zhuquanzhong 朱全忠 to his living palace and let him meet Queen He 何皇后, and bestowed on him a lot of belongings. Queen He said to

---

[17] Cf. Liufu 劉斧, *Qingsuogaoyi* 青瑣高議 (*Comment on the Various Historical Records*), fasc. 5 of Series II, Shanghai Classics Publishing House 上海古籍出版社, 1983, p. 147.
[18] Cf. *Jiutangshu* 舊唐書, fasc. 196A, p. 5226.
[19] Cf. Wangdang 王讜, *Tangyulin* 唐語林, fasc. 5, item 687, in Zhouxunchu 周勛初, *Tangyulinjiaozheng* 唐語林校證 (*A Correction and Study on A Collection Narrating the Tang*), Zhonghua Book Company 中華書局, 1987, p. 470.

Zhuquanzhong, "From now on, the safety of the couple of 大家 dajia depends on you completely." Then, she was very tearful.

The appellation 大家 was also used in the Five Dynasties. I am not going to make a detailed discussion about it here, but want to discuss another designation similar to it, namely, 宅家 zhaijia. Huangchaoying 黃朝英 cited a poem written by Songzijing 宋子京 in his *Jingkangxiangsuzaji* 靖康緗素雜記: "The tenth day of new year is just the Beginning of Spring, all people of the imperial city drink for celebrating emperor's birthday. Everyone rejoice and give his warm congratulation on the sovereign, wish the 宅家 Zhajia lives forever."[20] Obviously, the term "宅家 Zhaijia" was an honorific title for the emperor. In addition, this appellation seemed to be very popular in the Tang Dynasty, because Husanxing 胡三省 said in his note on the history of the Tang that "In the Tang era, people in the palaces call the emperor as 宅家 Zhaijia."[21]

Why is the emperor called 宅家 Zhaijia? Likuangai 李匡乂 explains it in his *Zixiaji* 資暇集 that because the whole country was the emperor's *Residence* 宅, and the whole world was his *Home* 家, the 宅家 becomes a metaphorical name of the emperor, and is same as *Your Majesty* 陛下[22] Although this interpretation is rather farfetched, his next statement seems to be reasonable, namely, when "大家" is pronounced quickly, it might sound like "宅家". The fact is that in Middle Chinese the pronunciation of "宅" is dák。, while the "大" is pronounced as d'â。, so the two words have a similar pronunciation, and could be confused with each other. If that is the case, both the 大家 and 宅家 are quite possibly the transliteration names from non-Chinese words.

During the period of the Han and Tang, there were frequent exchanges between China and foreign regions, and numerous cases of linguistic mutual references have been also found. That is to say, Chinese words might be the phonetic borrowings of the foreign languages, and vice versa. I believe that the Chinese term 大家 or 宅家 is not only one of the

---

[20] Cf. Huangchaoying 黃朝英, *Jingkangxiangsuzaji* 靖康緗素雜記, Supplement, item 7, punctuated and proofread by Wuqiming 吳企明, Shanghai Classics Publishing House 上海古籍出版社, 1986, p. 93. The Chinese text is as follows: "新年十日逢春日, 紫禁千觴獻壽觴。寰海歡心共萌達, 宅家慶祚與天長。"

[21] Cf. *Zizhitongjian* 資治通鑑, fasc. 264, p. 8630.

[22] Cf. Likuangai 李匡乂, *Zixiaji* 资暇集, fasc. B, in *Sikuquanshu* 四庫全書, Book 850, p. 159.

loanwords but also a *Buy Back* product in some form. A brief analysis is as follows.

As a proper name for "China", 大漢 Dahan was adopted by people of Central Asia in early times, and gradually transformed into one of their daily words. Thus, they called the Chinese emperor *Tabyač Qaghan*, meaning the *Qaghan of Tabyač* 大漢可汗. Such an appellation is seen frequently in the ancient Turkic Inscriptions, and obviously, it existed universally in ancient ages. The Altaic nomads called their sovereign Qaghan, so it is reasonable that they called the Chinese emperor Qaghan too.

As pointed out above, -č is a suffix in ancient Turkic, so the stem of *tabyač* should be *tabya*, and when the *tabya qaghan* is read quickly, three guttural sound after *tab-* would be pronounced as one syllable. This syllable is similar to the pronunciation of 家 in ancient Chinese, namely, *ka*. Therefore, the Chinese term 大家 or 宅家 was formed. In the Sui and Tang period, the emperor was often called 大家 or 宅家, which may be related to the frequent communications between China and the nomads of Central Eurasia. The above conclusion appears to be confirmed.

By the way, some scholars think that the appellations 國家 and 官家 for emperor are transliterations of *Qaghan*. It is not impossible, but I will not discuss this topic in depth here.

Finally, the conclusion of this chapter is as following. The name *Tabyač* referring to China by ancient foreigners initially came from the honorific appellation 大漢, the powerful and lasting regime of the Han. Later, this name was combined with *Qaghan* to refer to the Chinese Emperor. Chinese people adopted this designation and read it as a similar pronunciation 大家 or 宅家. From the *Exportation* of 大漢 dahan to the *Buying Back* of 桃花石 taohuashi, 大家 dajia or 宅家 zhaijia, this is a typical case of cultural communication between ancient China and foreigners, especially the nomads in Central Eurasia.

Chapter 6

The *Prehistoric* Habitations of the Turks and Their Migration

The ancient nomads of Central Eurasia had a close relationship with the Silk Road. First, the feature of their life was "following the water and grass", that is to say, in order to obtain the best grazing surroundings, they had to migrate continually. Therefore, as a result, along with their migration activities, various traffic routes were opened up, and formed parts of the so-called Silk Road network. Second, as the nomads promoted the opening and developing of traffic routes in Eurasia, especially Central Eurasia, they also introduced advanced civilizations from all over the world through these roads, forming a complementary relationship with other peoples. This chapter will take the Turks of the Asena/Ashina clan 阿史那氏 as an example, discussing their early habitations and the later migration routes, to reveal the close relations between the nomads and the Silk Road.

In the middle of the 6th century, the Asena tribe 阿史那氏 of the Turks[1] established a powerful khanate in the hinterland of the Eurasian continent. Scholars studied a lot on the race, original habitations and migrating course of the Asena Turks. I think the acceptable view may be

---

[1] According to the Chinese historical literatures, initially, the word 突厥 *Tujue* only referred to the Turkic Khanate's ruling clan Asena 阿史那. However, later, this term was gradually used to refer to the whole ethnic group speaking in the Turkic language. In order to avoid confusion of this word's broad sense and narrow sense, I generally name the Turks of the 6th–8th centuries the *Asena Turks* 阿史那突厥.

as follows: The Asena Turks had undergone several migrations,[2] that is to say, before the Turk Khanate was established, their early or *prehistoric* habitations were more than one. What I will discuss in this Chapter is the region of the Caspian Sea, namely, the northern Caucasia Mountains west of the Caspian Sea and the lower reaches of the Volga River north of the Caspian Sea, which may be the *earliest* habitation of the Asena Turks, the so-called *Western Sea* 西海.[3]

1. Historical Facts Revealed by Legends of the Turkic Origin

The origin legends of the Asena Turks helped to prove that this tribe once lived in the region of the Caspian Sea.

According to Chinese literatures, there are four kinds of origin legends, which could be summed up as statements of "the she-wolf and kid without feet",[4] "the hybrid barbarians in Pingliang 平涼 Region",[5] "the Suo country 索國 north of the Desert"[6] as well as "the descendants

---

[2] For example, Xuezongzheng 薛宗正 holds this proposition. Cf. his "On the legends of Ancestors of Tujue", in *Social Science of Xinjiang* 新疆社會科學, No. 1 of 1987. He supposes that this Turk tribe migrated from the Aral Sea to the North of Desert 漠北, then went to Pingliang 平涼, then to Gaochang 高昌, finally to the South of Altai Mountains.

[3] About the discussion of the early habitation of the Asena Turks, cf. my paper "On the prehistoric habitations of the Asena Turks 阿史那人史前居地考", in *Northwestern National Minorities Researches* 西北民族研究, No. 2, 1991.

[4] Cf. *Zhoushu* 周書, fasc. 50, p. 907. The Chinese text is as follows: "突厥者,蓋匈奴之別種,姓阿史那氏。別爲部落。後爲鄰國所破,盡滅其族。有一兒,年且十歲,兵人見其小,不忍殺之,乃刖其足,棄草澤中。有牝狼以肉飼之,及長,與狼合,遂有孕焉。彼王聞此兒尚在,重遣殺之。使者見狼在側,並欲殺狼。狼遂逃於高昌國之北山。... 經數世,相與出穴,臣於茹茹。居金山之陽,爲茹茹鐵工。"

[5] Cf. *Suishu* 隋書, fasc. 84, Zhonghua Book Company 中華書局, 1973, p. 1863. The Chinese text is as following: "突厥之先,平涼雜胡也,姓阿史那氏。後魏太武滅沮渠氏,阿史那以五百家奔茹茹,世居金山,工於鐵作。"

[6] Cf. *Zhoushu* 周書, fasc. 50, Zhonghua Book Company 中華書局, 1971, p. 908. The Chinese text is as follows: "或云突厥之先出於索國,在匈奴之北。... 大兒爲出火溫養之,咸得全濟。遂共奉大兒爲主,號爲突厥,即訥都六設也。訥都六有十妻,所生子皆以母族爲姓,阿史那是其小妻之子也。"

of the Sea Goddess".⁷ The first and third legends were recorded in *The Biography of Tujue* 突厥傳 of *Zhoushu* 周書; the first and second legends were recorded in *The Biography of Tujue* 突厥傳 of *Suishu* 隋書; the first, second and third ones were in *The Biography of Tujue* 突厥傳 of *Beishi* 北史; and the fourth legend was in *Youyangzazu* 酉陽雜俎.

Generally speaking, *Beishi* 北史 only copied three legends in *Zhoushu* 周書 and *Suishu* 隋書, making little substantive revisions. However, *Suishu* and *Beishi* gave a noticeable supplementation on the legend *she-wolf and kid* of the *Zhoushu*. *Suishu* added a sentence, "their ancestors established a country in the region of Western Sea", and revised the sentence "the wolf escapes to the Northern Mountain of Gaochang state 高昌國" into "just like flying, the wolf runs to a mountain east of the Sea in a moment." *Beishi* inserted two sentences: "their ancestors lived in the region west of the Sea" and "as if being carried by deities, the wolf is sent in a moment to the east of Western Sea." Since the reliability of *Suishu* and *Beishi* is better than that of *Zhoushu*,⁸ there must be a reason for their emphasis on the *Western Sea*. In addition, though the characters and plots in the legend of *Youyangzazu* 酉陽雜俎 are different from the other three books, it also distinctly depicts the close relationship between the Turks' ancestors and the Western Sea.

We have to admit that there are some real historical facts behind these mythological legends. That is to say, before they migrated eastward to the Altai area and established a powerful khanate, the Asena Turks lived in the land west of the *Western Sea*.

There are many waters named "Western Sea" in ancient Chinese literatures. Shiratori Kurakichi 白鳥庫吉 summed it up as follows: the Qinghai 青海 (Blue Sea) of the Former Han was called *Western Sea*. In the reign of Emperor Wudi 武帝 of the Han, Zhangqian 張騫 was dispatched to visit countries in Western Regions 西域, both of the Caspian Sea and the Persian Gulf, which were named *Western Sea*. In the Later

---

⁷Cf. *Youyangzazu* 酉陽雜俎 (*A Miscellany of Ancient History*), fasc. 4 of Book I, punctuated and proofread by Fangnansheng 方南生, Zhonghua Book Company 中華書局, 1981, p. 44.

⁸Both *Suishu* and *Zhoushu* were completed in 636, but the former had a strong team of editors, while the latter was criticized as "incomplete information". *Beishi* was completed in 659. Its editor Liyanshou 李延壽 had read almost all the books of the country, and was involved in the writing of *Suishu*. Therefore, *Beishi* might be the best one among the three kinds of standard history.

Han Dynasty, people called the Indian Ocean *Western Sea*. Up to the Tang Dynasty, in *Jingxingji* 經行記 written by Duhuan 杜環, the Mediterranean was called *Western Sea*. Thus, the so-called *Western Sea* possibly referred to different oceans at different times.[9]

Nevertheless, the Western Sea here was probably the Caspian Sea. This is because, according to the records of Byzantine historian Menander, in 576 AD, the Turk ruler Turxanthos met with the Byzantine envoy Valentinus in a place near Yayiq River, which was the residential place of Turxanthos.[10] The so-called Yayiq River is the present Ural River. Obviously, at that time, the territory of the Asena Turks had already expanded to regions of the Caspian Sea. Besides, according to the *Biography of Tujue* 突厥傳 in *Zhoushu* 周書, in the earlier period of the Turk Khanate, its territory extended "westward to the Western Sea", and this "Western Sea" apparently referred to the Caspian Sea. Therefore, the early residential area of the Asena Turks should be the present Caspian regions.

2. The Name "阿史那" Manifests Its Origin of Caspian Sea

In addition to the origin legends of the Asena Turks, the tribe name 阿史那 (Ashina/Asena) also helps to trace back their early habitat to the Caspian region, thereby showing a closer relationship between the Asena Turks and the Caspian region.

Kliaštornyi believed that *Ashina/Asena* originated from *Āsāna*, meaning *valuable*, *aristocratic* and *noble*. It is a word in the Saka dialect of the Iranian language family.[11] Many scholars accept this opinion. But, I think the appellation 阿史那 *Ashina/Asena* probably came directly from an existing tribe name *Asiani*.

Ptolemy mentioned that in the reaches of the Kama River lived the peoples of Asaei, Alani as well as the Alauni. Marquart believed that these

---

[9] Cf. Shiratori Kurakichi 白鳥庫吉, *Studies on the History of Western Regions* II 西域史研究 (下), Iwanami shoten 岩波書店, 1944, pp. 276–277.
[10] Cf. I. Bekker and B.G. Niebuhr ed., *Dexippi, Eunappi, Petri Patricii, Prisci, Malchi, Menandri historiarum quae supersunt*, Bonnae, 1829, p. 400.
[11] Cf. S. G. Kliaštornyi, *Drevetiukskie runičeskie Pamiatniki kak istočnik po istorii Sretnei Asii*, Moskva, 1964, pp. 111–112.

names were closely related even if they are not completely identical.[12] Bretschneider pointed out that in later generations the people Alani were known as Ās (Asaei) or Asi (Asy or Yasy in Russian).[13] And, the Ās were exactly the ancestors of the Osset living in present Northern Caucasia. Thereby, a successive or identical relationship is established among the Alān, Ās and Osset.[14]

According to *The Records of the Grand Historian* 史記, the country Yancai 奄蔡 or Hesu 闔蘇 was located in the northwest of Kangju 康居, facing the sea; the *Biography of Western Regions* 西域傳 of the *History of Later Han* 後漢書 said that, later, 奄蔡 Yancai changed its name to 阿蘭 Alān. Thus, Alani, Alān and 奄蔡 Yancai are identical. Hirth thought the Yancai 奄蔡 was the Aorsi mentioned by Strabo.[15]

In terms of the geographical location, Yancai should be in the region of the Caspian and Aral seas; the Aorsi, especially the Northern Aorsi, dominated most of the coasts of the Caspian Sea.[16] Obviously, the Alan, As, Aorsi and Yancai 奄蔡 are regarded as the same or similar by many scholars, so the main living area of these tribes should also be in the Caspian region.

In the works of Strabo and Ptolemy, there are some other names similar to *Asaei*, such as *Asii*, *Assaei* and *Asiani*. According to Tarn's opinion, *Asaei* is the adjective form of Asii in the Iranian language.[17] Regardless of whether this viewpoint is correct or not, the pronunciation of the Chinese word 阿史那 is consistent with that of *Asiani*, as the pronunciation of 阿史那 in Middle Chinese is ā-si-nā. This identification affirms further the supposition that the prehistoric residence of the Asena Turks was in Caspian region, especially the western coast and northern coast of this sea.

Interestingly, the ruling family name of the Khazar mentioned in *Hudūd al-Ālam* (*The Regions of the World*) is similar to 阿史那 ā-si-nā: "Ātil, a town divided by the river Ātil. It is the capital of the Khazars and

---

[12] Cf. J. Marquart, *Über das Volkstum der Komanen*, in Abh d. K. Ges d. Wiss. Gottingen, N.F. XIII, 1914, p. 182.

[13] Cf. E. Bretschneider, *Medieval Researches* II, London, 1910, pp. 84–85.

[14] Minorsky said, the Alān, namely, the later Ās, was the ancestor of present Osset. Cf. V. Minorsky, *Hudūd al-'Ālam*, Oxford University Press, 1937, p. 445.

[15] Cf. F. Hirth, *China and the Rome Orient*, Shanghai, 1885, p. 139, note 1.

[16] Cf. *The Geography of Strabo*, tr. By H.L. Jones, London, 1916, p. 243.

[17] Cf. W.W. Tarn, *The Greeks in Bactria and India*, Cambridge University Press, 1951, p. 284.

the seat of the king, who is called Ṭarkhān Khāqān and is one of the descendants of Ānsā."[18] The Ātil River is the present Volga River; and the main territory of the Khazar Khanate was in Caspian region, particularly its northern and western coasts. Therefore, if Ānsā is really a slight deformation of Āšinā,[19] it is another piece of evidence to prove that the Asena Turks had a close relationship with the Caspian Sea. Besides, the tribal names Asen and Asan were associated with the second Bulgarian Empire and the personal names of princes and dignitaries of the Golden Horde, such as Asanak, Asanuna and Asan, might be another form of 阿史那 Ašina/Asena.[20]

We could find the origin of the Asena Turks by means of the tribal names Alan, As and Asii, and they already existed prior to the Turk Khanate. We can also find some traces about the Asena 阿史那 through the historical records of regimes established later, such as the Khazar, Bulgar and Golden Horde. However, all this information can only affirm the fact that the Asena Turks once lived in the Caspian region, rather than testifying that the Asena Turks were the same ethnic group as one of the tribes there.[21]

Roman historian Ammianus said that, just like the Persians, the Alans defeated every tribe they met and annexed them into their regime, also calling them Alan.[22] Hence, one can see that the tribes titled *Alan* did not necessarily all belong to the Indo-European ethnic group. Therefore, in the early period, the Asena Turks were quite possibly one of the nomadic tribes of the non-Indo-Europeans conquered by the Alan/As. They lived in adjacent areas of the Alans, and had to take *Alan* (*As*) as their regime appellation.

---

[18] Cf. V.Minorsky, *Hudūd al-Ālam*, Oxford University Press, 1937, pp. 161–162.
[19] About this viewpoint, cf. M.I. Artamonov, *Istoriia Xazar*, Leningrad, 1962, pp. 170–171.
[20] Cf. P.B. Golden, *Khazar Studies*, I, Budapest, 1980, pp. 220–221.
[21] Some scholars believe that the Asena Turks contained Indo-European blood, because the pronunciation of its name is similar to 烏孫 Wusun and Asii, and the latter belongs to the Indo-European race. Cf. Qianboquan 錢伯泉, *On the Name, Origin and Early History of the Turks* 突厥族名、族源傳說和初期史實考, in *Symposium of Northwestern Minorities* 西北民族文叢, No. 2, 1984; Yutaishan 余太山, *A Study on the Wusun* 烏孫考, in *Historical and Geographical Review of Northwest* China 西北史地, No. 1, 1988.
[22] Cf. Ammianus Marcellinus, *Res Gestae*, XXXI, 2, 13, ed. and tr. By J.C. Rolfe, Harvard University Press, 1963.

3. The Asena Turks were Expert in Smelting of Iron

An important factor for the rise and prosperity of the Asena Turks was the iron smelting industry. At the same time, some obvious traces related to the iron smelting industry were found among the *As* or other tribes residing in North Caucasus west of the Caspian Sea.

According to Chinese literatures, before the establishment of their regime, the Asena Turks lived in the south of the Altai for a long period. They were vassals to the powerful nomadic regime Rouran 柔然, acting as its blacksmiths. Apparently, in the earlier period, the Asena Turks were ironmaking workers. Certain scholars believe that, because of their excellent skills in metallurgy, the Turks overthrew their suzerain Rouran and flourished in the Altai region; later, the Turks were able to maintain a powerful khanate for a long time also because of their outstanding iron technology and iron products.[23] It shows that the iron was of great importance for the Asena Turks, while the same thing was also reflected in the As living in North Caucasus.

The region of Caucasus was one of the most famous metallurgical centers in the ancient world, and there were numerous excellent metallurgical technicians in that area. In the legends circulating among the Ossetes of the North Caucasus, the stories relating to blacksmiths occupy a prominent position, as the Ossetes are the descendants of the As. The most famous legend is one about the transcendental blacksmith Kurdalagon, the protector god of all smiths and armorers. This iron god even forged the giant god Batradz with heavenly forge, making him stronger.[24]

In such legends, the status of the iron smelting industry and ironworkers was lifted so high that even the gods had to seek help from them. In fact, this is a kind of worship of iron. In many places of the Caucasus, every iron furnace was regarded as a holy spot, and the hammer and iron anvil were sacred objects. For example, in Abkhazia, the iron anvil was used as an altar at the annual prayer service. In addition, the solemn oath-taking ceremony was also held in front of the iron anvil. In another region,

---

[23] Cf. Matsuda Hisau 松田壽男, *A Study on the Historical Geography of the Tianshan Mountains in Ancient Times* 古代天山歷史地理學研究, tr. by Chenjunmou 陳俊謀, Minzu Academy Press 中央民族學院出版社, 1987, pp. 284–285.

[24] Cf. G. vernadsky, *The Origins of Russia*, Oxford, 1959, p. 40.

people held a ceremony every Saturday. Ironworkers lit candles on the iron anvil, and every apprentice knelt down and worshiped it, kissing it. The belief that the iron anvil can effectively cure various diseases circulated widely in Samurzagan.[25] Correspondingly, the status of blacksmiths was also lifted. In many villages of the Caucasus, both the blacksmiths and their apprentices enjoyed great privilege.

The Chinese records also indirectly indicated the Asena Turks being ironworkers in the early period and taking pride in this specialty: Their chief Bumin Qaghan 土門可汗 proposed marriage to the ruling family of their suzerain Rouran 柔然, because they valued their own social status very much. When they were scolded as *ironworking slaves* 鍛奴, they immediately rebelled against Ruoran, because they thought it was a great insult. Apparently, their ideas were in line with that of ironworkers on the western coast of the Caspian Sea.

Besides, the Mongol rulers of the 13th century held a grand ceremony on New Year's Eve annually, summoning the ironworkers to the palace to pound iron, in memory of their ancestors' ironwork industry.[26] Many scholars believe this ceremony was a custom inherited from the Turks. That is to say, the ancient Turks also had such a custom.[27]

A ceremony of iron pounding mentioned by Gibbon is similar to the one described above, which is believed to have been also held by the Turks: "The annual ceremony, in which a piece of iron was heated in the fire, and a smith's hammer was successively handled by the prince and his nobles, recorded for ages the humble profession and rational pride of the Turkish nation."[28]

In addition to the descriptions recorded by later historians, the contemporary data of the Asena Turks also affirmed the fact that they had the custom of worshiping the iron smelting industry and iron products;

---

[25] Cf. B.E. Degen-Kovalevstky, *K Istorii zenleznogo proizvodstva Zakavkazia*, IGAIMK, CXX, 1935, p. 376.
[26] Cf. M. D'Ohsson, *Histoire des Mongols*, Vol. I, Chapter 2, tr. by Fengchengjun 馮承鈞, Zhonghua Book Company 中華書局, 1962, p. 32.
[27] Cf. Matsuda Hisau 松田壽男, *A Study on the Historical Geography of the Tianshan Mountains in Ancient Times* 古代天山歷史地理學研究, tr. by Chenjunmou 陳俊謀, Minzu Academy Press 中央民族學院出版社, 1987, p. 276.
[28] Cf. Edward Gibbon, *The History of the Decline and Fall of the Roman Empire*, Vol. IV, Chapter 42, London: Strahan and Cadell, 1783, p. 224.

just like the ironworkers in the Caucasus, they also believed the iron objects had wonderful functions.

According to Byzantine historian Menander, Byzantine ambassador Zemarchus was dispatched to the Turks in 568. When the Byzantines arrived at the territories of the Sogdians, certain Turks presented some iron and its products for sale, or probably in order to show off their rich iron mines in the country. Yule cited the viewpoint of Deguigenes that the Qaghans of the Turks instituted in memory of their origin the ceremony of annually forging a piece of iron. So, the presentation of iron to the Byzantine envoys may have had some similar signification.[29] Shiratori Kurakichi 白鳥庫吉 thought that the Turks attempted to dispel the evil influences brought by the Byzantine ambassadors with either the fire or the iron.[30] It appears that the statement of selling iron was just Menander's own assumption instead of the real purpose of the Turks showing iron.

In my opinion, though the Asena Turks were eager to be friendly with the Byzantines, they might not have attempted to immediately sell iron while the ambassadors arrived in their country. That is rather ridiculous and ineffective. So, the opinion of Menander is not correct. On the contrary, the two matters of *Presentation of Iron* and *Ritual of Fire* occurred at the same time, which seems to show both having a similar functions, namely, *Expelling Evil*. The ancients, especially the culturally backward nomads, often confound medicine and sorcery. Therefore, they were very apt to believe the iron has the efficiencies both of disease-curing and evil-dispelling. In short, iron was regarded as a holy object by both the Asena Turks and the people who live west side of the Caspian Sea. This is another piece of evidence to testify the *Caspian Origin* of the Asena Turks.

4. The Asena's Institutions were Similar to that of the Khazars

The Khazars lived in the Caspian region. According to historical records, their regime was a vassal of the Western Turk Khanate in the second half

---

[29] Cf. H. Yule, *Cathay and the Way Thither*, Vol. I, revised by H. Cordier, London, 1915, p. 208.
[30] Cf. Shiratori Kurakichi 白鳥庫吉, *Studies on the Mongolian Words in the Korean History*, in Toyo Gakuho 東洋學報, Vol. XVIII, No. 2, pp. 166–168.

of the 6th century. After the decline of the Western Turk Khanate in the late 7th century, the Khazar became a powerful force in the Caspian region. The political institutions of the Asena Turks and Khazars were very similar, and one of them is the inauguration of Qaghan.

The Biography of the Tujue 突厥傳 of *Zhoushu* 周書 depicted the inauguration of the Turk Qaghan as follows: "As soon as their Qaghan is confirmed, courtiers and ministers carry him with a felt, go around the sun nine times. After every turn all officials kneel down and salute. Then they mount him on a horse and tighten his neck with a silk belt until the Qaghan almost faints, then loose it and ask him immediately, 'how many years will you rule for?' Being not quite conscious, the Qaghan might give a random number, but it would be the grounds to check his reign term."

In addition, the Islamic writer Istaxri also described the inauguration of the Khazar Qaghan. Before appointing a Qaghan, they tightened a silk belt around him until he nearly choked. They asked him at once, "how long do you want to be in reign?" If he dies before this deadline, it would be regarded as a good omen for the whole regime; if the opposite is true, the Qaghan would be put to death after the deadline.[31]

Both the Asena Turks and Khazars tightened their ruler's neck with a silk belt, forcing him to be in an almost unconscious state. Apparently, they believed that at this moment the answer given by the Qaghan is in fact the reply of the god attached to him, and thereby the command of the god must be executed.

Although this ceremony is rather superstitious, it actually had certain practical significance. Ibn Faḍlān mentioned the following about the Khazar Qaghan: "the length of their rule is forty years. If the king exceeds it by a single day, the subjects and his courtiers kill him, saying his reason has failed and his understanding is become disordered."[32]

Masʿūdī expressed more clearly the cause of the Qaghan being executed. "When the Khazars suffer from famine or some other calamity strikes their land, or if the fortunes of war turn against them or some nation declares them an enemy, if then, any disaster befalls them, the people and the nobles rush to the king and say: 'this Xāqān whose reign presages nothing but disaster, augurs no good for us, put him to death or turn him over to us so that we may kill him.' Sometimes, the king

---

[31] Cf. Istaxri, *Kitab Masalīk wa'l Mamālik*, ed. by M.J. de Goeje, Leiden, 1870, p. 224.
[32] Cf. A.Z.V. Togan, *Ibn Faḍlān's Reisebericht*, in *Abhandlungen für die Kunde des Morgenlandes*, XXIV, 3, Leipzig, 1939, p. 101.

abandons him to them and they kill him and sometimes he has him commit suicide and sometimes, taking pity on him he defends him, saying that he has not committed any crime which merits punishment."[33] Actually, the convention that Khazars killed their Qaghan when his reign's term was not over or over was helpful in choosing an excellent ruler with sufficient physical strength, intelligence and talent for their regime.

Two other pieces of information recorded in *Biographies of Zhangsuncheng* 長孫晟 and *Tujue* 突厥 of *Suishu* 隋書 appeared to reflect such convention and purpose. The former said that Zhangsuncheng sent spies to inquire about the domestic situation of the Turks, and was informed that there were frequent natural disasters recently in their capital. The red rainbow was found in the night, shining hundreds of *li* 里; a meteor shower lasted three days, and shooting stars fell into the barracks with loud noises. Two months later, their ruler Dulan Qaghan 都藍可汗 "is murdered by his subordinates". In addition, the *Biography of Tujue* 突厥傳 said that the tent of Išbara Qaghan 沙鉢略可汗 was suddenly burned down by fire. The Qaghan was very depressed and died a month later.

According to my opinion, it was not to be trusted that the natural disasters were the omens of the Qaghans' death. As compared to this statement, a more reasonable explanation might be that the Turks were convinced deeply about it, so they killed their rulers in keeping with gods' will. Therefore, we have good reason to think the Asena Turks and the Khazars had similar ideas in dealing with the Qaghan's reign.

If we try to confirm that the Asena Turks lived in the Caspian region during their *prehistoric period*, we have to prove first that the Khazars had also existed there at the same time. Otherwise, a possibility could not be ruled out that the Turk Khanate expanded westwards and spread their cultures to the Khazars after the establishment of their powerful regime. Actually, the Khazars were active in the Caspian region in quite an early age, though their powerful regime was established after the Turk Khanate.

According to the Armenian materials, in the 4th century, the Khazars invaded Transcaucasia.[34] The Islamic writings also mentioned a war

---

[33] Cf. Al-Mas'ūdī, *Murūj adh-Dhahab wa Ma'ādin al-jawhar*, II, pp. 12–13; quote from Peter B. Golden, Khazar Studies, Budapest, 1980, p.100.
[34] Cf. Movsēs Dasxuranci, *The History of the Caucasian Albanians*, tr. by C. Dowsett, London, 1961, p. 70.

between the Khazars and the Persian king Kavadh I (488–531).[35] Some modern scholars support the viewpoint of the Khazars having been active in the Caspian area since earlier times. For instance, Artamonov thought that in the period of the 5th and 6th centuries, one of the new tribes reorganized by some aboriginal peoples of Northern Caucasus was the Khazar. Together with other indigenous tribes, the Khazars accepted the Turk's suzerainty status around 570. Later, the Khazars gradually blended with the Turks, becoming the backbone of the regime in Northern Caucasus, and established the Khazar Khanate soon after.[36] Dunlop believed that the statement that the Khazars began to be mentioned in the reign of Kavadh (r. 488–531) and Khosrau (r. 531–579) is credible. "The growing number of increasingly precise indications seems to prove that they are indeed upon the scene."[37]

In view of the fact that before the Asena Turks established their Khanate and expanded westwards, the Khazars already lived in the region west of the Caspian Sea, the cultural similarity between the Turks and Khazars demonstrates that the Asena Turks also inhabited the same region or its vicinity in their *prehistoric period*.

5. The Asena's Official Titles were Similar to that of the Khazars

The official titles of the Asena Turks and Khazars were also very analogous. A number of official titles were mentioned in some Chinese historical records, such as 可汗 kehan (Qaghan), 可賀敦 kehedun (Qatun), 特勤 teqing (Tegin), 設 she (Šad), 啜 chuo (Čor), 達干 dagan (Tarqan), 頡利發 xielifa (El-täbär), 吐屯 tutun (Tudun), 俟斤 Sijin (Irkin) and 叶護 yehu (Yabγu). *Tongdian* 通典 said that the Turkic regime divided their senior official rank into ten levels and the lower rank into twenty-eight levels. This showed that the Turk's bureaucratic system was quite perfect. Apparently, such a complex administrative system could not be completed in a short period; in other words, there must have taken a long time to form this system before the Asena Turks established the powerful regime

---

[35] Cf. P.K. Hitti, *The Origins of the Islamic State*, New York, 1916, pp. 305–306.
[36] Cf. M.I. Artamonov, *O čerki drevneišei Istorii Khazar*, Leningrad, 1936, pp. 88–134.
[37] Cf. D.M. Dunlop, *The History of the Jewish Khazars*, Princeton University Press, 1967, p. 22.

in middle of the 6th century. However, only few precedents of such official titles were found among the Rouran 柔然 and nearby nomads of the Altai region. On the contrary, almost all these official titles appeared among the Khazars in the Caspian Sea. This fact demonstrates once again that in their *prehistoric stage*, the Asena Turks might have lived in the Caspian region for a long period.

Just like the Turks, the Khazars also took *Qaghan* as the title of their sovereign, and had great respect for it. The Islamic writer Ibn Xurdādhbih said that the rulers of the Turks, Tibetans and Khazars were all called *Qaghan*, but the king of the Qarluq as titled *Yabγu*.[38] Obviously, the author emphasized the sacredness of the title *Qaghan*, which was not allowed to be used arbitrarily. The Qarluq destroyed the last remnant of the Western Turk Khanate; even so, the Qarluqs' ruler seemed to dare not claim himself as *Qaghan*, but adopted only the designation "Yabγu". Therefore, the fact of the Khazars' monarch being titled *Qaghan* reveals their close relations with the Asena Turks.

Qatun 可敦/可賀敦 was the designation referring to the wife of the Turk ruler. It was slightly different in the Khazars. For instance, a daughter of the Khazar Qaghan Bağatur was married to the governor of Armenia around 760; she was also titled Qatun.

Yabγu 葉護 was a very honorable title among the Asena Turks; for the Western Turks, it seemed to be of more particular significance, because some rulers of the Western Turk Khanate took Yabγu as a part of their names, such as Tong Yabγu 統葉護 and Si Yabγu 肆葉護. This title was also seen in the Khazars. For example, according to the Georgian records, in 627–628, the Khazar army entered Transcaucasia to help the Byzantine emperor Heraclius to fight back against the Persians. The Khazars besieged Tbilisi city, with their commander who was called Yabγu. Besides, other Byzantine historians, such as Simocatta/Simocattes and Menander, also mentioned the title Yabγu of the Khazars in an earlier age of the late 6th and early 7th centuries.

Tegin was a high official rank of the Asena Turks. *Tongdian* 通典 said that only the sons or other juniors of the ruling family were qualified to be titled Tegin. Dasxuranci once mentioned a tribal chief of the Northern

---

[38] Cf. Ibn Xurdādhbih, *Kitāb al-Masālik wa'l-Mamālik*, ed. by M. deGoeje, Leiden, 1906, p. 16.

Caucasus of the late 7th century, who was named El-Tegin, and his tribe was a vassal of the Khazars.[39]

The *Biography of Tujue* 突厥傳 of *Zhoushu* 周書 states, "The military commander of an independent portion of the country is called *Šad*." In other Chinese records, 設 she (Šad) was also written as 殺 sha or 察 cha. This was a high official rank and usually held by members of the ruling family. Among the Khazars, Šad had enormous authority, second only to the Qaghan. A *Šad* mentioned by Dasxuranci was the nephew of Yabɣu Qaghan, the sovereign of the West Turks and Khazars.[40]

According to the Chinese historical materials, 頡利發 Xielifa (El-täbär) was the title awarded to the vassal ruler by the Asena Turk regime. For example, after conquering all countries in the Western Regions, Tong Yabɣu 統葉護, the Qaghan of the Turks, appointed their rulers as *El-täbär*. The Russian historian Barthold concluded that the regime taking *El-täbär* as its ruler was regarded as inferior to the one taking *Qaghan* as its ruler.[41] A Huns tribe of the North Caucasus was the vassal of the Khazar, while its chief was called *Alp El-täbär*.

The *Biography of Tujue* 突厥傳 of *Tangshu* 唐書 recorded that after the countries of Central Asia submitted to the Western Turk Khanate, its Qaghan Tong Yabɣu 統葉護 appointed a Tutun 吐屯 to manage them and supervise the tax affairs. From this, we know that *Tutun* 吐屯 may be an official title for the supervisor. Theophanes said that during the reign of Justinian II, an envoy sent to Byzantium by the Khazar government was titled *Tutun*.[42]

The title *Tarqan* 達干 was frequently seen in Chinese and other foreign sources. According to the *Biography of Tujue* 突厥傳 of *Tangshu* 唐書, Qutluɣ, the founder of the Later Turk Khanate, appointed Ashideyuanzhen 阿史德元珍, his capable minister, as Alp Tarqan to specially manage military affairs. Therefore, at that time, the position of Tarqan seemed to mean "senior military chief". The Asena Turks used this official title universally; it also appeared among the Khazars and was

---

[39] Cf. Movsēs Dasxuranci, *The History of the Caucasian Albanians*, tr. by C. Dowsett, London, 1961, p. 168.

[40] Cf. Movsēs Dasxuranci, *The History of the Caucasian Albanians*, p. 88.

[41] Cf. W. Barthold, *Zwölf Vorlesungen über die Geschichte der Türken Mittelasiens* 中亞突厥史十二講, tr. by Luozhiping 羅致平, Chinese Social Sciences Press 中國社會科學出版社, 1984, p. 35.

[42] Cf. Theophanes, Chronographia, I, ed. by C. de Boor, Lipsiae, 1883, pp. 378–379.

mentioned in numerous historical records in Armenian, Persian and Arabic.

6. The Asena's Customs were Similar to those of the Peoples in the Caspian Region

There were still many other similarities between the Asena Turks and tribes in the Caspian region. For instance, Dasxuranci described the burial customs of the North Caucasian Huns as follows: "Possessing completely anarchical minds they stumble into every sort of error, beating drums and whistling over corpses, inflicting bloody saber and dagger cuts on the cheek and limbs, and engaging naked in sword fights — O hellish sight — at the graves ... Numerous groups wrestled with each other and in the orgy performed swift gallops on horseback, wheeling this way and that. Some were occupied in weeping and wailing, others in a game of diabolical fury ..."[43]

The *Biography of Tujue* 突厥傳 of *Zhoushu* 周書 gave a similar description of a Turkic funeral: "When one of them dies, his corpse is laid out in a tent. All the children and grandchildren, male and female relatives of the deceased each slaughter a sheep and a horse and place it in front of the tent as an offering. Then they ride on horseback around the tent seven times and each time, when they come to the entrance of the tent, they cut their face with a knife. Then they wail so that the blood and tears flow down together ..." Obviously, the most similar aspects of the funeral customs between the two tribes were the running horse and cutting face.

In addition, the ideas on deer held by the Asena Turks were also very close to those of the Alans or its eastern branch, the Sakas. The deer was worshiped by both the Alans and Sakas; according to some scholars, the deer appeared to be the patron divinity of their tribes. Abaev thought that the word *saka* derives from *sag* in the Alanian dialect, meaning deer.[44] In Ossetic folklore, a brave soldier is called *sagtae*, namely, the plural form of *sag*.

The deer often played a sacred role in folklore of the Alan and Saka. A Buddhist legend said that a certain person of the Saka killed many foemen, violating the Buddhist precepts, and thus was driven out of his

---

[43] Cf. Movsēs Dasxuranci, *The History of the Caucasian Albanians*, pp. 155–156.
[44] Cf. V.I. Abaev, *Osetinskii Iazyk I Foklor*, I, Moskva, 1949, p. 179.

homeland by his clan members. Later, he came to a country and became its king. He ordered his subjects not to harm the deer.[45] An Ossetic story said that the beautiful bride went to the groom's house; she drove a carriage towed by seven stags, which was the present given by the hunter's patron deity. Another story states that a white deer was chased by a deity; at last, it changed into a beautiful princess with golden plaits and golden wings.[46]

There were many similar stories relating to the Asena Turks in ancient records. Volume One of *Datangxiyueji* 大唐西域記 mentioned the summer resort Qianquan 千泉 of Tong Yabγu 統葉護, the Qaghan of the Western Turk Khanate: The Turk Qaghan often went to Qianquan for the summer. There were numerous lovely deer there, very tame and much favored by the Qaghan. He warned his subjects that if anyone dared kill a deer, he will be put to death immediately.

A story about Turks' origin in *Youyangzazu* 酉陽雜俎 showed more clearly that the deer had an important status in the life of ancient Turks: Every day, the sea goddess sent white deer to carry the Turk chief Shemo 射摩 to enter the sea and take him home the next morning. They had done so for several decades. If Shemo wanted to be a permanent husband of the sea goddess, he had to shoot the white deer with golden antlers, which would run from the ancestral cave of the Turks in a moment. The function of this white deer was analogous to that of the deer driven by the beautiful princess.

Interestingly enough, in the folk song of the Serbs who once lived in North Caucasus, the golden antlers are a symbol of the sun rays.[47] It is exactly the meaning indicated by the golden antlers in the legend of Turkic origin: it symbolized fleeting time, namely, precious opportunity; if Shemo missed the target, he would lose forever the opportunity to be with the sea goddess.

The alphabet and writing system of the Asena Turks led to the opinion of scholars that the Turks once lived in the Caspian region in their prehistoric stage. The dialect spoken by them was differently named, such as Old Turkic, Blue Turkic, Runic Turkic and Orkhon Turkic. This dialect is

---

[45]Cf. J. Przyluski, *Nouveaux aspects de L'histoire des Scythes*, Revue de L'univrsité de Bruxelles, XLII (1936–1937), pp. 214–219.
[46]Cf. V. Dynnik, *Skazaniia o Nartakh*, Moscow, 1944, p. 76.
[47]Cf. A.N. Afanasiev, *Poetičeskie vozzreniia slavianna prirodu*, I, Moscow, 1866, p. 630.

known to us through the inscriptions found in several monuments of the Turk leaders, which are located mainly in the basin of the Orkhon River.

Most of the contemporary scholars seemed to agree with the opinion of Thompsen: the letters of Old Turkic came from those of the Aramaic. However, there are many different views on the formation of Old Turkic. Some think that it was the Iranians, especially the Sogdians of Central Asia, who transmitted the Aramaic letters to the Asena Turks, while some others objected to it. For instance, Thompsen believed that there was communication between the Aramaic and Old Turkic, and the Iranians could not possibly be their intermediary.[48] Pedersen completely denied the Iranian intermediary between these two sets of alphabets.[49]

Therefore, if the Turks really directly learnt Aramaic letters from the Semites, the main communication spot was more likely to be the Caspian region than the regions of Orkhon or Yenisei Rivers. It is possible that the Asena Turks already had their own writing system before the establishment of the Khanate;[50] in addition, the Khazar alphabet was quite similar to the Old Turkic.[51] If these statements are true, it is unnecessary

---

[48] Cf. V. Thompsen, *Inscriptions de L'Orkhon déchiffrées*, Helsingfors, 1896, p. XLXXX.

[49] Cf. H. Pedersen, *The Discovery of Language, Linguistic Science in the Nineteenth Century*, Bloomington, 1962, p. 199.

[50] The reasons for this conclusion may be summarized briefly as follows. First, the Sogdians were generally called 胡 *Hu* (foreigners/barbarians). Since the Turkic writing was claimed to be "similar with that of the *Hu*" in *Zhoushu* 周書, this writing system was certainly the Turks' own language rather than the Sogdian dialect. Second, *Beiqishu* 北齊書 distinctly stated that Liushiqing 劉世清 translated the Buddhist sutras into *the Turkic dialect* 突厥語. Third, Menander clearly called the Turks *the Scythians*; in 568 AD, the credentials they presented to the Byzantine emperor were written in Scythian. Therefore, the so-called *Scythian* undoubtedly referred to the true Turkic dialect. All these pieces of description are very definite; thus, we can infer that the Old Turkic had already circulated at least in the middle of the 6th century. Tekin held the same view. He said that the invention and application of the Old Turkic script "is certainly older than the Turkic inscriptions which date from the first half of the eighth century A.D ... The Turkic runic script probably began to be used as early as the middle of the sixth century, as the official alphabet of the Turkic Empire." Cf. Talāt Tekin, *A Grammar of Orkhon Turkic*, Indiana University, 1968, pp. 29–30.

[51] Nemeth said that there were many noticeable similarities between the Turkic script and the Khazar alphabet. Cf. J. Cf. Nemeth, "The Runi-form Inscriptions from Nagy Szent-Mikios and the Runi-form Scripts of Eastern Europe", in *Acta Linguistica*, 21, 1971, pp. 48–49.

to discuss the formation of the Old Turkic base on the close contacts between the Turks and Sogdians in the later period. On the contrary, we may explore such a topic against the background that the Asena Turks once lived in the Caspian region during their *prehistoric age*.

7. Other Elements in the Culture of the Asena Turks

In the culture of the Asena Turks there were not only cultural elements of the peoples in the Caspian region but also other elements originating from more distant areas. For example, the Byzantine envoy Zemarchus found that the golden throne of the Turk Qaghan Istami was supported by four golden peacocks. The cultural element of this throne probably derived from the Indian civilization, because in the Hindu mythology, the peacock is the mount of Shiva's son, the war god Kaetikeya.

Besides, the high-ranking official title *Yabyu* used generally by the Turks was regarded as a word originating from dialects of the Kushans and Sakas, namely, *yavuga<yam*, meaning commander and leader. *Šad* was believed to come from the Persian *šah* or Sogdian *xšyd*. As for *Istemi*, the name of one of the founders of the Turk Khanate, it was considered to be a derivative term of *Istanu*, the name of the sun god of the Hittites.

Why did such a wide variety of cultural elements mix together among the Asena Turks? The only reasonable answer perhaps was that during their *prehistoric* age, the Asena Turks once lived in the Caspian region. The Caspian region was exactly located where the nomads and settlers coming from everywhere in the Eurasian Continent communicated frequently, so they were apt to assimilate other groups' cultures.

The Volga is the longest river in Europe, which flows through central Russia and into the Caspian Sea. Due to its geographical situation, the Volga played an important role in the communication of people between east and west, as well as south and north. One could go westward from the Volga and arrive at Kiev through the ways connecting the Volga and the Don-Donets water–land networks. These roads continued to extend westerly and connect with Western Europa. Starting from the Volga reaches, one may also go to Byzantium through the water course of the Dnieper River and the Black Sea.

Northward, the trade network of the Volga extended to the White Sea region through rivers of Dvina and Sukhona. A large quantity of amber was produced in the White Sea and its vicinity, which was exported to many parts in the South, especially in the Mediterranean, where it could be sold at a high price.

One could sail southward along the Volga, entering the Caspian Sea, then land in Persia, finally reaching Mesopotamia. To the East, one could go from the Volga region, passing through land roads and the Kama River, reaching the Ural Mountains, Ural River, Siberia and Khorazm. Khorazm was a very important link on this long trade chain. From there, the raw materials coming from the Slavs and Finno-Ugrians were resold to Khorasan and Mesopotamia, and the finished products coming from these two areas were resold to the Caspian region and Volga Basin.

The Arabic geographer Xurdādhbih described the trades and exchanges among the countries of the Eurasia Continent as follows: The trade roads of the Jews are called Rādhānīyah. They speak multiple languages, such Arabic, Persian, Greek, French, Andalusian and Slavic. They travel all over the world through both of waterways and land ways. In the western end of the Mediterranean they load the cargo on board, sail eastward along its southern coast, arrive at the northern coast of the Red Sea. Then, a large part of these goods might be resold to Jidda, the important port on the middle of the Red Sea's eastern coast. They used to sail to India and China. Sometimes they select the land way, namely the route that sets out from Byzantium, across the Russian territory, arriving country of the Khazars, then crossing the Caspian Sea, entering Central Asia, next, going to Mongolia, and reaching China finally.[52]

It was well known that since very early times, the Jews had been very good at engaging in trade. Thus, although this paragraph was written in the middle of the 9th century, we may infer that in the *prehistoric age* of the Asena Turks, the Caspian region was already an area with well-developed traffic and an important component of the whole transporting network of the Eurasian Continent.

Based on the analysis above, the following conclusion could be drawn. The habitations of the Asena Turks in their *Prehistoric Age* were probably the western and northern shores of the Caspian Sea, namely, the North Caucasus and the lower reaches of the Volga. The main reasons could be as follows: First, several origin legends of the Turks indicate that their earlier habitation was located "west of the Western Sea". Second, the

---

[52] Cf. Ibn Xurdādhbih, *Kitāb al-Masālik wa 'l-Mamālik*, ed. by M. deGoeje, Leiden, 1906, pp. 153–155.

culture of the Asena Turks was very similar to that of the peoples in the Caspian region. Third, there were multiple cultural elements in the Turks' culture, such as Semitic, Iranian and Indian ones; it proves that the Turks once lived in a region of well-developed intercourse. Therefore, only the opinion of the Caspian region being regarded as the *Prehistoric Habitation* of the Asena Turks can reasonably explain the special cultural phenomenon of the Turks.

8. The Possible Routes of Migration of the Asena Turks

The so-called *She-Wolf Legend* claimed that, initially, the Asena Turks "establish their country in the Western Sea", thereby indicating that the Western Sea was the earliest inhabitation area of these Turks. Thus, the place "north of the Suo 索 country" mentioned in another legend could be regarded as the region after the Turk's migration. The record said that this region was located north of the Xiongnu 匈奴, so the time when the Turks lived in the Suo country 索國 appears to be the same as the flourishing period of the Xiongnu, namely, the 3rd–2nd century BC.

Later, they migrated southward to the region of Pingliang 平涼 (the eastern part of present Gansu 甘肅), seemingly attempting to get foods and goods from China more conveniently. They lived there until the middle of the 5th century at least. In 439 AD, the Northern Wei Dynasty 北魏 destroyed the regime of the Northern Liang 北涼. After that, at some point, the Turks appeared to become the vassal of the Rouran 柔然. Then, the Asena Turks migrated once again; on the way, they made a short stay in Turpan (高昌 Gaochang) and continued to march northwestward. Finally, they arrived at the region south of the Altai (金山 Golden Mountains) and formally became the ironworkers of the Rouran regime. A few generations later, they overthrew their suzerain Rouran.

In summary, the migration routes of the Asena Turks before they established the Khanate can be inferred as follows: At a very archaic age, the Asena clan of the Turks lived in the Caspian region. Later, they were forced to migrate eastward as a result of being expelled by certain nomadic tribes, and arrived at the region north of the Lake Baikal. At that time, the Xiongnu 匈奴 had risen and were becoming powerful. As they developed, the Turks migrated southward once again and inhabited the region of the Pingliang 平涼, the present eastern part of Gansu Province, until the middle of the 5th century. Soon after, the Turks moved to Gaochang 高昌, the present Turpan region, but stayed there for a short period. Finally, they migrated to the region south of the Altai Mountains. These Turks assumed a role of the subjects and ironworkers of the nomadic regime Rouran 柔然 for several generations until they overthrew their suzerain in the middle of the 6th century.

When the Asena Turks lived in the Caspian region during their earlier times, they benefited from the excellent geographical location, thereby mixing multiple cultural elements, such as that of the Greeks, Romans, Iranians and Indians, into their own civilization. Afterward, along with their eastward migration, some oriental cultures, such as Mongolian and Chinese, blended into their civilization. Briefly, because of their frequent migration on the Silk Road, the Asena Turks developed into an ethnic group mixed with various cultures.

Part II

The Sogdians, the Special Role on the Silk Road

Among the people who often went to and from the Silk Road and had frequent intercourses with China, in addition to the nomadic barbarians in the North, there were many settled groups. They were generally called Western Barbarians 西胡, such as the Persians coming from West Asia, the Indians coming from South Asia and the Sogdians from Central Asia. The latter, in particular, played an important role in the exchanges between the East and the West for a thousand years. They once had a great impact on the economy, culture, etc., of Eurasia.

About the Sogdians, the Danish scholar Asmussen briefly and vividly described some of their features:

In Central Asia, the Sogdian was known as the merchant par excellence. He loved trading and profit, say the Chinese sources. This is probably not without basis, since words such as the Sogdian *pwrc*, "debt", and *mr'z*, "hired servant", have been adopted into the Turkish language. The Iranian in general, and particularly the Sogdian, was so much of a merchant that all other commercial activities in which the Iranian now and then appears, according to the surviving historical information, are quite overshadowed. He was a merchant who took the rough with the smooth.

The Sogdian trading colonies — often of significant proportions — that are known from, for example, Tun-huang and Lob Nor, of course played their part in establishing this reputation. But throughout the ages the trader has done more than merely offer his goods for sale; he was also the messenger bringing tidings of all things new and strange from other regions. He was the great colporteur of religions, a popular figure in Buddhist *Jātaka* and *Avadāna* literature, in Manichaean narratives and in Christian — particularly Syriac — literature. So popular was he that among the Buddhists a mercantile title such as Sārthavāha, "caravan leader", came to be regarded as worthy of use when referring to the great teachers, tathāgatas, bodhisattvas, and among the Manichaeans (doubtless following a Buddhist model) Mani himself, "the great caravan leader" (*wzyšt srtw'*).[1]

Here, Asmussen mentions two characteristics of the Sogdians: Being good at trading and being keen to preach religions. However, he seems to ignore another outstanding specialty of the Sogdians, namely, valiancy and skill in fighting. Although judging from the modern concepts, the last feature appears to contradict the other two, all three features were naturally embodied in the Sogdians, the *Western Barbarians* 西胡. In this Part, we are going to discuss this special character played by the Sogdians on the Silk Road.

---

[1] Cf. Jes. P. Asmussen, "The Sogdian and Uighus-Turkish Christian Literature in Central Asia before the Real Rise of Islam", in L.A. Hercus etc. ed. *Indological and Buddhist Studies: Volume in Honour of Professor J.W. de Jone on His Sixties Birthday*, Canberra, 1982, p. 13.

Chapter 7

On the Distinction Between 粟特 Sute and 粟弋 Suyi

The main contents of this chapter involve two aspects. The first one is an introduction for Soghd and the Sogdians, including their geographic environment and political history. Second, a small country 粟弋 recorded in *Houhanshu* 後漢書 will be discussed in detail; for a long time, this country was confused with 粟特 sute.

1. The Geographic Environment and Political History of Soghd

(1) Names of 粟特 and its geographical scope

"粟特國" (Sute Country) was recorded in the *Biography of the Western Regions* 西域傳 of *Weishu* 魏書. It said that this country lay in the "west of Congling 葱嶺", its merchants used to go to Liangzhou 梁州 for trading, its king once redeemed the captives from the Northern Wei regime and so on. Later, this "粟特" was used by modern Chinese scholars to refer to Soghd/Sughd of the western languages; "粟特人" (Sogdians) accordingly became the proper designation for its aborigines.

In the classical literatures of the West, there are many names pronounced similarly to that of *Soghd*, such as *Sugda* or *Suguda* in Persian, and *Suγδa* or *Suχδa* in Avestan, which was named *Sogdiana* by the Greeks; in the Sogdian literatures, it was called *Swyδ*, *Suyδ*, *Suwδ* and *Syuδ*. In the Chinese sources, there were also various names for this region, such as 屬繇 zhuyao, 窣利 suli, 速利 suli, 孫鄰 sunlin and 蘇哩 suli.²

The toponym Soghd 粟特 was mentioned in numerous literatures coming from the Orient and Occident; the Sogdians were also frequently found in many regions of the Eurasian Continent. Apparently, this was a very active ethnic group. Indeed, these Sogdians lived in Central Eurasia at least for a thousand years. However, Soghd was not a powerful nation with a large population and vast territory; on the contrary, in terms of its population and the area of its native land, it was probably only a *weak nation* or *weak regime*.

First, let us examine its territory. Soghd once existed as a country or an administrative division. Though its exact boundaries were unclear, the territory of it was surely not large. The earliest materials mentioning Soghd were the Behistun Inscription and the Naqsh-e Rustam Inscription. Unfortunately, neither inscription points out the specific location of Soghd. Later, the Greek scholars spoke about the Sogdians and their homeland in their writings, but only roughly located it between the present Amu River and Syr River instead of giving exact boundaries. After the expedition eastward of Alexander the Great in the 4th century BC, the geographical scope of Soghd became more explicit, and it was referred to as the region lying in the lower reaches of the River Zarafshan.

According to the Islamic sources, Soghd was also situated in a small region of the lower reaches of the Zarafshan River; generally, it included two important cities Samarkand and Bukhara, which belong to the present Republic of Uzbekistan. Most of the writers regarded Samarkand as the capital of Soghd, but Ya'qūbī believed that its capital was Kish/Kass, 50 kilometers south of Samarkand. Istakhri claimed that Soghd was a small country, and even the cities Bukhara, Kish and Nasaf were not listed as Sogdian territory. Mas'ūdī said that Soghd was just a region between Samarkand and Bukhara; thus, these two metropolises were excluded from Soghd. Among many Islamic geographers, only Yākūt divided

---

²They could be seen respectively in *weilüexirongzhuan* 魏略西戎傳 (*Biography of the Western Barbarians in Weilüe*), *datangxjyueji* 大唐西域記 (*Great Tang Records on the Western Regions*), *datangxiyue qiufagaoshengzhuan* 大唐西域求法高僧傳 (*Biography of the Eminent Buddhist Monks who had Traveled the Western Regions in the Tang*), *fanyuqianziwen* 梵語千字文 (*A Thousand Words in Sanskrit*) and *fanyuzaming* 梵語雜名 (*Various Sanskrit Words*).

Soghd into two portions: *Samarkand Soghd* and *Bukhara Soghd*. In sum, all the Arabic writers thought that Soghd was a small country.

Comparatively speaking, in Chinese sources, the scope of Soghd is larger. 康國 Kangguo (Kang Country), an area centered on Samarkand, was indisputably considered to be *Soghd*. The *Biography of the Western Regions* 西域傳 of *Suishu* 隋書 described the origin of Soghd as follows. Initially, its king's family name was 溫 Wun. In the early times, they once lived in Zhaowu 昭武 City, north of the Qilian Mountain 祁連山. Later, they were driven by the Xiongnu 匈奴 forces, migrating westward and crossing the Pamir Plateau, then settling in Central Asia. The descendants of each branch established a regime near the Kang Country, and adopted Zhaowu 昭武 as their surname in memory of their origin.[3]

According to this statement, every city-regime whose surname is Zhaowu 昭武 was of the same race as the Kang Country 康國; in other words, all of them were Sogdians. On the basis of the Chinese records, in Central Asia, there were altogether fourteen countries with *Zhaowu* as their surname. *Suishu* 隋書 listed countries of 康 Kang, 安 An, 鏺汗 Pohan, 米 Mi, 史 Shi, 何 He, 烏那曷 Wunahe, 穆 Mu and 漕 Cao as *Zhaowu Countries* 昭武國, while *Xintangshu* 新唐書 listed the countries of Kang, 安 An, 曹 Cao, 石 Shi, Mi 米, He 何, 火尋 Huoxun, 戊地 Wudi, 史 Shi and 東安 Dongan. Thus, with the exception of repeated names, there are fourteen countries which took *Zhaowu* 昭武 as their surname, namely, Kang, An, Pohan, Mi, Shi 史, He, Wunahe, Mu, Cao 漕, Cao 曹, Shi 石, Huoxun, Wudi and Dongan. Therefore, the phrase "Nine Clans of Zhaowu" 昭武九姓 applied in *Xintangshu* 新唐書 was just a rough expression rather than an exact statistic. In other words, it does not mean that in the Sui 隋 and Tang 唐 period, there were merely nine regimes in Central Asia which took Zhaowu as their surname.

According to the studies of many scholars, the approximate locations of those Zhaowu city-states might be as follows. Kang Country centered on present Samarkand; An Country 安國 centered on present Bukhara; both the countries lay in the basin of Zarafshan River.

Pohan 鏺汗 was a transliteration of Ferghana, roughly the present Ferghana Basin, located on the upper reaches of the Syr River, now

---

[3] Cf. *Suishu* 隋書, fasc. 83, p. 1848. The Chinese text was as follows: "康國者, 康居之後也。遷徙無常, 不恆故地, 然自漢以來相承不絕。其王本姓溫, 月氏人也。舊居祁連山北昭武城, 因被匈奴所破, 西逾蔥嶺, 遂有其國。支庶各分王, 故康國左右諸國並以昭武爲姓, 示不忘本也。"

belonging to Republic of Uzbekistan and Republic of Kyrgyzstan, respectively. Mi Country 米國 was named 弭秣賀 Māymurgh recorded in *Datangxiyueji* 大唐西域記, situated southwest of Samarkand, and was nearly 500 *li* 里 in circumference during the Tang period.

Shi Country 石國 was 者舌 Zheshe recorded by *Weishu* 魏書, 赭時 Zheshi in *Datangxiyueji* 大唐西域記 and 柘支 Zhezhi in *Xintangshu* 新唐書. They were transliterations of the Persian word *Chach* and Sogdian word *C'c*, meaning stone. It is the approximate equivalent of the present Tashkent and its surrounding areas, north of the Syr River, and now belongs to the Republic of Turkmenistan and Republic of Uzbekistan, respectively.

Huoxun Country 火尋國 was 貨利習彌 Huoliximi recorded in *Datangxiyueji* 大唐西域記, namely, Khwarizm, located on both sides of the lower reaches of the Amu River; at present, this region, respectively, belongs to the Republics of Turkmenistan and Uzbekistan. Besides, some scholars supposed that Mu Country 穆國 was the present Merv of Turkmenistan, and Wunahe 烏那曷 was the present Balkh of Afghanistan. The two countries are located south of the Amu River (Amu Darya).

Although the last identification was not necessarily accurate, generally speaking, the range of these Zhaowu countries was much vaster than the Zarafshan River valley, even extending to the north of the Syr River and south of the Amu River. Therefore, if the Zhaowu countries were regarded the same as the Sogdia, the territory of the 粟特 Sute in Chinese literatures was obviously much larger than the Soghd of the records in non-Chinese languages.

However, according to *Datangxiyueji* written by Xuanzang 玄奘, the scope of Sogdia was wider than the Zhaowu countries. He said, "The region between the city 素葉 Suye (Suyab) and the country 羯霜那 Jieshuangna (Kasanna/Kusāna) is called 窣利 Suli. Its people, scripts and language also take the same designation."[4]

Here, the toponym 窣利 Suli is the transliteration of the Sogdian *Sγwlik*, while 粟特 Sute is the transliteration of the Sogdian *Sγwδik*, and the meaning of the two names is exactly the same. The letter δ of the earlier Sogdian dialect is pronounced as *l* in the later Sogdian; as a result, two different words *Sγwδik* and *Sγwlik* appear. That is to say, 粟特 is exactly

---

[4]Cf. Xuanzang 玄奘, *Datangxiyueji* 大唐西域記 (*A Record of the Western Regions in the Tang*), fasc. 1, proofread and punctuated by Zhangxun 章巽, Shanghai People's Publishing House 上海人民出版社, 1977, p. 8.

the same toponym as 窣利 in the Chinese language. The city 素葉 Suye or 素葉水 Suyeshui mentioned by Xuanzang 玄奘 was also called 碎葉 Suiye in other writings. It lay near Tokmok on the west bank of the Issyk-Kul. As for the country 羯霜那, it is Shahr-i-sebz, 75 kilometers south of the present Samarkand. Some believed it to be Shi Country 史國, one of the so-called *Nine Clans of Zhaowu* 昭武九姓.

According to this description of Xuanzang 玄奘, the range of 粟特 (Sogdia) should start from Issyk-Kul and Chu River valley in the north and extend southward to the north bank of the Amu River. In other words, in addition to the Zarafshan River valley, its territory included also a wide area north of the Syr River. Why did Xuanzang think the Sogdia was so large in scope? It may be closely related to the environment of that time: in the first half of the 7th century, Xuanzang travelled to India; it was exactly an era when the Sogdians flourished on the Eurasian Continent. The Sogdians set a lot of settlements outside their homeland, including the region north of the Syr River, so Xuanzang mistook it for their native country.

In sum, on the basis of the Chinese or foreign sources, it is comparatively reasonable to regard both the region centering on Zarafshan River valley and that of Tashkent and its surrounding regions as Sogdia. Though this area was not vast, it lay on a key point of the Eurasian traffic. So, its people blended multiple classical civilizations of Eurasia and spread them all over the world. The Sogdians became a unique excellent intermediary of the ancient civilizations.

(2) Advantageous location of Sogdia

Most of the ancient civilization centers lie on the Eurasian Continent. For example, as long ago as the first half of the 1st millennium BC, there were already intercourses between China of East Asia and foreign regions; since the establishment of the Han Dynasty in the 2nd century BC, the Chinese had more frequent exchanges with countries in the West. India lying in South Asia communicated with West Asia and Europe at a very early age; in the 2nd millennium BC, the Aryans invaded the subcontinent on a large scale and dominated it. The Greek and Roman civilizations circulated in the Mediterranean region. Mesopotamia of the West Asia was one of the main sources of classical civilizations. Sogdia lying in Central Asia was just like an important transport hub for all these civilizations.

The geographical location of Samarkand makes the whole Sogdia of great importance in the exchange of world civilization. This topic involves the so-called *Silk Road*. According to the contemporary concept about the Silk Road, its range already expended greatly, even spreading all over the Asia, Europe and Africa. Generally speaking, it was divided into two kinds, namely, the *Land Silk Road* and the *Maritime Silk Road*. The Land Silk Road can be subdivided again into two main lines, the *Steppe Silk Road* and the *Oasis Silk Road*, which cross over the great steppe of the nomads and the oasis region of the settlers, respectively. We find that Sogdiana, the homeland of the Sogdians, was of great importance to both the Steppe Silk Road and the Oasis Silk Road.

The main route of the Oasis Silk Road was roughly as follows. It went along the Yellow River westward, being divided into several roads at the end of the Hexi Corridor 河西走廊. One of the roads passed the northern side of Tarim Basin, crossing over the Pamir Plateau west of the present Kashgar, then going through the Ferghana Basin and Samarkand region, continuing westward. Another road passed the southern side of Tarim Basin, crossing over the Pamir Plateau west of the present Shache 莎車, then going through the upper and middle reaches of the Amu River, meeting with the first road at Merv of Turkmenistan. Afterward, this thoroughfare passed the southeastern coast of the Caspian Sea, through the present countries of Iran, Iraq and Syria, reaching Antioch at the Mediterranean's northeastern corner; from there, people could go to every place along the coast of the Mediterranean. The third road went northwestward from the Hexi Corridor, after passing Hami 哈密, then going to the north foot of Tianshan Mountains, connecting the Steppe Silk Road lying in the Ili, Chu and Talas river valleys.

The outline of the Steppe Silk Road was less distinct than that of the Oasis Silk Road. It crossed over the expansive and deserted grassy plain, and hardly got the attention of the historians of the ancient civilized world, while the native inhabitants left few written records because of their backward cultures. Thus, modern scholars can only roughly infer the routes of the Steppe Silk Road on the basis of very scanty written materials and some archaeological data.

The Steppe Silk Road was characterized by its wide distribution and multiple branches. One of such Steppe Roads was closely related to the Oasis Roads, and the general situation of its route may be as follows. It started from North China with several branch lines, going northward to the Mongolian Plateau, coming to the Orkhon River valley and Baikal coasts. Here, one could go westward along the course of the present

Siberian railway, arriving at Eastern Europe, or cross over the Hangay Mountain 杭愛山, and go westward along the Altai Mountain, then turn southward to the grasslands north of the Tianshan 天山. Subsequently, the road passed the valleys of Ili, Chu, Talas and Syr rivers in succession, reaching the north coast of the Aral Sea. This road continued to the west, passing the valleys of Ural, Volga and Don rivers, leading to the north coasts of the Caspian Sea, Azov Sea and Black Sea. It could also lead to regions further west, such as Dnieper, Vistula and Danube river valleys.

Both the Oasis Road and Steppe Road had many branch lines just like a spiderweb. For instance, in the upper reaches of the Amu River some thoroughfares were separated from the Oasis Silk Road, turning southerly and entering the territories of present Afghanistan, Pakistan and India. Along the coast of the subcontinent, it joined the *Maritime Silk Road* of the Indian Ocean. Besides, one of the branch lines of the Steppe Silk Road extended northward along the Irtysh River, leading to Omsk and other regions. The branch roads of the Syr River basin led either southeastward to Ferghana or southward to Sogdiana. In the lower reaches of the Volga River, some branch roads led northerly to the Kama River valley and southerly to the Caucasia, and so on.

Let us take Samarkand as an example to demonstrate the developed traffic network of Sogdiana. If someone started out from Ura-Tjube and went eastward, after passing cities in the Ferghana Basin, crossing over the Pamir Plateau, he would arrive at Kashgar, the western end of the Tarim Basin. From there, if he went easterly along the road lying on the northern side of the Tarim, after passing Aksu, Kuqa, Yanqi and Hami, he would reach the Hexi Corridor, then onward to the Central Plains of China.

This route corresponded to the *Middle Road* recorded by Peiju 裴矩 (cf. *Biography of Peiju* in *Suishu*). Obviously, this road could join the so-called *South Road* at a certain spot south of Kashgar, while the South Road lay on the southern side of the Tarim Basin, and directly led to Afghanistan. In addition, there were many paths in the Tianshan Mountains, using which people could cross the Tianshan Mountains easily. That is to say, people could easily change their route of the *Middle Road* into that of the *North Road*, or vice versa.

Going northward from Samarkand and crossing the Syr River, one could arrive at Tashkent, Dzhambul and other regions. Dzhambul/Jambyl lay on the Taraz/Talas River and was the site of the ancient city Talas. According to Xuanzang's *Datangxiyueji* 大唐西域記, in the city Talas, "a lot of foreign traders inhabit there". Apparently, it was once a flourishing commercial metropolis. The Byzantine historian Menander recorded that, in 568 AD, the Byzantine envoy Zemarchus was sent to the Turks. On his way home, he met with the sovereign of the Western Turk Khanate Istami in the city of Talas. It clearly showed the political and economic importance of Talas; hence, it might have been one of the significant regions of the "*Middle Road*" recorded by Peiju 裴矩, which traversed the northern region of Eurasia and was a part of the Steppe Silk Road. Continuing eastward from here, the road led to the city Suyab and its surrounding Chu River valley, reaching the south coast of the Issyk-Kul; going further east, one could arrive at the Central Plain of China through the ways of the *Tianshan South Road* or the *Tianshan North Road*. Going west from Dzhambul/Jambyl/Talas, one may take the way of the northern coasts of the Aral and Caspian Sea, reaching South Russia and Asia Minor finally.

West of Samarkand, also in the Zarafshan River valley, was another famous oasis metropolis Bukhara. Going southwestward from Bukhara, crossing Amu River, passing Merv of the present Republic of Turkmenistan, and then crossing through North Iran, one could reach Damghan, Hamadan and the present Iraq's capital Baghdad. From here, the road led farther to Syria and the important port Antioch of the present South Turkey.

The thoroughfare led southward from Samarkand; after crossing the Amu River, it entered the territory of the present Afghanistan. After passing Mazari Sharif, Bagram and crossing the Hindu Kush Mountains, it reached Kabul. From there, these roads led to everywhere in the Indus River Basin of the present Pakistan; going further southeast, the roads entered India, and joined the *Maritime Silk Road* of the Indian Ocean's coast.

Obviously, although Sogdiana which centered on Samarkand was not a large area, it can be reasonably regarded as a pivot in the traffic network of ancient Eurasia, not only because the most famous Oasis Silk Road crossed through the Samarkand region but also because one of the Steppe Silk Roads passed by the north part of Sogdiana. In addition, the oriental civilization originating from China, the Occidental civilization coming from Greece and Rome as well as Mesopotamia spread to India through Sogdia and its surrounding regions. Correspondingly, in the course of the spreading of the ancient Indian civilization to Europe, West Asia, East Asia and North Asia, it was also transferred through Sogdia by the Sogdians.

It was precisely because of the advantageous geographical position and distinguished traffic network of the Sogdiana that this region and its people played an important role in the intercourses and integrations between the ancient Occident and Orient. The Sogdians went abroad, all over the world. They were actively involved in the economic, cultural, diplomatic, political and even military affairs of the native people, attaining a lot of remarkable achievements. The Sogdians were really a legendary minority in the ancient world.

(3) A brief history of the Sogdians
The Sogdians were the eastern branch of the Iranian people, who were sometimes called the *Iranians of Central Asia* and were thought to be an Indo-European race. They had a protruding nose, deep eyes, golden beard and so on. In the period of the Achaemenid Empire (550–330 BC), at least in terms of its language, the Sogdians seemed to be an individual ethnic group; as for the political affiliation, their regime might have belonged to the Persian Empire. Darius (ca. 522 BC–486 BC) and Xerxes (ca. 486–465 BC) often mentioned the provinces in the eastern part of the Persian Empire, such as Sugda, Bāxtriš, Uvārazmiš and Haravia. A palace inscription of the winter capital Susa recorded that the Gems of lapis lazuli and carnelian were produced in Sogdiana and shipped to Persian capitals in large quantities.

In the 4th century BC, the political unity of the Iranian nationalities broke up with the collapse of the Achaemenid Empire, and hence the Sogdians began to enjoy greater autonomy. Soon after the expedition eastward of Alexander the Great, the capital Marakanda of the Sogdians was captured by the Greeks. However, instead of succumbing to the Greeks, the Sogdians resisted resolutely. Clitus, the governor of Bactria and Sogdia, complained to Alexander and said that the people of Sogdiana frequently rebelled against the Greeks. They were unyielding and almost unconquerable. As a governor of this country, he seemed to have been thrown into the beast herd.

Many Sogdians were forced to move to other countries; those who stayed in the native land never gave up their resistance to the invaders. After the death of Alexander, though there were still several Greek governors ruling Bactria and Sogdia, they appeared to control only a part of this region. Later, in the Seleucid Dynasty (312 BC–63 BC), the situation of Sogdiana was approximately the same as before, and its center region, the Zarafshan River basin, appeared to be always outside the political borders of the Seleucid Empire.

During this period, the Sogdians established their own minor kingdom, enjoying greater autonomy. However, not long after, their independence was threatened due to the invasion of the Darouzhi 大月氏. The latter was a nomadic tribe originally living in Northwest China; being forced by the powerful Xiongnu 匈奴, they had to move westward and finally came to the region south of the Syr River. In the 40s BC, the Darouzhi invaded Sogdiana and occupied some part of this country. In addition, the Sogdians also suffered invasions from the Scythian tribes of Central Asia, who had close ethnic relations with the Sogdians.

After the Darouzhi consolidated their base in Central Asia, Emperor Wudi 武帝 of the Han dispatched Zhangqian 張騫 as the envoy to visit countries in the Western Regions. The main purpose was to join forces with the Darouzhi, opposing the Xiongnu together. Having overcome countless hardships, Zhangqian reached many regions of Central Asia including Sogdiana. Although he failed to convince the Darouzhi to jointly attack the Xiongnu, these diplomatic activities made a tremendous contribution to the large-scale exchanges of economy, culture and politics between the Chinese government and these countries. Over a long period since then, Chinese silk and other goods were shipped continually to the West through the oasis settlers of Central Asia and the Steppe nomads of North Asia, while Indian Buddhism, Greek and Iranian cultures and arts were also introduced into China proper. The Sogdians played a very important role in these intercourse activities.

It is unknown whether Sogdiana was once occupied by the Parthian Empire of Iran. However, it should be true that the Kusana Dynasty centered in Bactria once crossed northward past the Amu River and occupied a part of Sogdiana. We can reasonably infer that the Kusana once dominated Sogdiana, the Ferghana Basin and even the Kashgar region of the present China. However, the history of the period from the reign of Kanishka (ca. the first half of the 2nd century) to the establishment of the Sasanian Persian Empire (225 AD) became unclear once again. In the middle of the third century, Sogdiana became one of the provinces under the rule of Shapur I of the Sasanian Empire. This situation probably remained until late the 4th century.

In the 370s AD, another nomadic invasion tide appeared in Transoxiana,[5] the conquest from the Hephthalites. The Hephthalites were

---

[5] *Transoxiana* is a toponym for the region north of the Amu River. It was regarded the same as Sogdiana by some scholars. Generally speaking, however, the range of Transoxiana was

a nomadic tribe, possibly deriving from the Yifu 乙弗 clan among the Xianbei 鮮卑 ethnic group in North China. Around the early 370s, they crossed the Altai Mountains and migrated westward to Sogdiana, dominating the Zarafshan River Basin. The Ephthalite regime, however, was not very strong then; it had once been vassal to the emerging nomadic power Rouran 柔然. By the 420s, the Ephthalites grew strong enough to expand their territories; they crossed southerly past the Amu River and invaded the land of the Sasanian Empire.[6] In light of this, in the earlier period, though Sogdiana was occupied by the Ephthalites, the Sogdians were not necessarily dominated firmly by them.

In the early 550s, a Turkic tribe Asena rose in the Altai region. These Turks not only freed themselves from the bondage of Rouran but also established a powerful nomadic khanate in the Asian hinterland. In the late 50s and the early 60s, the Turks allied with the Sasanian Persians, defeated and destroyed the Ephthalite regime together with the Persians, and divided up its territory. The lands north of the Amu River belonged to the Turks, while the lands south of the river belonged to the Persians. Thus, Sogdiana and many parts of Transoxiana became the domain of the Turk Khanate.

The Turk Khanate set its base in the Mongolian Plateau and had a vast territory. In the east, it started from the northeastern part of China, and extended westward to the Aral and Caspian regions; in the South, it extended from the north banks of the Yellow River and the north borders of Tarim Basin to Transoxiana. In short, the territory of this nomad khanate almost adjoined that of the three civilization centers of China, Iran and Byzantium. Under the rule of the Turks, the Sogdian metropolises with a high level of urban civilization enjoyed autonomy to some extent, just like the situation in the Ephthalite period. Besides, the Sogdians played quite an active role in the Turk government, making significant contributions to the politics, economy and culture of the Turks. The Turk Khanate dominated Central Eurasia for more than a hundred years, and much of this achievement should be attributed to the participation of the Sogdians.

---

larger than that of Sogdiana; it included all lands between the Syr River and Amu River (Oxus River).
[6] About the origin of the Ephthalites and the dates they entered Sogdiana, all cite from Yutaishan 余太山, *A Study on the History of Ephthalite* 嚈噠史研究, Qilu Publishing House 齊魯書社, 1986, pp. 1, 31, etc. His viewpoints are different from those of other scholars abroad.

Not long after the establishment of the Turk Khanate, it was divided into two parts of the east and west, which were nearly independent of each other. In 630 AD, during the reign of Emperor Taizong 太宗 of the Tang, the so-called Eastern Turk Khanate was destroyed by Chinese forces, while the Western Turk Khanate which controlled Sogdiana experienced serious chaos, and was destroyed finally by Emperor Gaozong 高宗 of the Tang in 657.

In 659 AD, Gaozong issued an imperial edict, claiming that in lunar September of that year, the former countries Shi 石, Mi 米, Shi 史, Da'an 大安, Xiaoan 小安, Cao 曹, Ferghna 拔汗那, Ephthalite 悒達, Shule 疏勒, and Zhujuban 朱駒半 of Central Asia would be set into 127 states and counties.[7] The Shi 石, Mi 米, Shi 史, An 安, etc., were all typical *Countries of Zhaowu Clans* 昭武國, namely, the regimes in Sogdiana. Apparently, at that time, Sogdiana was already placed under the control of the Tang Dynasty. Generally speaking, for the countries outside of China proper, the Tang government adopted the policy of high autonomy and pacification, that is to say, as long as these countries nominally recognized the Tang as the supreme authority, they could enjoy in fact a very high autonomy. Therefore, when the Sogdians "succumb to the Tang", they could exchange with Chinese more conveniently, but would not be forced to change their inherent cultures at all.[8]

Half a century later, the situation changed greatly. The Arabs who already established the Muslim Dynasty in Iran launched the expedition to the east, and Sogdiana became one of the first objects of this conquest. The Sogdians fought hard against the invaders, but still failed to withstand the heavy blows of the Arabic forces. In 712 AD, the Arabic governor Qutaiba occupied Samarkand and conquered Tashkent and other regions north of the Syr River. The policy of the Arabs was quite different from that of the Tang; they enforced the policy of *Islamization* in the locality. Thus, the Zoroastrian shrines, Buddhist temples and some other religious buildings were all destroyed and converted into mosques. The native people were forced to renounce their own traditional religions and convert to Islam. If anyone dared disobey the Arabic rulers' order, he could suffer

---

[7] Cf. *Zizhitongjian* 資治通鑑, fasc. 200, p. 6317.
[8] About the Sogdian brief history, may cf. B. Gharib, *Sogdian Dictionary (Sogdiam-Persian-English)*, Tehran, 1995, pp. xiii–xviii; Ehsan Yarshater (ed.), *The Cambridge History of Iran*, Vol. 3 (I), Chapter 6 (by E.V. Emmerick), Cambridge University Press, 1983.

physical injury and financial loss. The traditional cultures of the Sogdians began to disappear in the locality.

In the second half of the 9th century, the Samanid family, which descended from the Sasanian aristocracy, was gaining more and more power in Central Asia. In 874 AD, Nasr, one of the members of this family, established his own regime, taking Samarkand as the capital, and issuing his own silver coins. The Abbasid imperial government of Bagdad had to admit the fait accompli, appointing Nasr as the governor of Transoxiana to manage all territories north of the Amu Darya. Ismail, the successor of Nasr, took Bukhara as the Capital. The Samanid Dynasty greatly flourished in the first half of the 10th century, with the economy prospering, the cultures being brilliant and the metropolises Samarkand and Bukhara being famous for their cultures and sciences. During this period, the Iranian classical cultures were rehabilitated to certain extent. In 999 AD, the Samanid Empire was destroyed by the Karakhan Dynasty and the Ghaznavid Dynasty, and its territory was divided up by them.

The Karakhan Dynasty lay east of the Samanid Dynasty, within the territory of present Xinjiang 新疆. It was ruled by the Turks who believed in Islam. Their domination of Sogdiana ended forever the rule of the Iranian ethnic group over this region. Previously, though this region was often controlled by the foreign nationalities, its traditional features of the ethnic, linguistic and religious respects did not change greatly, and sometimes they even got free development. However, the Turkic rulers of the Karakhan Empire not only expelled the Iranian political forces from Sogdiana but also implemented *Turkification* in language, religion and other respects; Islamism dominated the whole country. As a result, Sogdians who were unwilling to be assimilated by the Turks left their homeland. Finally, the situation became so bad that the Sogdian dialect remained only in the Republic of Tajikistan.

One century later, the domination of the Karakhan Empire in Sogdiana was challenged by the Khitan 契丹 in the east. The Liao 遼 Dynasty was a powerful regime founded by the Khitan tribe in North China. Yelüdashi 耶律大石, a member of its royal family, clashed with the emperor in 1124, leading all his men to migrate westward. They crossed over the Mongolian Plateau, reaching regions of Kirghiz, Uighur and Semiryechye in succession. Around 1134, they conquered Kashgar and Khotan which were previously occupied by the eastern branch of the Karakhan Empire. In 1141, taking advantage of the civil strife in Sogdiana, Yelüdashi marched southward, defeating the Seljuk reinforcement of the Karakhan Empire, and occupied Sogdiana. This regime of Central Asia established by Yelüdashi was called 西遼 (The Western Liao) by the Chinese, because it originated from the Liao Dynasty in the East.

Though the Western Liao conquered Sogdiana, it was not directly involved in local administration, but only dispatched some officials to levy a tax on them. Generally speaking, as long as the conquered acknowledged the supreme authority of 葛爾罕 Geerhan, the title for monarch of the Western Liao, and paid a small amount of taxes, they could live without trouble. Therefore, the Karakhan regime of Sogdiana could still exist in the name of a vassal state.

In the early period of the 13th century, the Western Liao gradually declined, while Khwarizm centered in the lower reaches of the Amu River was getting more powerful. Mohammed, the king of Khwarizm, was unwilling to submit to the Western Liao anymore, so he did his best to escape its control and expand his own influential scope. Around 1209–1210, the Karakhan ruler of Samarkand tried to oppose the suzerainty of the Western Liao. Geerhan sent troops to suppress them, but immediately withdrew because of the rebellion in east part of his country. Taking advantage of this opportunity, the Khwarizm army marched to Samarkand at once and forced the Karakhan ruler to yield. Then, their joint forces defeated the army of the Western Liao in the Talas region. Khwarizm forced the Western Liao out of Sogdiana, and replaced the Western Liao, becoming the new master of Sogdiana.

As a result, the situation of Central Asia changed into a direct confrontation between Khwarizm and the rising Mongolian power. There were once some commercial and diplomatic exchanges between the Mongolians and Khwarizm. The last contact was in 1218 when Genghis Khan sent a caravan with about 500 members to Otrar, a border city of Khwarizm. Unfortunately, Mohammed killed all of them and plundered all their possessions. His excuse was that an Indian trader among these members offended him.

This silly behavior infuriated Genghis Khan. In the autumn of 1219, an army with 200000 soldiers led by Genghis Khan reached Otrar, and divided into several routes to attack Khwarizm. Genghis Khan and his youngest son Tuolei 拖雷 advanced on the center of Sogdiana, and captured Bukhara and Samarkand, respectively, in February and March of

1220. Mohammed had to flee, and in the same year, died on an island in the southeastern Caspian Sea.[9]

Generally speaking, since the Arabs had conquered Sogdiana, Soghd had been declining as a political entity. In their homeland, the traditional features of the Sogdians were altered to some extent. Later, this situation became more serious. After the Mongolian conquest of Central Asia, the typical Sogdian cultures, such as Sogdian dialect, Zoroastrianism and Manicheism, no longer existed in Sogdiana proper. Therefore, from then on, the history of this region almost did not relate to the Soghd discussed in this book. On the contrary, in terms of the intercourses between the Sogdians and Chinese regimes, the most flourishing period was in fact prior to the *Five Dynasties* 五代 in the 10th century. There were few exchanges between the Western Regions 西域 and the Song 宋 Dynasty, especially the Southern Song 南宋. Thus, whether based on the history of the Sogdian homeland or on the relationship between the Sogdians and Chinese, the interchanges of the two ethnic groups ended approximately in the times of the Five Dynasties and Northern Song.

2. An Investigation on 粟弋 Suyi

According to the description above, nearly every definition regards the region between the Syr River and Amu River, or including their surrounding areas, as Soghd/Sogdiana. Besides, in both ancient and modern times, people seemed to deliberately or unintentionally equate 粟弋 Suyi with 粟特 Sute (Soghd), while the former was actually a small country in the Caspian region, though it was only briefly mentioned in Chinese historical records. I am going to discuss this topic as follows.

As the name for a regime in ancient Central Eurasia, 粟弋 Suyi rarely appeared in Chinese literatures, and was depicted extremely briefly. A biography of this country was listed in the *Biography of the Western Regions* 西域傳 of *Houhanshu* 後漢書. However, there were only twenty-seven Chinese characters in this biography, and 粟弋 Suyi was miswritten as 粟弌 liyi in the later editions. The whole text said, "The country Suyi 粟弋 is a vassal of Kangju 康居. Its native products are good

---

[9] About the Sogdian political history, cf. Wangzhilai 王治來, *Zhongyashigang* 中亞史綱 (*An Outline of the History of Central Asia*), Hunan Education Publishing House 湖南教育出版社, 1986, pp. 244–252, 312–316, 350–354, 386, 394, 424–436.

horse, cattle, sheep, grapes and other fruits. There are fertile land and rich water in this country, so it is very famous for the wine."[10]

In addition, a sentence in *Biography of Kangju* 康居傳 of *Jinshu* 晉書 mentioned Suyi: "The country Kangju 康居 lies about two thousand *li* 里 northwest of 大宛 Dawan. It is adjacent to 粟弋 and 伊列 Yilie."[11]

Finally, there was a *Biography of Suyi* 粟弋傳 in *Tongdian* 通典. It contained a paragraph of less than eighty Chinese characters: "The country 粟弋 Suyi begins to interchange with China in the period of the Later Wei 後魏. It is a large country lying in the Congling 葱嶺 Mountains. It is also named 粟特 Sute or 特拘夢 Tejumeng. Its native products are fine horse, cattle, sheep, fruits of grape, etc., and good wine. There are fertile land and rich waters in this country. Besides, a kind of big crop grows there, about three to four meters tall, its fruits are like beans. It lies fifty *li* north of Parthia, with vassals of more than 400 cities. In the reign of emperor Taiwu 太武 of the Northern Wei, it sends envoys to pay tribute."[12]

In fact, the *Biography of Suyi* of the *Tongdian* 通典 possibly mixed the two records from *Biography of Suyi* 粟弋傳 in *Houhanshu* 後漢書 and *Biography of Sute* 粟特傳 in *Weishu* 魏書, thereby leading to great confusion. The *Biography of Sute* in *Weishu* said, "The country Sute lies west of Congling Mountains, namely the ancient Yancai 奄蔡, also named Wennasha 溫那沙. It is adjacent to the great water area, lying northwest of Kangju, 16000 *li* from the capital of the Wei. Initially, the Xiongnu kill their king and occupy their lands. It has been three generations since the king Huni 忽倪. Previously, merchants of this country often come to Liang Prefecture for trading. After this region is taken by the Wei regime, all of them are captured. Early in the reign of emperor Gaozong, the king of Soghd dispatches envoys to China, asking for redemption. Gaozong accepts this request. Since then they no longer send missions and pay tribute."[13]

---

[10] Cf. *Houhanshu* 後漢書, fasc. 86, Zhonghua Book Company 中華書局, 1965, p. 2922. The Chinese text is as follows. "粟弋國屬康居，出名馬牛羊、蒲陶眾果，其土水美，故蒲陶酒特有名焉。"
[11] Cf. *Jishu* 晉書, fasc. 97, Zhonghua Book Company 中華書局, 1974, p. 2544.
[12] Cf. *Tongdian* 通典 (*Encyclopaedic History of Institutions*), fasc. 193, p. 1043.
[13] Cf. *Weishu* 魏書, fasc. 102, Zhonghua Book Company, 1974, p. 2270. The Chinese text is as follows. "粟特國，在葱嶺之西，古之奄蔡，一名溫那沙。居於大澤，在康居西北，

Because of the confusion of original sources, nearly all the scholars of the later generations equated 粟弋 Suyi with 粟特 Sute, and located them either in the region of Caspian Sea and Black Sea or in the region of Syr River and Amu River. But, my opinion is that 粟弋 Suyi was a country completely different from 粟特 Sute; the former lay in the region north of the Caspian Sea, adjacent to Yancai 奄蔡 and Yan 嚴, while the latter lay in the region of the Syr River and Amu River. The analysis and argumentation are given as follows:

(1) According to *Houhanshu*'s narrative rules, Suyi should lie in the Caspian region

In the *Biography of the Western Regions* 西域傳 of *Houhanshu* 後漢書, all these countries were narrated in a highly orderly manner. The whole Western Regions was divided into five districts, and the countries in each district were described according to the arrival sequence of the traffic routes. The arrangement order of the countries is listed as follows:

A. Group of the South Road: The thoroughfare along the south edge of Tarim Basin was called South Road 南道 by the Chinese. In this *Biography*, it crosses in a southerly way the Kara Kunlun Mountains, entering Kashmir, and finally reaching 烏弋山離 Wuyishanli, the present Herat of Afghanistan. The *Biography* successively recorded the states of 鄯善 Shanshan, 且末 Qiemo, 精絕 Jingjue, 拘彌 Jumi, 于闐 Yutian, 皮山 Pishan, 西夜 Xiye, 子合 Zihe, 德若 Deruo, 烏秅 Wudu, 罽賓 Jibin and 烏弋山離 Wuyishanli/排特 Paite.

B. Group of the West Asia: The countries in this region were mentioned sequentially as 條支 Tiaozhi, 安息 Anxi, 阿蠻 Aman, 斯賓 Sibin, 于羅 Yuluo and 大秦 Daqin. According to the present concepts, the countries of Tiaozhi, Aman, Sibin and Yuluo approximately lie in the valley of the Tigris River and the mouth of the Persian Gulf; Anxi (Parthia) lies in the present Iranian Plateau; and Daqin is the Roman Empire which occupies the Italian Peninsula and Asia Minor.

C. Group of the South Asia: The members of this group were successively 大月氏 Darouzhi, 高附 Gaofu, 天竺 Tianzhu and 東離 Dongli. In its early period, Darouzhi occupied the region north of the Amu River and northern part of present Afghanistan. Generally, Gaofu was equated with the region centered on present capital of Afghanistan; but, it was already

---

去代一万六千里。先是，匈奴殺其王而有其國，至王忽倪已三世矣。其國商人先多詣涼土販貨，及克姑臧，悉見虜。高宗初，粟特王遣使請贖之，詔聽焉。自後無使朝獻。"

the vassal of Darouzhi when the *Biography of the Western Regions* was finished. Tianzhu was usually the name for the present North India. As for Dongli, some scholars think it lay on the northeastern coast of India, while others situated it on the northwestern coast.

D. Group of the Caspian Sea: There were three countries in this group, namely, 粟弋 Suyi, 嚴 Yan and 奄蔡 Yancai. All of them were said to be the vassals of Kangju 康居. Thus, Kangju should have been narrated prior to these three countries. However, because the narrative rule of this *Biography* is that it "only records the countries established after Jianwu 建武 period (25–55 AD), and those countries that their situations are changed", Kangju was not recorded here. Kangju was a powerful nomadic regime; except for a part of Sogdiana, its main body of territory lay in the Kazakh grassland. Since the narrative rule of this *Biography* is on the basis of sequence of reaching the traffic routes, it is quite possible that Suyi, Yan and Yancai all lay beyond Kangju, that is to say, they were located at the Caspian region.

E. Group of the North Road: The *North Road* here referred to the traffic roads along the north side of the Tarim Basin. The countries were described successively as follows: 莎車 Shache, 疏勒 Shule, 尉頭 Weitou, 溫宿 Wensu, 姑墨 Gumo, 龜茲 Qiuzi, 焉耆 Yanqi, 蒲類 Pulei, 移支 Yizhi, 東且彌 East Qiemi, 車師前部 Front Cheshi and 車師後部 Rear Cheshi. Apparently, they were arranged in an orderly manner.

As the analysis above shows, all these countries were described one by one strictly according to their geographical positions. Therefore, it is almost impossible that only the single country Suyi 粟弋 violated this editorial regulation. Apparently, Suyi surely lay in the Caspian region rather than Sogdiana.

(2) According to the *Biography*, Suyi was not the familiar Soghd for the Chinese

It is easy to see a distinctive writing style in this *Biography*, namely, describing a country according to the sequence of regime name, capital, the distance to the Chinese capital or a certain administrative center, populace, soldier number, customs, native products, political situation, etc. The countries were comparatively powerful or near China; in fact those more familiar to the Chinese were depicted in more detail by the *Biography*.

This *Biography of Western Regions* consisted of 22 biographies of countries; among them, the Front Cheshi 車師前部 and the Rear Cheshi 車師後部 were in the same biography. Most of these biographies fit the features mentioned above. In order to conveniently compare and analyze,

I listed the following in a table, showing the contents of each biography being either detailed or brief: In the item "Content", "1" represents its capital; "2" represents the distance to the residence of the chief of the Chinese border force; "3", the distance to Luoyang 洛陽, eastern capital of China; "4", the distance or location to other countries; "5", the number of its populace; "6", the number of its troops; "7", its customs and native products; "8", its domestic political situation; "9", whether is there a biography of it in *Hanshu* 漢書; and "10", the number of Chinese characters in its biography. In addition, "★" shows that this item exists in its biography, while "○" shows that this item did not exist in its biography.

On the basis of this table, we can draw the following conclusions:

(A) The biographies containing the least number of words are that of Yan 嚴, Zihe 子合, Suyi 粟弋 and Yancai 奄蔡. Because there is already a single biography of Zihe and Xiye 西夜 in *Hanshu* 漢書, and Yancai is also mentioned slightly in Biography of Kangju 康居, the Yan and Suyi seem to be the most briefly recorded countries since the former Han regime.

(B) All four items of 2, 3, 5 and 6 are missing from some biographies, such as Tiaozhi, Daqin, Gaofu, Tianzhu, Dongli, Suyi, Yan and Yancai. In fact, the detail or brevity and existence or absence of the four items are the key indicators to judge Chinese familiarity with these countries.

A Comparison Table of the Countries in *Biographies of the Western Regions of Houhanshu*

Regime Name	Content 1	2	3	4	5	6	7	8	9	10
Jumi 拘彌	★	★	★	★	★	★	○	★	★	215
Yutian 于闐	★	★	★	★	★	★	○	★	★	527
Xiye 西夜	○	○	★	★	★	★	○	○	★	65
Zihe 子合	★	○	○	★	★	★	○	○	★	25
Deruo 德若	○	★	★	★	★	★	○	○	○	51
Tiaozhi 條支	★	○	○	★	○	○	★	○	★	57
Anxi 安息	★	○	★	★	★	★	★	○	★	91
Daqin 大秦	○	○	○	★	○	○	★	★	○	589
Darouzhi 大月氏	★	★	★	★	★	★	○	★	★	83
Gaofu 高附	○	○	○	★	○	○	★	○	○	81

(*Continued*)

(Continued)

Regime Name	1	2	3	4	5	6	7	8	9	10
Tianzhu 天竺	○	○	○	★	○	○	★	★	○	286
Dongli 東離	★	○	○	★	○	○	★	★	○	67
Suyi 粟弋	○	○	○	○	○	○	★	○	○	27
Yan 嚴	○	○	○	★	○	○	★	○	○	15
Yancai 奄蔡	★	○	○	○	○	○	★	○	★	32
Shache 莎車	○	○	★	★	○	○	○	★	★	1459
Shule 疏勒	○	★	★	★	★	★	○	★	○	430
Yanqi 焉耆	★	★	★	★	★	★	○	★	★	219
Pulei 蒲類	★	★	★	★	★	★	★	★	★	143
Yizhi 移支	○	○	○	★	★	★	★	○	○	49
East Qiemi 東且彌	○	★	★	★	★	★	★	○	★	59
Front Cheshi & Rear Cheshi 車師前後部	★	★	★	★	★	★	○	★	★	846

The countries Tianzhu, Dongli, Tiaozhi and Daqin are far away in South Asia, West Asia and even Europe, so it is understandable that the biographies do not record the distance from them to Chinese capital Luoyang 洛陽. Even so, there are numerous indirect materials about their geographical positions. For example, "Tianzhu 天竺, is also named Shendu 身毒, lying several thousand *li* southeast of Rouzhi 月氏 … It faces broad waters … The lands west of Rouzhi and Gaofu, southward to the West Sea and from Panqi 磐起 in the east, all are the territories of Shendu." "The country Dongli takes Qisha 奇沙 city as its capital, more than 3000 *li* southeast of Tianzhu. It is a big country." "The capital of Tiaozhi lies on the mountains, its perimeter is about 40 *li*. This country faces the West Sea, the water surrounds it in the south, east and north, only the northwestern corner connects the lands … Turning to the north, then to the East, after a course of horse-riding for more than 60 days, reaching Anxi 安息." "The country Daqin is also called Lijian 犁健 or Haixi 海西 because of its position west of the sea. It possesses a territory of thousands li, and more than 400 cities."

In contrast with them, the information related to the geographical position of Yancai, Yan and Suyi is very rare. Yancai 奄蔡 is only mentioned in the *Biography of the Western Regions* 西域傳 of *Hanshu* 漢書: "The country Yancai locates around 2000 li northwest of Kangju 康居."

About the country Yan 嚴, it is only mentioned in the Biography of the Western Regions of *Houhanshu* 後漢書: "It lies north of Yancai." As for Suyi 粟弋, there is no record speaking of its geographical location. Therefore, among all the countries listed in *Biography of the Western Regions* of *Houhanshu*, Suyi is the most geographically unknown regime.

C. Besides, there are some biographies without a description of their domestic political situation, such as Xiye 西夜, Zihe 子合, Deruo 德若, Tiaozhi 條支, Anxi 安息, Gaofu 高附, Suyi 粟弋, Yan 嚴國, Yancai 奄蔡, Yizhi 移支 and Eastern Qiemi 東且彌. However, Xiye 西夜, Zihe 子合, Tiaozhi 條支, Anxi 安息 and Eastern Qiemi 東且彌 were already recorded in *Hanshu* 漢書; in the *Biography of Gaofu* of the *Houhanshu*, the relationship between Gaofu and its suzerain is talked about very specifically. Thus, Suyi was one of the few countries without any description on its domestic political situation.

In view of the three conclusions listed above, Suyi was the only regime of the Biography for which the following were not mentioned: the distance to Luoyang, populace, the number of troops, the exact geographical location and the domestic political condition. In other words, Suyi was a country of the Western Regions most unfamiliar to the Chinese during the 200 years since the Han Dynasty. Of course, Yan and Yancai were similar to Suyi.

In contrast to Suyi, Soghd/Sogdiana was particularly well known to the Chinese. This region had been a dense confluence of thoroughfares in the Eurasian Continent since early times. It was generally believed that the Zarafshan River valley including the cities of Samarkand and Bukhara was the center of Sogdiana, Or, the basin of Zarafshan River, in a narrow sense, was Sogdiana. From there, the roads stretched eastward, passing through the southern Tianshan Mountains, reaching the Central Plains of China. Other roads crossed northward past the Syr River, passing by the northern coasts of Aral Sea and Caspian Sea, leading to South Russia and Asia Minor. After crossing the Amu River, the roads extending southward could lead to present Afghanistan, Pakistan and India. Finally, the roads leading westerly from Sogdiana could reach West Asia and Asia Minor.

Early in the reign of Emperor Wudi 武帝 of the Han (r. 141 BC–87 BC), Zhangqian 張騫 visited many countries in Central Asia, such as 大宛 Dawan, 大月氏 Darouzhi, 大夏 Daxia and 康居 Kangju. In addition, he indirectly got to know some other neighboring countries. Afterward, Zhangqian once again dispatched his vice-envoys to Dawan, Kangju, Yueshi and Daxia, while these regimes also sent their diplomats to China. From then on, "The diplomatic missions dispatched by Chinese government are up to more than a dozen or around six annually. It takes them ten or several years to return their homelands."[14] Obviously, at that time, there were frequent intercourses between China and Central Asia, even South Asia and West Asia.

After that, Liguangli 李廣利 once launched expeditions to Dawan 大宛 (Ferghana). The Chinese army led by Chentang 陳湯 and Ganyanshou 甘延壽 had military conflicts with Kangju 康居; in the Later Han Dynasty, Banchao 班超 had a lot of military and diplomatic dealings with the Darouzhi and Kangju. All these facts were enough to acquaint the Chinese with Sogdiana. The *Biography of the Western Regions* of *Hanshu* stated that the Darouzhi 大月氏 passed through Dawan 大宛, conquered Daxia 大夏 and set their capital north of the Amu River. Besides, from Dawan westerly to Anxi 安息, the dialects everywhere were approximately similar. The people featured deep eyes, a dense beard and were skilled in business.

Therefore, many pieces of evidence show that in the period of the Former Han and Later Han, the Chinese were quite familiar with Sogdiana lying between the Amu River and Syr River. If Suyi 粟弋 was really Soghd/Sogdiana, as many scholars believe, why was it so unfamiliar to the authors of *Houhanshu* 後漢書? Thus, the most reasonable answer can only be that Suyi was by no means Soghd/Sogdiana.

(3) The Product similarity of Suyi and Sogdiana is not the ironclad proof for equating the two countries

The *Biography of the Western Regions* of *Houhanshu* stated that Suyi's "native products are good horse, cattle, sheep, grapes and other fruits. There are fertile land and rich water in this country, so it is very famous for the wine." This paragraph is often cited by many scholars as the main evidence to prove that Suyi equates to Soghd/Sogdiana, for their local specialties were analogous.[15] In fact, this opinion is not convincing,

---

[14] About Zhangqian's visitation to the Western Regions, cf. *Hanshu* 漢書, fasc. 61, 1962, pp. 2687–2698.

[15] For example, Cenzhongmian 岑仲勉 thought that the descriptions of wine in *Biography of Dawan* in *Shiji* 史記 and *Biography of Kang* in *Suishu* 隋書 equated to the wine described in *Biography of Suyi* in *Houhanshu* 後漢書, therefore, "It is undoubtable that 粟弋 Suyi and 粟特 Sute is Soghd." Cf. his *Corrections and Explanations on the Geographical Locations about The Biography of the Western Regions in Hanshu* 漢書西域傳地里校釋, pp. 272–273. In addition, Xiaozhixing 蕭之興 also believed this passage

not only because many other countries had such products too but also because the local products of the Caspian region were the same as those recorded in the *Biography of Suyi*.

According to the *Biography of the Western Regions* 西域傳 of *Hanshu* 漢書 and *Houhanshu* 後漢書, the following were produced: the country Qiemo 且末 produced "grape and other fruits"; Nandou 難兜 "grow grain, grape and other fruits"; "the countries near to Dawan 大宛 make wine with grapes. The rich men usually store wine up to more than 600 tons; which can be kept its good quality for decades"; "the lands of Yiwu 伊吾 fit for growing grain, mulberry, hemp and grape"; Shanshan 鄯善 "is rich in donkey, horse and camel"; Wusun 烏孫 "is rich in horse; the rich man usually possesses up to 5000 horses"; Pulei 蒲類 "produces cattle, horse, camel and sheep. They are able to fabricate bow and arrow. There are many fine horses there"; "the lands of Wulei 烏壘 are very fertile"; Yixun 伊循, Daxia 大夏, Yiwu 伊吾 and Liuzhong 柳中 were also claimed as the *fertile lands*. Apparently, the areas characterized by fertile land, rich water, abundant horse, sheep and grape as well as wine were all over the *Western Regions*, and Soghd/Sogdiana was only one of them. We must not regard all these areas as Soghd/Sogdiana!

Suyi lay approximately in the same region as Yan 嚴 and Yancai 奄蔡, while the territory of Yancai should include the land north of the Caspian Sea and the lower reaches of the Volga River and Ural River. The main sphere of influence of the Khazars was believed to be in this region; they established the powerful regime in the early seventh century. Thus, the native products of the Khazar Khanate mentioned by ancient writers would be conducive to learn about Suyi.[16]

Ibn-A'tham al-Kūfi said that the Khazars possessed a kind of camel. They were perhaps of a particular breed, small size and distinct from the Bactrian two-humped variety. The Burtās who lived in the Volga valley possessed not only camels but cattle as well. The Bulgars apparently also bred camels. Muqqadasi mentioned that there were numerous sheep in the

---

in *Biography of Suyi* "is exactly same as the description on the Zarafshan River valley." Cf. his *On the Course of Xiongnu's Migration Westward* 關於匈奴西遷過程的探討, in Lingan 林幹 ed., *A Symposium on the History of the Xiongnu* 匈奴史論文集, Zhonghua Book Company 中華書局, 1983, p. 152.

[16] The information about the products of the Khazars cited below come from the Muslim historians of that time, recorded in D.M. Dunlop, *The History of the Jewish Khazars*, Princeton, 1954, pp. 224–228.

country of Khazar. According to Ibn-Sa'īd, the riding animals of the Khazars were unusually big, presumably referring to the horse. During the Arab invasion of Khazaria in 737 AD, Marwān destroyed many large studs in the course of his march up the Volga. There were some agricultural areas in Khazaria. Iṣtakhri spoke of the farming fields extending around the capital for a distance of 60 or 70 miles. Crops of millet and rice were raised there. Both Muqaddasi and Gardīzi mentioned abundant honey, to which Gardīzi added excellent wax. There was much honey in the Burtās country, which stretched from Khazaria proper toward the Bulgars' inhabitation. The province of Samandar, lying on the northern side of the Caucasus, appeared to be rich and fertile. Iṣtakhri and Ibn-Ḥawqal mentioned its gardens and vineyards. As for the latter's number, Iṣtakhri's figure was 4000, while Ibn-Ḥawqal's figure increased to 40000. Elsewhere too, in Khazar territory, gardens were mentioned by Gardīzi.

Hundreds of years prior to the time of these Muslim writers, the Roman historian Ammianus Marcellinus mentioned the Alans also living in the Caspian Regions. It was said that they possessed two famous local products, namely, fine horses "Saurag" and beer. The beer was regarded as *State Wine* by the Alans; it appeared at all important official and private banquets. Even in modern times, the two products are still the main feature of the Ossetes, who are descendants of the Alans, now living north of the Caucasus.[17]

Consequently, the local products of Suyi were similar to that of the Caspian region, just as its products were similar to that of Soghd/Sogdiana. So, if only in terms of the native products, the region north of the Caspian Sea can also be regarded as the location of Suyi.

(4) *Biography of Kangju* in *Jinshu* indicated that Suyi lay in the Caspian Region

The *Biography of Kangju* 康居傳 in *Jinshu* 晉書 said the following: "Kangju is about 2000 *li* northwest of Dawan 大宛, adjacent to Suyi 粟弋 and Yilie 伊列. Its king resides in the city Suxie 蘇薤. The customs, facial feature and costume of its people are similar to that of Dawan. This country is rather warm, rich in tung, willow and grape; in addition, cattle, sheep and fine horse are also bred abundantly. In the middle of the reign Taishi 泰始 (265–274), its king sends envoys to China to pay tribute, and

---

[17]Cf. George Vernadsky, *The Origins of Russia*, Oxford, 1959, p. 73.

present the sturdy steeds."[18] This passage described mainly the customs and products of Kangju, and incidentally mentioned the relative position between Suyi and Kangju. Even so, it conveyed some meaningful information.

The location of its capital Suxie 蘇薤 was already identified basically by scholars. Chavannes believed that *Suxie* was the transliteration for *Soghd*. *Xintnagshu* 新唐書 equated it with 佉沙 qusha, namely, Kesh, the present Shahr-i-Sabz south of Samarkand. This opinion was supported by Muslim sources.[19] Cenzhongmian 岑仲勉 said that since 蘇薤 Suxie was the transliteration of 粟特 Soghd, and Samarkand was the capital of Soghd, it was reasonable to infer Suxie to be the later Kang 康 country.[20] However, because the king of Kangju 康居, namely, one of the five Minor kings of Kangju, resided in Sogdiana, the Suyi mentioned in *Jinshu* 晉書 could not possibly lie in Sogdiana too; it was surely located beyond the whole territory of Kangju.

According to the sentence "(Kangju being) adjacent to Suyi 粟弋 and Yilie 伊列" in *Jinshu*, Suyi was obviously in the same region as Yilie, both of them lying in a similar geographical position relative to Kangju. At least, the two countries could not be too far apart, that is to say, it was impossibly that one could be adjacent to Kangju's north border, while the other was adjacent to the south border. If this happened, the text would be a different type, such as "(Anxi 安息 being) adjacent to Kangju in the North and adjacent to Wuyishanli 烏弋山離 in the South" (cf. *Biography of the Western Regions* in *Houhanshu* 後漢書).

The country Yilie 伊列 was also mentioned in *Biography of Chentang* 陳湯 in *Hanshu* 漢書. A speech of Chentang was quoted in his *Biography*: "Now Zhizhi Chanyu 郅支單于 of the Xiongnu is known all over the world. He often harasses Wusun 烏孫 and Dawan 大宛, and attempts to dominate Kangju. The Xiongnu persuades Kangju to invade Wusun and Dawan, says, if capturing these two countries, it could attack Yilie in the North, take Anxi in the West, defeat Darouzhi and Wuyishanli in the South. Thus the city-states of the Western Regions will be in great

---

[18] Cf. Jinshu 晉書, fasc. 97, Zhonghua Book Company 中華書局, 1974, p. 2544.
[19] Cf. E. Chavannes, *Documents sur les Tou-kiue (Turks) occidentaux* 西突厥史料, tr. by Fengchengjun 馮承鈞, Zhonghua Book Company 中華書局, 1958, p. 135, note 1.
[20] Cf. Cenzhongmian 岑仲勉, *Corrections and Explanations on the Geographical Locations about The Biography of the Western Regions in Hanshu* 漢書西域傳地里校釋, p. 251.

danger." Here, the positions of Yilie, Anxi and Darouzhi were clearly relative to Kangju, so Yilie might lie north of Kangju.

伊列 Yilie was usually supposed to be 伊犁 Yili, but I do not think so. First, Yilie was distinctly a name of a regime, while Yili was a name of a region. There was never a regime in the Yili region called Yili. Second, in terms of the geographical position, the region Yili could only be regarded as lying *east of Kangju* instead of *north of Kangju*. Finally, according to the words of Chentang, Kangju had to conquer Wusun and Dawan first, then "attack Yilie in the North". It was well known that the base of Wusun was located in the Yili region. Therefore, it was unnecessary to completely attack northward Yilie after conquering Wusun, if Yilie was the same as Yili. Apparently, Yilie 伊列 was surely not Yili 伊犁.

The Record of the History of the Three Kingdoms 三國志 cites a passage from *Biography of the Western Barbarians* 西戎傳 in *Weilüe* 魏略, saying, "The new North Road turns northwest, leading to Wusun and Kangju. The Wuyibie 烏伊別 country lies north of Kangju. There are other countries of Liu 柳, Yan 巖 and Yancai 奄蔡 in these areas; the last one is also called Alan, has customs similar to that of Kangju." This Wuyibie 烏伊別 also lay north of Kangju, and its pronunciation was almost the same as that of Yilie 伊列. So, they possibly referred to the same country.

Yangxianyi 楊憲益 argued the following persuasively: "Apparently, 伊列 Yilie in *Jinshu* 晉書 is exactly 烏伊別 Wuyibie in Weilüe 魏略. The Chinese character 別 is a clerical error of 列. The western scholars usually equate 伊列 with the later Ili valley, it is an inexcusable mistake. In terms of the geographical position, in the Han Dynasty, Kangju is adjacent to Dawan and Wusun in the East, but it is never adjacent to the Ili River Basin. Besides, in the period of the Han 漢 and Jin 晉, Chinese character 伊 is pronounced as U or O, just like the Sanskrit word *Upasaka*, being transliterated as Chinese term 伊蒲塞; its pronunciation is completely different from that of the later *Ili* 伊犁."[21]

Taking a look at various records, it could be concluded as follows: the *Biography of Chentang* in *Hanshu* located Yilie 伊列 north of Kangju; the *Biography of the Western Regions* in *Houhanshu* put Yancai, Yan and Suyi in the same region; in the *Biography of Kangju* of *Jinshu*, Suyi and Yilie are in a similar geographical position; and the *Biography of the Western*

---

[21] Cf. Yangxianyi 楊憲益, *Yiyuoushi* 譯餘偶拾, The Joint Publishing Company 三聯書店, Beijing, 1983, p. 252.

Barbarians in *Weilüe* put Wuyibie/Yilie, Liu, Yan and Yancai north of Kangju. Undoubtedly, the approximate location of Suyi should also be *north of Kangju*, that is to say, in the same region of Yancai, Yan, etc., or the areas north or northwest of the Caspian Sea.

(5) The evidence of names of the Tiele 鐵勒 tribes in the Caspian Region
The *Biography of Tiele* in *Suishu* 隋書 recorded that the Tiele tribes were scattered over the lands east of the Western Sea. They lived in the valleys, stretching endlessly. "North of Kang Country, along the banks of the Ade 阿得 River, there are 訶咥 Hedie, 曷嶻 Hejie, 撥忽 Bohu, 比干 Bigan, 具海曷 Juhaihe, 比悉 Bixi, 何嵯 Hecuo, 蘇拔 Suba, 也末 Yewei and 渴達 Keda, etc. They possess troops of around 30000. There are 蘇路羯 Sulujie, 三 San, 索咽 Suoyan, 蔑促 Miecu and 薩忽 Sahu, etc., in the east and west sides of 得嶷 Deyi Sea."[22]

The *Biography of Kang Country* 康國傳 in *Suishu* 隋書 claimed that the Kang Country was the descendant of Kangju 康居 and a powerful regime, possessing many vassals in the Western Regions, and hence the writer of the *Biography* surely regarded Kang as a country with an extensive territory rather than a region limited only in the Zarafshan valley. In this case, the north border of Kang Country perhaps extended to the banks of Syr Darya, so the *lands north of Kang* should refer to those north of the Syr River or the northern coast of the Aral Sea. It was widely accepted that the *Ade River* is the present Volga River, while the *Deyi Sea* is the present Caspian Sea. Therefore, these Tiele tribes listed above probably lay in the areas north of the Syr River and north of the Aral Sea, as well as the middle and lower reaches of the Volga River north of the Caspian Sea.

In the *Biography of the Western Regions* in *Houhanshu* the countries of Yancai, Yan and Suyi were most briefly mentioned. However, the successors of their names could be found among the Tiele tribes of the Caspian region after several hundred years.

I have already pointed out in my paper *A New Study on the Tiele Tribes* that the tribe 何嵯 Hecuo (pronounced as *ya-ts'ie* in ancient Chinese) was 曷薩 Hesa in the *Biography of Huoxun* 火尋傳, 可薩 Kesa in the *Biography of Bosi* 波斯傳 and 阿薩 Asa in *Youyangzazu* 酉陽雜俎,

---

[22] There are various opinions on the names and locations of the Tiele tribes in *Biography of Tiele*. I hold some new views different from the former, cf. my paper *A New Study on the Tiele Tribes* 鐵勒部落新考, in *Gansu Minorities Research* 甘肅民族研究, 1991, No. 1–2. The tribe names adopted here all follow that paper.

namely, the Khazars rising up in the lower reaches of the Volga River in the early 7th century. Besides, its pronunciation was also the same as that of 闔蘇 (ɣap-sa). The *Historical Records* 史記 said that Yancai 奄蔡 was named 闔蘇 Hesu. Therefore, it is quite possible that the Tiele tribe Hecuo 何嵯 of the Sui Dynasty was the descendant of Yancai 奄蔡 of the Han and Wei period, which lay about 2000 *li* northwest of Kangju, and faced the extensive waters.

The ancient pronunciation of 也未 was *ia-mjwei*, similar to that of 嚴 (國). In old Chinese, 嚴 was pronounced as *ngim*; later, the *ng-* transformed into *y-*, that is to say, in ancient Chinese, the pronunciation *ng-* equated with *y-*. Pulleyblank believed that in the Han period, because the Middle Chinese initial *y-* was not yet formed completely, the velar nasal continuant *ng-* seemed to have been the closest that could transliterate a foreign palatal continuant *y-*.[23] As for the Chinese character 未, it can be used to transliterate the letter M, just like the character 姆. Thus, it is reasonable to suppose that there was a successive relationship between Yewei 也未 and Yan 嚴 (國).

索咽 Suoyan had the Middle Chinese pronunciation of *sak-ien*, while 粟弋 was pronounced as *siwk-d'ik* in Old Chinese and *siwok-ik* in Middle Chinese. Apparently, the first character of the two names was almost the same; the second character was only different slightly. So, the name Suyi 粟弋 seemed to leave its mark in the Caspian region, too.

The country names of 奄蔡 Yancai, 嚴 Yan and 粟弋 Suyi in the *Biography of the Western Regions* in *Houhanshu* seemed to have their counterparts among the Tiele tribes of the Caspian region in the Sui Dynasty. Obviously, it was by no means an occasional phenomenon, so the logical conclusion should be the following: Suyi 粟弋 in the period of the Han and Wei was a country like Yancai 奄蔡 and Yan 嚴, also lying in the region north of the Caspian Sea; it was completely different from Soghd 粟特 or Sogdiana.

---

[23] Cf. E.G. Pulleyblank, *The Consonantal System of Old Chinese*, Part I, in *Asia Major*, 8, 1962, p. 93.

Chapter 8

The Economic and Cultural Activities of the Sogdians in China

In the ancient Chinese records, the Sogdians were famous mainly for the designation of the *Nine Clans of Zhaowu* 九姓昭武. The so-called nine clans of Zhaowu included surnames of 康 Kang, 安 An, 石 Shi, 史 Shi, 米 Mi, 曹 Cao and 穆 Mu. These were also the names of their countries. In the period of the Sui 隋 and Tang 唐, the *barbarians* originating from these Zhaowu countries participated more frequently in Chinese social life. Although the *Western Barbarians* 西胡 xihu of that time also included the Persians and Indians, the leading role in the Xihu still belonged to the Sogdians from Central Asia. They played a significant part in Chinese economic and cultural life.

1. 酒家胡 Jiujiahu in Inland China

The *Biography of Kang* in *Jiutangshu* 舊唐書 described the cultures and customs of the country Kang 康, the homeland of the Sogdians. It said that Kang Country 康國 of the Tang Dynasty was, namely, Kangju 康居 of the Han Dynasty. The surname of its king was Wen 溫, and its people belonged to the Rouzhi 月氏 ethnic group. Initially, they lived in Zhaowu 昭武 city north of Qilian Mountains 祁連山. Later, they were defeated by other nomads, hence crossing the Pamir Plateau and occupying the lands they came to have. In memory of their ancestors, all their branches took the surnames of Zhaowu as their royal family surnames. Their facial features included deep eyes, a prominent nose and a dense beard. The men usually had their hair cut or braided. The king wore a felt hat decorated with jewels. The women generally wore the black headscarves decorated with golden flowers. They were very fond of wine and liked to sing and dance on the street. As soon as a son was born, they put honey in his mouth and put glue in his hand. This symbolized the hope that when the baby grew up he would talk with sweet words and firmly hold wealth. They spoke and wrote in a foreign language. They were good at trading. Men went abroad when they were only twenty; they went to China and any other place where they could make money.[1]

Apart from the features of their appearance and costume, the most noticeable characteristic of the Sogdians was their tradition of paying attention to trade and being good at business. In contrast, the Chinese traditional idea and policy was attaching importance to agriculture and despising commerce. Therefore, to the Chinese people, the characteristic of *Being Good at Business* of the Sogdians seemed to be more peculiar; thus, much related information was left in historical records.

Generally speaking, the commercial activities of the Sogdians were reflected in the following aspects. A lot of rare products from foreign countries, including peculiar jewels and even strange birds and animals, were imported into China by the Sogdians. The most famous and valuable Chinese specialty exported by them was the silk in various kinds, including raw silk and silk products. The silk could be sold at a very high price in distant civilized countries, such as Persia, Greece and Rome. Such commercial activities of the Sogdians were recorded in numerous writings. I am not going to describe them in detail here. Instead, I will give a brief introduction on the wine shops managed by the Sogdians in Chinese cities, especially the metropolises. Such wine shops flourished particularly in the Tang Dynasty, and the managers of the shops were called 酒家胡 Jiujiahu, meaning "the barbarians/foreigners who run wine shops." However, *Jiujiahu* was also used to refer to the wine shops managed by the foreigners. Although these *foreigners* or *barbarians* involved

---

[1] Cf. *Jiutangshu* 舊唐書, fasc. 198, p. 5310. There are some slight mistakes in the Chinese text. I copy this passage as follows for the readers to correct: "康國, 即漢康居之國也。其王姓溫, 月氏人。先居張掖祁連山北昭武城, 爲突厥所破, 南依蔥嶺, 遂有其地。枝庶皆以昭武爲姓氏, 不忘本也。其人皆深目高鼻, 多鬚髯。丈夫剪髮或辮髮。其王冠氈帽, 飾以金寶。婦人盤髻, 幪以皂巾, 飾以金花。人多嗜酒, 好歌舞於道路。生子必以石蜜納口中, 明膠置掌內, 欲其成長口常甘言, 掌持錢如膠之粘物。俗習胡書。善商賈, 爭分銖之利。男子年二十, 即遠之傍國, 來適中夏, 利之所在, 無所不到。"

more than one ethnic group, the main members of it were the Sogdians. I will discuss several issues concerning the Jiujiahu as follows.[2]

(1) The management features of the Jiujiahu
One feature of the Jiujiahu was its high-quality wine. Wangji 王績 was an official in the late period of the Sui and early period of the Tang. He was so fond of good wine that he once volunteered to be a junior official to conveniently get this alcoholic drink. Naturally, he also frequented the wine shops run by the Sogdians. He wrote a poem to depict his relationship with the Jiujiahu. This poem stated that both he and his guests were fond of the wine sold by the Sogdians, but he often could not afford to drink. So, he was very ashamed of his repeated debts for wine.[3] Obviously, this wine was of a very high quality and Wangji could not resist its temptation, thereby he would rather be in debt to get it.

Actually, there were several kinds of vintage wines in such wine shops. Wangji mentioned at least two famous wines in his poem. "The *Bamboo Leaf* shows bluish green, while the *Grape* is colored deep red. Let us drink up for this reunion, otherwise, there will be few opportunities to drink together henceforth."[4] Here, the *Bamboo Leaf* was a trademark for a famous wine, named 竹葉青 zhuyeqing in Chinese; its color was green. The *Grape*, of course, refers to the wine made from grapes; it was red. It is said that the wine Zhuyeqing was invented in Shanxi 山西 province during the period of the Southern and Northern Dynasties; it was obviously a native product of China. However, the grape wine undoubtedly originated from foreign lands. In particular, since people believed that winemaking technology was introduced in the reign of Emperor

---

[2] Although *Jiujiahu* had already appeared in China by the Later Han Dynasty, the most prosperous age for them was the Tang Dynasty. Thus, the inquiring topic here is mainly the Jiujiahu in the Tang Dynasty. About this subject, cf. my paper "A Study on the Jiujiahu of the Tang 酒家胡述考", in *Quarterly Journal of the Shanghai Academy of Social Sciences* 學術季刊, 1993, No. 2, pp. 159–165.

[3] Cf. Wangji 王績, *Five Poems on the Wine Shops* 過酒家五首, the fifth one, in *The General Anthology of Tang Poetry* 全唐詩, fasc. 37, Zhonghua Book Company 中華書局, 1960, p. 484. The Chinese text was as follows: "有客須教飲，無錢可別沽。來時常道貰，慚愧酒家胡。"

[4] Cf. Wangji, *Five Poems on the Wine Shops* 過酒家五首, the third one, in *The General Anthology of Tang Poetry* 全唐詩, fasc. 37, p. 484. The Chinese text says: "竹葉連糟翠，葡萄帶麴紅。相逢不令盡，別後爲誰空？"

Taizong 太宗 of the Tang,[5] the grape wine in the period of Wangji was distinctly a purely exotic product.

Although the date of introduction of grapes and grape wine into inland China could be rediscussed, the fact that they originated from foreign lands is undoubted. For example, *Shiji* 史記 said that Dawan 大宛, the present Ferghana Basin, and the countries near it "make wine with grapes. The rich man usually stores wine up to more than 600 tons; which can be kept good quality for decades."[6] *Houhanshu* 後漢書 stated that the country Suyi 粟弋 planted grapes, and their grape wine was particularly famous.[7] *Jinshu* 晉書 recorded that many local people of Qiuzi 龜茲 possessed a large quantity of wine, up to more than 60 tons, which could retain its quality for ten years.[8] All this information shows that initially, the grapes grew in foreign lands, and the technology of winemaking also came from the foreign countries. Therefore, in the early times, grape wine was so rare and valuable in China that Mengtuo 孟佗 only paid a bribe of ten kilograms of wine to exchange for a high-ranking official position, as governor of Liangzhou 涼州.[9]

A reasonable supposition may be that the Jiujiahu 酒家胡 flourished in inland China, so the sales of quality wine must have been great. Thus, it was uneconomical and unrealistic to always import wine on a large scale from its country of origin far away from China. In contrast, it was quite possible that these *barbarians* or foreigners made wine by themselves locally at their wine shops. If that was true, the introduction of the technology of winemaking and the presence of Jiujiahu in China may have occurred simultaneously. This was a typical example of the Sogdians

---

[5] The grape wine was mentioned in *Cefuyuangui* 冊府元龜 (*Outstanding Models from the Storehouse Literature*), fasc. 970, said, "This wine was presented formerly by the foreigners, but nobody had acquaintance with it. After Gaochang 高昌 was conquered by emperor Taizong 太宗, he transplanted the grapes into the palace, and had mastered the technology of wine making. Emperor Taizong made the grape wine personally, and divided it into eight types, being very fragrant and delicious. The emperor invited all officials to taste these wines; henceforth the Chinese had acquaintance with the grape wine."

[6] Cf. *Shiji* 史記, fasc. 123, p. 3173.

[7] Cf. *Houhanshu* 後漢書, fasc. 86, p. 2922.

[8] Cf. *Jinshu* 晉書, fasc. 122, p. 3055.

[9] About this hearsay, cf. some historical records, such as *Biography of Eunuchs in Houhanshu* 後漢書·宦者列傳, *Chronicle of Mingdi of the Wei* 魏書·明帝紀 in *The Record of the History of Three Kingdoms* 三國志, and *Sanfujueluzhu* 三輔決錄注 as well as *Xuhanshu* 續漢書.

(the principal part of Jiujiahu) spreading sciences and technologies while doing business.

Grape wine is the most characteristic and the most competitive famous wine sold by the Sogdians, but it seemed to be only one of the good wines imported from foreign countries. According to *A Supplement of the History of the Tang* 唐國史補, during the Tang period, there were many famous wines coming from abroad. "As for the wine, there are Fushui 富水 of Yingzhou 郢州, Ruoxia 若下 of Wucheng 烏程, Tukuchun 土窟春 of Yingyang 滎陽, Shidongchun 石凍春 of Fuping 富平, Shaochun 燒春 of Jiannan 劍南, Qianhe Grape 乾和蒲萄 of Hedong 河東, Lingxi 靈溪 and Boluo 博羅 of Lingnan, Jiuyun 九醞 of Yicheng 義城, Benshui 溢水 of Xunyang 潯陽, Xishiqiang 西市腔 of the Capital 京城, Langguanqing 郎官清 and Apoqing 阿婆清 of Xiamaling 蝦蟆陵. In addition, there are also Sanlejiang 三勒漿 (Three types of liquids); it is similar to wine, and its zymotechnics comes from Persia. So-called Sanle 三勒 is namely Anmole 菴摩勒, Pilile 毗梨勒 and Helilf 訶梨勒."[10] The 西市腔 Xishiqiang mentioned here was probably derived from the *Western Barbarians* 西胡. The so-called 西市 (Western Market) in the capital Changan 長安 was the largest residential area of the foreign merchants and also the special district for shops run by the foreigners. Thus, the wine named 西市腔 was quite possible a kind of liquor made by the foreigners coming from the western countries.

Besides, the Sanlejiang 三勒漿 could undoubtedly be traced back to its foreign origin because of its *zymotechnics coming from Persia*. A contemporary scholar studied Sanlejiang. He believes that it originated from India and was a beverage similar to an alcoholic drink. It was synthesized from āmalaka, vibhītaka and harītakī, and had therapeutic and health benefits, good taste, helps digestion and was intoxicating. Later, it was introduced into Persia, the three components were named, respectively, in Persian as *amola*, *balīla* and *halīla*, thereby this beverage was called 三勒 (three *la*) in Chinese, and became a high-grade alcoholic beverage.[11] The Sanlejiang seemed to begin to circulate in China during the Tang period, while it was exactly the time that the Jiujiahu was flourishing in inland

---

[10] Cf. Lizhao 李肇, *A Supplement of the History of the Tang* 唐國史補, Shanghai Classics Publishing House 上海古籍出版社, 1979, p. 60.

[11] About the discussion on this topic, cf. Chenming 陳明, *Foreign Medicine and Culture in Medieval China* 中古與外來文化, Chapter 6, Peking University Press 北京大學出版社, 2013, pp. 466–489.

China. So, it is certain that Sanlejiang 三勒漿 was sold and spread mainly by Jiujiahu.

Another feature of the Jiujiahu was to solicit customers with exotic music, dance and song. The main role of this business was held by female Sogdians, namely, 胡姬 huji (Foreign Girls) as called by the Chinese. There were many descriptions on the Huji 胡姬 in poems written by the literati of the Tang Dynasty. For example, Libai 李白 wrote that the beautiful Huji played the moving music with the pipa and accompanied the poet to drink, intoxicating and bewitching him.[12] In another poem, he depicted the scene of the poet drinking and enjoying snow with two Huji, accompanied by their songs and dances.[13] Hechao 賀朝 also wrote a poem on Huji and their wine shop: "The wine shop run by Huji is still full of music late at night. The moonlight shines on the scarlet carpet, the person in marten coat sits facing the thin frost. The jade plate is filled with delicious carp, and the mutton is cooking in the golden pot. The honored customers gather together, enjoy the songs and dances these girls perform."[14] Apparently, in the wine shops run by the Sogdians, there were songs, music, dances and good wine, as well as charming girls. It was really a good place for the rich literati and officials to enjoy themselves.

In addition to the songs and dances, many musical instruments of Jiujiahu 酒家胡 also had a strong extraterritorial flavor. The pipa, upright konghou 箜篌 (harp), bili 篳篥 (reed pipe) and some other instruments were all introduced from the Western Regions. The orchestral music mentioned in the above poems was surely played by the pipa, harp and bili. In the popular *Qiuzi Music* 龜茲樂 of the Tang Dynasty, bili 篳篥 played the main role. Qiuzi Music was one type of foreign music, which involved the sheng 笙, horizontal flute and xiao 簫 (vertical flute). The scene of playing wind music by the Sogdians could be found in many poems of the

---

[12] Cf. Libai 李白, A Cup of Wine, in *The General Anthology of Tang Poetry* 全唐詩, fasc. 162, p. 1686. The Chinese text is as follows, "琴奏龍門之綠桐，玉壺美酒清若空。摧弦拂柱與君飲，看朱成碧顏始紅。胡姬貌如花，當壚笑春風。笑春風，舞羅衣，君今不醉將安歸。"

[13] Cf. Libai 李白, *Dedicating to Wangliyang* 贈王歷陽, in *Quantangshi* 全唐詩, fasc. 171, p. 1758. The Chinese text says the following: "書禿千兔毫，詩裁兩牛腰。筆蹤起龍虎，舞袖拂青霄。雙歌二胡姬，更奏遠清朝。舉酒挑朔雪，從君不相饒。"

[14] Cf. Hechao 賀朝, *To Huji of the Wine Shop* 贈酒店胡姬, in *Quantangshi* 全唐詩, fasc. 117, p. 1181. The Chinese text of it is as follows: "胡姬春酒店，弦管夜鏘鏘。紅毺鋪新月，貂裘坐薄霜。玉盤初鱠鯉，金鼎正烹羊。上客無勞散，聽歌樂世娘。"

Tang Dynasty, such as the verses "girls play flute in painted tower, Jiujiahu serves good wine with golden cup" written by Wangwei 王維 and "drink with Huji upstairs in the evening, the sound of her vertical flute fills the whole building" written by Zhangxiaobiao 章孝標.[15]

Correspondingly, the dances of the Jiujiahu also had a strong extraterritorial flavor. In ancient China, the dances were divided into several categories according to their peculiarities, such as 健舞 jianwu (healthy dance), 軟舞 ruanwu (soft dance), 花舞 huawu (flower dance) and 馬舞 mawu (horse dance). Some scholars believed that the *Jianwu* was generally a dance with a sword, displaying a sturdy and vigorous style, while *Ruanwu* was a dance without sword, showing a feminine and pliable taste. If true, most of the dances performed by the Jiujiahu were probably *Ruanwu*. On such occasions, the customers seemed more willing to enjoy soft feminine beauty rather than a combative style.

Generally speaking, the Jiujiahu's business covered only wine, song and dance, but did not involve the sex transaction. However, some information indicated that such deals appeared to exist occasionally. For instance, a poem written by Shijianwu 施肩吾 states, "The young Mr. Zheng drinks happily, in the spring he relaxes at the wine shop. If Huji invites him to sleep there tonight, he would surely stay and let his horse also rest."[16] Although this poem only made fun of the young Zhengshenfu, it actually hinted that there were occasions of the customers spending the night in the wine shop. This was also one of the allures of the wine shops managed by the Sogdians.

(2) The Male Members of the Jiujiahu
The so-called Jiujiahu 酒家胡 consisted of not only the female member Huji 胡姬 but also the male member. In fact, the male members were no less important than the female ones. As mentioned above, the Sogdians were good at business; males went abroad at the age of twenty, going everywhere as long as they could make money. Obviously, the Sogdian traders coming to China were mainly males. Even if there were a similar

---

[15] Cf. Wangwei 王維, *Passing by Suifuma Hill* 過崔駙馬山池, in *Quantangshi* 全唐詩, fasc. 126, p. 1274; Zhangxiaobiao 章孝標, *The Lads* 少年行, in *Quantangshi* 全唐詩, fasc. 106, p. 5756.

[16] Cf. Shijianwu 施肩吾, *Making Fun of Zhengshenfu* 戲鄭申府, *Quantangshi* 全唐詩, fasc. 494, p. 5608. The Chinese text was as follows: "年少鄭郎那解愁，春來閒臥酒家樓。胡姬若擬邀他宿，掛卻金鞭繫紫騮。"

number of women, they were mostly the wives and daughters of the Sogdian traders, because there appeared to be no corporations consisting of women only.

The male Sogdians also actively participated in the management of the wine shops. This fact could be reflected by a device urging people to drink, which was called 酒胡子 jiuhuzi (perhaps meaning *the drinking foreigner*). It was also named 勸酒胡 quanjiuhu (the foreigner who urged drinking); a vivid depiction of it was given in a book of the Five Dynasties.

Tangzhiyan 唐摭言 quoted a paragraph from the writing of Luzhu 盧注, an official of the Tang. In his later years, Luzhu wrote a poem to describe the interesting device *jiuhuzi* 酒胡子. It said that one day Luzhu drank with several friends in a restaurant. One of them showed a jiuhuzi, an object with a human figure; on the table, it could swing forward and backward and spin. The one who faced it when it stopped moving had to drink a cup of wine. Its movement and speed, of course, were controlled by people rather than by itself. Thus, Luzhu wrote a poem titled 酒胡歌 *Jiuhuge* (*Song of the Drinking Foreigner*), its main content being as follows:

I am drinking with some good friends, and have the jiuhu 酒胡 (drinking foreigner) as a device for urging drinking. The jiuhu swings ceaselessly in a plate, we all think it is very interesting. This jiuhu swings and spins at random, pitilessly urges people to drink. Oh, dear jiuhu, though you do not farm, you will not be hungry; though you do not keep silkworms, you dress well. Your eyes cannot distinguish between nobility and humbleness, your mouth cannot distinguish between right and wrong. Your nose is very high, your eyes are so green. You wear emerald green cap and red dress, what a lovely statue! Notwithstanding your name is *Drinking Foreigner* 酒胡, you have never had a drink.[17]

---

[17]Cf. Wangdingbao 王定保, *Tangzhiyan* 唐摭言, fasc. 10, in *Sikuquanshu* 四庫全書, Taibei 臺北: The Commercial Press 商務印書館, 1986, p. 767. The Chinese text is as follows: "(盧注) 晚年失意, 因賦《酒胡子》長歌一篇, 甚著。序曰: '二三子逆旅相遇, 貰酒於旁舍, 且無絲竹以用娛賓。友蘭陵掾淮南王探囊中, 得酒胡子, 置於座上, 拱而立令曰: 巡觴之時, 人心俛仰, 旋轉所向者舉杯。其形類人, 亦有意趣, 然而傾側不定, 緩急由人, 不在酒胡也。作《酒胡歌》以誚之曰: 同心相遇思同歡, 擎出酒胡當玉盤。盤中飽飢不自定, 四座親賓注意看。可以不在心, 否以不在面, 徇俗隨時自圓轉。此物五藏屬他人, 十分亦是無情勸。爾不耕, 亦不饑; 爾不蠶, 亦有衣。有眼不曾分齦齪, 有口不能明是非。鼻何尖, 眼何碧, 儀容本非天地力。彫鐫匠意若多端,

In light of this, the so-called *jiuhuzi* 酒胡子 or *quanjiuhu* 勸酒胡 referred to a device like a foreigner; it rotated on the table for a while and eventually fell down, and the person it pointed to had to drink a full cup of wine. The writings of the Song Dynasty also gave such descriptions. For instance, *Mozhuangmanlu* 墨莊漫錄 depicted a device being used to urge drinking at feasts. It was carved into a human figure with the pointed lower part. It spun on a plate, swinging ceaselessly, just like a dancer. Then, the plate was passed in turn to everyone at the wine table. When this statue fell, the person holding the plate must have a drink. It was called 勸酒胡 quanjiuhu, meaning "the foreigner who urges drinking". Someone once wrote a poem to describe this quanjiuhu. There is another type of quanjiuhu. It was not passed on successively, but rather pointed to a person after it stopped spinning, and that person must have a drink.[18]

Apparently, both the two types of quanjiuhu were popular in the period of the Tang and Song. They were called 勸酒胡 quanjiuhu or 酒胡子 jiuhuzi because of their appearance being like a *foreigner* or *barbarian*, with the Chinese character 胡. As mentioned above, Luzhu 盧注 described the appearance of jiuhuzi 酒胡子 in his poem 酒胡歌 *Jiuhuge*: "nose is high, eyes are green" and "wear green cap and red dress". This was exactly the facial features and costume of the Iranians or Sogdians. In addition, Xuyin 徐夤 of the Tang also portrayed the jiuhuzi as a foreigner: "it is like a real person, wearing fur robe and has a bushy beard."[19]

Therefore, I think, the so-called *jiuhuzi* meant not only "the foreigner who urges persons to drink" but also "the drinking persuader who has a bushy beard" because the Chinese character 胡 hu means both *foreigner/barbarian* and *beard*. It is possible that because the beard was one of the remarkable facial features of the foreigners, especially the western

---

翠帽朱衫巧裝飾。長安斗酒十千酤，劉伶平生爲酒徒。劉伶虛向酒中死，不得酒池中拍浮。酒胡一滴不入腸，空令酒胡名酒胡。'"

[18] Cf. Zhangbangji 張邦基, *Mozhuangmanlu* 墨莊漫錄 (*Miscellany of Mozhuang*), fasc. 8, in *Sikuquanshu* 四庫全書, Taibei 臺北: The Commercial Press 商務印書館, 1986, pp. 864–875. The Chinese text is as follows: "飲席，刻木爲人，而銳其下。置之盤中，左右欹側，傲傲然如舞狀。久之力盡，乃倒，視其傳籌所至，酬之以盃。謂之勸酒胡。程俱致道，嘗作詩云：'簿領青州掾，風流麴秀才。長煩拍浮手，持贈合歡盃。屢舞回風急，傳籌向羽摧。深慚偃師氏，端爲破愁來。'或有不作傳籌，但倒而指者當飲。"

[19] Cf. Xuyin 徐夤, *Jiuhuzi* 酒胡子, in *The General Anthology of Tang Poetry* 全唐詩, fasc. 708, p. 8141. The Chinese text is as follows: "紅筵絲竹合，用爾作歡娛。直指寧偏黨，無私絕覬覦。當歌誰擐袖，應節漸輕軀。恰與真相似，氈裘滿頷鬚。"

foreigners, they and their beard were usually named using the same word 胡 by the ancient Chinese. So, the *jiuhuzi* or *quanjiuhu* invented in the Tang Dynasty probably took the appearance of the male *jiujiahu* 酒家胡 for reference. All Sogdians, men and women, played important roles in the wine shop management of China.

(3) The Prosperity and Decline of the Jiujiahu 酒家胡 in the Tang Dynasty

All the information involving the Jiujiahu of the Tang was mostly found in the poetry of the same period. Thus, if we give an analysis on the contents of these poems, an outline of the development of the jiujiahu may be deduced.

According to a rough statistic, there are at least more than 20 poems involving the jiujiahu and their managing features, written by about fourteen poets. They lived in different periods of the Tang; specifically, one poet (王績 Wangji) lived in the first half of the 7th century, the reign of Taizong 太宗; four (賀朝 Hechao, 李白 Libai, 王維 Wangwei, 岑參 Cencan) lived in the first half of the 8th century, the reign of Xuanzong 玄宗; eight (元稹 Yuanzhen, 楊巨源 Yangjuyuan, Zhangxiaobiao 章孝標, 杜牧 Dumu, 張祜 Zhanhu, 溫庭筠 Wentingjun, 施肩吾 Shijianwu, 姚合 Yaohe) lived in the first half of the 9th century, the reigns of Dezong 德宗, Xianzong 憲宗 and Wenzong 文宗; and one (羅隱 Luoyin) in the second half of the 9th century. If other factors, such as lack of information and preference of a certain theme, are not taken into account, we may suppose that in the earlier period of the Tang, there were few jiujiahu in China; they were popular in the flourishing period of the Tang, even more prosperous in middle period of the Tang and the first part of the late Tang, and gradually declined in the final period of the Tang.

This conjecture is approximately in line with the developing trend of Sino-foreign exchanges of the Tang Dynasty, so it is comparably reliable. After the Tang regime was established, it was not effectively controlling some countries of the Western Regions until it destroyed the Turkic Khanates in the 30s–50s of the 7th century. Therefore, it is reasonable that the jiujiahu was not very popular in the earlier period of the Tang. The reign 開元 kaiyuan of Emperor Xuanzong 玄宗 was a period of the so-called 胡化 huhua (*foreignization*) being greatly prosperous. At that time, "the foreign music is popular in the imperial court. The eminences are fond of foreign foods; the ladies like foreign costume very much."[20]

---

[20] Cf. *Jiutangshu* 舊唐書, fasc. 45, p. 1958.

Thus, it was a normal phenomenon that during this period the jiujiahu was flourishing.

As for the reason for the jiujiahu being more prosperous than before in the middle and even late period of the Tang, it may be attributed to the rebellions of Anlushan 安祿山 and Shisiming 史思明. In order to save his regime and recover the lands occupied by the rebels, the Chinese emperor invited the Uighur troops to China. At last, by the help of the Uighurs, the Chinese government defeated and destroyed the rebels. The Uighurs became the great hero of the Chinese regime. There were a lot of Sogdians in the Uighur Khanate, and they had a major impact on the economics, politics and religions of the Uighurs. It was exactly these Sogdians who demanded that the Chinese government *open* to foreigners as much as possible. The Chinese rulers dared not disobey them. As a result, larger-scale *foreignization* 胡化 emerged in China.

A poem written by Yuanzhen 元稹 depicts the prosperous foreign culture in China after half a century of the Anlushan-Shisiming rebellion: Since the Uighur cavalry had come into China, persons wearing fur coats appeared everywhere, especially in the capital regions. Most women imitated the barbarians, wearing foreign costumes; actors and actresses sang the foreign songs and played the foreign music. The music and singing of foreign flavor were popular everywhere. In fifty years, a lot of exotic music, ornaments, costumes and foreign horsemen appeared in China.[21] Against this background, the jiujiahu was naturally more prosperous than before.

The Uighur regime began to disintegrate in the early 40s of the 9th century, when its tribes divided into several groups and migrated to different regions. As a result, the Uighurs' influence in China diminished greatly. Besides, the barriers of the Sino-foreign traffic caused by wars and the economic decline of the Tang Dynasty worked against business development. So, it was logical that the jiujiahu gradually disappeared in China since then.

2. The Spread of Exotic Music and Dance in Inland China

The Sogdians came east along the Silk Road. They not only promoted Chinese economic development but also enriched the cultural life there.

---

[21] Cf. Yuanzhen 元稹, *Faqu* 法曲, in *Quantangshi* 全唐詩, fasc. 419, p. 4617.

Colorful foreign arts were introduced into inland China. Some cultures being regarded as *Chinese Quintessence* by modern people were in fact *foreign or barbarian cultures* originating from abroad in ancient times; they involve music, dance, musical instruments, magic and acrobatics. The Sogdians played an important role in these cultural communications.

(1) The spread and evolution of Pipa

Modern people often associate the "National Musical Instruments" of China with the pipa 琵琶, zither 箏, huqin 胡琴, vertical flute 簫 and drum 鼓. They are indeed the instruments commonly used in the Chinese "national music". In fact, however, just one or 2000 years ago, most of these instruments had been called "foreign music" or "foreign musical instruments" 胡樂, a typical one among them being the pipa 琵琶.

In his *Shiming* 釋名 (*Explanation of Terms*), Liuxi 劉熙 of the Han Dynasty mentioned a musical instrument called 枇杷/批把 pipa/piba, originating from the foreign countries. Generally, people played it on horseback. Plucking strings from the inside to outside was called 枇/批, while plucking strings from the outside to inside was called 杷/把.[22] This explanation may seem reasonable, but it was actually wrong, for it was well known that 枇杷/批把 probably was just the transliteration of the Sanskrit *barbhic* or Persian *barbat*, having nothing to do with the playing technique of the pipa. Just for this reason, this musical instrument could be called either 枇杷 or 批把, as well as other homophonic words in Chinese. The name 琵琶 pipa did not catch on until after the Jin 晉 Dynasty.

The pipa of the Qin 秦 Dynasty consisted of a round sound box and a long handle, with a straight neck. In the period of the Northern and Southern Dynasties, another type of pipa was introduced from the Western Regions; it was called 胡琵琶 hupipa (pipa coming from foreign countries), with a pear-form sound box, a curved neck, with four strings. Thenceforth, the pipa evolved gradually, especially making a bigger change in the later part of the Tang. The playing mode changed from holding the instrument horizontally into holding it vertically. Formerly, the player plucked the strings with a plectrum, but later he played the pipa

---

[22] Cf. Liuxi 劉熙, *Shiming* 釋名 (*Explanation of Terms*), fasc. 7, in *Sikuquanshu* 四庫全書, Taibei 臺北: The Commercial Press 商務印書館, 1986, pp. 221–415. The Chinese text is as follows: "枇杷, 本出於胡中, 馬上所鼓也。推手前曰枇, 引手卻曰把, 像其鼓時, 因以爲名也。"

with his five fingers of the right hand. The pipa finally evolved into the modern form, namely, the so-called "4 ledges and 13 frets 四相十三品" or "6 ledges and 24 frets 六相二十四品".

The cultural intercourses involving the pipa between China and foreign countries began at an early time. According to the historical records, when the princess of the Former Han married the king of Wusun 烏孫, she seemed to introduce the improved pipa and pipa music written by the Chinese government into this foreign country. Fuxuan 傅玄 wrote in his *Introduction of Pipa* 琵琶序 that in order to relieve the homesickness of the princess, Emperor Wudi 武帝 ordered the imperial musicians to compose particular pipa music for her, so as to amuse the princess on her way to the distant country of Wusun. The musical instrument they used was also called 枇杷. We do not know if this pipa was the original product from abroad or a modified one by the Chinese. In any case, the fact of the Chinese producing pipa musical compositions is indeed proof of a typical *pipa culture* interchange between China and the barbarians or foreigners.

Later, cultural exchanges like this appeared again in the intermarriage of Wangzhaojun 王昭君 and Xiongnu Chanyu. In the second half of the 1st century BC, the Chinese government took up the intermarriage policy once again for the sake of splitting the Xiongnu forces. The emperor sent Wangzhaojun, a court lady who failed to be chosen as a concubine, to marry Chanyu 單于 Huhanye 呼韓邪 of the Xiongnu 匈奴. The Han rulers also composed pipa music especially for Wangzhojun, just like they did when the Princess Xijun 細君 intermarried the king of Wusun 烏孫. Since then, the image of her leaving China with the pipa became the literary and painting theme passed down through the years.

During the period of the Northern and Southern Dynasties, the imperial families of the Northern Wei 北魏, Northern Qi 北齊 and Northern Zhou 北周 all derived from the *Barbarian Tribes* 胡族 (Xianbei 鮮卑). They were fond of the so-called foreign music or barbarian music, so it was natural that the pipa was becoming more and more popular in China. Among these rulers, Emperor Houzhu 後主 (r. 565–577) of the Northern Qi was a typical example. He often summoned others to play music for amusement, sometimes playing the pipa himself. He indulged in foreign music so much that he even completely ignored state affairs. Thus, the music that he was fond of was called "music of destroying the regime" by later historians. At the same time, there were indeed also distinguished pipa players among his officials, one of them being Heshikai 和士開, probably a person coming from Sogdiana.

Generally speaking, although there were many remarkable pipa players among the Chinese, some foreigners, especially the so-called *Western Foreigners* 西胡 (such as the Sogdians) were more famous in this respect. In the Northern Qi 北齊 regime, the Sogdians outstandingly displayed their excellent performance skills on the pipa and in other foreign music. The regime Northern Qi lasted only less than thirty years. Its military force and political influence were not very powerful, but the prosperity of its *foreign music* far outweighed that of other countries.

The later historical records talked about the flourishing foreign music of the Northern Qi, and said that, when Gaocheng 高澄, the elder brother of the first emperor of the Northern Qi, was in charge of the Northern Wei's government, he was fond of foreign music, such as the vertical flute and pipa, and foreign dance. After their family established its own regime, most members of their family were keen on foreign music. In particular, since the time of Emperor Wucheng 武成 (r. 561–565), foreign music was more popular. Emperor Houzhu 後主 indulged in foreign music so much that he greatly favored these foreign musicians, and even promoted them to high office. For instance, the Sogdian musicians 康阿馱 Kangatuo, 穆叔兒 Mushuni, 曹僧奴 Caosengnu, 曹妙達 Caomiaoda, 安未若 Anweiruo, 安馬駒 Anmaju, 何海 Hehai, 何洪珍 Hehongzhen, 何朱弱 Hezhuruo and 史醜多 Shichouduo were all granted the title *Prince*. Houzhu often sang foreign songs with pipa accompaniment by himself. He also composed new music and wrote new lyrics. Besides, taking trips with these Sogdian musicians was also his favorite recreation; they sang and danced on the way as well as playing instruments on horseback.[23]

Caosengnu 曹僧奴 and Caomiaoda 曹妙達 mentioned above were distinguished pipa players. As we know, Sogdiana consisted of the so-called *Nine Clans of Zhaowu* 昭武九姓. The Country Cao 曹國 was one of them, located north of Samarkand of the present Uzbekistan. During the period of the Northern Wei 北魏, a Sogdian named Caobrahman 曹婆羅門 immigrated to Qiuzi 龜茲, the present Kuche 庫車 of the Xinjiang Autonomous Region. From a fellow townsman, he learnt the playing technique of the foreign pipa calling *Qiuzi Pipa* at that time. Later, his playing skills reached an extremely high level. Caobrahman became a professional pipa player, and taught this skill to his children. Caosengnu 曹僧奴 was son of Caobrahman, and had two daughters and two sons. All of them were good at playing the pipa. Finally, Caosengnu and his children went

---

[23] About the related descriptions, cf. *Suishu* 隋書, fasc. 14, p. 331.

to the Northern Qi, and were highly valued by Emperor Houzhu. Caosengnu was appointed as the Prince of Rinan 日南; one of his daughters married the emperor as his concubine; Caosengnu's sons, Caomiaoda 曹妙達 and his younger brother, were appointed as county princes.

Among them, Caomiaoda 曹妙達 achieved the most. The names of all three generations were transliteration or free translations from Sanskrit. The Chinese name 婆羅門 of the grandfather is of course a transliteration of the Sanskrit *Brahmā* (*Brahman*); the father's name 僧奴 is possibly a mix of the transliteration *saṃgha* and the free translation *dāsa* (slave). As for the Chinese name (曹)妙達, it would involve another name 蘇祇婆 Suzhipo. The Sanskrit word *su* means excellent and wonderful, so its free translation could be 妙, and the transliteration could be 蘇. The Sanskrit *jiva* means spirit, vitality and wisdom, so its free translation could be 達, and the transliteration could be 祇婆. Therefore, (曹)妙達 seems to be exactly 蘇祇婆 recorded in other documents; he was also a famous musician coming from the *Western Regions*.[24] I accept this viewpoint and will discuss it on this basis.

In 568, Caomiaoda 曹妙達 followed the Turk Queen, who was going to marry Emperor Wudi 武帝 of the Northern Zhou 北周, reaching China. Caomiaoda was good at the so-called Qiuzi Music 龜茲樂, which originated from the Indian and Persian Music, and was different from the traditional music of China. However, he was not given enough attention by the rulers, thus he soon went to the Northern Qi. His specialty in foreign music was exactly in keeping with the hobby of Emperor Houzhu, so he was given the title *Prince*. After the Northern Qi was destroyed by the Northern Zhou in 577, Caomiaoda went to the Northern Zhou as a musician in 579. Both he and another famous musician Wanbaochang 万寶常 were followers of Zhengyi 鄭譯, and Zhengyi was the confidant of Yangjian 楊堅, the most powerful official in the imperial court.

Yangjian established his own regime Sui 隋 in 581. As a follower of Zhengyi, Caomiaoda also became an official of the Sui. In the next year, Emperor Wendi 文帝 of the Sui ordered his officials to develop a new music system for the new dynasty. According to the suggestion of Caomiaoda, Zhengyi offered a new music system. However, the emperor and many conservative traditionalists had a great prejudice against foreign

---

[24] About the discussion of 曹妙達 and 蘇祇婆 being the same person, cf. Yangxianyi 楊憲益, *A Supposition on the Identity of Suzhipo* 關於蘇祇婆身世的一個假設, in his *Yiyuoushi* 譯餘偶拾, The Joint Publishing Company 三聯書店, Beijing, 1983, pp. 26–38.

music, and they stated that such music was not orthodox and even had an *inauspicious sound*. Thus, the foreign music proposed by Caomiaoda was not accepted by the government.

Unfortunately, these traditionalists were not able to offer any appropriate reform program of music except to blame others. Several years later, the emperor finally could not stand such a condition, threatening to punish them. In this case, Caomiaoda was again valued, and was appointed as a supervisor of the Imperial Music Department. Although the so-called *Seven Musical Scales* passed on to Zhengyi by Caomiaoda had not been adopted and advertised by the government, this foreign music was becoming more and more popular among the common people. At last, the Chinese traditional *Five Musical Scales* was reformed.

The distinguished pipa playing technique of Caomiaoda and his family, as well as his descendants, had a great impact on the music of the Sui and Tang Dynasties. In the later part of the 8th century, Caobaobao 曹保保, his son Caoshancai 曹善才 and his grandson Caogang 曹綱 all became first-rate pipa players of their own time. Peixingnu 裴興奴, a contemporary of Caogang coming from Kashgar, was also good at playing the pipa. Caogang was skilled in plucking with the right hand, while Peixingnu was expert in playing with the left hand. Therefore, such a sentence was circulated at that time: "Caogang has right hand, Xingnu has left hand."

Lianjiao 廉郊 was an excellent disciple of Caogang. He once spent the night in a villa. He enjoyed the beautiful night scene of a gentle breeze and bright moonlight, playing the pipa with a tone of Ruibin 蕤賓 by the pond. Suddenly, there was a sound of fish jumping from the water. This sound disappeared when Lianjiao played other musical tones, but appeared again while he played the tone of Ruibin. Then, he deliberately played hard; after a short while, an object jumped out of the water, falling on the ground. It was a piece of Ruibin Iron 蕤賓鐵! This phenomenon made Lianjiao realize that because his playing technique was wonderful, the pipa musical tone of Ruibin had telepathizes with the things of its own kind. Although this story is rather mysterious, it indeed reflects the distinguished pipa playing skill of Lianjiao. At the same time, it could be inferred that Lianjiao's teacher Caogang was probably a better player of the pipa.

Because of the marvelous pipa playing technique of the Cao clan, many poets of the Tang wrote poems on this topic that were prevalent for thousands of years. For example, the famous poet Baijuyi 白居易 wrote poems such as *Listen to the Pipa Music Playing by Caogang* and *Pipa Disciple Thanks Female Teacher Caogongfeng* 曹供奉. In addition, there were the poems *Mourn for Caoshancai* 曹善才 written by Lishen 李紳, *Listen to the Pipa Music Playing by Caogang* written by Xuefeng 薛逢 and *Caogang* 曹剛 written by Liuyuxi 劉禹錫. Here, 曹剛 Caogang was, namely, 曹綱 Caogang; 曹供奉 Caogongfeng was a woman who taught the pipa playing technique, and was obviously also a member of the Cao clan.

During the Tang period, many Sogdians were famous for their excellent skills on the pipa, one of them being Kangkunlun 康昆侖. His name shows clearly that he came from Kang Country, namely, Sogdiana of Central Asia. *Miscellanea of Music Bureau* 樂府雜錄 and some other literatures mentioned the story of Kangkunlun. In his childhood, Kangkunlun learnt the pipa technique from a female neighbor; the latter was a native of the Western Regions, and believed in a certain religion. Later, Kangkunlun went to China by sea, soon becoming a follower of Yuanbohe 元伯和, the eldest son of a powerful high official Yuanzai 元載. At that time, there was an excellent Chinese pipa player Duanshanben 段善本; Kangkunlun learnt about him, and was eager to get the music score *Western Liangzhou* 西梁州 composited by Duanshanben himself, but failed to do so. However, an official of Fujian Province presented this music score to him for the sake of pleasing Yuanbohe. As a result, this admirable music score was handed down. Although both Yuanzai and Yuanbohe were put to death by Emperor Daizong 代宗 late in his reign, Kangkunlun still got the favor of the emperor because of his distinguished skill of pipa playing. When Weiyingwu 韋應物, the governor of Suzhou 蘇州, got Kangkunlun's lost pipa, he specially sent the pipa to the capital in order to show the emperor his friendship for Kangkunlun.

In the reign of Zhenyuan 貞元 (785–804) of Dezong 德宗, Kangkunlun once competed to prove his pipa playing skills with the Chinese player Duanshanben 段善本. In that year, the capital Changan 長安 suffered a severe drought. The emperor ordered people to hold governmental and civilian ceremonies praying for rain. One program of this ceremony was a *Music Competition* 鬥樂, in which each side of the two teams chose a master to compete for their pipa playing skills. The competitive stages were set in Tianmen Street 天門街, with one lofty pavilion located east of the street and the other west of it.

Kangkunlun went up the east storied pavilion first, and the musical composition *Lüyao* 綠要 played by him won full acclaim. All his supporters believed he would win the game. Then, a beautiful girl holding a pipa appeared in the west pavilion, and she also played the music *Lüyao*. All the spectators were shocked by her marvelous playing skills, and they burst into thunderous applause. Kangkunlun himself was also deeply moved, and hence eager to learn from her. He immediately went to the west pavilion and sincerely expressed his willingness to treat her as a teacher. Instead of meeting Kangkunlun soon, this girl entered the inner chamber first to change her clothes. When she reappeared in public, she was dressed as a man. It turns out that it was a man, the top pipa player Duanshanben 段善本 of China; he was invited by the team of the west pavilion to wound the pride of the east team.

Next day, both Kangkunlun and Duanshanben were summoned by the emperor, and they played the pipa in front of him. Finally, according to the emperor's judgment, Duanshanben excelled over Kangkunlun in pipa playing skill. Accepting the emperor's suggestion, Duanshanben and Kangkunlun learnt much from each other on the pipa playing technique. Thereafter, the foreign music including pipa culture was more popular all over China.

Although this story is rather legendary, it displays a historical background that in the Tang Dynasty the Sogdians had good pipa playing skills and there were frequent musical communications between the Chinese and foreigners.

(2) The Foreign or Barbarian Music and Dance in China
It is well known that for the sake of allying with many foreign countries, resisting against the Xiongnu 匈奴, Emperor Wudi 武帝 of the Han dispatched Zhangqian 張騫 to the Western Regions, initiating the earliest Sino-Foreign exchanges on a large scale. As a result, a lot of colorful material cultures and spiritual civilizations were introduced into China. Among them, the so-called Foreign Music 胡樂 was one of the famous cultures, spreading soon all over China. A musical instrument called 橫吹 hengchui (horizontal blowing), namely fife, was ascribed to Zhangqian's introduction. According to 古今樂錄 *Gujinyuelu* (*Records of the Ancient and Modern Music*), hengchui was a kind of foreign musical instrument, and Zhangqian introduced this instrument and its playing technique into the capital Changan 長安 at an early time. Only a single musical composition relating to this instrument existed, titled 摩訶兜勒 *Mohedoule*. Later, Liyannian 李延年 developed this composition, and listed it as a kind of martial music. Down to the period of the Later Han, the fife and martial

music were generally played only by the generals and soldiers of the bordering garrison; there were some scores of the fife music, such as 黃鵠 *huanghu* (*Yellow Swan*), 隴頭 *Longtou* (*Frontier Fortress*), 出關 *Chuguan* (*Exiting Pass*), 入關 *Ruguan* (*Entering Pass*), 出塞 *Chusai* (*Exiting the Frontier*) and 入塞 *Rusai* (*Entering the Frontier*).

With the development of Sino-Foreign exchanges, foreign music was increasingly introduced into China. This spread, however, was not always smooth on account of the Chinese traditional ideology. Confucianism believed that music was the expression of ethics and morality; only the true educated person comprehended music. Besides, music was divided into the righteous one and the evil one; the righteous music leads to a peaceful regime and prosperous society, while the evil one leads to a decaying world. Therefore, music was the essential element of a person's character and politics.

In view of such ideas, Emperor Lingdi 靈帝 (r. 168–189) of the Later Han was condemned for his hobby of foreign music and wares. According to the *Houhanshu* 後漢書, Lingdi was particularly interested in things from outside, such as foreign costumes, foreign tents, foreign beds, foreign foods, foreign konghou 箜篌 (a plucked stringed instrument), foreign flute and foreign dances. All these things were indispensable enjoyments in his daily life. Since the monarch set an example, the officials and nobles were racing to imitate; soon afterward, this trend of *Foreignization* 胡化 prevailed among the populace. This phenomenon was regarded as an omen of the rebellion soon launched by Dongzhuo 董卓, who led the barbarian troops, plundered the palace and disturbed the whole society.[25]

Whether this trend of *Foreignization* was indeed an ill omen is unknown, but it was a distinct fact that in the late period of the Han, the so-called *Foreignization* was very popular. Emperor Lingdi's favorite *foreign flute* 胡笛 as mentioned above was the horizontal flute 橫笛 introduced at least as early as the time of Zhangqian 張騫. The konghou 箜篌 is said to been invented in the reign of Emperor Wudi 武帝; it was played by plucking seven strings, just like playing the pipa. The so-called *Foreign Konghou* 胡箜篌 was also named *Vertical Konghou* 豎箜篌, because it was played in an erect state. This musical instrument had 22 strings, and had to be played with both hands. Wuzimu 吳自牧 of the Song Dynasty concretely depicted it: The vertical konghou is about three feet tall, and is shaped like half of a comb. It has a pedestal and 25 strings;

---

[25] Cf. *Houhanshu* 後漢書, "*Wuxingzhi* 五行志", p. 3272.

the player has to kneel and play it.²⁶ Obviously, it was very much like the harp of ancient West Asia; in fact, the *foreign konghou* 胡箜篌 was probably the harp derived from Persia.

The ruling clans of the Northern Dynasties were all foreigners or barbarians, so it was natural that their rulers, such as Emperor Houzhu 後主 of the Northern Qi, were fond of and even indulged in foreign music. Foreign music flourished much in the Sui Dynasty. The *Music Annal* 音樂志 of the Sui Dynasty recorded that at the beginning of the Sui, the government set up seven kinds of music including *Korean Artistry* 高麗伎, *Indian Artistry* 天竺伎, *An Country Artistry* 安國伎 and *Qiuzi Artistry* 龜茲伎. In addition, musical compositions originating from Vietnam, Sogdiana, Turks and Japan were involved. The nine kinds of music instituted during the period of Yangdi 煬帝 included the musical compositions of *Western Liang* 西涼, *Qiuzi* 龜茲, *India* 天竺, *Kang Country* 康國, *Kashgar* 疏勒, *An Country* 安國 and *Karea* 高麗. Evidently, there were a lot of foreign elements in the official music of the Sui regime. From Korea and Japan in the east to India and Sogdiana in the west, as well as the Indochina Peninsula in the south, almost all of Asia's musical features were integrated into Chinese music.

It is well known that the rulers of the Tang regime were very open to foreigners/barbarians and their cultures, hence the foreign music was popular all over China during this period. The *Foreignization* 胡化 of the Tang was a progressive development. It began in the early Tang Dynasty, and flourished during the reign of Emperor Xuanzong 玄宗. After the rebellion of Anlushan 安祿山 and Shisiming 史思明 (755–763), the popularity of foreign cultures seemed to be at a peak.

Taking costumes as an example, such a trend was displayed clearly. During the period of the reign of Wude 武德 (618–626) and the reign of Zhenguan 貞觀 (626–649), when the court ladies rode outside the palace, they had to wear a full-length gown to cover their faces and bodies, just like people did in the Northern Dynasties, Southern Dynasties and Sui Dynasty. Women of noble and official families followed the same rule. After the reign of Yonghui 永徽 (650–655), they only covered their face with a special hat instead of covering the whole body with a gown; a veil hanging from the hat could cover the face, but did not necessarily cover the neck. Though the emperor once prohibited wearing such a hat, this

---

[26] Cf. Wuzimu 吳子牧, *Menglianglu* 夢梁錄, fasc. 3, in *Sikuquanshu* 四庫全書, Taibei 臺北: The Commercial Press 商務印書館, 1986, pp. 590–527.

rule was not fully adhered to. Later, in 671, Emperor Gaozong 高宗 issued a ban once again, and women were forbidden from wearing the hat with a veil and riding in an open sedan chair.

However, after the reign of Wuzetian 武則天 (684–704), the hat with the veil was greatly popular, and almost no one wore covering robes any more. Since the reign of Zhongzong 中宗 (705–709), the court rules and regulations were becoming more relaxed, and neither the court ladies nor the female populace would wear the gowns covering the whole body. In the early reign of Kaiyuan 開元 (713–741), the court ladies riding horses all wore a *foreign cap* 胡帽, and their faces were completely uncovered. Accordingly, the populace imitated them successively. Soon afterward, the Chinese women stopped wearing caps, and they even clothed themselves in manly dresses. The foreign or barbarian costume became a fashion.[27]

At the same time, the foreign music accepted by the government was growing gradually; foreign foods were becoming more and more popular; and foreign costumes were more fashionable among both men and women. After the rebellion of Anlushan and Shisiming late in the reign of Tianbao (742–755), such a *Foreignization* phenomenon reached the most prosperous stage.

As mentioned above, the famous poet Yuanzhen 元稹 of the Tang depicted the flourishing foreign cultures among the Chinese in the early 9th century. He wrote that Emperor Xuanzong 玄宗 (r. 712–756) was fond of foreign music and dance, and thus many foreign cultural elements were integrated into traditional Chinese culture. However, the most prosperous era of *Foreignization* came decades later: Since the Uighur cavalry had come into China, people wearing fur coats appeared everywhere, especially in the capital regions. Most women imitated the barbarians, wearing foreign costumes; actors and actresses sang the foreign songs and played the foreign music. Music and singing of foreign flavor were popular everywhere. In fifty years, a lot of exotic music, ornaments, costumes and foreign horsemen appeared in China.[28] Obviously, the poet attempted to

---

[27] Cf. Liusu 劉肅, *Datangxinyu* 大唐新語 (*A New Narration of the Great Tang*), fasc. 10, punctuated and proofread by Xudenan 許德楠, Lidingxia 李鼎霞, Zhonghua Book Company 中華書局, 1984, p. 151.

[28] Cf. Yuanzhen 元稹, *Faqu* 法曲, in *The General Anthology of Tang Poetry* 全唐詩, fasc. 419, p. 4617. The Chinese text of this poem is as follows: "明皇度曲多新態, 宛轉侵淫多沉著。赤白桃李取花名, 霓裳羽衣號天落。雅弄雖云已變亂, 夷音未得相參錯。自

express the idea that because of the barbarians participating in the Chinese civil war, the so-called *Foreignization* was greatly promoted in China.

Although this opinion is debatable, the prosperous foreignization of that time is a reality. In addition, this phenomenon was closely related to the rulers' enthusiasm and hobby; they promoted such foreign or barbarian cultures intentionally or unintentionally. As mentioned above, the popularity of foreign costumes of the women throughout the country began with the clothing of the ladies in the imperial palace; only after the foreign/barbarian music was listed in the statutory musical institution did it become more and more beloved among the populace; in a like manner, because the monarchs were keen on the foreign dance, it flourished in China.

Anlushan's father was a Sogdian native (An 安 is one of the nine surnames of Zhaowu 昭武 clan) and his mother was a Turk, so he was a typical *hybrid foreigner* 雜胡. Hence, Anlushan was good at foreign dance, and this specialty became his skill to please the emperor. According to *Jiutangshu* 舊唐書, Anlushan was fat, weighing about 150 kilograms, and normally, he had to walk with the help of someone else. However, he could dance in front of the emperor. Generally, he danced *Huxuan* 胡旋 (*Foreign Rotating Dance*), which involved the actor's characteristic rapid spin. Emperor Xuanzong was very fond of this dance, so his beloved wife Concubine Yang 楊貴妃 also learned to perform *Huxuanwu* 胡旋舞.

Xuanzong 玄宗 often enjoyed the foreign dances performed by Anlushan 安禄山. One day, Xuanzong joking to Anlushan, pointing to his fat abdomen, asked, "What is there in it? Why it is so big?" Anlushan replied immediately, "The biggest organ inside my body is the sincere heart to Your Majesty!" Apparently, Anlushan was very alert and even cunning. Xuanzong, however, was unaware of Anlushan's hidden ambition. He always favored him, giving him a lot of money and luxury residences. Besides, in Qinzhenglou 勤政樓 (Administering Pavilion), he even set up a specialized seat next to his throne for Anlushan.[29] Therefore, considerable responsibility for the rebellion led by Anlushan must be placed on Xuanzong.

從胡騎起煙塵，毛毳腥羶滿咸洛。女爲胡婦學胡妝，伎進胡音務胡樂。火鳳聲沉多咽絕，春鶯囀罷長蕭索。胡音胡騎與胡妝，五十年來競紛泊。"

[29] Cf. *Jiutangshu* 舊唐書, fasc. 200 A, p. 5368; *Xintangshu* 新唐書, fasc. 225 A, p. 6413.

The so-called *Huxuanwu* 胡旋舞 (*Foreign Rotating Dance*) was generally thought of as one of the Sogdian musical dances, namely, Music of Kang Country 康國樂. This dance was performed usually by a pair of dancers. The dancer wore a short red jacket and green silk trousers, with a white ribbon around the waist and red boots on the feet. Rapid spinning and agile movements were the main characteristics of *Huxuanwu*. It was said that some actors could even dance on a ball; no matter how his feet moved, he would not leave the ball. Whether this is true or not is unknown, but it was certain that a dancer of *Huxuanwu* must be very flexible in pace and movement. Therefore, this dance was performed mostly by women; dancing by a fat man such as Anlushan was only probably a legend or an exceptional case.

Generally speaking, the music for this dance consisted of wind music and percussion, the instruments including two flutes, two drums and cymbals. According to the poem *The Foreign Dancing Girl* 胡旋女 written by Baijuyi 白居易, this dance was also accompanied by plucked music. It depicted a girl dancing to the rhythm of the strings and drum; with her sleeves lifted high, she was spinning and fluttering rapidly, faster than the rotating wheel and whirlwind.[30] A brief and vivid depiction showed a wonderful scene.

Another foreign dance, which was also derived from Sogdiana of Central Asia, was called *Hutengwu* 胡騰舞 (*Foreign Squatting Dance*). This dance featured frequent and rapid kicking of the feet and squatting. It needed adequate physical strength, so this dance was performed commonly by men. The poems of the Tang also depicted such *Hutengwu*; for example, Liuyanshi 劉言史 wrote the following: The dancer comes from Shi Country 石國 of Sogdiana; when dancing, he swiftly and frequently squats, like a flying bird. He wears a foreign cap with a pointed top, and dresses a leather jacket with narrow sleeves. Accompanying by the horizontal flute and pipa as well as the bells of his belt, the dancer nimbly jumps, spins, squats and kicks, so that fibers of the carpet are flying and floating in the air.[31]

---

[30] Cf. Baijuyi 白居易, *Huxuannü* 胡旋女 (*The Foreign Dancing Girl*), in *The General Anthology of Tang Poetry* 全唐詩, fasc. 426, pp. 4692–4693. The Chinese text is as follows: "胡旋女，胡旋女，心應弦，手應鼓。弦鼓一聲雙袖舉，回雪飄飄轉蓬舞。左旋右旋不知疲，千匝萬周無已時。人間物類無可比，奔車輪緩旋風遲。"

[31] Cf. Liuyanshi 劉言史, *Yeguanwuhuteng* 夜觀舞胡騰 (*Enjoy the Dance Huteng in the Evening*), in *The General Anthology of Tang Poetry* 全唐詩, fasc. 468, p. 5324.

From this poem, we know that the dancer was a Sogdian; he dressed in typical foreign costume, namely, a pointed cap, tight jacket and soft boots. As for the accompanying musical instruments, they were the wind instrument horizontal flute and plucked instrument pipa. A poem written by Liduan 李端 more vividly depicted the *Hutengwu*. It said that the dancer belonged to the Iranian race, with white skin and a high nose (胡騰身是涼州兒, 肌膚如玉鼻如錐); he appeared to wear flimsy and soft clothes with long ribbons (桐布輕衫前後捲, 葡萄長帶一邊垂); his cap was decorated with pearls (紅汗交流珠帽偏); he wore soft leather boots on the feet (雙靴柔軟滿燈前); sometimes his dance actions appeared to be gentle and fragile (醉卻東傾又西倒); sometimes he rapidly rotated and kicked to the rhythm of the music (環行急蹴皆應節); the musical instruments included plucked or string ones, as well as the horns (絲桐忽奏一曲終, 嗚嗚畫角城頭發).[32]

The third kind of foreign dances were named *Zhezhiwu* 柘枝舞, it were thought to originate from Shi Country 石國 of Sogdiana, because this country was also called 柘枝/柘支 Zhezhi. According to *Yueshu* 樂書 (*Musical Book*), Zhezhi Dance was performed by two slender girls. They would dress in a colorful silk garment, with a silver belt around the waist. Their clothes would be considerably loose and thin, so the body was not well covered, often being half-naked. A feature of it was that both the dress and cap of the dancer were decorated with golden bells, which would make a pleasant sound when they danced. At the beginning of the dance, the two dancers would appear in two blooming lotuses and then dance lissomely.

Zhezhiwu prevailed in the Tang Dynasty. Although it still existed in the Northern Song Dynasty, its flavor seemed to have changed, and people were no longer very familiar with this foreign dance. Shenkuo 沈括 of the 11th century said that the famous politician Kouzhun 寇準 (961–1023) was very fond of Zhezhiwu; he often spent a lot of time watching and enjoying this dance, so he was given the nickname of *Zhezhi Fans* 柘枝顛. Several decades later, however, an old nun, who was a dancer in

---

The Chinese text is as follows: "石國胡兒人見少, 蹲舞樽前急如鳥。織成蕃帽虛頂尖, 細氎胡衫雙袖小。手中拋下葡萄盞, 西顧忽思鄉路遠。跳身轉轂寶帶鳴, 弄腳繽紛錦靴軟。四座無言皆瞪目, 橫笛、琵琶遍頭促。亂騰新毯雪朱毛, 傍拂輕花下紅燭。酒闌舞罷絲管絕, 木槿花西見殘月。"

[32] Cf. Liduan 李端, *Hutenger* 胡騰兒 (*Huteng Dancer*), in *The General Anthology of Tang Poetry* 全唐詩, fasc. 284, p. 3238.

the time of Kouzhun, told people that the movements and musical compositions of the present Zhezhiwu were far less than the dance several decades ago, being only two-tenths or three-tenths of the former.[33] Obviously, as the Sogdians faded away from the historical arena, their indigenous cultures also gradually disappeared.

---

[33] Cf. Shenkuo 沈括, *Mengxibitan* 夢溪筆談 (*Brush Talks from Dream Brook*), fasc. 5, in Wang Hong 王宏 and Zhao Zheng 趙崢 tr., *Brush Talks from Dream Brook*, in *Library of Chinese Classics* 大中華文庫, Sichuan People's Publishing House 四川人民出版社, 2008, pp. 138–139.

Chapter 9

The Influence and Domination of the Sogdians on the Nomads

For the ancient Chinese regimes, the most ferocious foreign enemies were the nomads, who generally lived north or northwest of China. They often invaded southward into Chinese border areas, plundering and killing people. Therefore, many Chinese historians were very concerned about these nomadic tribes and powers. In their writings, these nomads were either the terrible enemies of China or friendly allies; in short, they often played important roles in the politics, economics and culture of China. However, an easily overlooked fact is that a group of foreigners coming from more civilized areas were secretly supporting and manipulating these barbarian nomads. These *hidden* foreigners were the Sogdians, who had a special role in the Silk Road. Taking the Turk Khanate and Uighur Khanate as examples, this chapter will discuss the great influence and domination the Sogdians exerted upon the nomadic regimes.

1. The Sogdians and the Turk Khanate

In 552 AD, the nomadic Turks (Tujue 突厥) overthrew their suzerain Rouran 柔然, and established their own regime, with the ruling family of the Asena (Ashina 阿史那) clan. They founded a vast nomadic khanate in Central Eurasia, frequently exchanging with the Northern Zhou, Northern Qi, Sui and Tang successively, lasting more than one hundred years. It was called *The First Turk Khanate* 突厥第一汗國 by Chinese historians. During this period, the intercourses between the East and the West were more prosperous than ever, and the political situation, social and cultural environment of Central Eurasia, even the whole Eurasian Continent, changed greatly. Some modern scholars attribute this phenomenon to the Turks, who established a powerful khanate at that time. For instance, Sinor said the following:

> Even if their political power was short-lived, the eighty years during which the Türk held the key-points of Central Eurasia exercised an incalculable effect on history, because it was a period of intense interchange between different civilizations. Indeed, the interpenetration had begun before the Türk conquest. The pre-Türk mural paintings discovered in Chinese Turkestan already show the importance of Greek, Indian and Iranian influences, but under the Türk shield communications became easier and contacts more frequent. The Türk Empire linked four civilizations: Byzantium, Iran, India and China. It was more than a simple vehicle of spiritual and material exchange: it was also a mixing pot in which the elements of different origins were amalgamated and were tinted with the specific Türk civilization. It does not appear that this last influence was of particular importance, but foreign civilizations were enabled to penetrate deeply into Central Eurasia through Türk channels. It is fascinating to think that a Türk envoy who had spent several years in Constantinople might have been sent to China on his next mission, and that Buddhist monks from India or from China might have discussed religion with Greek Christians or Persian disciples of Zoroaster at the court of the Türk ruler.[1]

Denis Sinor stressed both the prosperity of world civilization exchanges and the great contribution of the Turks, but he did not mention the role played by the Sogdians in these civilized exchanges. I shall discuss this subject as follows:

(1) The Sogdians participated in the political and diplomatic affairs of the Western Turks *Zhoushu* 周書 talked about the diplomatic activities between the Western Wei and the Turks: "In the 11th year of the reign Datong 大統 (545), emperor Taizu 太祖 dispatches a mission to the Turks, which is led by Annuopantuo 安諾槃陀, a foreigner of Jiuquan

---

[1] Denis Sinor, "The Historical Role of the Turk Empire", in his *Inner Asia and its Contacts with Medieval Europe*, London: Variorum Reprints, 1977, p. 433.

酒泉. All people of their country celebrate each other and say: 'We will certainly prosper, inasmuch as the envoys of the great power come here.'"[2] This is the earliest record of Chinese sending a mission to the Turks. There are two probable why the Turks were eager to have friendly exchanges with Chinese regimes. First, because of economic considerations, they were keen to trade with China to gain various goods, especially silk. The latter could be resold to the distant western countries for high profits.[3] Second, the Turks also had political ambition. They were still ironworkers of the Rouran 柔然 at that time, and hence were anxious to get out of slavery by the help of other powerful regime.

In this situation, a friendly relationship with the Western Wei 西魏 was more significant to the Turks; it was exactly the reason for all Turks' celebrations. The envoy with the important mission of communicating the relationship between the two regimes was a Sogdian, named Annuopantuo. *An* 安 was one of the Nine Surnames of Zhaowu 昭武九姓, namely, another Chinese name for the Sogdians. Besides, 諾槃陁 Nuopantuo was a Chinese transliteration for Sogdian words. The Sogdian word *Nahid* was the famous goddess Anahita, which could be transliterated into the Chinese character 諾 nuo; the Sogdian word *βande* meant slave, servant, which could be transliterated into the Chinese characters 槃陁 pantuo.[4] Thus, the original meaning of Nuopantuo 諾槃陁 should be "Servant of Goddess Anahita", an ordinary name of the Sogdians.[5]

Obviously, Annuopantuo accomplished this mission quite successfully, because the Turk Qaghan soon sent emissaries to "present tribute" to the Western Wei the next year; in the next five or six years, the two powers intermarried with each other, and there were at least three round

---

[2] Cf. *Zhoushu* 周書, fasc. 50, Zhonghua Book Company 中華書局, 1971, p. 908.

[3] In fact, long before this, the Turks distinctly expressed such a wish, as mentioned by *Zhoushu*: "In the reign of Bumin Kaghan, the tribe becomes flourished gradually, and begins to buy silks in the Chinese border areas. They are eager to exchange with China." ("其後曰土門, 部落稍盛, 始至塞上市繒絮, 願通中國") cf. *Zhoushu* 周書, fasc. 50, p. 908.

[4] On the meaning of the two Sogdian words, cf. B. Gharib, *Sogdian Dictionary*, item 5836 (p. 234), item 2656 (p. 105), Tehran: Farhangan Publications, 1995.

[5] About this identification, cf. J. Harmatta, "Iran Turica", in *Acta Orientalia Hungaricae*, Vol. 25, 1972, p. 273.

trips of diplomatic missions between them.⁶ It is unknown whether the Sogdians continued to participate in these frequent diplomatic activities, but it is certain that the Sogdians played a very positive role in the first friendly exchange between the Turks and the Chinese regime.

Another typical example displays the important part played by the Sogdians in the complicated rivalry of the Western Turks, Persia and Byzantium more than twenty years later. Its background and process are mentioned in Chapter Two of Part One of this book, and here a brief summarization will be given as follows.

At that time, Istami, the ruler of the Western Turks, allied with Persia, defeated and destroyed the Ephthalites, thus dominating Sogdiana and many other countries of Central Asia. If the Turks further expanded the market of silk coming from China, they could gain much more profit. Therefore, some Sogdians advised Istami to open up the Persian silk market. The Qaghan adopted their recommendation, and dispatched a mission to Persia; this delegation almost entirely consisted of Sogdians, and the leader was Maniakh. Apparently, the Sogdians gained the trust of the Turk rulers, thereby participating in this important diplomatic activity.⁷

The Turks twice sent missions to Persia, but failed. On the first occasion, much silk was burnt by the Persians; on the second occasion, many members of the Turkic mission were killed with poison. Nevertheless, taking into account the overall interests, the Turks adopted the tactic of alliance with Byzantium instead of immediately retaliating against the

---

⁶During the period of several years, the diplomatic exchanges between the two regimes could be listed as follows. In 547–550, the Turks defeated the Tiele 鐵勒 tribe, but failed to intermarry with Rouran 柔然, thus becoming hostile to it. Prior to lunar March 28 in 551, the Turk Kaghan made a proposal of marriage to the emperor of the Western Wei, and was granted permission. Emperor Wendi 文帝 died in lunar March 28 in 551, and the Turkic mission came to mourn and presented 200 horses. In lunar August 16 in 551, Princess Changle 長樂公主 of the Western Wei left for the Turk Khanate to intermarry with its ruler. About the discussion on all these events, cf. Hilda Ecsedy, "Trade and War Relationship Between the Turks and China in the Second Half of the 6th Century", in *Acta Orientalia Hungaricae*, Vol. 21, 1968, pp. 154–155.

⁷About the rivalries among the Turks, Persia and Byzantium, cf. "Extracts Readings Intercourses between the Turkish Khans and the Byzantine Emperors", in Henry Yule, *Cathay and the Way Thither*, Vol. I, Munshiram Manoharlal Publishers, 1916, pp. 205–212. It includes some fragments of the *Greek History* written by Byzantine historian Menander.

Persian with martial forces. It was Maniakh, a Sogdian and the former mission leader, who offered this proposal to the Turk Qaghan.

Maniakh explained to the Qaghan that there was a wider silk market in Byzantium and other western countries, so a direct trade with them could make more profit. In addition, the alliance of the Turks and Byzantium was quite helpful for holding Persia back, as Byzantium was the great political power. Maniakh volunteered to lead the mission to Byzantium, namely, the East Roman Empire, to promote the establishment of friendly relations between the Turk Khanate and Byzantium.

This proposal was readily adopted by Istami Qaghan. Then Maniakh left for Byzantium in 567, bringing with them a letter to the Byzantine emperor by the Turk Qaghan and a large quantity of silks and many other valuable gifts. This Turk diplomatic mission went westward along the so-called *Steppe Roads*, passing through the northern coasts of the Aral Sea and Caspian Sea, then crossing southward over the Caucasus, entering the territory of Byzantium. When they arrived at the destination in early 568, they were warmly received by the Byzantine emperor.

According to the historical record, the Qaghan's letter to the emperor "is written in Scythian". Many modern scholars tend to think this dialect was likely to be Sogdian. It showed that the Sogdians not only led the nomads into the international political struggle but also promoted cultural exchanges among various regions of the Eurasia Continent.

For the next decade, there were frequent diplomatic communications between the Turk Khanate and Byzantium. As for the Byzantine mission leaders who left their names in historical records, there were Zemarchus, Anankhast, Eutychius, Herodian, Paul, Valentin, etc. Some of them were dispatched to the Turk Khanate more than once.

Naturally, many Turks also went to Byzantium. The son of Maniakh was appointed as one of the Turkic envoys. According to Menander, Maniakh died around in 568 or 569, and his successor was Tagma, who had an official title of *Tarkhan*. The son of Maniakh was one of the mission chiefs, and was second only to Tagma in power and position; this apparently had to do with his father's great feats for the Turk Khanate.

The Turkic–Byzantium *Strategic Partnership* schemed by the Sogdians had a significant impact on the political situation of Central Asia and West Asia in the second half of the 6th century. It restrained the Sasanian Persians from further expansion, or at least brought the three powers of the Western Turks, Persia and Byzantium to a certain balance. More importantly, along with the frequent intercourses between the Turks and Romans, many other nomadic tribes along the Steppe Roads also enthusiastically participated in the cultural exchanges between the East and West, thereby promoting the development of world civilizations. It is just from this era that the Byzantine historians received rich records about the Far East; it was not until more than 600 years later that the Greek and Latin writings relating to the Orient gradually increased again.

(2) Influences of the Sogdians on the East Turk Khanate
The Sogdians not only actively participated in the political and diplomatic affairs of the western Turks but also had a great impact on the eastern Turks who took the Mongolian Plateau as the core base.

At the end of the Sui Dynasty, all factions tried to fight for power, and the whole of China was in turmoil. Liyuan 李淵, a warlord occupying Shanxi 山西 province, titled as Duke Tang 唐公, attempted to seize the power of the Sui regime with the help of Turk forces. He humbly sent a letter to Shadpit Qaghan 始畢可汗, offering to trade and ally with the Turks. The Qaghan thought this proposal would benefit the Turks, and so accepted it and sent a mission led by a high-ranking official Kangshaoli 康鞘利 to China. A force of cavalry came along with this Sogdian[8], intending to boost the morale of Liyuan. In addition, Kangshaoli sold thousands of horses to Duke Tang, satisfying him greatly.[9]

It seemed that the Sogdians influenced and manipulated the Turk rulers more and more. For example, in the reign of Shadpit Qaghan (609–619), Peiju 裴矩 distinctly told Emperor Yangdi 煬帝 of the Sui 隋 that because of the instigation of the Sogdians, the Turks always hated and harassed China. Hence, it was better to kill the leaders of the Sogdians. A detailed description on this matter is given in *Suishu* 隋書:

---

[8] Cenzhongmian 岑仲勉 believes Kangshaoli is a Sogdian native for the reason that the ancient pronunciation of Chinese characters 鞘利 is *sau li*, which is almost same as *su li* 窣利; while the latter is also a transliteration of Soghd/Sogdiana, just like 粟特. Cf. Cenzhoongmian 岑仲勉, *Tujuejishi* 突厥集史 (*A Comprehensive History of the Turks*), Zhonghua Book Company 中華書局, 1958, p. 111.

[9] About the detailed descriptions on the alliance of Liyuan and the Turks before the establishment of the Tang Dynasty and the important part played by Kangshaoli in the intercourses between the Chinese and Turks, cf. Wundaya 溫大雅, *Datangchuangyeqijuzhu* 大唐創業起居注 (*Records of the Tang Dynastic Founder's Daily Activities*), punctuated and proofread by Lijiping 李季平 and Lixihou 李錫厚, Shanghai Classics Publishing House 上海古籍出版社, 1983, pp. 8–14, 30.

Peiju says to the emperor: "The Turks are originally honest, apt to be deceived, but the Sogdians among them are very cunning, instigate the Turks to be evil. I heard that the particular sly one is Shishuhuxi 史蜀胡悉, the favored official of the Qaghan. Therefore, he must be killed." The emperor agrees with this plot. Then Peiju sends to Shishuhuxi, lies: "The emperor furnishes a large quantity of valuable goods in the town Mayi 馬邑, wants to trade with foreigners. People go there would certainly benefit much." Shishuhuxi is very greedy, so he immediately rushes to Mayi, bringing with his tribe members and a lot of cattle. He does not inform the Qaghan, because he tries to make the most profit by trading with the Chinese as soon as possible. Peiju lays an ambush at the city gate, kill Shishuhuxi easily. Thereupon, emperor Yangdi sends a letter to the Turk Qaghan, saying, "Shishuhuxi suddenly comes to Mayi, claims that he will betray the Qaghan, requests my acceptance. But I think you are my real subject, I do not permit anyone to betray you. Thus, I execute him, and acquaint you with the fact." However, Shadpit learns the truth, so he no longer pays tribute to the Sui Dynasty.[10]

This passage reveals at least two facts. First, in order to change the bad situation for itself, the Sui government did everything to destroy the Sogdians' impact on the Turks, even by means of murder. This fact shows clearly the important and critical role played by the Sogdians in the political affairs of the Turk Khanate. Second, it was the whole *tribe* rather than some members of the tribe that followed Shishuhuxi to Mayi. Obviously, there were numerous Sogdians inside the Turk Khanate, thereby their power and influence were surely great.

El 頡利 Qaghan (r. 620–630) was the successor of Shadpit 始畢 and the last ruler of the East Turk Khanate. During his reign, the Sogdians were so influential in the political affairs that they were almost out of control. According to *Jiutangshu* 舊唐書, "El Qaghan often entrusts important tasks to the Sogdians, but has little faith in his own people. These foreigners 胡人 are very greedy and cunning, thereby lead to frequent violations of the law and even armed disturbances. The Turks are very disgusted with them, many tribes are no longer completely loyal to the Qaghan."[11]

---

[10] Cf. *Suishu* 隋書, fasc. 67, Zhonghua Book Company 中華書局, 1973, p. 1582.
[11] Cf. *Jiutangshu* 舊唐書, fasc. 194A, Zhonghua Book Company 中華書局, 1975, p. 5159.

In the passage above, the Chinese character 胡 refers exclusively to the Sogdians, though in other records it may also mean the barbarians of other ethnic groups. In 630, the Chinese forces led by Lijing 李靖 suddenly attacked the Turks, and El Qaghan hurriedly ran away. After that, the Sogdian chief Kangsumi 康蘇密 brought Queen Xiao 蕭后 of the Sui and Yangzhengdao 楊正道 together to surrender. Both Queen Xiao and Yangzhengdao were members of the imperial family of the Sui 隋, and were the opponents or enemies of the Tang 唐. Evidently, they were given to the Tang government as captives. This showed that Kangsumi and other Sogdians had considerable power in the Turk regime.

There were some 胡部 hubu (the Foreign Tribe) in the East Turk Khanate; these *hubu* were the Sogdian communities. These *hubu* did not disappear with the collapse of the East Turk Khanate; on the contrary, they continued the development of their communities; their settlements flourished even more than before.

First, after the Tang government destroyed the East Turk regime, the Chinese rulers had a heated debate on how to settle the Turks who surrendered to the Tang. Eventually, the proposal offered by Prime Minister Wenyanbo 溫彥博 was adopted. Five autonomous prefectures were set up along the line from Youzhou 幽州 to Lingzhou 靈州, including Shunzhou 順州, Beifuzhou 北撫州, Beikaizhou 北開州, Beiningzhou 北寧州 and Beianzhou 北安州. All of these towns were for the inhabitants of the former East Turk Khanate. Among them, two prefectures were for the Sogdians; the Sogdian chief Kangsumi 康蘇密 was appointed as the governor of Beianzhou, while Shishanying 史善應 was designated the governor of Beifuzhou. Actually, there were numerous Sogdian immigrants in North China.

Second, nearly forty years later, the Tang government set up the so-called *Six Foreign Prefectures* 六胡州 in the region of the Great Bend of the Yellow River, for the Sogdian immigrants to live in. According to *Jiutangshu* 舊唐書, in 679, Luzhou 魯州, Lizhou 麗州, Hanzhou 含州, Saizhou 塞州, Yizhou 依州 and Qizhou 契州 were set up in the southern part of Lingzhou 靈州 and Xiazhou 夏州 for the people who had surrendered to China; it was named Liuhuzhou 六胡州 (*Six Foreign Prefectures*) and was governed by Chinese officials.[12]

---

[12] *Ibid.*

The geographic scope of the Liuhuzhou was about the equivalent of the northeastern part of present Etuoke Banner 鄂托克旗 and Etuoke Front Banner 鄂托克前旗 of the Inner Mongolia, the regions west of Uxin Banner as well as the northern part of Yanchi county 鹽池縣 of Ningxia 寧夏. At that time the administrating principle for the foreign tribes remained the same as that of the beginning of the Tang, such as "maintenance of the entire tribe", "keeping their traditional customs" and "settling in sparsely populated areas".[13] Therefore, the Sogdians appeared to still live in the form of organized tribes or communities; they occupied vast regions, and had a considerable military force, financial resources and .political influence.

Third, in the 8th century, during the reign of Emperor Xuanzong 玄宗, the Sogdians in Liuhuzhou held a large rebellion, forcing the Tang government to send a powerful army to suppress it. In lunar April 721, Kangdaibin 康待賓 claimed himself to be *Yabghu* 葉護, launching an armed uprising against the Tang court. Some other Sogdian chiefs participated in this rebellion, such as *Yabghu* Anmurong 安慕容, "Great General" or "General" Heheinu 何黑奴, Shishennu 石神奴 and Kangtietou 康鐵頭. They led troops of 70000, soon occupying Changquan 長泉 count, capturing Liuhuzhou and approaching Xiazhou 夏州. The emperor hastily appointed Wangjun 王晙 and other officials to lead the resistance and counterattack. It was only in lunar July of that year that the governmental army finally defeated the rebels. Kangdaibin was captured alive, and the Sogdian cavalrymen numbering 35000 were killed.[14]

In next lunar September, Kangyuanzi 康願子, a remnant partner of Kangdaibin, claimed himself as Qaghan and rebelled again. Not long after, he was suppressed by defense minister Zhangyue 張說. In consideration of their powerful strength and disloyalty, the Tang government removed more than 50000 Sogdians from Liuhuzhou, forcing them to live scattered in Xuzhou 許州, Ruzhou 汝州, Tangzhou 唐州, Dengzhou 鄧州, Xianzhou 仙州 and Yuzhou 豫州.[15] Nevertheless, as a complete unit, the Sogdians continued to exercise a great impact on the nomads of Central Eurasia.

---

[13] Cf. *Xintangshu* 新唐書, fasc. 37, pp. 974–975.
[14] Cf. *Jiutangshu* 舊唐書, fasc. 8, p. 182; *Zizhitongjian* 資治通鑑, fasc. 212, pp. 6745–6746.
[15] Cf. *Zizhitongjian* 資治通鑑, fasc. 212, p. 6752.

2. The Sogdians and the Uighur Khanate

In the third century, Manicheism was founded in Persia; later it survived and developed in Central Asia, and was spread by the Sogdians to the East, including the Mongolian Plateau and China proper. This opinion had already been accepted by the academic circle. Therefore, the fact that Manicheism was popular among the nomadic Uighurs, and eventually became the *State Religion* of the powerful Uighur Khanate, is strong evidence to prove that the Sogdians had a great influence on the Uighur regime. I will discuss this example as follows.

There was only little information involving the Manichean faith of the Uighur rulers; a majority of the records about this fact are seen in Turkic fragment TM 276a and 276b, which were unearthed in Turpan, titled *A Record on Bögü Khan's Conversion to Manicheism* 牟羽可汗入教記. The writer described the Uighur Qaghan Bögü's conversion to Manicheism, and his proclamation of the faith as the official state religion in 762/763. Although this text is somewhat legendary and exaggerated, a number of valuable historical facts are still included. In order to conveniently discuss, I will give a quotation of the English translation of Klimkeit as follows, refer to the German translation of Bang and Von Gabain.[16]

(1) *A Record on Bögü Khan's Conversion to Manicheism*
The Qaγan said: "I am Tängri, I will go to the Realm of the Gods together with you."

The elect[17] gave this answer: "We are holy, we are elect. We execute God's commands perfectly. When we die, we will go to the Realm of the Gods, because we fulfill God's commandment to the word ... and because we have borne great oppression and grave dangers. Therefore, we shall reach the Realm of the Gods. Your Majesty, if you yourself trespass against the Law of the Eternal One, your whole kingdom will fall into

---

[16] Cf. Hans Joachim Klimkeit, *Gnosis on the Silk Road: Gnostic texts from Central Asia*, New York, 1993, pp. 364–370; Bang and Von Gabain, *Türkische Turfan-Texte II*, SPAW, Juli 1929, pp. 411–422.

[17] The Turkic word *dïndar/dïntar* derives from the Sogdian word *δēndār*, while the latter has the same meaning as Parthian *dyn'br* (*dēnāβar*), namely, religious, devout, righteous, believer, etc. These words are used to refer to the professional monk in Manicheism of Central Asia. In English, it is generally written as *Dēnwarā* or *Elect*.

confusion; all these Turkish people will sin against God, and wherever they find elect, they will suppress them and kill them. And if these four … holy elect who are from the land of China[18] will have to go back with their four wishes (demands?), … then great danger and oppressions will arise for the Law, that is, religion. Wherever they find auditors[19] and merchants they will kill them all, leaving not even one alive."

"In this your realm, great, meritorious deeds are being done at your command, and have already been done in this realm of yours up to the coming of the … Tarqan.[20] Your Majesty, if you yourself discharge this Tarqan, then the good laws and the good works will endure. But if the … Tarqan brings such great difficulties upon the land, evil deeds will be done and your kingdom will perish … The path on which you will have to walk from now on will have to be another one. And the divine Teacher[21] … will hear of these things (if you do not), and he will not approve of them at all."

Then the divine king and the elect discussed these things for two days and nights. On the third day the king searched himself fully … Then the mind of the divine king was troubled because he heard that this soul would never be liberated on account of that deed. Therefore he was afraid

---

[18] Apparently, the sentence "four holy elect who are from the land of China" denotes the four Manichean preachers who accompany Bögü Qaghan back to the Uighur Khanate from China in 763. The Chinese inscription of the *Monument of Uighur Qaghan Bilg ä* mentions a similar fact.

[19] The Turkic *nïyošak* derives from the Sogdian word *nγ'wšn'k*, meaning hearer auditor, audience, etc. It is also a Manichean term, used to refer to a secular believer of Manicheism. This appellation is relative to the professional monk "elect".

[20] The Turkic word *tarχan* is a high official title of the ancient nomads, seeming to derive from the title *Chanyu* of the Xiongnu's monarch. In the earlier Turkic, it probably meant the official primarily responsible for administrative matters. But, in Mongolian, the loan-word *darχan* only refers to those being tax free, even the craftsmen. Here, one or several words are missing before the *tarqan* (*tarχan*), so the lacking part may be either the name of this Tarqan or a certain adjective. Nevertheless, this *Tarqan* is surely a high-ranking representative of a powerful group which opposes the Uighurs to believe in Manicheism.

[21] The Turkic *možaj* is a loanword, equivalent to Sogdian *mwj'q*, Parthian *'mwc'g* (*ammōžāg*) and Middle Persian *hmwc'g* (*hammōžāg*). Its original meaning is "teacher". In Manicheism, however, it is the title of a high-ranking position second to Mani, the founder of Manicheism. The Turkic phrase "tngrimožag" of the text here should be translated more appropriately as "divine možag", meaning the chief of the Manichean Oriental Church.

and trembled and his mind was not at rest. Then the divine king Bögü Qaγan himself came to the assembly where the elect was; he fell down on his knees before the elect and asked for the remission of his sins, respectfully saying, "Since ... I have caused you distress ... I thought ... by hunger and thirst. By such searching I have come to a decision. May you have mercy upon me, support me in the faith and make me a chosen one. Up to now, my mind has not been firm. I do not like being in the world, or in my home at all.[22] My reign, the joys of the body, and my ... and my ... have become completely worthless in my eyes. My courage is failing and I fear ..., because you told me, 'By this kind of deed your soul will never be liberated, but rather if you come to the faith by way of the elect, and if you constantly do good works ...' If you elect so desire, I will walk in accordance with your words and your counsel. For you have said to me: 'Try to regain courage, Your Majesty, and give up sin.'"

At that time, when the divine King Bögü Qaγan had spoken thus, we elect and all the people in the realm were filled with great joy. We cannot fully express this joy of ours. Then they told each other what had happened over and over again and were glad. Crowds of thousands and ten thousand came together and came to ..., engaging in many kinds of sports. Up to the morning they rejoiced greatly, and many were the joys in which they were glad ... And when the new day dawned, it was the time of the Minor Fast.[23] The divine King Bögü Qaγan and all the elect in his entourage mounted their horses, and all the great princes and princesses and high officials and the leading nobles, the great and the small, that is, all the people, proceeded to the gate of the city in great joy and festivity. Then the divine king entered into the city, put the crown on his head, clothed himself with his ... red robe and sat down on his gilded throne. Then he issued an order to the nobility as well as for the common people, saying: "Now you all ... bright ... be happy, especially you elect ...; having calmed my mind, I entrust myself to you again. I have come anew, and have seated myself on my throne. I command you: When the elect admonish you, and when they urge you

---

[22] According to Manichean doctrine, this secular world is a prison for the *Light Elements*, i.e., the soul, so every believer must do his best to get rid of the fetter of world, returning back to the *Light World*.

[23] The Turkic *kičig* means "minor", *bačaγ* means "fast", so the phrase *kičig bačaγ* is translated as Minor Fast, but the exact meaning is unknown. It can only be discussed later.

to partake of the sacred meal,[24] and when they urge you to ... and admonish you, act in accordance with their words and admonitions. And in love show ... your respect."

When the divine Bögü Qaγan had issued this order, the many crowds and the common people paid homage to the divine king and rejoiced in his presence. And also to us, the elect, they paid homage and expressed their joy. Everyone ... was full of joy. For a second time, anew, the loved God ... and believed in Him. Then they unceasingly did "soul service" (gave alms) and performed good works. And the fortunate king constantly exhorted all the people to do good works, and he urged them to do so continually. Furthermore, the divine king decreed and issued this law: For every ten men, one man is to be appointed as their head, and shall be made their *tavratyučï* (one who encourages them) with respect to good works and the performance of "soul service". And if anybody grew slack in the religion and fell into sin, he gave him ... good instruction ...

(2) Information Revealed by this Record

To sum up, the main ideas of TM 276 were the negotiation process between the Manichean church of the Uighur Khanate and the Uighur ruler Bögü Qaghan. The Manicheans, dominated by the Sogdians, urged the Qaghan to protect Manicheism, even convert to Manicheism himself. After carefully examination, some facts relative to the Sogdians/Manicheans could be found in this file.

First, the spread of Manicheism in Uighur Khanate experienced considerable twists and turns. What the Elects said to the Qaghan shows this fact. "We are elect. We execute God's commands perfectly" — this sentence shows that at that time Manicheism was already popular with the Uighurs. But, the Manicheans suffered a strike from a group led by a certain Tarqan: "In this your realm, great, meritorious deeds are being done at your command, and have already been done in this realm of yours up to the coming of the ... Tarqan" and "If the ... Tarqan brings such great

---

[24] The Turkic phrase *üzüt ašï* was translated as the German *Seelen Mahle* by Bang and Von Gabain, meaning Soul Meal, while Klimkeit translated it into the English *Sacred Meal*. In my opinion, the former was more precise, because the light elements or souls were believed to be imprisoned in foods, especially fruits and other plants; Manicheans must eat these foods to liberate them and lead them back to their home, the Light Lands. Compared with this teaching, the term Sacred Meal was only a Christian concept, seemingly not suitable to be used here.

difficulties upon the land, evil deeds will be done and your kingdom will perish." However, the Qaghan seems unconcerned about the disaster of opposing the Manicheism, as showed in this sentence: "Your Majesty, if you yourself trespass against the Law of the Eternal One, your whole kingdom will fall into confusion; all these Turkish people will sin against God, and wherever they find elect, they will suppress them and kill them." In addition, Bögü Qaghan himself seemed to have once given up on Manicheism: "Since ... I have caused you distress."

Under strong pressure from the Manichean church, Bögü Qaghan had a long negotiation with the Manicheans, and in the end promised to protect them, as shown in this sentence: "Then the divine king and the elect discussed these things for two days and nights. On the third day the king searched himself fully." Finally, the Qaghan issued an edict, distinctly declaring that all his people and himself will convert to Manicheism: "having calmed my mind, I entrust myself to you again. I have come anew, and have seated myself on my throne. I command you: When the elect admonish you, and when they urge you to partake of the sacred meal, and when they urge you to ... and admonish you, act in accordance with their words and admonitions. And in love show ... your respect."

Second, it was under the pressure of the church that the Qaghan believed in Manicheism. As cited above, the Elects exhorted the Qaghan in the name of God, stating, "if you yourself trespass against the Law of the Eternal One, your whole kingdom will fall into confusion." But, the greatest threat is seen in this sentence: "And the divine Teacher (možag)[25] ... will hear of these things, and he will not approve of them at all." Since the *možag* was the leader of Manichean Oriental Church, he had enough power to make trouble for the Qaghan. That is to say, if Bögü Qaghan did not accept the Elects' demand, he could be hit hard militarily, politically and economically. It was possibly the real cause of the Qaghan's conversion to Manicheism.

Third, Manicheism had been popular among Uighur populace for quite some time. According to the document TM 276, the sentence

---

[25] The Turkic *možag* was a loanword, equivalent to Sogdian *mwj'q*, Parthian *'mwc'g* (*ammōžāg*) and Middle Persian *hmwc'g* (*hammōžāg*). Its original meaning was "teacher". In Manicheism, however, it was the title of a high-ranking position second to Mani, the founder of Manicheism. The Turkic phrase "tngrimožag" of the text here should be translated more appropriately as "divine možag", meaning the chief of the Manichean Oriental Church.

"(great, meritorious deeds) have already been done in this realm of yours up to the coming of the ... Tarqan" indicates that Manicheism had already been popular in the Uighur Khanate prior to this *Tarqan* suppressing it. Besides, when the Qaghan declared that he believed in Manicheism again, and Manicheism will be the state religion, "we elect and all the people in the realm were filled with great joy. ... Crowds of thousands and ten thousands came together and came to ..." Apparently, numerous Manicheans must have existed for a long period, and they impossibly appeared there in a short time. Therefore, the spread and popularity of Manicheism in Uighur Khanate must have been much earlier than when the Qaghan declared it the state religion.

Fourth, Manicheism once occupied a high position in the Uighur regime. As TM 276 shows, when the Qaghan held the grand ceremonies, the Manichean professional monks *Elects* accompanied him as personal attendants: "The divine King Bögü Qaγan and all the elect in his entourage mounted their horses, and all the great princes and princesses and high officials and the leading nobles, the great and the small, that is, all the people, proceeded to the gate of the city in great joy and festivity." The people not only saluted the Qaghan but also hailed the Elects of Manicheism: "When the divine Bögü Qaγan had issued this order, the many crowds and the common people paid homage to the divine king and rejoiced in his presence. And also to us, the elect, they paid homage and expressed their joy." In addition to this Turkic text, other Chinese texts also authenticated the honorable status of the Manicheans in the Uighur regime.

(3) Historical Facts Manifested by Chinese Materials

Some Chinese records clearly reveal the relationship between the Uighur regime and the Manicheans or Sogdians. For example, *Xintangshu* 新唐書 said that in the early 9th century, the Uighurs came to China with Manicheans to pay tribute. According to Manichean commandments, the followers did not eat until evening; meats, wines and even fermented drinks were forbidden. They ran the country together with the Qaghan. The Manicheans often came to western market of the capital, and the businessmen there sometimes colluded with them, doing immoral and criminal things.[26] Obviously, the Manicheans or the Sogdians, especially

---

[26] Cf. *Xintangshu* 新唐書, fasc. 217A, p. 6126. The Chinese text is as follows: "元和初, (回鶻) 再朝獻, 始以摩尼至。其法日晏食, 飲水茹葷, 屏湩酪, 可汗常與共國者也。摩尼至京師, 歲往來西市, 商賈頗與囊橐爲奸。"

their high-ranking monks, had a high political status in the Uighur regime, and thereby they were regarded as a part of the ruling class. In addition, so-called *Western Market* 西市 of the capital Changan 長安 was in fact a market especially for the foreign merchants; among them, there were numerous Sogdian tradesmen. Hence, the Manicheans close to these foreign businessmen were actually also Sogdian businessmen.

Many other Chinese materials supplied the evidences of these Manicheans' active political involvements. For instance, *Jiutangshu* 舊唐書 said that in lunar December of 813, the government hosted a banquet for eight Uighur envoys, who were going to return home soon. Not long before, they were sent by the Uighur Qaghan to request intermarriage with China. Considering the ongoing fighting inside the country, the emperor of the Tang did not accept this proposal of marriage.[27] In the same *Biography of Uighurs* 回紇傳, another passage records that in lunar May of 821, a Uighur mission came to China to welcome and receive the Chinese princess who was to marry the Qaghan. This mission consisted of 573 members, including a prime minister, governors, princesses and Manicheans; all of them resided in the Ministry of Foreign Affairs. The edict declared that Princess Taihe 太和公主 will be married to the Uighur Qaghan as his queen. The senior general Huzheng 胡證 was appointed as the chief envoy of the mission to escort the Princess to Uighur Khanate; Lixian 李憲 and others served as deputy envoys or held other positions.[28] These two paragraphs indicate that the so-called *Manichean Monks* 摩尼僧 of the Uighur regime had been quite involved in Uighur politics, at least frequently participating in its diplomatic activities.

It is precisely the great impact of Sogdians or Manicheans on the Uighur rulers that led to the popularity of Manicheism in China proper. The Chinese government was forced to accept the demand of spreading Manicheism in China, because the Uighurs had once helped them to quell

---

[27] Cf. *Jiutangshu* 舊唐書, fasc. 195, pp. 5210–5211. The Chinese text was as follows: "(元和八年)十二月二日,宴歸國回鶻摩尼八人,令至中書見宰臣。先是,回鶻請和親,憲宗使有司計之,禮費約五百萬貫,方內有誅討,未任其親,以摩尼爲回鶻信奉,故使宰臣言其不可。乃詔宗正少卿李孝誠使於回鶻,太常博士殷侑副之,諭其來請之意。"

[28] Cf. *Jiutangshu* 舊唐書, fasc. 195, p. 5211. The Chinese text was as follows: "五月,回鶻宰相、都督、公主、摩尼等五百七十三人入朝迎公主,於鴻臚寺安置。敕:太和公主出降回鶻爲可敦,宜令中書舍人王起赴鴻臚寺宣示;以左金吾衛大將軍胡證檢校戶部尚書,持節充送公主入回鶻及冊可汗使;光祿卿李憲加兼御史中正,充副使;太常博士殷侑改殿中侍御史,充判官。"

the rebellion of Anlushan 安禄山 and Shisiming 史思明; more importantly, the Uighurs possessed a powerful army.

Actually, the monarchs of the early stages of the Tang seemed rather cold and even hostile to Manicheism. For example, *Fozutongji* 佛祖統紀 (*General History of Chinese Buddhism*) recorded that in 694, a bishop of Manicheism, who was a native of Persia or Byzantium, came with a *Scripture on the Two Principles* 二宗經 to preach the false doctrines ("延載元年 ... 波斯國人拂多誕 (西海大秦國人) 持《二宗經》偽教來朝。" cf. fasc. 39). The fact that one of the most important Manichean scriptures was contemptuously regarded as "false doctrine" clearly shows the unfriendly and suspicious attitude toward Manicheism. Although this might have been the opinion of the Buddhists instead of the rulers of the Tang, for decades after that, no direct or indirect information on Manicheism in China was found. Therefore, it could be inferred that the Chinese government of that time really had no interest in Manicheism, namely, the so-called *false religion*.

Nearly thirty years later, a record of their request to spread Manicheism in China appeared again. According to *Cefuyuangui* 冊府元龜, in lunar June of 719, some countries in West Asia, South Asia and Central Asia sent missions to China to pay tributes. The king of Jaghanyan 支汗那 recommended to the Chinese emperor an astronomer, who was also a high-ranking monk of Manicheism, titled Možag 慕闍 (Teacher). The king praised the Možag's astronomical knowledge, and asked the emperor to allow him to set up a religious building and preach Manicheism.[29]

As a *Grand Možag* 大慕闍, he was a high-ranking Manichean monk, and also an excellent astronomer. Besides, he brought with him a king's recommendation; however, he still dared not directly request for dissemination of Manicheism, but just first used his astronomical knowledge to please the emperor. This implies that during the decades since the late 7th century, Manicheism seemed to have no development in China; it was not known to the public and not accepted by the rulers.

---

[29]Cf. *Cefuyuangui* 冊府元龜, fasc. 971, Zhonghua Book Company 中華書局, 1982, p. 11406. The Chinese text was as follows: "(開元七年) 六月, 大食國、吐火羅國、康國、南天竺國遣使朝貢。其吐火羅國支汗那王帝睑上表獻解天文人大慕闍: '其人智慧幽深, 問無不知。伏乞天恩, 喚取慕闍, 親問臣等事意及諸教法, 知其人有如此之技能。望請令其供奉, 並置一法堂, 依本教供養。'"

More than thirty years later, government of the Tang officially prohibited the Chinese people from believing in Manicheism. Emperor Xuanzong 玄宗 issued an edict in 732, saying, "Manicheism is originally a heresy. It pretends to be Buddhism, attempting to deceive the masses, so must be banned. As for the *Western Foreigners* 西胡, because Manicheism is their own religion, they can continue to practice this religion without punishment."[30] Here, Manicheism is severely accused of being "a heresy" and "deceiving the masses", which shows that the Chinese government deeply resented this religion. Besides, the real reason the *Western Foreigners* (mainly consisting of the Sogdians and Persians) were allowed to embrace Manicheism could be because of these merchants' impact on the Chinese economy. Hence, rulers of the Tang never really accepted Manicheism.

In contrast, the Uighurs were keen on spreading Manicheism in China. In fact, just after Manicheism was claimed as the *State Religion* of the Uighur Khanate, this religion began to flourish in China proper. That is to say, it was the Uighur regime that promoted the spreading and prosperity of Manicheism in China.

Many historical materials mention the popularity of Manicheism in the country of the Tang. For instance, "The Uighur Qaghan orders Manicheans to spread their religion in China. In lunar June 29 of 768, Chinese emperor builds temples for the Uighur Manicheans, and bestows it a plaque inscribing 大雲光明 Dayunguangming (Grand Cloud Light). In lunar January of 771, Manichean temples are built respectively in Jingzhou 荊州, Hongzhou 洪州 and Yuezhou 越州, etc., titled *Grand Cloud Light*" (cf. *Zizhitongjian* 資治通鑑, fasc. 237). A similar record was found in *Fozutongji* 佛祖統紀: "The Uighurs request to build Manichean temples of *Grand Cloud Light* in Jingzhou 荊州, Yangzhou 揚州, Hongzhou 洪州 and Yuezhou 越州, etc." (*Fozutongji* 佛祖統紀, fasc. 41). The prefectures of Jing, Yang, Hong and Yue were located, respectively, in the present provinces of Hubei 湖北, Jiangsu 江蘇, Jiangxi 江西 and Zhejiang 浙江. Apparently, due to promoting by the Uighurs, Manicheism rapidly extended to vast regions south of the Yangtze River. Of course, there were also many Manichean temples in North China, for example, "In lunar January of 807, the Uighur envoy requests to build three Manichean temples in provincial capitals of Henan

---

[30] Cf. *Tongdian* 通典 (*Encyclopaedic History of Institutions*), fasc. 40, Zhejiang Classical Publishing House 浙江古籍出版社, 2000, p. 229.

河南 and Taiyuan 太原, and is granted" (cf. *Cefuyuangui* 冊府元龜, fasc. 999).

An imperial edict cited in a book of the Prime Minister Lideyu 李德裕 distinctly reveals the fact that accompanying the vicissitude of the Uighur regime, Manicheism also underwent corresponding prosperity and decline in China: "Before the period of Tianbao 天寶 (742–755) Manicheism is banned in China. Thereafter, people are allowed to practice this religion because the Uighurs believe in it. It is popular in the basins of Yangtze River and Huai 淮 River. Recently, according to the reports of many provinces, since the Uighur regime has disintegrated, the rules and regulations are gradually destroyed, the foreign Manicheans here seem hard to live normally. The aboriginals south of Yangtze River do not seem so kind as to give alms to them. In addition, every religious believer should practice his religion in line with the suitable objective conditions, rather than being compelled to do so. In order to properly settle down these foreign Manicheans, I demand them only preach and worship in two capitals and Taiyuan 太原. The temples in basins of Yangtze River and Huai River are no longer used for religious services until the Uighur regime is steady again" (cf. Lideyu 李德裕, *Huichangyipinji* 會昌一品集, fasc. 5).

According to this imperial edict, the Tang government suspended the religious activities of the foreign Manicheans in the basins of the Yangtze River and Huai River, as if in consideration for their lives. Actually, the Chinese rulers just took advantage of the decline of the Uighurs to restrict and exclude Manicheism. Formerly, they were forced to accept Manicheism only because they feared the powerful strength of the Uighurs. In fact, it was mainly the Sogdians who encouraged and urged the Uighurs to spread Manicheism in China. Thus, this example clearly shows the Sogdians had a significant impact on the nomads and even the sedentary Chinese.

Chapter 10

Military and Political Advantages of the Sogdians: Taking the Five Dynasties as an Example

The Sogdians were good at business and had a keen interest in spreading religion, which have already been discussed in the previous chapters. As for their skills in military affairs and politics, I am going to examine and analyze in detail as follows:[1]

1. The Sogdians were Valorous and Adept at Fighting

As an overall perspective, most of the Sogdians of the Five Dynasties were famous for their valor and martial skills. They held high military positions, led conquests and triumphed, and seemed quite different from the Sogdian merchants and entertainers of the Sui and Tang Dynasties. It was an interesting phenomenon. In order to inquire into this subject deeply, we have to first be aware of the relationship between the Sogdians and the famous tribe Shatuo 沙陀.

---

[1] About this topic, cf. my paper "On the Sogdians' Activities in China Proper of the Five Dynasties" 五代時期中原地區粟特人活動探討, in *Historical Review* 史林, No. 3, 1992, pp. 7–13.

(1) The Ethnic Group of Shatuo 沙陀

When Shatuo is mentioned in Chinese historical materials, it is usually called *Shatuo Tujue* 沙陀突厥, meaning "the Shatuo people belonging to the Turk race." In fact, however, the ethnic composition of the Shatuo was probably not so pure. *Xintangshu* 新唐書 talked about its ethnic origin as following: "The Shatuo derives from Chuyue 處月 tribe, a branch of the Western Turk. In the earlier times the territory of former Wusun 烏孫 is respectively occupied by the Eastern Turk and Western Turk; the Turks are mixed with Chuyue 處月 and Chumi 處蜜…. When the Western Turk grows stronger, a civil war breaks out, a grand chief Yipiduolu 乙毗咄陸 sets his capital west of Zuhe Mountain 鏃曷山, which is called Northern Court 北廷. Chuyue and other tribes are subordinate to this Turkic regime. Chuyue lives south of Jinsuo Mountain 金娑山 and east of Pulei 蒲類. There is a vast desert named Shatuo there, so this tribe is called Shatuo Turk."[2]

Some facts can be summarized from this paragraph, such as the following. The name *Shatuo* originated from the toponym of a desert. This region was a part of the lands in which the Chuyue tribe resided; fearing of the powerful force of the Western Turks, the Chuyue yielded to it and became its *branch*. The homeland of Chuyue, Chumi and other tribes was the country of the former Wusun. Apparently, it was precisely because of the Turks occupying this area that the Shatuo were connected to the Turk. Thereby, the Shatuo did not necessarily belong to the same ethnic group as the Turks. On the contrary, because Chuyue lived in the lands of the former Wusun, its people were quite possibly the same ethnic group as that of Wusun. It is almost accepted by all modern scholars that the Wusun people belonged to the Indo-European race.[3] Therefore, as a part of the Chuyue, the Shatuo probably merged with a certain Indo-European bloodline.

The records of the late Tang Dynasty and the period of the Five Dynasties also indicate that the so-called *Shatuo Turk* 沙陀突厥 included a large proportion of Sogdians. For instance, the Tang government ordered Senior General Kangchengxun 康承訓 to suppress the rebellion led by Pangxun 龐勛; Kangchengxun asked the emperor to allow the Shatuo Three Tribes 沙陀三部落 and Tuyuhun 吐谷渾 to join the war too.

---

[2] Cf. *Xintangshu* 新唐書, 218, 1975, p. 6153.
[3] On the ethnic origin of the Wusun, cf. Yutaishan 余太山, *Saizhongshiyanjiu* 塞種史研究 (*A Study on the History of the Scythians*), Commercial Press 商務印書館, 2012, p. 210.

The so-called *Shatuo Three Tribes* were regarded as a tribal alliance of three tribes, namely, Shatuo 沙陀, Sage 薩葛 and Anqing 安慶.⁴ *Xintangshu* 新唐書 provided more information on these three tribes: "After Huangchao 黃巢 captures Tong Pass 潼關 and occupies the capital, Chenjingsi 陳景思 is sent to attack the rebels. At that time, Shatuo governor Liyoujin 李友金 owns the Xingtang Army 興唐軍, while Sage chief Mihaiwan 米海萬 and Anqing governor Shijingcun 史敬存 own the Ganyi Army 感義軍."⁵ In addition, in lunar October of 878, Shatuo chief Anqing 安慶 and Sage chief Mihaiwan 米海萬 assisted the Tang troops in suppressing Liguochang 李國昌 and his son; in lunar June of 880, Shatuo chief Liyoujin, Sage governor Mihaiwan and Anqing governor Shijingcun surrendered to the Tang government.⁶

We can affirm that at least two of the *Shatuo Three Tribes* consisted of Sogdians, or mainly consisted of Sogdians. First, the tribe name Sage 薩葛 pronounced as *sât-kât* in middle Chinese, may be another transliteration for Suɣδ (Soghd). In addition, other Chinese names, such as Xuege 薛葛 and Suoge 索葛,⁷ were apparently also the transliterations of Suɣδ. Second, these Shatuo tribes not only named their tribe *Soghd* but also took the typical Sogdian surnames as the family names of their chiefs. For example, the chief of the Sage Tribe was Mihaiwan, while Mi 米 was one of surnames of so-called *Nine Clans of Zhaowu* 昭武九姓. Similarly, both the *An* 安 of the Anqing Tribe and their Chief's surname *Shi* 史 were the surnames of *Nine Clans of Zhaowu*. Hence, the Sage and Anqing tribes of the Shatuo quite possibly consisted of Sogdians.⁸

Since the Shatuo were not a pure Turkic ethnic group, but included a lot of Sogdians, it was not proper to think of someone as a Turk when he was said to belong to the *Shatuo* ethnic group. For instance, according to *New History of the Five Dynasties* 新五代史, general Kangfu 康福 "is of

---

⁴Cf. *Zizhitongjian* 資治通鑑, fasc. 251, Note of Husanxing 胡三省, Zhonghua Book Company 中華書局, 1956, p. 8131.
⁵Cf. *Xintangshu* 新唐書, fasc. 218, p. 6158.
⁶Cf. *Zizhitongjian* 資治通鑑, fasc. 253, pp. 8209, 8227.
⁷*Jiutangshu* 舊唐書, fasc. 19B records that in lunar October of 877, Shatuo 沙陀, Anqing 安慶 and Xuege 薛葛 as well as other governmental forces and tribes were sent to suppress the rebels Liguochang. (p. 700) *Xinwudaishi* 新五代史, fasc. 51 says, Ancongjin 安從進 was a member of the Suoge 索葛 tribe (p. 586).
⁸About this opinion, cf. E.G. Pulleyblank, "A Sogdian Colony in Inner Mongolia", in *T'oung Pao*, Vol. 41, No. 4–5, 1952, pp. 343–344.

Barbarian descent", "his appearance is similar to that of foreigner", "proficient in several languages" and "he often claims that he derives from the Shatuo ethnic group".[9] Obviously, Kangfu was more likely to be a Sogdian rather than a Turk. First, his surname *Kang* was included in *Nine Clans of Zhaowu* 昭武九姓, namely, Sogdians. Second, the term *Foreigners* 胡 in the period of the Sui and Tang usually referred to the Sogdians or Persians. Third, the Sogdians traded all over the world, so knowing many kinds of languages was one of their significant features. As for claiming that he "derives from the Shatuo ethnic group", it was precisely because "the barbarians all honor the Shatuo." So, Kangfu was not a real Shatuo aboriginal.

Some historians think that the imperial families of the Later Tang 後唐 (923–936), Later Jin 後晉 (936–946) and Later Han 後漢 (946–950) all derived from the Shatuo descent. But, this statement seems incorrect. The first emperor of the Later Jin Dynasty is Shijingtang 石敬塘. *Xinwudaishi* 新五代史 mentioned his lineage and said that his father's was Nieleji 臬捩雞, originating from the western barbarians; it is unknown why Shijingtang was surnamed Shi 石.[10] There is no mention here of his Shatuo origin. On the contrary, Shijingtang was said to originate from the Western Barbarians 西夷, and had the surname Shi 石, a typical name of the *Nine Clans of Zhaowu*. Therefore, Shijingtang possibly came from Shi Country in Sogdiana.[11]

There are many similar examples in other records, so when the Sogdians of the Five Dynasties are talked about and discussed, careful attention must be paid to the so-called *Shatuo*.

(2) Military Officers Originating in the Sogdians
According to the *Biography of Anshuqian* 安叔千 in *Jiuwudaishi* 舊五代史, Anshuqian originated from the *Shatuo Three Tribes*. His surname "An 安" distinctly revealed his Sogdian ethnic origin. One of his characteristics was poor cultural literacy, thus having a nickname "Illiterate". However, he had great martial arts, and was especially good at riding and archery. In his youth, he followed Licunxu 李存勗, the first emperor of the Later Tang, to create the new regime. Later, he assisted

---
[9]Cf. *Xinwudaishi* 新五代史, fasc. 46, pp. 514–515.
[10]Cf. *Xinwudaishi* 新五代史, fasc. 8, p. 77.
[11]About this opinion, cf. Cenzhongmian 岑仲勉, *Suitangshi* 隋唐史 (*History of the Sui and Tang*), Zhonghua Book Company 中華書局, 1982, p. 546.

Shijingtang 石敬瑭, the first emperor of the Later Jin of the future, to defeat the Khitans, and was appointed as the governor of Zhengwu 振武. After the establishment of the Later Jin 後晉, he successively served as governor of Binzhou 邠州, Cangzhou 滄州, Xingzhou 邢州 and Jinzhou 晉州, as well as Senior General. In addition, he was also a high-ranking official in the regimes of the Later Han 後漢 (946–950) and Later Zhou 後周 (951–960).[12]

Although all these regimes in the period of the Five Dynasties lasted only a short time, it was a remarkable achievement that Anshuqian 安叔千 was able to take military power in four dynasties of the Later Tang, Later Jin, Later Han and Later Zhou. This achievement was closely related to his outstanding military talents. It is noteworthy that Anshuqian's military expertise was taught by his family. The Sogdians came to the East with their entire family, even entire tribe; they learnt martial arts and had been good at fighting already for several generations. For example, Anshuqian's father Anhuaisheng 安懷盛 was also a general. He followed Likeyong 李克用, the father of Licunxu 李存勖, to defeat many opponents, and was famous for valor and skills in fighting.

Another similar case is Shiyan 史儼. *Jiuwudaishi* 舊五代史 said that Shiyan was a native of Daizhou 代州. He was good at riding and archery, thus serving in an entourage of Likeyong, father of the future emperor Licunxu. Shiyan was very brave, and an expert in setting up ambushes and capturing enemies alive; he won every battle.[13] Daizhou was the equivalent of the northeastern part of present Shanxi Province. In ancient times, the people living there were nearly entirely foreigners. Moreover, the surname *Shi* indicated that Shiyan was a Sogdian, for it belonged to the *Nine Clans of Zhaowu*. As a janissary of Likeyong, Shiyan assisted him to suppress the rebellion of Huangchao 黃巢; later, in the middle of the 890s, he protected Emperor Zhaozong 昭宗 of the Tang from rebel killings. Since Shiyan helped Yangxingmi 楊行密, the founder of the Wu 吳, the latter's military power and reputation rose to a high degree. Apparently, comparing Shiyan with Anshuqian, the former was not only good at individual combat but also had high military leadership. Therefore, he was far more excellent than Anshuqian, for the latter was only "an illiterate warrior".

---

[12] Cf. *Jiuwudaishi* 舊五代史, fasc. 123, Zhonghua Book Company 中華書局, 1976, p. 1622.
[13] Cf. *Jiuwudaishi* 舊五代史, fasc. 55, p. 743.

Kangsili 康思立 was also a valiant general originating from the Sogdian ethnic group.[14] He came from the tribes of Yinshan Mountains 陰山; more and more "western foreigners" or Sogdians lived there since the Turk Khanate had been established. Kangsili was expert in riding and archery since his childhood, thereby serving as a janissary of Likeyong 李克用 when he was young. After the Later Tang was established, Kangsili became an important official under Emperor Zhuangzong 莊宗. He got great battle achievements, serving as a high-ranking civil or martial official successively. In the reign of Mingzong 明宗, he was appointed as a supervisor of the Northern Tribes, governor of the Zhaowu Army 昭武軍 and commander of the Western Route Army in succession. He still held important military posts in his later years. Kangsili was simple and very generous, so he was praised greatly by his soldiers and the general public. During the reigns of all the four emperors of the Later Tang, he was always trusted by them and entrusted with heavy tasks.

As for Kangyicheng 康義誠,[15] he was stated to be "a native of Three Tribes in the north." Apparently, this *Three Tribes* referred to "Three Tribes of the Shatuo", namely, the tribal alliance of Shatuo 沙陀, Sage 薩葛 and Anqing 安慶. As frequently mentioned above, a person surnamed Kang surely had origins in Sogdiana. Kangyicheng was also good at riding and archery, and served as a janissary of Licunxu 李存勖 in his earlier days. When Licunxu ascended the throne, Kangyicheng was appointed as the commander of the elite cavalry. In the reign of Mingzong 明宗, he served as governor of Fenzhou 汾州. He was a master of military skills, and held several important military posts during the whole period of the Later Tang. In his later years, he had a greater impact on the monarch.

The Five Dynasties period was not far from the period of the rebellion of Anlushan and Shisiming. These rebels of Sogdian origin once captured enormous political and economic interest by means of military force. This set an attractive example for their Sogdian descendants with political ambition. The particular exciting fact was that in the struggle for hegemony, many foreigners or barbarians realized their dreams by force. Naturally, numerous Sogdians followed suit; Ancongjin 安從進 was one of them.

---

[14] For his experiences and achievements, cf. *Biography of Kangsili* 康思立傳 in *Jiuwudaishi* 舊五代史, fasc. 70.

[15] For his experiences and achievements, cf. *Biography of Kangyicheng* 康義誠傳 in *Xinwudaishi* 新五代史, fasc. 27.

According to historical records, Ancongjin[16] was a member of the Suoge 索葛 tribe in the region of Zhenwu 振武. Both his grandfather and father were cavalry generals in the Later Tang Dynasty. The territory of the Zhenwu Army is located in present Horinger County and its surrounding areas of Inner Mongolia, where there was a traditional settlement of the Sogdians. *Suoge* 索葛 is a transliteration of *Soghd*, while *An* is one of the surnames of the Nine Clans of Zhaowu, so Ancongjin doubtlessly originated from the Sogdian ethnic group. The fact that his grandfather and father were cavalry generals proves that martial arts were being handed down from generation to generation; at the same time, it indicated that Ancongjin and his tribal members had lived there for long time.

At first, Ancongjin followed Licunxu to fight for hegemony of China; after Licunxu became the first emperor of the Later Tang Dynasty, Ancongjin served the commander of the cavalry, and the governor of Guizhou 貴州. Later, he was appointed as governor of Baoyi 保義 and governor of Zhangwu 彰武 successively. In the regime of the Later Jin 後晉 established by Shijingtang 石敬塘, Ancongjin was given the rank of prime minister. Although Ancongjin held high-ranking official positions, he was not satisfied with them, because he pursued greater fame and power, just like his former lord Licunxu and the present monarch Shijingtang.

Ancongjin secretly recruited outlaws, taking them as his private army. Besides, he robbed official and private supplies transported from the South to the North, which went past Xiangyang 襄陽. His close ally was his fellow countryman Anchongrong 安重榮; they echoed each other. In 941, Ancongjin publicly rebelled. He relied on the solid defense of the Xiangyang city, so that the government forces could not capture it for a long period. He fought with the army of the Later Jin 後晉 till was breached in the next August. It was said that "Ancongjin burns himself to death together with all his kindreds" (安從進舉族自焚),[17] but we do not know whether the term "kindreds" meant his family or his clan, or even his tribe. Nevertheless, surely a lot of Sogdians were involved in his rebellion and eventually were killed by the governmental forces.

---

[16] For his experiences and achievements, cf. *Biography of Ancongjini* 安從進傳 in *Xinwudaishi* 新五代史, fasc. 51.
[17] Cf. *Zizhitongjian* 資治通鑑, fasc. 283, p. 9239.

Another famous general involved in this rebellion was Anchongrong 安重榮, also a Sogdian.[18] His nickname was *Iron Foreigner* 鐵胡, showing his foreign origin; in addition, his surname was *An*, belonging to the so-called *Nine Clans of Zhaowu*, so he was doubtlessly a Sogdian. Similar to other Sogdian military generals, Anchongrong was also taught martial arts by his family. His grandfather Ancongyi 安從義 once served as governor of Lizhou 利州; his father Anquan 安全 held the positions of governor of Shengzhou 勝州 and commander of the cavalry and infantry of Zhenwu 振武.

Anchongrong was depicted as "being muscular, good at riding and archery." So, in the Later Tang Dynasty, he once served as commander of the patrol force of the Zhenwu Army 振武軍. One story reflects his outstanding archery skills: In the early days, Shijingtang 石敬瑭 secretly tried to recruit Anchongrong, asking him to assist Shijingtang fight for hegemony.

This proposal was accepted by Anchongrong, but strongly opposed by his mother and elder brother, because the latter feared the failure of this rebellion. Then, Anchongrong used divination to predict the success or failure of the matter. He first said, "If Shijingtang will be the emperor in the future, I can hit the target center 100 meters away with only one arrow." He shot an arrow and exactly hit the target center. Then, he prayed again, "If I can be promoted to governor in the future, I will hit the bull's eye with only one arrow." Sure enough, he hit the target center again. Naturally, now the whole family agreed with Anchongrong getting involved in Shijingtang's rebellion. Apparently, this so-called *divination* or *prediction* completely depended on the archery of Anchongrong rather than the fortunes of him and Shijingtang. This result only proves Anchongrong's excellent shooting skills.

After the establishment of the Later Jin 後晉 Dynasty by Shijingtang, Anchongrong was appointed as the governor of the Chengde Army 成德軍. Being promoted from a common warrior to a high-ranking official, Anchongrong was very pleased to get wealth and rank in such violent and martial way. He was more ambitious when he witnesses Shijingtang and others' experiences of seizing regimes by violence. He often said to others, "Anyone who wants to be emperor, he must rely on his troops instead of his noble birth." Thus, he secretly gathered strength, waiting for

---

[18] For his experiences and achievements, cf. *Biography of Anchongrong* 安重榮傳 in *Xinwudaishi* 新五代史, fasc. 51.

the chance of rebellion. When Ancongjin 安從進 rebelled in 941, Anchongrong immediately responded to him. At that time, Zhenzhou 鎮州 suffered a severe insect disaster; Anchongrong attacked the lands of the Jin together with tens of thousands of victims. Unfortunately, Anchongrong was defeated at last, and was captured and executed, failing to fulfill the *Dream of being Emperor*.

2. The Sogdians were Good at Politics

In the period of the Five Dynasties, the political situation was very chaotic and complex. In this case, the Sogdians displayed not only their excellent martial arts and military skills but also the extraordinary political talent. As we may easily find, there were numerous politicians of Sogdian origin in this age, and many high-ranking officials even emperors were among them.

(1) Politicians Originating in the Sogdians

In the Five Dynasties, Anchonghui 安重誨[19] was a comparatively famous politician among the officials originating from Sogdiana. He was said to be a native of Yingzhou 應州; while this prefecture was located in northern part of the present Shanxi Province, for a long period, it was a foreign settlement. The ancestors of Anchonghui were originally "the chief of the north tribe", namely, the chief of *Foreign Tribe* 胡部. In addition, he had the surname of *An*, a typical surname of the Sogdians. Therefore, Anchonghui was undoubtedly a Sogdian. His father, named Anfuqian 安福遷, was "known for bravery"; he had been a military general, and died in battle at last. Besides, his uncles Anfushun 安福順 and Anfuqing 安福慶 were also famous cavalry generals serving the royal family. The fact that they were called *Foreign Generals* 蕃將 reveals the foreign origin of this family.

When he was young, Anchonghui followed Lisiyuan 李嗣源, the future emperor Mingzong 明宗 of the Later Tang 後唐. Anchonghui was smart and capable, and very strict in his work, thereby gaining the trust of the emperor, and being involved in the discussion and decision-making of

---

[19] For his experiences and achievements, cf. *Biography of Anchonghui* 安重誨傳 in *Jiuwudaishi* 舊五代史, fasc. 66 and *Biography of Anchongrong* 安重榮傳 in *Xinwudaishi* 新五代史, fasc. 24.

important state affairs. After Mingzong succeeded to the throne, Anchonghui was appointed as grand general and defense minister in succession. Several years later, he was promoted to prime minister. So, his power grew stronger than any other official. According to the historical records, since Anchonghui became the chief secretary of the privy council, he was trusted by the emperor, dealing with all important state affairs. He had more power than everyone else. "Since Anchonghui makes it his duty to govern the world, he is trying to consolidate power internally, control other hegemonies externally." Obviously, Anchonghui of that time already unconsciously regarded himself as a master or lord of the entire regime, thereby he was no longer careful and even dared to decide what should have been decided by the emperor.

For example, the Prime Minister Renyuan 任圜 once argued with Anchonghui because of different opinions on official business. Renyuan failed and resigned on the pretext of illness. Later, when Zhushouyin 朱守殷 rebelled in Bianzhou 汴州, Anchonghui pretended to follow the emperor's order, sending some killers to murder Renyuan, and accused him of rebellion with Zhushouyin. Even if the emperor had doubts about Anchonghui, he dared not inquire directly. However, Anchonghui was afraid of being condemned by public opinion, thus he cut taxes by two million without authorization. Emperor Mingzong had no choice but to agree with this decision. There were many other similar cases, which clearly showed that his pursuit and control of power had reached a very dangerous extent.

It is true that Anchonghui's monopolistic power caused the officials to resent and resist; more importantly, the emperor was also very wary of him. Therefore, under the double pressure of emperors and high officials, Anchonghui was gradually deprived of important positions and powers. In the end, he was framed as a rebel, and executed together with his wife in his own house by the imperial envoy. Anchonghui was not a corrupt official, but still could not avoid the extermination of his entire family.

Among the Sogdians who had a great impact on the politics of the Five Dynasties, there were members of the royal family in addition to generals and civil officials. As shown above, Shijingtang, the founder of the Later Jin regime, was of Sogdian origin. Here, a more detailed discussion about the relationship between this Sogdian clan and Chinese politics will be given.

First, *Shi* 石 was a main surname of the *Nine Clans of Zhaowu*, so Shijingtang 石敬塘 was apparently derived from the Sogdians.

In addition, some records claimed the family of Shijingtang "originating in the Western Barbarians 西夷"; this also indicated his foreign ethnic element. Second, the surnames of Shijingtang's relatives displayed obvious Sogdian features. For instance, his great-grandmother's surname was *An* 安, his grandmother's surname was *Mi* 米 and his mother's surname was *He* 何; his nephew Shichonggui 石重貴 succeeded him as the emperor, whose mother's surname was *An* 安.[20] It was well known that *Shi* 石, *An* 安, *Mi* 米, *He* 何, etc., were all the Sogdian surnames designated in Chinese historical literatures. This information indicates that Shijingtang's clan seemed to intermarry only with the Sogdians, hence the Sogdians related to this *royal family* of Shi were surely numerous.

As a Chinese regime, the Later Jin 後晉 Dynasty lasted only for ten years (936–946), but the participation of its royal members in a struggle for hegemony was much longer. Therefore, these Sogdians had correspondingly a much greater impact on the political situation of late the Tang and the Five Dynasties.

According to *Jiuwudaishi* 舊五代史, during the reign Yuanhe 元和 (806–820) of the Tang, the fourth generation grandfather of Shijingtang, named Shijing 石璟, followed the Shatuo 沙陀 army from Linwu 靈武 to surrender to the Tang government. Linwu was about the equivalent of the present Yinchuan 銀川 of the Ningxia 寧夏 Autonomous Region, a settlement inhabited mainly by the foreigners. In order to reward his attachment, Emperor Xianzong appointed Shijing as a middle-ranking officer of Yinshan 陰山 prefecture. Later, Shijing was gradually promoted as the governor of Shuozhou 朔州 because of his brilliant military exploits in border areas. The great-grandfather of Shijingtang was named Shichen 石郴, who died in his youth, but was awarded an honorary title for his contribution to the Tang regime. Shijingtang's grandfather Shiyi 石翌 had been the military chief of Zhenwu 振武, and once had the title "Deputy Prime Minister". Shijingtang's father was named Nielieji 臬捩雞, evidently a Chinese transliteration of the Sogdian dialect, but its meaning is unknown. Nielieji was good at riding and archery, and had great military skills. He had been a subordinate of Likeyong 李克用 and Licunxu 李存勖 of the Later Tang Dynasty, building outstanding battle achievements, and serving as governor of Pingzhou 平州 and 洺州 Mingzhou in succession.

---

[20] Cf. *Jiuwudaishi* 舊五代史, fasc. 75 (pp. 977–978) and fasc. 81 (p. 1067).

As for Shijingtang himself, in many years prior to the establishment of his own regime, he was an official of the Later Tang Dynasty, holding some important posts successively, such as governor of the Bauyi Army 保義軍, governor of the Xuanwu Army 宣武軍, commander of the royal guards, military chief of Datong 大同 and prime minister. Therefore, this Sogdian clan, surnamed Shi, was active on the Chinese political and military stage for at least one and half centuries, exerting tremendous positive or negative influences on Chinese politics and society.

(2) The Character of Family Participating in Politics
Generally, the Sogdians moved eastward together with their family members, even the whole clan. Thus, they could easily set up their collective immigration bases in many places in China. Exactly for this reason, when the Sogdians participated in Chinese political or military affairs, they often got involved in it with many family members instead of doing it alone. Therefore, in the political circle of the Five Dynasties, there were usually a number of relatives who got involved in similar political or military business. They were often as many as seven or eight, including several generations. This phenomenon was rarely seen in the old days.

The family of Anjinquan 安金全[21] was a typical case of *Family Participating in Politics*. Anjinquan came from the Shatuo 沙陀 tribal alliance of the north end of China; and *An* 安 was one of the main surnames of the Sogdians. So, Anjinquan undoubtedly was of Sogdian origin. Several generations of his ancestors had been the military generals of the border regions. His father Anshansheng 安山盛 served as a Douxiao 都校 of Shuozhou 朔州, namely, the chief of 1000 soldiers; in addition, he was awarded a high-ranking honorary title *Taifu* 太傅.

Due to his patrimonial martial arts, Anjinquan was valorous and heroic in his childhood, and good at riding and archery. In his youth, Anjinquan served as a cavalry general, following Likeyong 李克用 to fight all over the country and achieving great things. During the reign of Zhuangzong 莊宗 (r. 923–926) of the Later Tang, he was promoted continually up to the position of governor. Later, he retired for reasons of age and health. However, while the mighty enemy attacked the empty

---

[21] For the experiences about Anjinquan and his family members, cf. *Biography of Anjinquan* and *Biography of Anshentong* 安審通 in *Jiuwudaishi* 舊五代史, fasc. 61; *Biographies of Anshenqi* 安審琦, *Anshenhui* 安審暉 and *Anshenxin* 安審信 in *Jiuwudaishi* 舊五代史, fasc. 123, and so on.

Bingzhou 并州, the ageing Anjinquan still led hundreds of his disciples and retired soldiers to give the enemy a sneak attack at night. They scared the enemy away until the reinforcements arrived. In the period of Mingzong 明宗 (r. 926–933), Anjinquan held some high-ranking positions, such as prime minister, governor of the Zhenwu Army 振武軍 and general supervisor of the Protectorate of Anbei 安北都護府.

Anshenqi 安審琦 was the son of Anjinquan. He was also quite valorous, and proficient in riding and archery. In his youth, Anshenqi was a follower of Licunxu, serving as legal secretary of the Yizhi Army 義直軍; later, he was promoted to commander of the Yizhi Army. Under the rule of emperors of the Later Tang, Anshenqi had served as bodyguard chief, cavalry commander, governor of Fuzhou 富州 and governor of the Shunhua Army 順化軍 in succession. Later, in the regime of the Later Jin 後晉, Anshenqi held successively the positions of deputy imperial preceptor, prime minister, governor of the Tianping Army 天平軍, deputy grand commandant, governor of the Jinchang Army 晉昌軍 and mayor of the capital.

The Later Jin regime was replaced by the Later Han Dynasty. Anshenqi still enjoyed the trust of the new monarchs. He was appointed as governor of Xiangzhou 襄州 and held a concurrent post of prime minister. Later, he was awarded the title *Duke of Qi State* 齊國公 for the great military exploits. In the Later Zhou 後周, the last regime of the Five Dynasties, Anshenqi gained more power and more honor. He was successively awarded *Prince of Nanyang* 南陽王 and *Prince of Chen* 陳王. Besides, he once governed Xiangzhou 襄州 and Mianzhou 沔州 as *Grand Commandant* 太尉 and *Grand Teacher* 太師, respectively. He was well governed, and highly praised by the public. Anshenqi was honored so much that when the emperor received him, he was treated as an *Imperial Elder*. His son Anshouzhong 安守忠 once served as governor of different prefectures of the Chinese regimes.

Another son of Anjinquan was Anshenhui 安審暉, the elder brother of Anshenqi. He was also a warrior, serving as a legal secretary of the army at first. He followed Licunxu to conquer Youzhou 幽州, Jizhou 薊州, Shandong 山東 and Henan 河南, accomplishing great battle achievements. Later, Anshenhui was successively appointed as governor of Weizhou 蔚州, deputy commandant of the Ruzhou 汝州 army and deputy governor of Fengxiang 鳳翔 and Xuzhou 徐州. Like his younger brother Anshenqi, he was also trusted greatly by the emperors of the Later Tang, Later Jin, Later Han and Later Zhou Dynasties. In the Later Zhou regime, he retired with the title 太子太傅 *Taizitaifu* (Grand Preceptor of Crown Prince), and was awarded as *Duke of Lu State* 魯國公, with 5000 households paying tax to him.

Anjinyou 安金佑 was the brother of Anjinquan. He was also a warrior originating from the Shatuo tribal alliance, and was famous for his outstanding martial arts among the people of the border regions. Both of his sons were active in the military and political fields of the Five Dynasties. In his youth, Anshentong 安審通 followed Licunxu to fight for hegemony, accomplishing great achievements and serving as vanguard commander. When Licunxu succeeded to the throne, Anshentong was appointed as general commandant of the cavalry, stationed in Fenghua 奉化. Later, in the reign of Emperor Mingzong 明宗, he held successively the positions governor of Shanzhou 單州, garrison commander of Qizhou 齊州, deputy grand preceptor and governor of Changzhou 滄州. After he died in battle, he was awarded the title of *Grand Commandant* 太尉.

Anshenxin was the younger brother of Anshentong. He was also adept at riding and archery, and once served as governor of Zhenwu 振武 in the reign of Emperor Mingzong of the Later Tang. After that, he held successively several high-ranking military positions in Changzhou 滄州 and other cities. At the end of the Later Tang Dynasty, Anshenxin turned to follow Shijingtang 石敬塘, and was trusted by him. However, his wife and two sons were killed by Emperor Modi 末帝 of the Later Tang. After Shijingtang became the emperor of the Later Jin 後晉 regime, Anshenxin served as governor of Fenzhou 汾州, governor of Hezhong 河中, deputy grand commandant, deputy prime minister, etc., in succession. In the Later Han regime, he was appointed as governor of Tongzhou 同州 and grand general. He was also a grand general of the Later Zhou 後周. Finally, he retired with the title *Grand Teacher of Crown Prince* 太子太師.

Thus, it can be seen that at least eight members of Anjinquan's family were recorded by the historical literatures. This Sogdian family experienced five Chinese regimes, exerting great impact on the political and military affairs during a period of four or five generations.

Another similar case was the family of Shijiantang 史建瑭.[22] The father of Shijiantang was Shijingsi 史敬思. In late of the Tang, when

---

[22] For the experiences about Anjinquan and his family members, cf. *Biography of Shijiantang* 史建瑭, *Biography of Shikuanghan* 史匡翰 and *Biography of Shiyi* 史懿 in *Jiuwudaishi* 舊五代史, fasc. 55, 88 and 124, respectively.

Likeyong 李克用 was the governor of Yanmen 雁門, he served as governor of the Nine Clans Prefecture. The so-called *Nine Prefecture* (九府 jiufu in Chinese) was an abbreviation of *Nine Surnames Prefecture* 九姓府. It was a settlement set up especially for the Sogdians (*Nine Clans of Zhaowu*), and was also a unique administrative district of the Tang Dynasty. So, the supreme head of the Jiufu 九府 was generally held by the Sogdians, and was hereditary. Shijingsi was one such character. He always followed Likeyong; as an outstanding military general, he accomplished great achievements, including defeating the rebels of Huangchao 黄巢 and other hostile forces. Unfortunately, it ended badly: when they were attacked by the enemy at night, in order to cover Likeyong's breakout, he valiantly stood up against the enemy, and was killed in the end.

Like his father, Shijiantang was also valorous and good at martial arts. In the late Tang, he was promoted to minister of works for his prominent achievements in the war. After the Later Liang 後梁 regime was founded by Zhuwen 朱溫, Shijiantang followed the family of Likeyong 李克用 to fight against this new dynasty. He defeated Zhuwen and caused him a great loss, hence gaining the nickname *Vanguard Shi* 史先鋒. Shijiantang successively held many important positions, such as governor of Chanzhou 澶州, governor of Beizhou 貝州, governor of Xiangzhou 相州 and commandant of imperial guards. He died from a stray arrow at forty-six, two years before the establishment of the Later Tang Dynasty.

Shiyi 史懿 was the eldest son of Shijiantang. He was only twenty when his father died in battle. Licunxu 李存勖 was very fond of Shijiantang, and thereby he appointed Shiyi as the military legal secretary of the Zhaode Army 昭德軍 at first, and soon promoted him as the chief of 1000 soldiers.

In the reign of Emperor Mingzong 明宗 of the Later Tang, Shiyi served as governor of Haozhou 濠州 and governor of Zhaozhou 趙州 in succession. In the period of the Later Jin, he held a number of military and political positions, such as the chief of local army of Mingzhou 洺州, military head of Fengzhou 鳳州, governor of Chanzhou 澶州, governor of Beizhou 貝州 and governor of Jingyuan 涇原. Besides, Shiyi served as the deputy grand commandant of the Later Han regime and deputy grand teacher of the Later Zhou, and was even promoted to *Duke of Bin State* 邠國公. After he died at sixty-two, the emperor of the Later Zhou awarded him the title *Prime Minister* 中書令.

Shikuanghan 史匡翰 was the second son of Shijiantang. In his youth, he succeeded to the position of *Governor of Nine Clans Prefecture* 九府都督, the hereditary position of his family. Later, in the period of the Later Tang, he served as patrol chief of Lanzhou 嵐州, Xianzhou 憲州 and Shuozhou 朔州. In addition, he held many other posts, such as deputy minister of revenue, governor of Xunzhou 潯州, infantry commandant of the Tianxiong Army 天雄軍 and cavalry commandant of Zhangsheng 彰聖.

After the establishment of the Later Jin, Shikuanghan was appointed as governor of Huaizhou 懷州, and married the younger sister of Emperor Gaozu 高祖 (Shijingtang 石敬塘). Thereafter, he served as governor of Hezhou 和州, military head of Zhengzhou 鄭州 and governor of the Yicheng Army 義成軍. Shikuanghan was famous for his resolute disposition, astuteness, outstanding military talent, strict military administration and being kind to subordinates. He died of illness at the age of forty. His son Shiyanrong 史彥容 was also an excellent politician, having served as general manager of the palace, governor of Puzhou 濮州, governor of Chanzhou 單州 and governor of Suzhou 宿州 in succession.

There are numerous cases similar to those described above. For example, there are at least five other family members besides Anchonghui 安重誨 to be involved in politics, such as Anchonghui's father Anfuqian 安福遷, his uncles Anfushun 安福順 and Anfuqing 安福慶, as well as his sons Anchongzan 安崇讚 and Anchongxu 安崇緒. In addition, in the family of Kangfu 康福,[23] with the exception of him, many other members were also active in the military and political fields. For instance, his grandfather Kangsi 康嗣 once served as standby governor and grand teacher of the crown prince; his father Kanggongzheng 康公政 served as military legal secretary of Pingsai 平塞 and grand preceptor; his eldest son Kangtingzhao 康廷沼 was governor of Suizhou 随州 and Zizhou 澤州; and his other sons Kangyanze 康延澤 and Kangyanshou 康延壽 held military or civil posts. All these facts show clearly that in the period of the Five Dynasties, the Sogdians usually participated in military and political affairs with almost all their male family members.

---

[23] For the experiences about Kangfu, cf. *Biography of Kangfu* in *Jiuwudaishi* 舊五代史, fasc. 91.

3. The Reasons for Thriving of the Sogdian Military and Political Officials

Apparently, in the period of the Five Dynasties the Sogdians were far more involved in military and political affairs than they were before. In other words, in this age, the Sogdians displayed more about their feature of being good at martial arts and politics rather than that of being adept at trade and preaching. As for the reasons for this phenomenon, it will be summarized as follows.

First, at the beginning of the Tang Dynasty, the Sogdian *Foreign Tribes* 胡部 inside the Turk Khanate grew stronger and more independent. Besides, after the collapse of the Turk regime, the Tang government set up *Six Prefectures for Foreigners* 六胡州 specially for the Sogdians. All these measures provided a good opportunity for the Sogdians to expand their political power.

In 630, the Eastern Turk Khanate was destroyed by the Tang government, and a lot of people surrendered and moved into China. As people who surrendered, many Sogdian immigrant groups migrated southward into the northern part of present Hebei 河北 province, the northern part of Shanxi 山西 province and Inner Mongolia south of the River Bend. They were the main body of the *Foreign Tribes* which was already well developed. Although in 639 they were once asked to return to the north bank of the Yellow River, four years later, the Tang government set up *Six Prefectures for Foreigners* for them, which was located between Shengzhou 勝州 and Xiazhou 夏州, namely, the region of present Inner Mongolia south of Hetao 河套. All chiefs of the six prefectures were Sogdians and were not replaced by a Chinese governor until 679. Decades of a highly autonomous management system greatly stimulated the Sogdians' ambition to pursue political power, and at the same time, it laid a solid foundation for this goal.

Second, during the Kaiyuan reign 開元 of Emperor Xuanzong 玄宗 (r. 712–741), the Sogdians of Six Prefectures staged a series of mass riots. Although all of them failed at last, it triggered their greater political ambitions.

In lunar April of 721, the Sogdians of Lanchizhou 蘭池州, Kangdaibin 康待賓, Anmurong 安慕容, Heheinu 何黑奴, Shishennu 石神奴 and Kangtietou 康鐵頭 initiated armed rebellion in Changquan County 長泉縣, and soon captured Liuhuzhou 六胡州 (Six Prefectures for Foreigners). The number of their soldiers rapidly expanded up to 70000, and then they advanced on Xiazhou 夏州. The Tang court urgently mobilized troops to resist, and after hard fighting for two or three months, the government army eventually defeated these *foreign rebels* 叛胡. It was said that in this war, 30000 Sogdian soldiers were killed. Obviously, the armed forces of the Sogdians were already very strong at that time.

In lunar August of the same year, Kangyuanzi 康願子, the remaining confederate of Kangdaibin, rebelled again. He claimed himself as Qaghan, getting a lot of momentum. The government was forced to fight as hard as it could. About one year later, in the next lunar September, the court eventually suppressed this rebellion. Thereafter, about 50000 of the remaining Sogdians were moved to Xuzhou 許州, Ruzhou 汝州, Tangzhou 唐州, Dengzhou 鄧州, Xianzhou 仙州 and Yuzhou 豫州, which was equivalent to the middle part of the present Henan Province. Several years later, about 730, Emperor Xuanzong 玄宗 sent Niuxianke 牛仙客 to placate the Sogdians in the northern regions. Yanzhou 鹽州, Xiazhou 夏州 and other prefectures, some areas with a good natural environment, were selected as the special districts for the Sogdians. Thus, numerous Sogdians were able to live in their original settlements, and continued to develop. These measures provided a suitable social environment for the Sogdians to participate in the rebellion of Anlushan 安禄山 and Shisiming 史思明 more than two decades later.

Third, the Sogdians were the main force of the rebellion of Anlushan and Shisiming (755–763). This rebellion lasted eight years, almost succeeding in replacing the Tang regime. This fact set a good example for Sogdians of the future who were keen on politics.

Anlushan and Shisiming doubtlessly originated among the Sogdians; there were also a lot of Sogdians among their relatives, trusted followers, mainstays and general supporters. For instance, Anlushan's stepfather Anyanyan 安延偃 and Anyanyan's younger brother Anbozhi 安波至 were naturally Sogdians. The eldest son of General Andaomai 安道買 and Anlushan once suffered together, while his second son Anzhenjie 安貞節 served as a high official of Lanzhou 嵐州. Ansishun 安思順, the governor of Hexi 河西, was a close friend of Anlushan, and they called each other "brother". The military generals Heside 何思德, Shidingfang 史定方, Heqiannian 何千年 and Anshenwei 安神威 were the subordinates of Anlushan, and they were all Sogdians. In addition, Shisiming's subordinate Kangmoyebo 康沒野波, Anqingxu's subordinate Anshouzhong 安守忠 and many other persons were also from Sogdiana. Before his rebellion, Anlushan asked the emperor to agree with his proposal of replacing 32 Chinese generals with foreign generals. There were surely many Sogdians among these so-called *foreign generals*. In 757, Shisiming defeated Anqingxu 安慶緒, the son of Anlushan, and forced him to flee north. Later, he offered amnesty and enlistment to the former subordinates of Anqingxu, which included many thousand Sogdians in Liuhuzhou 六胡州 (Six Prefectures for Foreigners).

During the Rebellion of Anlushan and Shisiming, the Sogdians not only firmly supported the rebels but also actively allied with other political forces to fight for hegemony. For instance, in 756, the Turk chief Asenali 阿史那禮 betrayed Anlushan and invited the Sogdians to participate in his alliance, attempting to capture the region of Helong 河隴; many thousand Sogdians were involved in this military operation. In the next year, Gaitinglun 蓋庭倫, the commandant of Hexi 河西, conspired with Sogdian businessman Anmenwu 安門物, killed the governor Zhoumi 周泌 and occupied Wuwei 武威 city. Their army numbered as many as 60000. There are many such examples, which show that during the Rebellion of An-Shi, a lot of Sogdians were involved in the military and political struggles of China, either actively or passively.

In short, the reason that the Sogdians of the Five Dynasties were good at fighting and keen to participate in politics was mainly the influence of the objective social environment. Since the period of the Sui and Tang, they established highly autonomous settlements in China and were often involve in political struggles and military conflicts of the Chinese, and thereby had political ambitions up growing. Besides, in their long process of migration eastward, the Sogdians had closely communicated with the warlike nomads, thus also having outstanding military arts and powerful armed forces. It provided a good condition for their future victories.

Chapter 11

On the Meaning and Origin of 曳落河 Yeluohe and 柘羯 Zhejie

The excellent military and political skills of the Sogdians have already been discussed in the previous chapter, while a kind of military institution of the ancient times will be analyzed in this chapter. It was possibly invented by the nomads, improved and spread by the Sogdians. This institution was once popular in Central Eurasia, and also found in China, which seemed to be rather helpful for improving combat effectiveness. It is the so-called 柘羯 zhejie and 曳落河 yeluohe in Chinese historical literatures.

1. Various Opinions about 曳落河 Yeluohe and 柘羯 Zhejie

The ancient Chinese historical materials, especially that of the Tang era, often mention two terms, namely, 曳落河/拽落何 yeluohe and 柘羯/赭羯/拓羯 zhejie, which are apparently the transliterations of non-Chinese languages. For example, *Xintangshu* 新唐書 said, "Tongluo 同羅 lies north of Xueyantuo 薛延陀, east of Duolange 多覽葛 ... When Anlushan 安祿山 rebels, he captures their soldiers as his own army, which is called *yeluohe* 曳落河, meaning *valiant fighter*."[1] "The country *An* 安 is also named Buhuo 布豁 and Buhe 捕喝 ... The valiant warriors are

---

[1] Cf. *Xintangshu* 新唐書, fasc. 217B, Zhonghua Book Company 中華書局, 1975, pp. 6140–6141.

enlisted as zhejie 柘羯, which is equivalent to *Warrior* in Chinese."² These records at least tell us two facts. First, both *yeluohe* and *zhejie* are a special name for a kind of valorous warrior who is good at fighting. Second, this military institution originated from either the nomads or the Sogdians of Central Asia.

Over the years, many scholars have discussed these two names. Shiratori Kurakichi thought that *yeluohe* 曳落河 was namely *yela* 拽剌 of *Liaoshi* 遼史 (*History of the Liao*), originating in *arlik* of the Turkic or *ere* of the Mongolian, meaning *manly, valorous, resolute,* etc., as well as persons with such character.³ Maejima Shinji believed that *yeluohe* is a transliteration of the Arabic word *ariqqa*, the plural form of *raqiq*. It referred to someone whose identity and functions were equivalent to zhejie 柘羯 among the Sogdians.⁴

Yeluohe was regarded by Chenshu 陳述 as the Yela Army 拽拉軍 of the Liao Dynasty. He analyzed various functions of the yeluohe and concluded the following: "曳落河 yeluohe, 拽落何 yeluohe, 裊羅箇 niaoluoge, 藥羅葛 yaoluoge, 耶剌里 yelali, 夜落紇 yeluohe, 夜落隔 yeluoge, 迭剌 yila, 迭烈 yilie, 迭剌葛 yilage, 迭剌哥 yilage, 曳剌 yela, 夜剌 yela, 拽剌 yela, 移剌 yila, 移剌答 yilada 移剌里 yilali and 伊剌阿 yilae, all these different Chinese words are found in various historical records, referring to army, tribe, official title, surname, character, mountain and river, etc … In fact, all these terms derive from the same foreign word; they are just different transliterations of it."⁵

As for the term zhejie 柘羯, there were more discussions and more opinions on it. Generally speaking, all these views could be divided into three kinds. The first category of viewpoints can be called "opinion of toponym". For example, Watters thought that the *zhejie* 赭羯 of Sogdiana

---

²Cf. *Xintangshu* 新唐書, fasc. 221B, p. 6244.

³Cf. the opinion of Shiratori Kurakichi 白鳥庫吉 白鳥庫吉 ("Study on the Tungus People" 東胡民族考 東胡民族考 東胡民族考 , in *Journal of History* 史學雜志 史學雜志, Vol. 23, No. 12) cited by Chenshu陳述 in his "On the Yeluohe and other Questions" 曳落河考釋及 曳落河考釋及 曳落河考釋及 其相關諸問題 其相關諸問題 其相關諸問題, in *Academia Sinica Bulletin of the Institute of History and Philology*, Vol.II, Part 4(1938), p.550.

⁴Cf. Maejima Shinji 前嶋信次, "Some Central Asia Words of the Time of Anlushan and Shisiming Rebellion", in *Memoirs of the Research Department of Toyo Bunko* 東洋文庫研究部歐文紀要, No. 36, Tokyo, 1977.

⁵Cf. Chenshu 陳述, "A Study on yeluohe and other Related Problems", in *Journal of Historiography and Linguistics Institute* 歷史語言研究所集刊, Vol. VII, Part 4, p. 572.

mentioned in *Great Tang Records on the Western Regions* 大唐西域記 was, namely, zhejie 柘羯 in *History of the Tang* 唐書. He cited others' opinions, saying one city Chalak lay northwest of Samarkand, the center of Sogdiana. The males of this city were tall, strong and muscular, fit to be soldiers. Thus, people often called the warriors or valorous fighters *Chalak*, which was transliterated into Chinese as 柘羯 zhejie.[6] Xiangda 向達 believed the etymon of 柘羯 zhejie is another place name: According to *Wenxiantongkao* 文獻通考 (*General History of Institutions and Critical Examination of Documents and Studies*), 柘羯 zhejie is also the name of Shi Country 石國. "The so-called 者舌 zheshe, 赭時 zheshi, 赭支 zhezhi, 柘支 zhezhi, 柘折 zhezhe and 柘羯 zhejie are all the transliterations of Persian word *Chaj*."[7]

The second kind of view regarded *yeluohe* and *zhejie* as the name of certain ethnic groups. Fujita Toyohachi tended to think 赭羯/柘羯 zhejie was a Chinese transliteration of *Sacae* or *Saka*, the ethnic name of the Scythians. He said, "According to *Jiutangshu* 舊唐書 and *Xintangshu* 新唐書, zhejie 赭羯/柘羯 is a specialized title for valorous warriors. Hence I think it is possibly a transliteration of the word *Sacae*, just with a slight error."

Fujita said again, "Since the ages of Cyrus and Darius, the Sacae/Saka has supplied the most excellent and valiant soldiers to the Persian troops. It is said that when Alexander the Great goes on an expedition eastward, this Sacae nation heroically fight for the Persians ... After many years, the name Sacae/Saka becomes a title referring to foreign mercenary who are good at war. Along with the expansion of the Turk powers, many warlike Turks serve as mercenaries of Iranian states in Sogdiana. They are still called as Saka, namely zhejie in Chinese. When the Arabians invade into Sogdiana, the fighters who resist against them are also zhejie 赭羯/柘羯."[8]

Chenyinke 陳寅恪 believed 柘羯 zhejie meant *Barbarians Jie* or *Foreigners Jie* 羯胡 jiehu, who were generally regarded as hybrid foreigners in Sogdiana, such as Anlushan 安祿山 and Shisiming 史思明. He said that Anlushan, Shisiming and their followers belonged to an ethnic group adept at fight, and were invincible at that time. This ethnic

---

[6] Cf. T. Watters, *On Yuan Chwang's Travels in India*, Vol. I, London, 1904, p. 94.
[7] Cf. Xiangda 向達, *Changan of the Tang and Civilizations of the Western Regions* 唐代長安與西域文明, The Joint Publishing Company 三聯書店, 1957, p. 102.
[8] Cf. Fujita Toyohachi 藤田豐八, "On the Ethnic Groups of Saka, Sei, Zhejie and Jiu Army" 論釋迦塞赭羯糺軍之種族, in his *Studies on the Western Regions* 西域研究, tr. by Yanglian 楊鍊, 1933, pp. 170–171.

group was called zhejie 柘羯 or jiehu 羯胡 (foreigners Jie) in the contemporary literatures. Zhejie 赭羯 was a name for an ethnic group.[9]

Third, some scholars think *zhejie* probably referred to persons with particular functions and special skills. The French scholar Chavannes agreed with the statement that 柘羯 zhejie was a transliteration of the Persian word *tchakar*. He said that *Great Tang Records on the Western Regions* 大唐西域記 claimed that the Samarkand Country 颯秣建國 "has a strong army; most of them are zhejie 柘羯." Both 柘羯 zhejie and 赭羯 zhejie were the transliterations of the same Persian word *tchakar*. In Sogdiana and its surrounding areas, this name meant *guards*.[10]

However, Shiratori Kurakichi thought that 柘羯/赭羯 zhejie and 煎 jian, the first part of Ferghana dialect 煎靡 jianmi, shared a common etymon. The original word was quite possibly *suguš* in Uighur and *šag* in Kusnezk, or some other words of similar pronunciation. It derived from the meaning *war* and *fight*, and was used to refer to warriors and soldiers. At that time, the native inhabitants were the Sogdians of the Iranian nation, while their rulers and soldiers were the warlike and valorous Turks. So, in their official language, the soldiers and fighters were called zhejie 柘羯/赭羯, namely, šagas, suguš.[11] This opinion was accepted by many scholars and was comparatively popular in the Chinese academic field.

Although the predecessors provided a lot of valuable viewpoints, there is still considerable scope for discussion about the relations between yeluohe 曳落河 and zhejie 柘羯, as well as their respective etymons and meanings. A discussion on this subject will be given as follows, attempting to prove that the two names in fact refer to two military institutions, which were invented by the nomads of Central Eurasia and improved by the Sogdians.

2. The Basic Features of *Yeluohe* and *Zhejie*

The basic characteristics of yeluohe and zhejie were analogous. They belonged to the same category, and there were only subtle differences between them. Their basic features can be summarized as follows:

---

[9] Cf. Chenyinke 陳寅恪, *On the Political History of the Tang* 唐代政治史述論稿, The Joint Publishing Company 三聯書店, 1956, pp. 29–30.
[10] Cf. Edouard Chavannes 沙畹, *Documents sur les Tou-Kiue (Turcs) occidentaux* 西突厥史料, tr. by Fengchengjun 馮承鈞, The Commercial Press, 1935, p. 103, Note 18.
[11] Cf. Shiratori Kurakichi 白鳥庫吉, "New Studies on History of the Western Regions" 西域史上の新研究, in his *Studies on History of the Western Regions* Part I, 西域史研究 (上), Iwanami Shoten 岩波書店, 1941, p. 99.

(1) Both *Yeluohe* and *Zhejie* were Military Institutions; Its Members were Selected from Different Ethnic Groups and were Good at War.

Yeluohe 曳落河 was first founded in the troops of Anlushan 安祿山. *Xintangshu* 新唐書 depicted the various initiatives adopted by Anlushan to actively prepare to rebel: "Anlushan builds a fortress north of Fanyang 范陽, names it Xiongwu City 雄武城, where the troops station, and a large quantity of grains are stored up there. Anlushan recruits eight thousand *yeluohe* as his foster sons, who come from different tribes of Tongluo 同羅, Xi 奚 and Khitan 契丹, etc. He trains also hundreds of bodyguards adept at archery."[12] In addition, *Story of Anlushan* recorded the following: "Anlushan revolts in 9 lunar November. His main forces consist of *yeluohe*, whom come from different tribes, such as Tongluo 同羅, Khitan 契丹 and Shiwei 室韋. They are called *the Army of Father and Sons*. Together with the troops of Fanyang 范陽, Pinglu 平盧, Hedong 河東, Youzhou 幽州 and Jizhou 薊州, there are one hundred thousand infantry and cavalry."[13] According to the above quotations, the *yeluohe* 曳落河 of Anlushan was apparently a special army. Its members were all valiant and good at fighting, and were selected from some nomadic tribes. It is interesting that they were nominally Anlushan's foster sons.

Husanxing 胡三省 discussed the *yeluohe* of Anlushan, saying that, according to historical records, Anlushan formed the surrendered Tongluo soldiers into a special army called *yeluohe*. In addition, it was said that Anlushan recruited 8000 surrendered soldiers of the Tongluo, Xi and Khitan tribes, and gave them the appellation "yeluohe 曳落河".

"*Yeluohe* is a foreign word, means warriors. At that time, the number of Tongluo *yeluohe* is a fifth of the total army's 50000, so the number of *yeluohe* is nearly ten thousand. Anlushan is then preparing for capturing of the capital, so he impossibly gives Shisiming his whole elite unit of 8000 persons. The truth should be that after the defeat and death of Abusi 阿布思, his tribe Tongluo surrendered to Anlushan. The latter select the elite fighters of Tongluo, Xi and Khitan, composes so-called *yeluohe*. Still a lot of other soldiers have not been incorporated into the *yeluohe*.

---

[12] Cf. *Xintangshu* 新唐書, fasc. 225A, p. 6414.
[13] Cf. Yaorunen 姚汝能, *Story of Anlushan* 安祿山事跡, fasc. 2, punctuated and proofread by Zengyifen 曾貽芬, in *Collection of Historical Records of the Tang and Song* 唐宋史料筆記叢刊, Zhonghua Book Company 中華書局, 2006, p. 94.

The troops being dispatched to assist Shisiming consist of common Tongluo soldiers and yeluohe, total of them are nearly ten thousand."[14]

Obviously, the so-called *yeluohe* of Anlushan was a special force composed of elite fighters who were selected from tribes of Tongluo, Khitan, etc. They were not named after a certain ethnic group, nor did they come from just a single tribe. In other words, *yeluohe* was an elite army whose members were selected from various tribes according to the level of military skill.

Here, Husanxing based his conclusion on the statement that "Anlushan recruits eight thousand *yeluohe* as his foster sons" of *Xintangshu* 新唐書, insisting that the total amount of Anlushan's *yeluohe* was only 8000. However, these 8000 *yeluohe* were in fact only the elite warriors recruited by Anlushan from some tribes before his rebellion; thereafter, he could have organized more such forces without any difficulty, if he wanted.

Therefore, in the An-Shi Rebellion, the *yeluohe* might have numbered far more than 8000. The words of Fangguan 房琯 hinted at this fact: He was dispatched by the emperor to recover two capitals from the rebels. Fangguan was very proud of his subordinate Liuzhi 劉秩, saying, "Though the *yeluohe* are so numerous, they will certainly be defeated by Liuzhi!"[15] As a commandant of a large army aiming at recovering capitals, Fangguan noticed and admitted that the *yeluohe* were *numerous*; it suggests possibly that the *yeluohe* of the rebels were far more than 8000.

Zhejie 柘羯 was similar to yeluohe 曳落河. According to *Biography of An State* 安國傳 in *Xintangshu* 新唐書, *zhejie* 柘羯 was the name for recruited warlike warriors. They undoubtedly belonged to the military combatants; in other words, *zhejie* was a certain specialized military organization. Just like the *yeluohe*, its members also came from different ethnic tribes. Since they were selected from numerous warriors adept at fighting, the most important criterion for selection was their martial skills; hence, it was impossible that it was only the natives of a certain country or ethnic group.

The truth is really like that. *Records on the Western Regions* 西域記 states that there were many *zhejie* 赭羯 in the country of Samarkand 颯秣

---

[14] Cf. Husanxing 胡三省, *Correction on the Notes of Comprehensive Mirror* 通鑑釋文辨誤, fasc. 10, in *Sikuquanshu* 四庫全書, Taibei 臺北: Commercial Press 商務印書館, 1986, pp. 312–341.

[15] Cf. *Zizhitongjian* 資治通鑑, fasc. 219, p. 7003.

建國 (Kang Country 康國); *Xintangshu* 新唐書 tells us that there were *zhejie* 柘羯 in An Country 安國; *Tongdian* 通典 says, "After El qaghan is defeated, his tribes flee to Xueyantuo 薛延陀 regime or Western Regions; in addition, a lot of people surrender to China. All the surrendered tribal chiefs are appointed as generals; their high-ranking generals are up to more than 100, almost half of the Chinese court officials. But only the *zhejie* does not come to surrender, then the emperor sends envoys to pacify them."[16]

Obviously, there were *zhejie* 柘羯 in both Sogdiana and the Mongolian Plateau; they seemed to have a wide sphere of activities. Besides, the words "only the *zhejie* does not come to surrender" show that members of the *zhejie* were very proud and unyielding, and would even rather die than surrender. This fit the meaning of the following statement in *Records on the Western Regions*: "The *zhejie* are valorous and strong-willed, facing death unflinchingly, so they are invincible."

Zhangxinglang 張星烺 pointed out the following: "Since the army of *zhejie* 柘羯 consists of recruited soldiers, its members are surely from various ethnic groups. Anyone who is valiant and good at war, and professional in fight could enlist it. Such fighters have no ethnic restrictions."[17] This opinion is reasonable. It exactly explains the character of *zhejie* and that it was based on candidates' level of martial arts rather than their ethnic classifications. Therefore, like the *yeluohe* 曳落河, *zhejie* 柘羯 was also a specialized elite army, which consisted of valorous fighters from various countries and ethnic groups.

(2) The Characteristics of *Yeluohe* and Foster Sons

Xintangshu 新唐書 says that Anlushan recruited 8000 *yeluohe* as his foster sons. The *Story of Anlushan* 安祿山事跡 tells us that because there were a lot of *yeluohe* in the rebelling troops of Anlushan, these forces were called *Army of Father and Sons*. This statement also shows the close relationship between *yeluohe* and the so-called *foster sons*. Although the *foster sons* could not be completely regarded as *yeluohe*, in the period of the An-Shi Rebellion and especially the late Tang, when many warlords struggled for hegemony, the so-called *foster sons* of those military chiefs

---

[16] Cf. *Tongdian* 通典, fasc. 197, pp. 1070–1071.
[17] Cf. Zhangxinglang 張星烺, *A Compilation of Historical Materials on the Intercourses between China and the Occident* 中西交通史料彙編, proofread by Zhujieqin 朱傑勤, Zhonghua Book Company 中華書局, 1977, 4, p. 297.

were basically the warlike warriors *yeluohe*. The characteristics of the *yeluohe* or foster sons can be briefly summarized as follows.

A passage in *Jiutangshu* 舊唐書 records a story of Libaochen 李寶臣, a foster son of general Zhangsuogao 張鎖高. Libaochen was originally a native of the Xi 奚 tribe; later, he became a foster son of Zhangsuogao, and thus he changed his name to Zhangzhongzhi 張忠志. He was good at archery since his childhood, and in his youth was appointed as an archery instructor by Anlushan, the governor of Fanyang 范陽. He once served as a military official in the palace of Emperor Xuanzong 玄宗. After the rebellion of Anlushan, Zhangzhongzhi fled back to Fanyang, and was recruited as a foster son of Anlushan, changing his surname to An 安. Later, he led a cavalry of 8000 persons to assault Taiyuan 太原 city, and kidnapped its governor Yangguanghui 楊光翽. When he retreated, 10000 warriors of the chasing army dared not approach him.[18] In addition, *Xintangshu* 新唐書 said that he once went deep into the savages' area to spy on the military affairs. When he was expelled and pursued by the barbarians, he shot six cavalrymen successively, escaping calmly.[19]

These records reveal some facts. First, this Libaochen 李寶臣 or Zhzngzhongzhi 張忠志, or Anzhongzhi 安忠志 was surely a member of the *yeluohe* because of his identity of Xi 奚 origin and as a foster son of the warlords. Second, he was so valiant and adept at military skills that even 10000 cavalry dared not approach him. In short, this case displays the feature of *yeluohe* or foster sons being valorous and good at war.

Since the most important selection criteria was "warlike", "valorous", "outstanding martial arts" or something like that, the moral character of the *yeluohe* might be neglected by the warlords, thereby their moral character possibly was very poor, even terrible. Sometimes, they behaved like thieves and robbers. For example, *Xintangshu* says that Shisiming's son Shichaoqing 史朝清 "is fond of hunting; he is as cruel as his father; his lust and drinking even exceeds his father. He trains three thousand fighters, all of them are brave, fierce and not fear of death."[20]

Apparently, these fighters recruited by Shichaoqing were also *yeluohe* or so-called *foster sons*, and their moral character was rather poor, similar to the outlaws. Relying on their own good martial skills and their lords' support, they often hurt others and even committed crimes. For instance,

---

[18] Cf. *Jiutangshu* 舊唐書, fasc.142, p. 3865.
[19] Cf. *Xintangshu* 新唐書, fasc. 211, p. 5945.
[20] Cf. *Xintangshu* 新唐書, fasc. 225A, p. 6432.

Lecongxun 樂從訓 was the son of Leyanzhen 樂彥禎; he recruited more than 500 outlaws, calling them *Son Generals* 子將. He trusted them very much, allowing them access to private rooms. Thus, these bodyguards did a lot of bad things without scruple, causing a backlash from other soldiers.[21] The reason why these outlaws were called *Son Generals* was apparently because they were the foster sons of Lecongxun. It is another instance which shows the feature of foster sons or *yeluohe* of that time.

(3) *Yeluohe* or Foster Sons were the Personal Escorts of the Warlords.
Based on above quotations and other materials, some facts may be summarized as follows. There was a very close relationship between yeluohe and their lord, like sons and father, thereby they were called *foster sons*. The *yeluohe* of Anlushan was a typical example, for it had the title "Army of Father and Sons". Besides, *yeluohe* seemed to be not only a kind of elite force in the formal battlefield but also the personal bodyguards of their master. A passage in *Xintangshu* 新唐書 gives a detailed description on such fighters:

Liyi 李錡 recruited many soldiers, and selected from them some persons being good at archery, giving them titles such as "Escorts with Bows and Arrows". In addition, fighters from the northern barbarians, western foreigners and Xi 奚 or like tribes composed another kind of army titled "Foreign Warriors". Liyi trusted them very much, paying them ten times more than other common soldiers, and asking them to call him *Adoptive Father*. Accordingly, these fighters were all quite willing to serve him.[22]

Here, though the text has not made it clear that these fighters are *yeluohe* or *zhejie*, they show all the characteristics of the *yeluohe* or *zhejie*. For instance, they came from various ethnic groups; they composed a certain military unit; they were all good at martial skills; they called their lord their *adoptive father*; and so on. These fighters were so well paid and privileged that they were willing to do their best to serve their master.

Under the chaotic situation of struggling for hegemony, it seemed to be quite common to compose the armed escorts in the form of *yeluohe* or foster sons. For example, Gaokaidao 高開道 also had hundreds of such foster sons: Gaokaidao recruited hundreds of warriors to guard him, and

---
[21] Cf. *Jiutangshu* 舊唐書, fasc. 181, p. 4690.
[22] Cf. *Xintangshu* 新唐書, fasc. 224A, p. 6382. The Chinese text is as follows: "錡得志，無所憚，圖久安計，乃益募兵，選善射者爲一屯，號'挽硬隨身'；以胡、奚、雜類、虯鬚者爲一將，號'蕃落健兒'，皆倚腹心，稟給十倍，使號錡爲假父，故樂爲其用。"

appointed Zhangjunli 張君立 and Zhangjinshu 張金樹 as their commandants. Later, Zhangjinshu betrayed Gaokaidao. He sent some trusted subordinates to pretend to play with the foster sons. At night, they quietly cut the bow strings and hid other weapons. Then, Zhangjinshu led his force to assault these foster sons. When the latter found that the weapons were missing or destroyed, they surrendered to Zhangjinshu. Gaokaidao knew that he could not escape from the misfortune, so he killed all his wives and children, then committed suicide at daybreak. Eventually, all these foster sons were executed by Zhangjinshu.[23] This case distinctly shows the foster sons' feature of serving as bodyguards.

In addition, Dufuwei 杜伏威 had thirty foster sons. They were all valiant warriors armed with excellent weapons, living with their lord every day.[24] Apparently, these foster sons or *yeluohe* were also the personal escorts of their commander in chief.

3. The Institution of Slave Army in the Ottoman Empire

The *yeluohe* and *zhejie* were founded in the East of the ancient world. Interestingly, there were also similar military institutions in the Ottoman Empire, which was located more west and was in a later era. Although the two kinds of military institutions were found in different regions and times, they possibly have a common origin, because the ruling clan of the Ottoman Empire derived from the Turks of Central Eurasia. First of all, a brief introduction about the military institution of the Ottoman Empire is given as follows.

The Ottomans belonged to a branch of the Turks, the latter springing up in Central Eurasia in the middle of the first millennium. When the Asena 阿史那 Turks established their khanate and the West Turks greatly expanded their power, the Ottomans lived in the Amu River basin of Central Asia. Later, in the 13th century, forced by the powerful Mongolian troops, the Ottomans had to move westward, just like their predecessors the Seljuk Turks. Finally, at the end of the 14th century, they established their independent regime in Asia Minor, and developed into a vast empire

---

[23] Cf. *Xintangshu* 新唐書, fasc. 86, p. 3715.
[24] Cf. *Xintangshu* 新唐書, fasc. 92, p. 3801.

spanning Asia, Europe and Africa over a period of more than two hundred years.

It is said that Kara Chalil Tschendereli, the founder of the Ottoman Janissary, once alleged, "The conquered are the property of the conqueror, who is the lawful master of them, of their lands, of their goods, of their wives, and of their children." "The new force would be recruited, not only out of the children of the conquered nations, but out of a crowd of their Christian friends and relations, who would come as volunteers to join the Ottoman ranks."[25]

It was under the guidance of such ideas that the Ottoman government recruited annually 3000 or 4000 male teenagers from their conquered lands. These new recruits were called *kullar* (singular form is *kul*), meaning slave and servant. Among these foreign teenagers, some were captives, some were slaves to the trade, some were "tributes" paid by the local governments to the central regime and some were "taxes" levied by the imperial court. These Kullar came from various regions, such as the Balkan Peninsula, Hungary, the western coast of Asia Minor and the Eastern coast of the Black Sea. The persons, being particularly muscular and capable, were generally Albanians and Yugoslavians living in mountainous areas. All these young kullar were sent to the capital for further classifying and training.

These teenagers were divided into two categories, one consisting of elites and another consisting of the ordinary majority. The persons with excellent physique and intelligence could get the best education, especially Islamic theology, Turkic language and other cultures. They could serve as the royal cavalry or palace guards in the future, and the most outstanding ones could even hold the important posts of the army and government. Naturally, such elites were few; generally, they numbered only a tenth of all enlisted kullar.

The remaining nine-tenths of the members had to get another type of education and training. It was mainly the physical exercises. It was believed that their physique was better than their intelligence, so were sent to do heavy and low jobs.[26] They were called *ajem-oghlan*, signifying "foreign youths"; this term was sometimes applied to all the young recruits. Their

---

[25] Cf. Edward S. Creasy, *The Ottoman Turks: from the Beginning of their Empire to the Present Time*, London, 1878, pp. 13–14.

[26] Cf. Paul Ricaut, *The History of the Present State of the Ottoman Empire*, London, 1868, p. 74.

training was largely physical, industrial and military, with oral instruction in the Turkish language and the principles of the Islamic system.

After a certain time spent in the stage of development, the majority of the ajem-oghlans were assigned, and most of them became *Janissaries* or "new soldiers", namely, the elite infantry corps that formed the sovereign's household troops, bodyguards and standing army. The *Solak*, who were one of three kinds of bodyguards, were selected from the Janissary and were veteran archers, and numbered about one hundred and fifty. They marched on foot beside the sultan wherever he went, with bows and arrows ready for instant use. Obviously, many elite ajem-oghlans (*foreign youths*) could serve as important fighters of the Turkish governments and Turkish monarchs. This was an obvious feature of the Ottoman military institution.

Another important feature of the Ottoman military system was that these recruited foreign slaves had a very close relationship with the monarch. The Ottoman Empire conquered their homelands, captured them, forced them to be slaves and demanded their absolute obedience. Ironically, most of these young slaves were not disgusted with their *Kul* (slave) status; on the contrary, they regarded it as an honorable title.

Then, what was the cause of this phenomenon? Actually, the reason is simple: in addition to instilling the ideas of absolute loyalty to the monarch, the sultan also provided opportunities for the teenagers to do their best. These *kullar* could get a promotion as long as they had excellent skills and worked hard; sometimes, they could even hold important civil or military posts, gaining great power and wealth. They would not be discriminated against; the freemen, officials, even the sultan might be willing to let their own daughters marry these excellent *kullar*. These slaves were protected by the laws of the state, and enjoyed the privilege of being exempted from all taxes. They were subject only to their superiors, imperial court and the sultan himself. Indeed, sometimes the sultan would severely punish those who disobeyed his orders, while he would also often generously reward those who did very well. The relationship between the sultan and his *kullar* appeared to be like that between the family patriarch and his children. The sultan of the Ottoman Empire and his *kullar* were really similar to a father and his sons in the same family. According to a contemporary historian of the Ottoman Empire, the sultans adopted the palace pages as their foster sons.[27]

---

[27]Cf. Albert Howe Lybyer, *The Government of the Ottoman Empire in the Time of Suleiman the Magnificent*, Harvard University Press, 1913, pp. 60–61.

Therefore, both the regular cavalry or infantry and royal bodyguards or palaces pages were actually under the direct control of the sultan. These armed elite fighters were centered on the sultan in both the ideas and forms. In times of battle, both the royal cavalry (*Spahi*) and infantry (Janissary) were responsible for defending the sultan: the Janissaries were aligned in the front, the Spahis proper, the elite cavalry, on the right and the other ordinary cavalry corps on the left and in the rear.[28] Apparently, the *ajem-oghlans* (foreign youths) or the *slaves* of Ottoman Empire were not only the regular cavalry and infantry but also the bodyguards and palace attendants of the sultan. Hence, the close relationship between the slave troop and the Ottoman monarch was mainly reflected in the slaves' status as foster sons and personal escorts.

Another characteristic of the slave troop was their similarity to bandits. As mentioned above, around a tenth of the recruited *ajem-oghlans* served as cavalry; the remaining majority would be infantry. The former were educated well and earned a lot, so they were more law-abiding, while the latter held comparatively low posts and got a lower salary, so they tended to do something illegal. Lybyer analyzed this fact, saying the following: "Since its members were physically trained beyond comparison with their intellectual education, since they were kept in poverty and hence were comparatively irresponsible, and since a large portion of them were in comparative idleness in time of peace, they were liable to act as an organized and very dangerous mob. They might start a riot on short notice, or burn a section of the city in order to pillage the neighboring houses, or rifle the shops of the Jews, or plunder the grand vizier's establishment. They could not easily be restrained from plundering cities which had capitulated or from violating terms of surrender."[29] Some cases are recorded in historical materials, for instance, Rhodes was pillaged after capitulation in 1521, and so were Ofen and Wychegrad in 1529 and 1544, respectively.

In summary, the slave troop of the Ottoman Empire had at least three characteristics. First, it consisted of elites of various ethnic origins. Second, there was a close relationship between its members and the monarch of the empire. Third, a majority of its members often behaved like

---

[28] Cf. Joseph von Hammer, *Geschichte des osmanischen Reiches* (10 vols), Vol. III, Pest, 1827–1835, p. 57.
[29] Cf. Albert Howe Lybyer, *The Government of the Ottoman Empire in the Time of Suleiman the Magnificent*, Harvard University Press, 1913, p. 92.

mobs and bandits. All these features were analogous to that of *yeluohe* 曳落河 and *zhejie* 柘羯 in the East. Now, I will discuss further the two groups of military institutions.

4. The Possible Common Origin of Yeluohe-Zhejie and Solak-Spahi

Although *yeluohe* 曳落河 and *zhejie* 柘羯 were similar to each other, as mentioned above, there were still some differences between them. For example, *yeluohe* was more like the infantry than the cavalry, at least a considerable part of it was so. Most modern scholars think *yela* 拽剌 of the Liao 遼 Dynasty was, namely, *yeluohe* 曳落河 of the Tang Dynasty. And, according to *History of the Liao*, "walking soldiers are called *yela* 拽剌."[30] Obviously, *yeluohe*/*yela* was classified as infantry. In addition, *Xintangshu* 新唐書 says, "Anlushan is appointed as the governor of Fanyang 范陽. At first he leads only two thousand cavalry and three thousand infantry of Tongluo 同羅 *yeluohe*. After several victories his army becomes the most powerful, thus he develops a stronger ambition of dominating China."[31] Here, the Chinese term was written as 步曳落河, which may be an abbreviation of 步卒曳落河 (infantry *yeluohe*), or missing a Chinese character 卒. So, the *yeluohe* was possibly the infantry.

Zhejie 柘羯, by contrast, showed more cavalry color. As recorded in *Xintangshu* 新唐書, after the death of Anlushan 安祿山, his son Anqingxu 安慶緒 dispatched a force of more than 100000 to attack Suiyang 睢陽. A *zhejie* army consisting of cavalrymen was included in these troops: "A chief in armor leads thousand cavalrymen, comes to challenge the soldiers guarding the city."[32] Besides, *Jiutangshu* 舊唐書 recorded that in lunar December of 755, the rebel forces of Anlushan rapidly marched westward, its vanguard arriving at Kuiyuan 葵園. The commander in chief Fengchangqing 封長清 sent the elite cavalry to fight against the *zhejie*, killing hundreds of them.[33] Though the text does not clearly mark that the vanguard of the rebel troops were the *zhejie*, the vanguard who rapidly marched must have been cavalry.

---

[30] Cf. *Liaoshi* 遼史, fasc. 46, Zhonghua Book Company 中華書局, 1974, p. 739.
[31] Cf. *Xintangshu* 新唐書, fasc. 225A, p. 6428.
[32] Cf. *Xintangshu* 新唐書, fasc. 192, p. 5537.
[33] Cf. *Jiutangshu* 舊唐書, fasc. 104, p. 3209.

Now, we can compare the yeluohe-zhejie with the slave troops of the Ottoman Empire as follows. As mentioned above, a majority of the recruited foreign youths served as Janissaries, while some elites Janissary archers were appointed as Solak, a kind of personal guards of the sultan. In Middle Chinese, the pronunciation "曳" was identical with that of s-; the pronunciation of the first letter γ- of "河" was identical with k-. Thus, the Chinese term 曳落河 and the Turkish word *Solak* might be different transliterations of the same original word.

In the Ottoman Empire, *solak* were the bodyguards of the Sultan, while in the Tang Dynasty, *yeluohe* 曳落河 were the personal escorts and foster sons of their lords. There is similarity between the two military institutions. Furthermore, *solak* means "left-handed", presumably because this army always marched on the left side of the sultan or their commander.

Although this supposition has not been proved by other pieces of evidence yet, the term *zhejie* 柘羯, quite probably being cavalry, was similar to the pronunciation of an Old Turkic word *sa:g*, with the latter meaning "right hand" or "right". Another interesting fact is that the royal cavalry of the Ottoman Empire, namely, the *Spahi of the Porte*, always kept the tradition of marching and encamping on the right hand of the sultan.[34]

Finally, a brief summary is given as follows.

In ancient times, a certain military institution was invented mainly by the nomadic Turks of Central Eurasia. The Sogdians who were active on the Silk Road perhaps did a lot for the improvement and dissemination of this system. After its application and development for many years, this military institution became *yeluohe* and *zhejie* in the East. Later, in Asia Minor, its elements were kept in the Janissary infantry and royal cavalry, which were the elites of the Ottoman slave army. The characteristics of this military institution were as follows:

First, this army consisted of warlike fighters recruited from various countries and ethnic groups, similar to mercenaries of modern ages.

Second, the elites of such an army usually served as the bodyguards of their master, having a close relationship with him, and they even called him "father".

---

[34] Cf. A.H. Lybyer, *The Government of the Ottoman Empire in the Time of Suleiman the Magnificent*, Harvard University Press, 1913, p. 250.

Third, the army consisting mainly of infantry transformed into *yeluohe* 曳落河 in the East and *solak* or other a similar infantry in the West. *Solak* might share the same pronouncing origin with *yeluohe*.

Fourth, the army consisting mainly of cavalry transformed into *zhejie* 柘羯 in the East and the royal cavalry in the West.

Fifth, *yeluohe* and *solak* possibly derive from the early military rules that they arrayed on the left side, for the Turkish word *solak* signified left side and left hand.

Sixth, the Chinese character 柘羯 zhejie can be regarded as a transliteration of the Old Turkic *sa:g*, meaning right side and right hand. The elite cavalry of the Ottoman Empire kept the tradition of arraying on the right side, therefore both *zhejie* and royal cavalry may be related to the ancient cavalry on the right.

Part III

Silk Road and the Spread of Religious Ideas

It is well known that the Silk Road in the broad sense is actually distributed over all regions of the ancient world. In terms of modern geographical concepts, the Silk Road leads to Asia, Europe and Africa. As for the contents exchanged through the Silk Road, in addition to various commodities, there were also a lot of intellectual creations; among them, the particularly important item is communication and spread of the religious thoughts. In this Part, I will discuss some topics on this aspect, paying more attention to the Manicheism in the East, which is called "Religion on the Silk Road" by many scholars.

Chapter 12

The Symbol Swastika in China

The word "symbol" here is defined as a "pattern or graphic character with symbolic meaning." Since the symbol contains "symbolic meaning", it displays not only a simple pattern but also expresses some abstract ideas, concepts and religious implications. Besides, the same symbol could be understood and explained differently in different regions. Therefore, as the symbols spread, rich ideas are fully exchanged. It reflects the important role played by symbols on the cultural communications of the ancient world. I will take the swastika as an example to talk about the cultural intercourses between ancient China and foreign countries.

1. The Date When the Swastika Becomes a Chinese Character

As a symbol and pattern, the swastika (卍) is found all over the world. There are numerous artworks decorated with the swastika in China, India, Persia, Mesopotamia, Greece, Cyprus, Roman, Egypt, Scandinavia, Northern Asia, and South and North America. These symbols can date back to at least the first or the second millennium BC, or earlier times. So, the swastika is regarded as one of the oldest symbols in the world.

However, as an exact word or character, the swastika 卍 exists only in the Chinese writing system. In contrast with the pattern swastika or the symbol swastika, the Chinese character swastika seems to have formed much later than the former, at least according to many modern scholars. In addition, most people tend to believe the symbol swastika was introduced into China from India; it was created as a Chinese character in the late 7th century, during the reign of Empress Wuzetian 武則天. Such opinions deserve further discussion, and some analyses are given as follows.

Like a pictograph, the swastika 卐 combines graphic and word, and composes a Chinese character. Almost all Chinese dictionaries ascribe this character 卐 to Wuzetian. For instance, the *Dictionary of the Sanskrit Terms of Sutras* says that, initially, there was no the character 卐, and the empress formally created it in 693, pronouncing it as *wan*, meaning "collection of all lucks and virtues."[1] *Ciyuan* 辭源 says, 卐 is originally a Sanskrit word rather than a Chinese character. It is the symbol on the breast of Tathagata, meaning lucky and happy. It also quotes the explanation in *Notes on Buddha vatamsaka mahavaipulya sutra* 華嚴經音義 that Empress Wuzetian lists it in Chinese characters in 693.[2]

Cihai 辭海 holds a similar opinion: "In ancient times, 卐 is found in India, Persia, Greece, etc., and used in Brahmanism, Buddhism and Jainism. It's called Śrivatsa 室利靺蹉 in Sanskrit, meaning *Auspicious Sea Cloud* 吉祥海雲. It is translated as 德 by Kumarajiva 鳩摩羅什 and Xuanzang 玄奘. Bodhiruci 菩提流支 of the Northern Wei Dynasty translates it as character 萬 in his *Notes on Daśabhūmi sutra* 十地經論. In 693, Wuzetian prescribes the pronunciation of this character as 萬, signifying *collection of all lucks and virtues*."[3]

Foguang Dictionary of Buddhism 佛光大辭典 talks a lot about the swastika 卐, including the statements cited above. It says, "The Sanskrit *Śrivatsalakṣana* is written as 万, 萬 and 卐 in Chinese; it is transliterated as 室利靺蹉洛剎曩 shilimochuoluoshanang, meaning *auspicious sea cloud* and *auspicious spiral*. This is one of the thirty-two special appearances of Buddha, also one of his eighty wonderful appearances. It is the virtuous appearance on the breast or elsewhere of Buddha and Daśabhūmi Bodhisattva." "There are some statements about the translation and transliteration of 卐. Kumarajiva and Xuanzang translate it as 德;

---

[1] Cf. Fayun 法雲, *Dictionary of the Sanskrit Terms of Sutras* 翻譯名義集, fasc. 55, in *An Index for Dictionary of the Sanskrit Terms of Sutras* 翻譯名義集易檢, Shanghai: Buddhism Book Company 佛學書局, 1935, p. 218. The Chinese text is as follows: "案卐字，本非是字。大周長壽二年，主上權制此文，著於天樞。音之爲萬，謂吉祥万德之所集也。"

[2] Cf. *Ciyuan* 辭源 (*Corpus of Chinese Words*), Commercial Press 商務印書館, 1988, p. 225.

[3] Cf. *Cihai* 辭海 (*Grand Dictionary of Words*), Shanghai Lexicons Publishing House 上海辭書出版社, 2010, p. 1931.

Bodhiruci translates as 萬, meaning *accomplishing one's charitable and pious deeds*. In addition, *Biographies of Eminent Monks of the Song Dynasty* 宋高僧傳 says, 萬 is not a free translation of 卐, but its transliteration. However, the pronunciation of 卐 is not found in Chinese sutras until Wuzetian prescribes this character's pronunciation and specifies its meaning as *collection of all lucks and virtues*."[4]

There are many other statements similar to those mentioned above. In other words, a conclusion accepted by most people is that in the earlier period of the Tang, 卐 became a Chinese character and was pronounced as 萬 wan. Furthermore, the symbol swastika 卐 was introduced into China along with Buddhism. The latter view is particularly prevalent in western academia. However, according to my opinion, there is still much room for discussion on this issue. First of all, I am going to inquire into the date of 卐 becoming a Chinese character initially.

The traditional Chinese character 萬, meaning *ten thousand*, is written as 万 in modern simplified form. However, in ancient times, it could also be written as 万. According to some archaeological data, 卐 could replace the character 万 on some occasions. For instance, there is an inscription "子孫千萬 (thousands descendants)" on a tile-end of the Former Han Dynasty. Among the four characters, character 萬(万) appears as a 卍 with its rotating arms turning left, as shown in Fig. 1.[5] This case indicates that

Fig. 1. The character 万 on the tile-end of the Former Han Dynasty.

---

[4]Cf. *Foguang Dictionary of Buddhism* 佛光大辭典, Taibei: Foguang Publishing House 佛光出版社, 1989, pp. 2202–2203.

[5]Cf. Wangrenshou 汪仁壽, *Dictionary of Epigraphy* 金石大字典, fasc. 22, Tianjing Classics Publishing House 天津古籍書店, 1982, p. 9. The editor says, "The character 万 of inscription 子孫千万 on the tile-end is so eccentric and archaic that it is surely the product of the Former Han Dynasty."

the Chinese character 卍, being pronounced *wan*, seems to appear initially in the Former Han instead of the Tang Dynasty. Wuzetian probably only officially confirmed this Chinese character; it had been popular for hundreds of years prior to her era.

Besides, the inscription "子孫千卍" raises two other questions. First, if the symbol swastika was really introduced into China together with Indian Buddhism, as most people thought, the introduction date of Buddhism should be during the Former Han Dynasty rather than the traditional statement of 67 AD. Second, if someone insists on the opinion that Buddhism was introduced early in the Later Han Dynasty, he has to admit that the swastika's initial introduction has nothing to do with Buddhism, at least there is no direct relation between the two. These two questions will be explained and answered as follows.

2. Swastika in Ancient China

Many scholars ascribe the introduction of the swastika to the eastward spreading of Buddhism. For example, d'Alviella says clearly that the swastika is not uncommon in China, Japan, Tibet, etc., "it is not difficult to prove that it must have come to them, with Buddhism, from India."[6] In addition, a similar opinion is held by Das Akhtar: "The orthodox Hindus regard the Buddha as one of the incarnations of the Sun-god Viṣṇu. The Buddhists inherited reverence of Swastika from this belief and carried it to Tibet, China, Japan and Korea."[7] As for the Chinese scholars, a majority of them keep the same view, as enumerated above.

However, these traditional opinions are incorrect and inexact, or at least quite one-sided. As I already point out above, in China, the symbol swastika and the character 卍 are different concepts. The former is purely a graphic, while the latter is both a graphic and a Chinese character. Furthermore, the latter was formed much later than the former, and its causes of formation probably differ from that of the former.

Basing on the materials currently available, the appearance of the swastika in China is much earlier than the introduction of Buddhism into

---

[6]Cf. Goblet d'Alviella, *The Migration of Symbols*, New York: University Books Incorporated, 1956, p. 73.

[7]Cf. Jamna Das Akhtar, *Introduction*, in Thomas Wilson, *The Swastika*, ed. by Jamna Das Akhtar, Delhi: Oriental Publishers, 1973, p. vii.

China, even much earlier than the creation of Buddhism, Jainism, etc., in India proper. It is an undoubted and well-known fact. Raozongyi 饒宗頤 discusses the earlier swastika of China in his paper *A Study on Swastika* 卍考. He says that the earliest swastika seems to be that found in the Xiaoheyan 小河沿 archeological site, the Aohan Flag 敖漢旗 of Liaoning Province. There are inscribed and painted primary graphics and characters on four pottery wares of the unearthed artifacts. Twelve symbols are decorated on the shoulders and abdomens of the wares, and seven symbols among them are the swastika. These swastika symbols could be classified into three categories, as shown in Fig. 2.

The first type is the *standard* swastika, its four arms bent at right angles, turning left or right. As for the second type of swastika, its four arms bend at right angles for several times, also turn to left. The third type of swastika also bends its arms left at right angles, but the bent arms are much thicker than the cross trunk. These pottery wares could date back to 2500 BC, corresponding to the times of the swastika in India and Asia Minor.

Later, many swastika symbols were found on the pottery wares of the Liuwan 柳灣 cemetery, located in Ledou County 樂都縣 of Qinghai Province 青海省. More than fifty symbols are decorated on the lower part or at the bottom of the pottery wares. Among them, symbols +, − and 卐 are the most common. The swastikas on the clay pots unearthed in Liuwan all turn their arms left. The swastikas on the flasks unearthed in Guanhutai 官戶台 of Minhe County 民和縣 are a little peculiar. By and large, they consist of four L, crossing each other at the right angle, and form a blank square in the center. The arms turn right or left. These pottery wares date back to the period of 2300 BC–2000 BC; obviously, these swastika symbols belong to the earlier ones of the world.

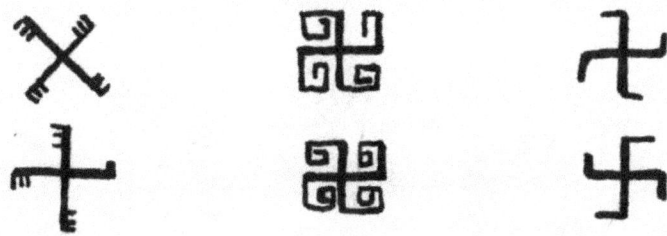

Fig. 2.   Three types of swastika of the Xiaoheyan site in Liaoning Province.

In addition to the prehistoric pottery wares, the swastika symbols also appear on the bronze vessels of the Shang 商 and Zhou 周 Dynasties. Figure 3 shows a partial scene of a bronze bottle of the Warring States period. On the upper part of the bottle, a hunting scene is depicted: three men are shooting birds with their bows and arrows. There is a row of swastika symbols on the lower part, their arms bend left, and a circular button is at the center of the swastika. All these arms are arc-shaped, and the ends of the arms are pointed. Such swastika could be seen frequently on bronze vessels and coins of the occidental world.

Some swastika symbols on the Zhongding Pot 仲丁壺 of the Zhou Dynasty are shown in Fig. 4. All these decorative patterns are divided into six layers, five on the body of the pot, one on the bottom. Swastika symbols occupy the upper four layers. The arm of this swastika is arc-shaped, and bends toward the left; the arms' ends are pointed; and a roundlet is at the center of the swastika. That is to say, its shape is very

Fig. 3.   Swastika on the bronze pot of the Warring States.

Fig. 4.   Swastika on the Zhongding Pot of the Zhou Dynasty.

like a fire flow from a fireball. So, it is thought to be a symbol of the sun. This Zhongding Pot seems to be made after the reign of King Xuan 宣王 (r. 827 BC–782 BC) of the Zhou Dynasty, apparently a quite archaic utensil.

A lot of swastika symbols appear on the pottery wares and bronze vessels of prehistoric and ancient times. All these objects can date back to the first millennium, the second and the third millennia BC; they are much earlier than the establishment of Buddhism, or at least contemporary with it. As for the date of Buddhism being introduced into China, among various opinions, even the earliest date[8] is later than the appearance of most Chinese swastika symbols.

Therefore, the cases of Chinese earlier swastika mentioned above prove that the view of "Chinese earlier swastika originating in Indian Buddhism" is unbelievable. However, it is unreasonable to deny completely that Chinese earlier swastika once had a certain relationship with the swastika abroad. What I am going to emphasize is that in the early ages, the swastika was introduced into China because of other causes instead of Buddhism.

3. The Relations between Chinese Character 卍 and Indian Cultures

Although the initial appearance of the pattern of the swastika in China cannot be ascribed to Buddhism, the Chinese character 卍 is definitely influenced by the Indian cultures.

According to some Buddhist writings, because the symbol 卍 means *ten thousand* in Indian Buddhism, it is pronounced as 万/萬 wan (meaning ten thousand) in Chinese. However, I do not think so. The truth should be that because of the similar shape or similar pronunciation of 卍 in Sanskrit, it is pronounced as *wan* in Chinese. For example, as Fig. 5

---

[8] The Chinese Buddhists often claimed that Buddhism already appeared in China prior to the era of Confucius (551 BC–479 BC); or, during the reign of the First Emperor of Qin, a Buddhist monk came to China with sutras; and so on. Cf. Tangyongtong 湯用彤, *History of the Buddhism in the Han, Wei, Two Jin and Southern-Northern Dynasties* 漢魏兩晉南北朝佛教史, Zhonghua Book Company 中華書局, 1983, pp. 1–10.

Fig. 5. The Sanskrit word for swastika in Chinese writings.

shows, this graphic is the Sanskrit word for symbol swastika.[9] It is easy to find that among the three components of this word, two of them are similar to the Chinese character 万. Hence, a likely supposition is that the ancient Chinese, especially the common people, took a part of this Sanskrit word to represent 卐 derived from India and replaced it with a Chinese character 万. This is the so-called "saying of analogous shape."

As for the "saying of analogous pronunciation", it means that the Chinese character 卐 is a transliteration of the swastika from India. A detail explanation on this issue is given in *Biographies of Eminent Monks of the Song Dynasty* 宋高僧傳. The author lists four rules for the translation from Sanskrit or other foreign languages into Chinese. The second rule, "translating pronunciation of the original word but keeping its shape, like 卐 on the breast of Buddha", seems to indicate the Chinese character 卐 is a transliteration of the Indian swastika.[10]

I think, the Chinese character 卐 is probably transliterated from the Sanskrit word *SWASTIKA*. Initially, this Sanskrit word only referred to the swastika symbols in India; later, it became a common name for all symbols of such type throughout the world, though they also have their own native names.

It was written as svastica, suastica, suastika, etc., in Latin; later, it was written as swastika in English and French. As for its etymon, this Sanskrit word is generally thought to mean fortunate, lucky, happy, etc.; it consists of *su*, *asti* and the suffix *ka*; both the *su* and *asti* means good and well.

In ancient Sanskrit, in addition to the word *swastika*, there is another term to refer to the same symbol, namely, *sauwastika* or *suavastika*.

---

[9]Cf. Huilin 慧琳, *Notes on Buddhist Sutras* 一切經音義, fasc. 21, in *Notes on Buddhist Sutras and the Continuation of the Notes on Buddhist Sutras* 正續一切經音義, Book I, Shanghai Classics Publishing House, 1986, fasc. 21, p. 12.

[10]Cf. Zanning 讚寧, *Biographies of Eminent Monks of the Song Dynasty* 宋高僧傳, fasc. 3, in *Sikuquanshu* 四庫全書, Book 1052, p. 34.

Max Müller believes that the symbol bending its arms toward the right is called swastika, it is the *standard* swastika, while the symbol bending its arms toward the left is called sauwastika. The difference between them is that the right-handed swastika symbolizes the progressive movement of the sun in the spring and summer, while the left-handed one represents the retrograde motion of the autumnal sun.[11]

A different interpretation is that the swastika 卍 with its arms turning right is an emblem of the god Ganesh. It represents the male principle, typifies the sun in its daily course from east to west, and symbolizes light, life and glory. The sauwastika 卐 with its arms turning left is a symbol of the goddess Kali. It represents the female principle, typifies the course of the sun in the subterranean world from west to east, and symbolizes darkness, death and destruction.[12] Besides, Burnouf says the word sauwastika may be a derivative or development of the swastika, and ought to signify "he who, or that which, bears or carries the swastika or a species of swastika."[13]

Undoubtedly, regardless of its different interpretations, the word *swastika* has long been a common name for the symbol 卍 in India and its neighboring countries. Therefore, when this Indian symbol was introduced into China, it was natural that the Chinese transliterated it into a character with a pronunciation similar to swastika. In the Chinese sutras, 卍 is generally transliterated into 塞縛悉底迦 saifuxidijia or 寶悉底迦 baoxidijia, apparently the transliterations of *swastika*. As for the latter, the first letter *S* is usually silent in the Chinese transliteration. Furthermore, the pronunciations b- and m- can replace each other in ancient Chinese. Thus, it is quite possible that the Chinese character 萬/万 wan is taken as an abbreviatory transliterated name for *swastika*.

If this deduction is true, the Chinese character 卍 is surely a result influenced deeply by Indian Buddhism or other cultures. The above example that 卍 is equated with 万 in the Former Han Dynasty ought to be regarded as evidence of the Indian cultures spreading into China in earlier ages.

---

[11] Cf. F. Max Müller's letter to Schliemann, in Henry Schliemann, *Iliod*, New York, 1881, p. 520.
[12] Cf. George Birdwood, *Report on the Old Records of the India Office*, London, 1891, pp. x–xi.
[13] Cf. Emile Burnouf, *Le Lotus de la Bonne Loi*, App. VIII, Paris, 1852, p. 626, note 4.

4. A Discussion on 室利靺蹉 Shilimocuo and 塞縛悉底迦 Saifuxidijia

As mentioned above, most of the Chinese literatures and dictionaries trace the Chinese character 卍 back to India, and claim that it derives from Sanskrit words. These transliterations of Sanskrit words are usually written as 室利靺蹉 shilimocuo or similar pronunciation. Obviously, they are quite different from *swastika*, which has been popular in ancient India. So, a question is raised: Is the current popular transliteration of 卍 correct?

In his *Yiqiejingyinyi* 一切經音義 Huilin 慧琳 explains the Chinese character 卍: "it is Sanskrit word 室哩末蹉 or 室利靺蹉"; the figure is drawn as a swastika with its four arms bent toward the right. Nearly all the later dictionaries adopt this concept, as mentioned above.

However, some other different names of the 卍 are also found in Chinese sutras. For instance, Huilin 慧琳 talks about many swastika graphics (卍字之形), and lists nine figures of them; all these swastika symbols belong to "the appearances of virtuous person", pronounced as 万 wan. He explains, according to the Sanskrit sutras, the symbol 卍 is originally the sign of a virtuous person rather than a word. There are many auspicious signs in Sanskrit sutras, such as 室利靺蹉 shilimocuo (s'rīvastaya), 難提迦物多 nantijiawuduo (nandyāvarta), 塞縛悉底迦 saifuxidijia (svastikā) and 拔折羅 bazheluo (vadjra).[14]

In terms of the pronunciation, the Chinese name 塞縛悉底迦 is undoubtedly the transliteration of the Sanskrit word swastika or svastika. However, in terms of the swastika graphics arranged by Huilin, the transliteration corresponding to the standard swastika is 室利靺蹉 (瑳). In my opinion, Huilin made a mistake in his account; the most proper Chinese transliteration for 卍 is 塞縛悉底迦 instead of 室利靺蹉 or some other names like that.

First, as a Chinese character, 卍 is pronounced *wan* 万; this pronunciation is more similar to that of *swastika* (塞縛悉底迦) rather than *Srivatsa* (室利靺蹉).

Second, according to the current materials, among the various Indian names referring to the symbol 卍, the term *swastika* is the

---

[14]Cf. Huilin 慧琳, *Notes on Buddhist Sutras* 一切經音義, fasc. 21, in *Notes on Buddhist Sutras and the Continuation of the Notes on Buddhist Sutras* 正續一切經音義, Book I, Shanghai Classics Publishing House, 1986, fasc. 21, p. 12.

most popular one. It is popular not only in India proper but also spreads to other regions of the world, as pointed out above. Therefore, the greatest possibility is that in earlier ages, the Indian symbol 卐 was introduced into China together with its common name swastika (塞縛悉底迦).

Finally, there is other evidence to support the view that 塞縛悉底迦 is the transliteration of swastika. For instance, *A Sanskrit-Chinese Dictionary* says in entry *s'rīvastaya*, "室利靺蹉 or 吉祥 lit. lucky omen. A mystic (star-like) diagram of good augury, the favorite symbol of Vishnuites and Jains." The entry *svastikā* says, "卐 or 塞縛悉底迦 or 穢佉阿悉底迦 or 寶悉底迦. Explained by 吉祥萬德之所集, lit. accumulation of innumerable virtues in one lucky sign, or by 佛心印, lit. the symbol stamped on Buddha's heart. (1) A mystic diagram (the cross cramponee) of great antiquity, mentioned in the Rāmāyana, found in (rock temples of) India, in all Buddhist countries, among Bonpos and Buddhists in Tibet and China, and even among Teutonic nations (as the emblem of Thor) (2) One of the 65 figures of the S'ripāda. (3) The symbol of esoteric Buddhism. (4) The special mark of all deities worshiped by the 蓮宗 Lotus School of China."[15]

According to this interpretation, although s'rīvastaya/srivatsa 室利靺蹉 is also a lucky sign, its shape is like star instead of 卐, while svastikā/swastika 塞縛悉底迦 is distinctly the typical shape of 卐. Furthermore, the Srivatsa seems to be applied only by Vaishnavism and Jainism, while the swastika is spread more widely. So, the name introduced into China along with the symbol 卐 is more possibly *swastika* 塞縛悉底迦.

As for the causes that many Chinese sutras and dictionaries ascribe the etymon of the Chinese character 卐 to the Sanskrit word *srivatsa*, it may be that the Buddhists once used various auspicious symbols of ancient India, but during the long spreading course they confused some signs, including Srivatsa and swastika. Therefore, among the *swastika graphics* listed by Huilin, the two symbols corresponding to *swastika* 塞縛悉底迦 and *srivatsa* 室利靺蹉, respectively, should be swapped with each other. That is the truth.

---

[15] Cf. Ernest J. Eitel, *A Sanskrit-Chinese Dictionary*, New Delhi: Cosmo Publications, 1981, pp. 158–159, 167–168.

5. The Meaning of Swastika in Ancient China

The meaning of 卐, as a Chinese character, is almost identical to the Buddhist explanation, such as "the appearance of virtues" or "auspicious signs", and so on. However, in the earlier periods, such as the Shang 商 and Zhou 周 Dynasties, or even earlier times, as a symbol, the swastika signified various meanings other than the Buddhist saying. A discussion on the symbolic meanings of swastika in ancient China is given as follows.

For a long time, people have tried to interpret the meanings of swastika throughout the world, or have been dedicated to explore its origin. But, the explanations are varied. Some believe the swastika is the symbol of genital organs; some think it signifies the female principle; some suppose it represents pregnancy and procreation; some say it is just a kind of ancient ornament or an emblem; and some believe it represents the four great castes of India, namely, Brahmin, Kshatriya, Vaisya and Sudra. Many other things are also thought to be the objects being symbolized by the swastika, such as fire, lightning, water, celestial phenomena, octopus and religious flag or military flag. Generally speaking, all these opinions can be divided into several categories as follows.

The first category of views is that the swastika is closely related with sex and procreation. For example, Hoffman regards the swastika as the symbol of coupling the male with the female principle; Birdwood thinks it is particularly the sign of the female sex.[16] Such views are supported by the fact that there are frequently swastika signs on the bodies of ancient goddesses and around them. These goddesses include Artemis, the Greek goddess of the hunt; Hera, the goddess of marriage and childbirth; Demeter, the goddess of harvest and agriculture, presiding over fertility; and Astarte, the goddess of the Middle East, being connected with fertility, sexuality and war.

Another piece of archeological evidence was found in the Troy site. This is a leaden idol, unearthed by Schliemann on the hill of Hissarlik. It is believed to be the goddess Artemis Nana of Chaldea. Characteristic figures of this goddess have been also discovered at Mycenae as well as in Cyprus. The vulva of the goddess is represented by a large triangle, and a swastika bending its arms to the left is in the middle of the vulva. Obviously, the swastika here symbolizes the sexuality and fertility of the goddess.

---

[16] Cf. Goblet d'Alviella, *The Migration of Swastika*, New York: University Books, 1956, p. 45.

The second category of views is that the swastika originates in natural phenomena, such as lightning or thunder. Some think the swastika represents lightning because it is like two crossed Z, while the letter Z is usually regarded as the sign of lightning. This is an explanation of the swastika from a pictographic perspective. In addition, some scholars reach the same conclusion according to the ancient Chinese characters. For instance, *lightning* 電 is written as 𖡄 in oracle bone inscription, and *thunder* 雷 is written as 𖡅. Their shapes are similar to that of the swastika, and thereby they are thought to be the objects which the swastika symbolizes.

Greg says that the swastika is the symbol of atmospheric phenomenon, or the emblem of the gods who dominate the atmospheric phenomenon. Among these atmospheric phenomena, the most typical ones are the thunderbolt and thunder-lightning god. There are varied thunder-lightning gods all over the ancient world, such as Indra of India, Thor of the Teuton and Scandinavian, Perun of the Slav, Zeus of the Greek and Jupiter of the Latin. Their distinct mark is the swastika.

The third category of views emphasizes the close relationship between the swastika and fire. A typical example is the Indian fire-god Agni. Burnouf makes the swastika the symbol of fire, or rather of the mystical twofold *arani*, namely, the fire-drill, which was used to produce fire among the early Aryans. He writes that the swastika sign "represents the two pieces of wood forming the *arani*, whose extremities were curved, or else enlarged, so that they could be firmly kept in place by four nails. At the point where they joined there was a small hole in which was placed the piece of wood, shaped like a spear, whose violent rotation, produced by whipping, made Agni to appear."[17]

Burnouf cites one hymn from the *Vedas* to emphasize the close relation between the Arani and fire-god Agni:

> Agni, thou art a sage, a priest, a king,
> Protector, father of the sacrifice;
> Commissioned by our men thou dost ascend
> A messenger, conveying to the sky
> Our hymns and offerings, though thy origin
> Be three folds, now from air and now from water,
> Now from the mystic double *Arani*.

---

[17] Emile Burnouf, *La science des Religions*, Paris, 1876, p. 240.

He says again, "The young queen, the mother of Fire, carried the royal infant mysteriously concealed in her bosom. She was a woman of the people, whose common name was Arani — that is, the instrument of wood (the Swastika) from which the fire was made or brought by rubbing."[18] Apparently, he regards the fire-drill as the prototype of the swastika.

The fourth category of views is that the swastika is a symbol of the sun. They think that most ancient people depict the sun with a graphic of a disc emitting lines. Later, the solar rays were simplified into a cross with the four arm ends bending to the right or left, to show the movement of the sun. Thus, the swastika is formed.

D'Alviella argues the view of "swastika symbolizing the sun" from four aspects.[19]

(1) In terms of the appearance of the swastika, its four arms undoubtedly represent the rays of the moving sun. Sometimes, these arms would be five or six, thereby this graphic is more like a sun.
(2) The so-called *triskèles* displays clearly that the swastika is the symbol of the sun. On Celtiberian coins, the face of the sun appears between three legs. To be specific, a circular human face is at the center; the face emits three bent legs. Three legs possibly signify three positions of the sun in its motion of a day, namely, dawn, noon and evening. Four legs are supposed to symbolize the four positions of the sun in a year, namely, Spring Equinox, Summer Solstice, Autumn Equinox and Winter Solstice.
(3) The swastika and the sun or sun-god often appear in the same picture. For example, Apollo is the famous sun-god in Greek mythology; swastikas usually appear on the Apollo portraits and other utensils related to Apollo. Most frequently, the swastika is combined with the solar disc. This pattern combination is found in ancient objects among the Greeks, Romans, Celts, Indians, Chinese, Japanese, etc.
(4) A number of materials confirm that the symbol swastika and graphic sun often replace each other. On the ancient coins of Ujjain and Andhra of India, the swastika and solar disc often substitute each other. In addition, Gardner once found a coin from the Mesembria city in Thrace; the city name *Mesembria* is marked on the coin, meaning

---

[18] *Ibid*, pp. 18, 252.
[19] Cf. Goblet d'Alviella, *The Migration of Symbols*, New York: University Books, 1956, pp. 45–83.

Midday City or Noon City.[20] However, other coins of this city mark the city name as ΜΕΣ卐, that is to say, the word "sun" of the original name "Mesembria" is substituted by the symbol 卐. Apparently, here, the swastika is identical to the sun.

In addition to the opinions of the swastika held mainly by foreign scholars as instanced above, the swastika is also given various symbolic meanings by the Chinese, and I think the primary object symbolized by it is the sun.

The most direct and distinct evidence of equating the swastika with the sun was seen during the reign of Empress Wuzetian 武則天 of the Tang. Empress Wu invented a number of new forms for Chinese characters already in existence, among which ㊋ was the word for sun, ☉ for moon, ○ for star, and so on. Obviously, the swastika sign 卐/卍 is completely identical to the sun. These Chinese characters were once very extensively used in ornamental writing, and even now the word ㊋ (sun) may be found in many of the famous stone inscriptions of that age, which have been preserved for us up to the present day. These inscriptions include that of *Famensi Stele* 法門寺碑, *Xinfasi Stele* 信法寺碑, *Wangrenqiu Stele* 王仁求碑, *Xiaoshiqiao Stele* 小石橋碑 and *Daiyueguan Stele* 岱岳觀碑.[21]

Empress Wu extensively promoted applying of the swastika; it seemed to indicate the Buddhist influence. In fact, the phenomenon of symbolizing the sun with the swastika already existed in China in the early times. The structure of the ancient Chinese character for sun is approximately the same as the swastika sign. As instanced in Fig. 6, four characters are on ancient bronzes, all of them are equivalent to the modern

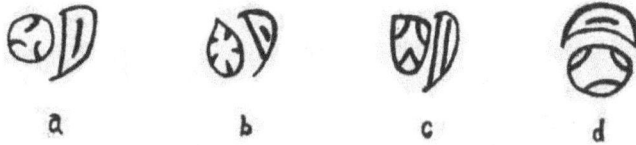

Fig. 6. Four characters for 明 on the ancient bronzewares.

---

[20] Cf. Percy Gardner, "Solar Symbols on the Coins of Macedon and Thrace", in *Numismatic Chronical*, Vol. XX (N.S.), p. 59.
[21] Cf. Thomas Wilson, *The Swastika*, ed. by Jamna Das Akhtar, Delhi: Oriental Publishers, 1973, Plate 2.

Fig. 7.   The character 囧 on the Gefuxin Tripod.

word 明, meaning *bright*, *light*, etc., consisting of 日 sun and 月 moon. It is easy to find that all the "sun" among these characters is roughly substituted by a solar disc and swastika with three or five arms. The three or five arms of the swastika possibly symbolize the solar flames or rays. The first "sun" is more like the so-called *triskèles*, namely, basically the standard swastika.

Another case is the ancient character 囧 jiong. Initially, 囧 meant 光 (light) and 明 (bright), while one of the ancient meanings of 明 was 日 (sun). Thus, the original meaning of 囧 seemed to be "shining sun." As shown in Fig. 7, it is the character 囧 on the Gefuxin Tripod 戈父辛鼎. This character is depicted as a disc with four short curves inside. These four curves look like the solar flames; if we connect them with a cross in the center, the whole graphic is more like a standard swastika.

The so-called *Fire Pattern* 火紋 or *Whirlpool Pattern* 渦紋 on the bronzewares of the Shang and Zhou Dynasties also displayed the close relationship between the swastika and the sun. Some scholars think the fire pattern is the sign of the sun. For example, Machengyuan 馬承源 says that the fire pattern is the symbol of the sun, its shape is round, there are four to eight curved flames along its periphery.[22] Indeed, the idea regarding the sun as heavenly fire or fire-spirit had been popular in China a long time ago. The *Biography of Xunshuang* 荀爽傳 in *Houhanshu* 後漢書 says, "On the earth it is fire, while in the sky it is sun." *Huainanzi* 淮南子 says, "The accumulated solar heat produces fire, the spirit of the fire is the sun." Therefore, the fire patters decorated on the ancient utensils ought to be symbols of the sun.

A good example is shown in Fig. 8. This is a graphic from a tile-end of the Qin 秦 Dynasty. There are two couples of bird in the picture, where

---

[22] Cf. Machengyuan 馬承源, ed. *Bronzewares of China* 中國青銅器, Shanghai Classics Publishing House 上海古籍出版社, 1988, pp. 338–339.

Fig. 8. The "two phoenixes worshiping the sun" tile-end of the Qin Dynasty.

Fig. 9. The fire pattern on a stemmed bowl of the Shang and Zhou Dynasties.

each bird faces another bird; between the two birds there is a fire pattern with three curves. This tile-end is titled as "two phoenixes worshiping the sun." It is very appropriate, for this fire pattern is undoubtedly the sign of the sun.

The fire patterns have been popular for a long time. They have been applied continuously from the period of the Erlitou Culture 二里頭文化 (1735 BC–1530 BC) up to the period of the Warring States (475 BC–221 BC). Another fire pattern is shown in Fig. 9; it appears on a stemmed bowl of the Shang 商 and Zhou 周 Dynasties. It is almost a *standard* swastika, with its four arms bent to the left.

The instances cited above reveal that in ancient China the swastika was mainly taken as the symbol of the sun. This symbolic meaning is the same as one of the symbolic meanings prevalent in foreign countries. So, the swastika sign of ancient China might be a product of the cultural exchanges between China and the foreign regions.

6. A Brief Conclusion

Basing on the discussion above, some conclusions can be given as follows.

First, the Chinese swastika could be divided into two types. That is to say, in the earlier period, the swastika was only a graphic or symbol which appeared on various utensils; this phenomenon can be called "symbolic type of swastika." Later, especially since the Tang Dynasty, the swastika also became a Chinese character 卍; this phenomenon may be called "character type of swastika." Generally speaking, the meanings, usages and even origins are different in these two types of swastikas. Hence "symbol swastika" and "character swastika" are two different concepts.

Second, the earliest appearance of the Chinese swastika can date back to the third millennium before Christ. In the earlier ages, when the swastika was only a symbol or a decorative pattern, it seemed to mainly symbolize the sun. This symbolic meaning is similar to that of the swastikas abroad. In view of the fact that the early swastikas are found only in the border areas of China, such as the present provinces of Qinghai 青海 and Liaoning 遼寧, the possibility of interaction between the Chinese swastika and the foreign swastika cannot be ruled out.

Third, the initial appearance of the swastika as a Chinese character 卍 ought to date back at least to the Former Han Dynasty instead of the Tang Dynasty. The early character 卍 possibly had less to do with Indian Buddhism, and was introduced into China by the common people. But, in later generations, the official formation of the Chinese character 卍 was obviously influenced by Buddhism, thereby causing the gradual disappearance of the early concept of the swastika.

Fourth, it is incorrect that the current Chinese dictionaries ascribe the etymon of the character 卍 to the Sanskrit word srivatsa 室利靺蹉; the most appropriate original word seems to be swastika 塞縛悉底迦.

Chapter 13

Discussion on the Relations between 饕餮 Taotie and Greedy Demon

The 饕餮 taotie is a curious and interesting term from ancient China. Generally, it refers to nothing more than the following: a certain evil greedy person, the fierce and cruel tribe, a kind of bloodthirsty monster as well as a type of symbol on ancient utensils, or a metaphor for gluttonous people. The definitions do not seem complicated. However, once the problems about its attributes, special meaning and origin are involved, it is difficult to reach a consensus. Many scholars have already offered a lot to this subject, while I have some new ideas on it, so I contribute them as follows. I should emphasize that the discussion in this chapter only deals with the name *taotie* in ancient Chinese records and its relations with the *greedy demon* of western religions, rather than matters involving the decorative pattern or symbol *taotie*.[1]

1. The Related Records in Chinese Ancient Literatures

Zuozhuan 左傳 (*Commentary on Spring and Autumn Annals by Zuoqiuming* 左丘明) says that the taotie is a greedy villain: In earlier times, the unfilial son of Dihong 帝鴻 was very vicious and did many evil

---

[1] About the designs and classifications of symbol taotie, cf. Hangxiaochun 杭曉春, "A Study on the Taotie Symbol of the Bronzewares" 青銅器饕餮紋研究述評, in *Palace Museum Journal* 故宮博物院院刊, 2005, No. 1, pp. 95–111.

things; so, he was given the nickname 渾敦 Hundun. The unfilial son of Shaohao 少皞 was treacherous and often snitched and slandered others; so, he was called 窮奇 Qiongqi. The unfilial son of 顓頊 Zhuanxu was very stupid and refused to be civilized, so, he was known as 檮杌 Taowu. In addition, the unfilial son of 縉雲 Jinyun was gluttonous and very greedy for money, but refused to help the poor, so he was named 饕餮 Taotie. These four evil persons did harm to the people for a long time till the ruling period of the sage Emperor Shun 舜. He exiled the four villains and their clans to the barbarian countries surrounding China, letting them live with devils and monsters.[2]

Here, the taotie 饕餮 was depicted to be an evil person, greedy for food and wealth, extravagant, indulgent and unsympathetic; thereby, together with his clansmen, he was exiled by the emperor to the barbarian deserts. According to this statement, Taotie was just a man, or a clan named Taotie.

Lüshichunqiu 呂氏春秋 (*The Spring and Autumn of Lübuwei*) says that 饕餮 taotie was the name of a ferocious tribe. Many barbarian tribes surrounded China, for example, Dajie 大解, Linyu 陵魚, Luye 鹿野 and Yaoshan 搖山 in the east; Fulou 縛婁, Yangyu 陽禺 and Huandou 驩兜 in the south; Boren 僰人, Zhouren 舟人 and Turen 突人 in west; as well as Taotie 饕餮, Qiongqi 窮奇 and Daner 儋耳 in the north. There was no sovereign in all these countries. The people living there were like animals; the old were in dread of the young, and the ferocious ones were honored. They kept fighting each other until they almost killed all the enemies.[3]

---

[2] Cf. *Zuozhuan* 左傳, fasc. 20, "the 18th year of Wen" 文公十八年, in *Interpretation on the Thirteen Classics* 十三經注疏, Book II, Zhonghua Book Company 中華書局, 1980, pp. 1862–1863. The Chinese text is as follows: "昔帝鴻氏有不才子, 掩義隱賊, 好行凶德, 醜類惡物, 頑嚚不友, 是與比周。天下之民謂之渾敦。少皞氏有不才子, 毀信廢忠, 崇飾惡言, 靖譖庸回, 服讒搜慝, 以誣盛德。天下之民謂之窮奇。顓頊氏有不才子, 不可教訓, 不知話言, 告之則頑, 舍之則嚚, 傲很明德, 以亂天常。天下之民謂之檮杌。此三族也, 世濟其凶, 增其惡名, 以至於堯, 堯不能去。縉雲氏有不才子, 貪於飲食, 冒於貨賄; 侵欲崇侈, 不可盈厭; 聚斂積實, 不知紀極; 不分孤寡, 不恤窮匱。天下之民以比三凶, 謂之饕餮。舜臣堯, 賓於四門, 流四凶族渾敦、窮奇、檮杌、饕餮, 投諸四裔, 以禦螭魅。是以堯崩而天下如一, 同心戴舜, 以為天子, 以其舉十六相, 去四凶也。"

[3] Cf. *Lüshichunqiu* 呂氏春秋, commentated by Gaoyou 高誘, fasc. 20 "Views on the Reason for Existence of Sovereigns" 恃君覽, in *Zhuzijicheng* 諸子集成 (*Philosophers Integration*), Book VI, Shanghai Book-shop Press 上海書店, 1986, pp. 255–256. The Chinese text is as follows: "非濱之東, 夷穢之鄉, 大解、陵魚、其鹿野、搖山、揚島,

The Taotie mentioned here was apparently the name of a belligerent tribe. They inhabited the *barbarian lands* outside China, just like the Taotie clan referred to by *Zuozhuan*. *Shenyijing* 神異經 (*Miraculous Stories*) also states that the *Taotie* was an ethnic group: "There is an ethnic group in the southwestern region. Their bodies are hairy, wear the pig head-like hats. They are ferocious and mean, keen to accumulate wealth but do not spend it. They rob others, bully the weak, and dare not to attack crowds but plundering who is alone. They are called Taotie. The tribe Sanmiao 三苗 are similar to them, so is called Taotie." A similar description is found elsewhere in the same book: "There is an ethnic group in the western wilderness. Their face, hands and feet are same as human, they have wings under the flanks but cannot fly. This is Miao people, who are gluttonous, greedy, indulgent, extravagant and morally corrupt, hence are exiled in this land."[4]

In addition to being depicted as a person or a tribe, *taotie* was also described as a symbol or a pattern. For example, *Lüshichunqiu* 呂氏春秋 states that in order to caution people against being too greedy, the government of the Zhou Dynasty decorated the tripod with the taotie design, for it symbolized the greedy character. *Shanhaijing* 山海經 (*Stories of Mountains and Seas*) says that there was a kind of beast in Gouwu Mountain 鉤吾山, with a sheep-like body and human face, with the eyes under the arms, its teeth the same as that of a tiger, sharp claws and a voice sounding like a baby. It was named Paoxiao 狍鴞, and fed on humans. Guopu 郭璞 of the Jin 晉 Dynasty explained it as follows: "It is gluttonous and greedy, fond of eating human, but before it swallows completely it hurts itself. Its figure is painted on the tripod of the Xia 夏 Dynasty, is namely the taotie 饕餮 mentioned in *Zuozhuan* 左傳."[5]

大人之居,多無君。揚、漢之南,百越之際,敝凱、諸夫風、余靡之地,縛婁、陽禺、驩兜之國,多無君。氐、羌、呼唐、離水之西,僰人、野人、篇笮之川,舟人、送龍、突人之鄉,多無君。雁門之北,鷹隼所鷙,須窺之國,饕餮、窮奇之地,叔逆之所,儋耳之居,多無君。此四方之無君者也,其民麋鹿禽獸,少者使長,長者畏壯,有力者賢,暴傲者尊。日夜相殘,無時休息,以盡其類。"

[4] Cf. *Shiji* 史記, fasc. 1, Zhonghua Book Company 中華書局, 1975, p. 38. *Shenyijing* 神異經, in *Sikuquanshu* 四庫全書, Book 1042, Taibei 臺北: The Commercial Press, 1983, pp. 1042–1269.

[5] Cf. *Shanhaijing* 山海經, fasc. 3, commentated by Guopu 郭璞, in *Sikuquanshu* 四庫全書, Book 1042, Taibei 臺北: The Commercial Press, 1983, p. 24. The Chinese text is as follows: "爲物貪惏,食人未盡,還害其身,像在夏鼎。《左傳》所謂饕餮是也。"

Lüdalin 呂大臨 of the Song Dynasty explained the design of the Gui Tripod 癸鼎 with the beast face of the taotie symbol. It was the taotie mentioned in *Lüshichunqiu* 呂氏春秋, which has only the head without the body. It also symbolized the unfilial son of Jinyun 縉雲, who was gluttonous, and was called Taotie. The ancients cast such a tripod as caution against extreme gluttony.[6] Here, the so-called *taotie symbol* was clearly linked to the person Taotie mentioned in *Lüshichunqiu* 呂氏春秋 and *Zuozhuan* 左傳. The *Antiquity Pictures* 博古圖 had a similar description when it introduced a tripod of the Shang Dynasty: The design on this tripod was like the so-called Taotie in legends, and so was named Taotie Tripod. Actually, the taotie symbol of the Zhou Dynasty was just imitation and improvement of the taotie of the Xia 夏 and Shang 商 Dynasties. So, the taotie symbol on the tripod did not originate in the Zhou Dynasty but in much earlier ages. As for its meaning, it could have been for cautioning people against a close relationship with evil and monstrous beings.[7] According to the discussion above, the ancients seemed to divide taotie's meanings into three categories: a certain evil person, a certain ferocious tribe as well as a symbolic design on the bronzewares.

2. The Main Viewpoints and Conflicting Opinions of Modern Times

A number of modern scholars have done useful research on taotie; among them, the studies conducted by Sunzuoyun 孫作雲 and Yangximei 楊希枚 were particularly detailed and exhaustive. A brief introduction and analysis of these opinions is summarized as follows:

---

[6] Cf. Lüdalin 呂大臨, *Kaogutu* 考古圖 (*Archeological Pictures*), fasc. 1, in *Sikuquanshu* 四庫全書, Book 840, Taibei 臺北: The Commercial Press, 1983, pp. 840–898.

[7] Cf. Wangfu 王黼, *Chongxiuxuanhebogutu* 重修宣和博古圖 (New Edition of Antiquity Pictures, edited in the reign of Xuanhe), fasc. 1, in *Sikuquanshu* 四庫全書, Book 840, Taibei 臺北: The Commercial Press, 1983, pp. 840–394. The Chinese text is as follows: "按，此鼎款識純古，仿佛饕餮之形。後人觀象立名，故取爲號。至周監二代，文物大備，凡爲鼎者，悉以此爲飾，遂使《呂氏春秋》獨謂周鼎著饕餮，而不知其原實啟於古也。按《春秋·宣公三年》，王孫滿對楚子問鼎之語曰：'昔夏之方有德也，遠方圖物，貢金九牧，鑄鼎象物，故民入川澤山林，不逢不若，魑魅魍魎，莫能逢之。'則商之爲法，亦基於夏而已，周實繼商，故亦有之耳。昔人即器以寓意，即意以見禮，即禮以示戒者如此。"

(1) Taotie being Regarded as a Symbol
Sunzuoyun divided the taotie symbols into five categories according to their appearance. First, the most common taotie symbol was the so-called *Beast Face Pattern* 獸面紋. The second one was the "taotie pattern with human face" 人面形饕餮紋; sometimes, it had all the facial organs of eyebrows, eyes, nose, mouth and ears. Third, it was depicted in the form of a beast head with a human body or a human figure. Fourth, it had the appearance of a real beast, but sat or knelt like a human instead of standing on its four feet like an animal. Fifth, it was shaped as a human face and snake body, though such cases were seldom seen.[8] Apparently, according to this view, a considerable part of the patterns on the utensils of the Shang and Zhou Dynasties should be called Taotie 饕餮.

Yangximei 楊希枚 was not sure which pattern the taotie belonged to, and he suspected that the ancients misunderstood the meaning of the taotie, or at least blurred it. He said that the pattern on tripods of the Shang and Zhou mentioned in *Kaogutu* 考古圖 and *Bogutu* 博古圖 was like a beast face, which consisted of two beasts connected at the heads. This appearance was quite different from the depiction of *Lüshichunqiu* 呂氏春秋 in that "it has only the head and no body 有首無身", so they were not necessarily the same being. In fact, if the patterns mentioned in *Lüshichunqiu* were really taotie 饕餮, those mentioned in *Kaogutu* and *Bogutu* cannot bet taotie, and vice versa.

In addition, *Lüshichunqiu* explained the taotie's meaning that as a result of gluttony, the taotie destroyed the body. Yangximei thought this saying was possibly just the opinion of the author or the popular explanation of the Qin 秦 Dynasty, rather than the initial concept of the Zhou Dynasty and earlier ages. Therefore, the symbolic meanings of such taotie patterns are not certain yet.

Besides, scholars of the Song Dynasty call the patterns on bronzes of the Shang and Zhou taotie 饕餮 because they misunderstand the words in *Lüshichunqiu*. The statements "it is similar to the appearance of taotie" and "the later people name it according to the image" show an uncertainty, so these authors perhaps only guess that these designs are *taotie*.[9]

---

[8] Cf. Sunzuoyun 孫作雲, *Collected Works of Sunzuoyun: Art Archeology and Folklore Studies* 孫作雲文集: 美術考古與民俗研究, Henan University Press 河南大學出版社, 2003, pp. 54–62.
[9] About the opinions of Yangximei, cf. his paper "On the Taotie and Taotie Symbol" 論饕餮與饕餮紋, in *Newsletter of Chinese Ethnology* 中國民族學通訊, No. 5, Taibei 臺北, September, 1966, pp. 1–13.

Sunzuoyun distinctly equated the taotie with Chiyou 蚩尤, the legendary character in Chinese myths. He repeated this view in several papers.[10] His arguments could be summarized as follows. First, 縉雲 Jinyun is 戩雲 Jianyun, and the name derives from the story of Huangdi 黃帝 (Yellow Emperor) destroying Chiyou 蚩尤. Therefore, the taotie, the unfilial son of Jinyun, is doubtless the Chiyou. Second, Taotie means gluttonous, while Jinyun's unfilial son Taotie was also gluttonous, so the Taotie was surely the Chiyou. Third, both Taotie and Chiyou had a snake-like appearance: Taotie's shape had a beast head and a snake body. So, Taotie is Chiyou. Fourth, according to the legend, Chiyou was the weapon inventor, while the knives and swords were often seen next to the Taotie pattern on the bronzewares. So, the Taotie is Chiyou. Fifth, Taotie pattern was applied to exorcise evil spirits and was called *Images of Intimidation* 畏图. The Chiyou image was used by Huangdi 黃帝 to deter the world, obviously also an *image of intimidation*. Thus, the Taotie 饕餮 is Chiyou 蚩尤. A number of other similar arguments listed by Sunzuoyun are also reasonable.[11]

Later, the opinion of Taotie being Chiyou was also held by Yuanke 袁珂. In his annotation on *Shanhaijing* 山海經 (*Stories of Mountains and Seas*), he believed the taotie symbol quite possibly referred to the Chiyou who opposed the Huangdi 黃帝. This is because the ancients said that in the Xia, Shang and Zhou Dynasties, the image of Chiyou was often decorated on sacrificial vessels to caution against greed and cruelty. This statement coincides with that of *Lüshichunqiu*. In addition, *Shiji* 史記 said that Jinyun's son Taotie was the descendant of Yandi 炎帝 (Blazing Emperor), surnamed Jiang 姜, while the Chiyou was also the descendant of Yandi, surnamed Jiang. Furthermore, *Dadailiji* 大戴禮記 said that Chiyou was a greedy person among the common people; apparently, his features were

---

[10] For example, "A Study on the Taotie 饕餮考", in *Zhonghe Monthly* 中和月刊, No. 5, Vol. 1, 2, 3, 1944; "On the Taotie 說饕餮", 1952, unpublished; "A Study on the Appearance of Taotie and Taotie's Legends 饕餮形象與饕餮傳說的綜合研究", 1960, unpublished; "Human-Face Square Tripod of the Shang Dynasty is Taotie Symbol Tripod 說商代人面方鼎即饕餮紋鼎", in *Newsletter of Henan Relics and Museology* 河南文博通訊, 1980, No. 1; and so on.

[11] Cf. Sunzuoyun 孫作雲, *Collected Works of Sunzuoyun: Studies on the Ancient Chinese Mythology (I)* 孫作雲文集: 中國古代神話傳說研究 (上), Henan University Press 河南大學出版社, 2003, pp. 305–325.

similar to that of Paoxiao 狍鴞 in *Shanhaijing* 山海經 and Taotie in *Shenyijing* 神異經. Based on these suppositions, the prototype of the Taotie may be the Chiyou.[12]

I think, probably, there was once certain cultural communication between the Chinese taotie symbol and the western exorcising mask. The taotie symbols on ancient Chinese utensils feature the eye, horn and snake-body, meaning "pursuing good fortune and avoiding disaster". On the other hand, the Humbaba head of Mesopotamia in the Assyrian period and the Gorgon head of Greece, which is said to be derived from Humbaba, are quite analogous to the taotie patterns. Hence, there is possibly a relationship between the taotie symbol and the exorcising masks of the West Asia.[13]

Besides, some scholars believe the taotie pattern is an artistic representation of a real animal.[14] For instance, Lizehou 李澤厚 roughly agreed with the view of taotie being an ox head[15]; Hanhuchu 韓湖初 said that, according to appearance, the taotie looked more like a bull[16]; Greel thought that the taotie represented the image of buffalo[17]; and Hentze believed the taotie represented the ox head and the curved ox horn symbolized the moon, thereby the taotie was the moon-god, meaning death and darkness.[18]

Another idea was to think of the taotie as a tiger head design. For example, Fengqiyong 馮其庸 said the following: "Its face is the idealized

---

[12] Cf. Yuanke 袁珂, *Corrections and Comments on Shanhaijing* 山海經校注, Shanghai Classics Publishing House 上海古籍出版社, 1980, pp. 374–375.

[13] Cf. Ruichuanming 芮傳明 & Yutaishan 余太山, *The Comparison of Symbols between China and the Occident* 中西紋飾比較, Shanghai Classics Publishing House 上海古籍出版社, 1995, pp. 331–352.

[14] About these statements, cf. Hangxiaochun 杭曉春, "A Study on the Taotie Symbol of the Bronzewares" 青銅器饕餮紋研究述評, in *Palace Museum Journal* 故宮博物院院刊, 2005, No. 1, pp. 95–111.

[15] Cf. Lizehou 李澤厚, *Meidelicheng* 美的歷程 (*History of Chinese Aesthetics*), Anhui Literature and Art Publishing House 安徽文藝出版社, 1999, p. 43.

[16] Cf. Hanhucnu 韓湖初, "A Brief Discussion on the Hideous Beauty of Taotie on the Bronzeware 略論青銅饕餮的猙獰美", in *Journal of South China Normal University* 華南師範大學學報, 1998, No. 4, p. 50.

[17] Cf. H.G. Greel, *Birth of China*, New York, 1937, p. 117.

[18] Cf. S. Allan, *History, Thoughts and Cultures of Earlier China* 早期中國歷史思想與文化, tr. by Yangmin 楊民, etc., Liaoning Education Publishing House 遼寧教育出版社, 1999, p. 231.

and stylized fierce beast, which is mainly the tiger head, I think."[19] Waterbury also thought the taotie was the symbol of a tiger, and it symbolized the solar god, having the functions of exorcising and protection of agriculture.[20] In addition, the goat head and deer head were also regarded by some scholars as the object that the taotie symbolized.

(2) Taotie being Regarded as an Ethnic Group

Yangximei 楊希枚 insisted on the opinion that the taotie is an ethnic group. He believed that the Taotie 饕餮 mentioned in *Zuozhuan* 左傳, *Lüshichunqiu* 呂氏春秋 and *Shenyijing* 神異經 certainly referred to a ferocious tribe which existed abroad early on. Although *Shiji* 史記 and *Shanhaijing* 山海經 claimed that the taotie was a ferocious beast or monster, just like Huntun 渾沌, QiongQi 窮其 and Taowu 檮杌, it is also true that Taotie is a tribal name.

The view of "taotie being Sanmiao 三苗" is not correct because it derives from a mistaken explanation since the Tang Dynasty. *Shenyijing*'s description of "its people are taotie 饕餮" meant actually that the Miao people were gluttonous and greedy, rather than that their tribal name was Taotie.

Besides, the saying "taotie is the name for ferocious beast" derives from a misreading of the related text of *Lüshichunqiu* and Guopu's mistaken explanation for Paoxiao 狍鴞. Finally, the author of *Zuozhuanzhengyi* 左傳正義 possibly forged some grounds to prove that taotie was a beast name. Therefore, Yangximei did not think taotie was the name for a monstrous beast.[21]

According to the Yangximei, Taotie 饕餮 ought to be the name for an ancient ethnic group known for ferocity. These people seemed to live in the plains near vast waters, probably in the region of Yancai 奄蔡 and Kangju 康居. The Taotie people appeared to have close relations with

---

[19] Cf. Fengqiyong 馮其庸, "The Meaning and Transformation of Beast-Face Human figure on the Jadeware of Liangzhu Period 良渚玉器上神人獸面圖形的內涵及其衍變", in *Chinese Cultures* 中國文化, December, No. 5, 1991.

[20] Cf. Frorance Waterbury, *Early Chinese Symbols and Literature*, New York, 1942.

[21] About these three opinions, cf. Yangximei 楊希枚, "On the Taotie and Taotie Symbol" 論饕餮與饕餮紋, in *Newsletter of Chinese Ethnology* 中國民族學通訊, No. 5, Taibei 臺北, September, 1966, pp. 1–13.

Xiongnu 匈奴, western barbarians 西戎 and Scythians. All these tribes may originate from a single ethnic group.[22]

Zhengshixu 鄭師許 insisted on the view that Taotie 饕餮 was Sanmiao 三苗, and the Chinese characters 饕餮 were the transliterations of the Miao dialect. Just like 夏 xia, 夷 yi, 蠻 man, 閩 min, 狄 di and so on, Taotie 饕餮 was initially also a totem for its ethnic group.[23]

To sum up, it is still difficult to identify distinctly the so-called *Taotie* 饕餮. It could be roughly classified into two categories, the living being and a symbol, while in a detailed classification, there are a lot of varied opinions. For example, some think it is an ethnic group, some think it is a human individual, or a person with magical powers, as well as a kind of curious beast. Even if one agrees with the view of Taotie being a tribal name, there are still varied opinions about the inhabiting region and national affiliation. As for the view of taotie being a symbol, there are also many different opinions about its meaning. Nevertheless, based on the numerous depictions of the taotie 饕餮, we may find that it contains concepts similar to that of the *Greedy Demon* in ancient religions of the West Asia, thereby seeming to hint that a certain communication had once existed between the *Taotie* and *Greedy Demon*. First of all, I will summarize the descriptions about the greedy demon as follows.

3. Āz or Greedy Demon in the West Asia

There is a villain in the mythology and religions of the ancient Iran, namely, the king of devils Āz. In most cases, especially in Manichean myths, it is a female being, the mother of devils. Her most noted characteristic is greed. Actually, in the Iranian languages, the original meaning of āz is greedy, lusted, desire and so on, which shows a lively image of the devil chief Āz.

The records related to Āz were mainly found in Iranian literatures of Zoroastrianism and Manicheism, as well as Chinese documents of

---

[22] Cf. Yangximei 楊希枚, "On the Ancient Taotie Tribe" 古饕餮民族考, in *Bulletin of the Institute of Ethnology, Academia Sinica* 中央研究院民族學研究所集刊, No. 24, Taibei, 1967, pp. 1–26.

[23] Cf. Zhengshixu 鄭師許, "A study on the Taotie" 饕餮考, in *The Eastern Miscellany* 東方雜誌, Vol. 28, No. 7, pp. 75–81.

Manicheism. Based on these materials, Āz is briefly portrayed as follows.

Initially, the name Āz appears in the myths of Zoroastrianism. As an evil spirit, Āz is a powerful destroyer; its partner is called Niyāz and has a close relationship with it. *Āz* means *greed*, while *Niyāz* means *desire*. On many occasions, they are regarded as being in the same category; both of them are supernatural devils.

The Avesta is the primary collection of religious texts of Zoroastrianism. The surviving texts of the Avesta consist of several parts.[24] The *Gathas* does not mention Āz, but it is mentioned many times in *Khorda Avesta*, *Vendidād* and *Bundahišn*. For instance, a paragraph in *Vendidad* says that Āz is the deadly foe to Ātar, while the latter is the son of good god Ahura Mazda, and is the fire god. He once repeatedly called for help because of Āz's serious threats:

> On the first part of the night, Ātar, the son of Ahura Mazda, calls the master of the house for help, saying: "Up! arise, thou master of the house! put on thy girdle on thy clothes, wash thy hands, take wood, bring it unto me, and let me burn bright with the clean wood, carried by thy well-washed hands. Here comes Āz, made by the Daevas, who consumes me and wants to put me out of the world.[25]

After this calling for help, Ātar again appealed for help twice: "On the second part of the night, Ātar, the son of Ahura Mazda, calls the husbandman for help, saying …"; "On the third part of the night, Ātar, the son of Ahura Mazda, calls the holy Sraosha for help, saying …" Then, the holy Sraosha woke up the bird named Parodarsh. The latter is in fact the rooster, and it crows loudly at the mighty demon. Apparently, Parodarsh cawing on "the third part of the night" symbolizes the cock crowing at dawn; hence, Āz, the foe of Ātar, is the symbol of darkness or evil.

Just like the manifestation of its name, the main evil of Āz is greed. The *Bundahishn*, which was written around the 8th and 9th centuries,

---

[24] The *Avesta* consists of literatures written in different periods and places. It is said that originally the *Avesta* included 21 Books, but the existing *Avesta* is only a little fraction of it, such as *Yasna*, *Gathas*, *Visperad*, *Vendidad* and *Khorta Avesta*. The *Gathas* is believed to have been composed by Zoroaster himself, reflecting most distinctly his thoughts.

[25] Cf. *Vendidad*, Fargard 18, II, digital edition, 1995; tr. by James Darmesteteramd, from *Sacred Books of the East*, American edition, Vol. 3, New York, 1898.

depicts Āz as follows: "The devil Āz is that which swallows things; when, owing to privation, nothing is obtained, it devours from its person. It is a deception which will not pile up, and will not be sated, when the entire wealth of the world is given to it. As one says, 'The eye of the covetous is an abode which has no boundaries.' ... This too one says, the strength of the devil Āz is owing to that person who is not content with his own wife, and abducts even those of others."[26] Obviously, the greed of Āz included gluttony, coveting wealth, and desiring and lusting, so he is really the destroyer of the world.

Now, let us examine Āz's identity and status in Zoroastrianism. In fact, the story of Āz derives mainly from Zurvanism,[27] a branch of Zoroastrianism. According to its myths, the divinity Zurvan is a primordial deity, who engenders equal-but-opposite twins, Ahura Mazda (Ohrmazd) and Angra Mainyu (Ahriman). The creation process of the twins is as follows.

In the beginning, the great God Zurvan exists alone. Desiring offspring that would create heaven, hell and everything in the world, Zurvan sacrifices for a thousand years. Toward the end of this period, Zurvan begins to doubt the efficacy of the sacrifice, and in the moment of this doubt Ahriman is conceived. Thus, Ohrmazd is born of the sacrifice, while Ahriman is born of the doubt. Upon realizing that twins are to be born, Zurvan resolves to grant the first-born sovereignty over creation. After knowing this decision, Ahriman preempts Ohrmazd by ripping open the womb to emerge first. Though Ohrmazd is fragrant and bright while Ahriman is stinking and dark, Zurvan has to concede Ahriman's sovereignty, but limits his kingship to a period of 9000 years, after which Ohrmazd would rule forever.

Interestingly enough, the weapon with which Ahriman destroys the world comes from Zurvan's gift; it is Āz, namely, greed and desires. Zadspram wrote the following in the 9th century:

> When first creation began to move, and Zurvān for the sake of movement brought that form, the black and ashen garment, to Ahriman, he made a treaty in this wise: "This is that implement like unto fire, blazing, harassing all creatures, that hath the very substance of Āz

---

[26] B.T. Anklesaria (tr.), *Iranian or Greater Bundahishn*, Chapter XXVII, Bombay, 1956.
[27] Zurvanism is a sect of Zoroastrianism, forms in as early as Achaemenid Dynasty; later, it has been regarded as a heresy. *Zurvan* means time or destiny in Pahlavi.

(concupiscence). When the period of nine thousand years comes to an end, if thou hast not perfectly fulfilled that which thou didst threaten in the beginning, that thou wouldst bring all material existence to hate Ohrmazd and to love thee — and verily this is belief in one Principle only, that the Increaser and the Destroyer are the same — then by means of these weapons Āz will devour that which is thine, thy creation; and she herself will starve; for she will no longer obtain food from the creatures of Ohrmazd — like a frog that liveth in the water; so long as it defileth the water, it liveth by it, but when the water is withdrawn from it, it dieth, parched."[28]

Here, the Āz is both a garment of desires and a female demon; by means of it or her, Ahriman attacks against the good god Ohrmazd. Besides, in the Manicheism, Āz is promoted to a status of *Mother of Devils*, as showed in the following Middle Persian texts of Manicheism:

Then that tricked Āz was filled with heavy anger. She began to desire a step forward, and she thought: "After those two forms — the female and the male — of God Narisah that I have seen, I will form those two creatures, the male and the female, so that they become my garment and veil. ... by me these two creatures shall not be taken away, and I will let no misery and wretchedness come over them." Thereupon the Āz from all that progeny of the demons that had fallen down unto the earth from the sky put on as a garment these two, the male Asrēshtār and the female Asrēshtār, lion-shaped, lustful and wrathful, sinful and terrible. She made them her own veil and garment and raged within them. And just as the Āz herself from the primeval beginning in that hell of Darkness, her abode, had taught the demons and witches, the demons of wrath, the Mazans and Asrēshtārs, male and female, lewdness and copulation, so again thereafter Āz began to teach also these, the other male and female Mazans and Asrēshtārs that had fallen unto the earth from the sky, lewdness and copulation so that they might become lewd and copulate and, with joined bodies, be mixed together and so that dragon progeny might be born from them, and so that Āz then might take and devour that progeny in order to make herefrom two creatures, a man and a woman. ...

---

[28] Cf. the quotation in R.C. Zaeher, *The Dawn and Twilight to Zoroastrianism*, New York, 1961, p. 223.

(Āz formed the first man.) And also from above, from the sky, she joined for him binding and connection with the Mazans and the Asrēshtārs and the zodiac and the planets so that upon him might rain wrath, lust and sinfulness from the Mazans and the zodiac, and so that the will might penetrate him to become more cruel and more Mazan-like, greedy and lustful. And when that male creature had been born, then she gave it the name of the "first man," namely Gēhmurd. ... She again in the same way formed and built another body, a female one, with bones, sinews, flesh, veins and skin. ...

(Āz formed the first woman.) And also for her, from the sky she joined binding and connection with the zodiac and the planets so that also upon her might rain wrath, lewdness and sinfulness from the Mazans and the zodiac, and so that the will might penetrate her to become more cruel and more sinful, filled with lewdness and lust, and so that she might deceive this man through lust, and so that from these two creatures mankind might be born in the world, and so that they might become greedy and lustful and behave wrathfully and maliciously and mercilessly, and so that they might strike water and fire, trees and plants and worship greed and lust, do what the demons want, and go to hell.[29]

Evidently, the noted characteristics of Āz are greed, lust, cruelty, ferocity, malice and so on. More abominably, Āz attempts to make all mankind possess these evil characteristics. Manicheism emphasizes this in particular; Ort says, "The names of those demons, Āz and Ahrmēn, appear in Manichaean literature. Āz is the demon of lust. Ahrmēn is the opponent of the primal man, Orhmizd. Ahrmēn and Āz very often represent the evil powers in Manichaean texts."[30] This depiction reveals the typical image of Āz, extreme greed and evil, so it is generally called Greedy *Demon*.

The following two instances also vividly display Āz's features.

Xormuzta tängri came and descended together with the Fivefold God in order at the command of all gods to fight the devil. He fought Šimnu[31]

---

[29] Cf. Jes P. Asmussen, *Manicchaean Literature: Representative Texts Chiefly from Middle Persian and Parthian Writings*, Delmar, New York, 1975, pp. 128–130.
[30] Cf. L.J. Rudolf Ort, *Mani, a Riligio-Historical Description of his Personality*, Leiden: E.J.Brill, 1967, p. 50.
[31] The name *Šimnu* in Turkic texts corresponds to *Ahrmēn* in Iranian texts.

with the evil deeds and with the five kinds of devils. Then at the time god and devil, light and darkness were mixed. Xormuzda tängri's son, the Fivefold God, our soul, fought for some time against the devil and was wounded. And being mixed with the evil knowledge of the uppermost one of all devils and the insatiable and shameless Āz devil's 140 myriads of devils, he became witless and weak-willed: He completely forgot the land of the immortal gods, in which he himself was born and created, and parted from the gods of light.[32]

This is a passage of the Manichean creation myth, telling us that the primal man (Xormuzta/Orhmizd) is defeated by the dark devils together with his five sons, who are in fact human souls. Owing to the allure of Āz, they lose their senses and forget their nature. Here, the Āz is depicted as *insatiable* and *shameless*. The same words are also found in another text:

> Because of evil deeds and sin we incur agony upon ourselves, and the light of the Fivefold God, which we in the course of day have eaten, goes to the evil place, because we ourselves, our souls, wandered in love of the insatiable and shameless Āz demon. For this reason, my God, we pray to be liberated from sin. Forgive my sin! For the sake of the divine omen of religion![33]

According to Manichean doctrine, the biggest sin is imprisoning souls, namely, causing them to be allured and imprisoned by the devils, losing intelligence (nous). The souls are light elements, which are homogeneous with the Light God, while the flesh bodies are dark devils.

The current chief Chinese Manichean literatures include 摩尼教殘經 Monijiaocanjing (*Fragmentary Manichean Treatise*), 下部讚 Xiabuzan (The Lower Section of the Manichean Hymns) and 摩尼光佛教法儀略 Moniguangfujiaofayilüe (*The Compendium of the Doctrines and the Styles of the Teaching of Mani, the Buddha of Light*). All of these texts derive from Iranian writings, but have a lot of Chinese Buddhist loanwords. The Iranian word *Āz* is precisely translated into 貪魔 Tanmo, *Greedy Demon*.

The name 貪魔 tanmo appears in these texts more than ten times. For example, *Monijiaocanjing* 摩尼教殘經 says, "Such flesh body is also

---

[32] Cf. Jes p. Asmussen, *Xᵘāstvānift: Studies in Manichaeism*, Copenhagen: Prostant Apud Munksgaard, 1965, p. 193.

[33] *Ibid.*, p. 198.

called Old Man, consisting of bones, sinews, veins, flesh, skin, grudge, annoyance, lust, wrath, foolishness, greed, gluttony and extravagance. These thirteen things compose a body, symbolizing the second dark night of the zone where there is no start and light; it is namely the evil thoughts of the greedy demon."

"There are two dark nights. The first dark night is the greedy demon. Its twelve hours are bones, sinews, veins, flesh, skin etc, as well as grudge, annoyance, lust, wrath, foolishness, greed, gluttony and so on. All these are impure poisons, symbolizing the first dark night of the dark land where there is no start and light." "The greedy demon builds a new impure city owing to the old one being broken. It spreads stupidity and five desires. …"

Xiabuzan 下部讚 says, "The dark mother of all the devilish kings, and the root and source of all evil and poisonous deeds. It is also the heart of the ferocious and venomous Yakṣas, and also the thought in the mind of the greedy devil." "How sad of the masses of living beings in the world! Being unable to believe devoutly and to discover the right road, they seek for wealth, day and night without a moment's pause, all for the sake of the flesh-body, the greedy, devilish lord."

Apparently, the obvious features of the greedy demon (*Tanmo*) are coveting wealth, lust, gluttony and so on.

4. On the Relationship Between Taotie 饕餮 and Greedy Demon

After a comparison of the Taotie and Greedy Demon, I will give some opinions about the relationship between them.

(1) The Common Traits of The Taotie and Greedy Demon
It is easy to find that the most noted commonalities between taotie and greedy demon are greed and lust. As shown in *Zuozhuan* 左傳 cited above, Taotie 饕餮, the son of Jinyunshi 縉雲氏, "is gluttonous of foods, coveting wealth, extravagant much, never contents. He accumulates numerous money and properties, but never helps the weak and the poor." So, his characteristics can be summarized as gluttony, greed, lust, extravagance and mercilessness. Besides, as an ethnic group, the old Taotie people were in dread of the young, while the ferocious ones were honored. They kept fighting each other until they nearly killed all the enemies

(cf. *Lüshichunqiu* 呂氏春秋). They were obviously very warlike, cruel and even killed their own tribal members and family members. As for the Taotie whose shape was monstrous, it "is fierce, likes sigh, fond of accumulation of wealth but spending nothing; being good at robbing people's grain, and very lusty" (cf. *Shenyijing* 神異經).

Although such depictions do not necessarily refer to a same being, the being named Taotie 饕餮 became the symbol of all these evil characters. In addition, interestingly, the characteristics of the greedy demon in the West Asia's religions were approximately the same as that of Taotie in the Orient. For instance, the devil Āz of the Zoroastrianism was the weapon with which the demon chief Ahriman opposed the good God, while the name Āz itself meant *greed*.

Later, Manicheism adopted this role and its name, but raised it to a status of *Mother of Devils*. This Āz attempted to make humans who were produced by her being as greedy, lustful and malicious as her. She was hence blamed as "being insatiable and shameless".

The Chinese Manichean writings properly translated Āz into 貪魔 Tanmo (greedy demon), revealing vividly the main characteristics of this devil. Tanmo was depicted as "being lustful, wrathful, stupid and greedy", as well as "vicious mind like the Yakṣa", "seeking for wealth day and night" and so on. Obviously, the image of Tanmo was almost the same as that of Taotie. In the course of westward spreading, Manicheism adopted a Greek term *Hylè* to replace the previous *Āz*. Nevertheless, the characteristic of the greedy demon did not change, still symbolizing the sin, thoughts of death, the creator of devils, and lustful, greedy, cruel features (cf. the Coptic literature *Kephalaia*). Therefore, there was possibly a certain relationship between the oriental Taotie and the occidental greedy demon.

(2) The Real Meaning of "Having a Head but no Body"

Another piece of evidence is recorded in *Lüshichunqiu* 呂氏春秋: "In the Zhou Dynasty Taotie pattern is decorated on the tripod. Taotie has a head but no body, supposedly means that it fails to swallow the human and destroys its own body instead. It signifies the retribution." Later, almost all writings discussing the Taotie referred to this information, and tried to explain its context; however, there were few satisfactory answers.

Chenqiyou 陳其猷 gave a comparatively detailed interpretation of these words. He said that, according to the description of chapter "Views on the Reason for Existence of Sovereigns 恃君覽" of *Lüshichunqiu*, the so-called Taotie 饕餮 were the most greedy and most cruel people imagined by the ancients. The sentence "fails to swallow the human" signified this phenomenon. As for the word "retribution", it indicated that the doers of evil deeds will be punished, just like the Taotie who, prior to hurting anyone, has its own body destroyed. Therefore, this Taotie symbol was warning people not to do any evil deeds.[34]

This Taotie pattern was depicted as merely a face or head but without the body, and this image was explained as Taotie's gluttony causing the ruin of its body. However, this interpretation leads to a question: Why does Taotie's gluttony cause its body to be destroyed? Thus, there is still room for discussion on this issue.

Now, we may first examine the legend about *Greedy Demon*. As cited above, the Zoroastrian document *Bundahishn* says, "The devil Āz is that which swallows things; when, owing to privation, nothing is obtained, it devours from its person. It is a deception which will not pile up, and will not be sated, when the entire wealth of the world is given to it. As one says, 'The eye of the covetous is an abode which has no boundaries.'" This passage reveals two major features of the greedy demon (Āz): first, it is so gluttonous that it even eats up its own body; second, its eyes open widely because of greed, that is to say, the greedy demon has very big eyes.

On the contrary, according to various Chinese literatures, Taotie is also depicted as "devours its own body". In particular, Guopu 郭璞 says that Taotie (Paoxiao 狍鴞) was very greedy, as it not only consumed other persons but also devoured itself (cf. Guopu, *Shanhaijing Illustration* 山海經圖讚). Apparently, both the Taotie 饕餮 of the Orient and the Greedy Demon (Āz, Hylè) of the Occident were depicted as a monster devouring itself because of its gluttonous character.

Lizehou 李澤厚 thought that no matter how one comprehends the ancient explanations, the basic meaning "devouring person" was completely in line with the image of the monstrous Taotie.[35] This opinion is distinctly correct. In fact, the Āz of Zoroastrianism and Manicheism also displayed the character of "devouring person". For example, as the description in Vendidad, Ātar, the son of good God Ahura Mazda,

---

[34] Cf. Chenqiyou 陳其猷, *Lüshichunqiujiaoshi* 呂氏春秋校釋 (*Correction and Interpretation on Lüshichunqiu*), fasc. 16, Academia Press 學林出版社, 1984, p. 955.

[35] Cf. Lizehou 李澤厚, *Meidelicheng* 美的歷程 (*History of Chinese Aesthetics*), Anhui Literature and Art Publishing House 安徽文藝出版社, 1999, p. 45.

repeatedly sought help: "Here comes Āz, made by the Daevas, who consumes me and wants to put me out of the world."

Based on the analysis above, Taotie's image "having a head but no body" could be possibly ascribed to it devouring itself. If it is understood like that, it is not only consistent with the description of Āz by *Bundahishn* but also more reasonable than the Chinese traditional explanations about Taotie "destroying itself".

In addition, interestingly enough, the second noted feature of Āz is its large eyes. In the *Bundahishn*, its eyes were even exaggeratedly depicted — as big as "an abode which has no boundaries". This feature of *large eyes* exactly coincided with that of Taotie image in the Orient.

Actually, despite various opinions on the meaning of Taotie symbols, people have an approximate consensus on the appearance of the Taotie pattern. That is to say, it is a stylized face of a certain beast, with a big mouth, widely opened eyes, a pair of erect ears or big horns on the forehead; sometimes, there are sawteeth and tusks in the mouth. Thus, the "large eyes" is one of the main characteristics of the Taotie pattern. As shown in the following Fig. 1, the two large eyes apparently play a principal role in the image.

Another type of Taotie symbol merely consists of two eyes, as shown in Fig. 2. It is found on the bronze goblet of Erligang 二里崗, present Zhengzhou 鄭州. Generally speaking, the main features of Taotie are greed and devouring human, its principal appearance is the absence of a body and large eyes. On the contrary, the similar qualities are also attributed to the greedy demon Āz, such as greed, lust, very large eyes, as well

Fig. 1. The Pattern on the Taotie Tripod Zhier 直耳饕餮鼎 (Adapted from *Kaogutu* 考古圖, fasc. 1).

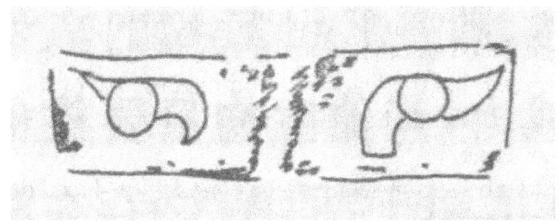

Fig. 2. Taotie symbols on the bronze goblet of Erligang, Zhengzhou.

as consuming others and even its own body. Therefore, there are probably some relations between Taotie and Āz.

(3) The Similarity between Taotie and Āz

Zuozhuan 左傳 claimed that Taotie was the son of Jinyun 縉雲; *Lüshichunqiu* 呂氏春秋 said that Taotie was a tribe living north of Yanmen 雁門. These two passages indicate that the Taotie was human; thereby, his appearance ought to be that of a human. However, other records either regarded it as half beast or completely called it a *beast*. Nevertheless, when talking about the appearance of Taotie, both the pictorial materials and literal files depicted it as a beast, especially the face of the beast.

As for the shape of the greedy demon, the related materials are rare; even so, an approximate appearance is given by some texts. For instance, the Manichean deity says to the greedy demon (Hylè): "How shall I heal thee, O Hylè, the lioness, the Mother of the world? For I am the physician that heals but thou art the wounder that wounds."[36] Here, the greedy demon is directly called *lioness*, hence its shape ought to be that of a real beast.

Besides, the devils subordinated to the greedy demon often look like lions, such as "The male Asrēshtār and the female Asrēshtār, lion-shaped, lustful and wrathful, sinful and terrible." "These two Asrēshtārs, the male and the female, lion-shaped, the garment of Āz, and full of lust."[37] Since the greedy demon is called "Mother of Devils", its appearance should be similar to her subordinates, namely, "lion-shaped". However, they are

---

[36] Cf. C.R.C. Allberry, *A Manichaean Psalm-Book (Part II)*, 221$^{5-7}$, Stuttgart, 1938.
[37] Cf. Jes P. Asmussen, *Manicchaean Literature: Representative Texts Chiefly from Middle Persian and Parthian Writings*, Delmar, New York, 1975, p. 128.

just indirect pieces of evidence. A specific depiction is seen in the Coptic Manichean Psalms: "The Saviour and his apostles and they that belong to the race of life revealed the Darkness and the essence of the Enemy; they wept for the body of death, the son of great … this lion-faced dragon, and his mother also, Hylē."

Here, the greedy demon seems to be called "lion-faced dragon", while the Chinese dragon (龍 long) is said to have nine sons, and one of them is Taotie 饕餮.[38] Then, it is not impossible that the Taotie also has a dragon-shaped body, just like the greedy demon. Although the appearance of the Chinese dragon (龍) is not exactly the same as that of the dragon in the occidental world, the two creatures are undoubtedly similar to each other, namely, both the Taotie and greedy demon have the shape of half man and half beast.

In addition, the genders of Taotie and greedy demon appear to be the same. In the Zoroastrianism or Manicheism literatures, the greedy demon is often described as female. For example, "Āz is the mother of devils"; "Āz is the evil mother of all devils"; "Hylè, the lioness, the mother of the world"; and "Hylè and her sons divided me up amongst them, they burnt me in their fire, they gave me a bitter likeness."[39]

Although there seems to be no direct evidence to indicate the Taotie being female, there are still indirect hints to show it is feminine. For instance, Shendefu 沈德符 of the Ming Dynasty mentioned the so-called *Nine Sons of the Dragon*, saying, "憲章 xianzhang is fond of imprisoning; 饕餮 taotie enjoys water; 蟋蜴 xiyi likes fishy smell; 蟃縷 wanquan prefers wind and rain; 螭虎 chihu is fond of literature; 金猊 jinni likes smoke; 椒圖 jiaotu features silence; 蚓蛇 diaoshe likes to take risks; 鰲魚 aoyu enjoys to swallow fire."[40] From this text, we know that the

---

[38] According to Liangzhangju 梁章鉅, *Langjixutan* 浪跡續談, the so-called *dragon's nine sons* could be listed as follows: the first one is 贔屓 bixie. It is capable of bearing a heavy load, so is used as the base under stele. The second is 螭吻 chiwen, which is used as the beast head on the roof because it likes to look out. The third is 蒲牢 pulao, which is used as the button loop of the bronze clock because it likes to bellow. The fourth is 狴犴 bigan, which is full of powers, thus is set in front of the prison gates. The fifth is 饕餮 taotie, which is gluttonous, so is decorated on the tripod lid. The other four *dragon sons* are 蚣蝮 gongxu, 睚眥 yazi, 狻猊 suanni and 椒圖 jiaotu, which are also weird animals. Cf. *Langjixutan* 浪跡續談, fasc. 8, Zhonghua Book Company 中華書局, 1981, p. 394.
[39] Cf. C.R.C. Allberry, *A Manichaean Psalm-Book (Part II)*, 54[17-18], etc.
[40] Cf. Shendefu 沈德符, *Wanliyehuobian* 萬歷野獲編 (*The Ming History Described by the Populace*), fasc. 7, Zhonghua Book Company 中華書局, 1999, p. 191.

Taotie is fond of water. Lurong 陸容 also mentioned it: "Taotie enjoys water, hence is built at the ends of a bridge."[41] Obviously, there is a close relationship between Taotie and the water; it is probably a kind of water deity. According to ancient Chinese ideas, the gender of water is feminine, so the water deity is a goddess. Just as stated in *Shuyuanzaji* 菽園雜記, "The heavenly imperial concubine has been known for long time. The ancients take the heaven as the emperor, the earth as the queen, and the water as the concubine; the last one is generally called water goddess …. Someone says, the water belongs to the feminine category, hence every water deity is shaped like a woman" (cf. fasc. 8).

Besides, the Chinese ancients believed that every trait or thing which is evil and greedy belonged to the feminine gender, such as expounded by *Wuxingdayi* 五行大義. In brief, goodness is masculine (positive) because it loves life, while evilness is feminine (negative) because it is fond of killing.[42] On the basis of these ideas, Taotie, who is characterized by greed, lust, cruelty and evilness, ought to be the feminine. Therefore, Taotie appears to have the same gender as the greedy demon or Āz, Hylē, etc.

(4) On the Possibility of Exchanges between the Taotie and Greedy Demon

According to Chinese records, the Taotie 饕餮 existed in as early as the Shang and Zhou Dynasties, even in earlier ages. Both the opinion of *ethnic group* and opinion of *symbol* claim that the Taotie originated outside China: it was either "exiled to barbarian regions" or living in the "north of Yanmen", "the southwestern wildness" and "Sanwei Country 三危國". For this reason, almost all scholars conclude that the Taotie originated extraterritorially instead of in China proper.

---

[41] Cf. Lurong 陸容, *Shuyuan* 菽園雜記 (*Miscellanea of Shuyuan*), fasc.2, Zhonghua Book Company 中華書局, 1985, p. 17.

[42] Cf. Xiaoji 蕭吉, *Wuxingdayi* 五行大義, fasc. 4, punctuated and proofread by Qianhang 錢杭, Shanghai Bookstore Press, 2001, pp. 106–107. The Chinese text is as follows: "《說文》曰: '情，人之陰氣，有欲嗜也。性，人之陽氣，善者也。'《孝經授神契》云: '性者，人之質，人所稟受產。情者，陰之數，內傳著流，通於五臟。故性爲本，情爲末。性主安靜，恬然守常; 情則主動，觸境而變。動靜相交，故間微密也。' 河上公章句云: '五性之鬼曰魂，爲雄; 六情之鬼曰魄，爲雌。此明性陽，情陰也。… 六氣通於六情者，好爲陽，惡爲陰，怒爲風，喜爲雨，哀爲晦，樂爲明。好爲陽者，陽爲好生，是以爲好。惡爲陰者，陰氣好殺，是以爲惡。'"

Yangximei said, "I think, the tribes Daner 儋耳, Taotie 饕餮 and Qiongqi 窮奇 etc. once inhabited in the Kirghiz steppes east of the Caspian Sea at the latest during the period of the late Zhou to the Qin and Han dynasties. It ought to be a reasonable ratiocination."[43] Whether this location is correct or not, one fact appears to be undoubted, namely, the *Taotie* either goes to foreign lands from China initially or comes to China from its native place outside. Both the possibilities reveal the fact that at least 3000 years ago, the Taotie 饕餮 was already an item exchanged between China and foreign lands. Actually, a lot of pieces of evidence show that there were frequent migrations of nationalities and cultural communications between the East and West several millennia ago. Against this historical background, it is unreasonable to expel the possibility that Taotie is a result of Sino-foreign communications. All we want to know is whether there is any communication between the Taotie and greedy demon, and if so, in what way they communicate.

I once had a discussion on this topic,[44] supposing that there are seemly some relations between the Taotie and the masks of mythological creatures of the West Asia. The Assyrian mythological poems around 2000 BC talk a lot about a monstrous giant Humbaba. Its distinctive head is possibly the prototype of the head of Greek enchantresses Gorgons, especially that of the third sister Medusa. Furthermore, a Gorgon mask of the 4th century BC was found in Pazyryk burials; the Gorgon mask of the 4th–3rd century BC in an ancient tomb of Hunan Province is very similar to the Gorgon mask of the Chiusi site in Italia, the latter made in the first half of the 1st millennium BC. The attributions and features of all these masks are analogous to that of the Taotie; hence, there may be a certain cultural exchange between them. Although this view has once been questioned,[45] I still believe that this possibility cannot be expelled completely. As for the Taotie and the greedy demon, they probably once learnt from each

---

[43] Cf. Yangximei 楊希枚, "*On the Ancient Taotie Tribe* 古饕餮民族考", in *Bulletin of the Institute of Ethnology, Academia Sinica* 中央研究院民族學研究所集刊, No. 24, Taibei, 1967, p. 13.

[44] Cf. Ruichuanming 芮傳明 & Yutaishan 余太山, *The Comparison of Symbols between China and the Occident* 中西紋飾比較, Chapter 8, Shanghai Classics Publishing House 上海古籍出版社, 1995.

[45] Cf. Hangxiaochun 杭曉春, "A Study on the Taotie Symbol of the Bronzewares 青銅器饕餮紋研究述評", in *Palace Museum Journal* 故宮博物院院刊, 2005, No. 1, pp. 103–104.

other directly or indirectly. On the contrary, they may also blend in other cultural factors, such as the Gorgon mask.

The role of Āz is seen in Zoroastrianism, but it was not paid particular attention until the 9th century. It may be one of the reasons used by some scholars to suppose the greedy demon concept derives from Indian Buddhism.[46] Regardless of whether this opinion is right or wrong, it is quite possible that the concept of greedy demon once drew lessons from other cultures. Both Zoroastrianism and Manicheism were initiated in the West Asia. The founder of Manicheism had been to Central Asia and South Asia before his religion forming; later, numerous Zoroastrian believers moved to India; Manicheism also spread over Central Asia and China. Against this historical background, these two religions could possibly absorb some oriental ideas, or spread their own ideas to other cultures.

Based on the discussion above, I can conclude the following. Both the Taotie 饕餮 and the greedy demon are evil creatures; greed, lust and cruelty characterize them. Both the symbol taotie and its related legends and ideas were probably initiated in the distant lands outside of China, and gradually absorbed the cultural factors of China, Central Asia, West Asia and South Asia. The main ideas about the greedy demon contain not only the traditional cultural factors of the West Asia but also that of South Asia and China; among them, the Taotie concept possibly exerts more direct influence on it. Later, people had no clear idea on the meaning of Taotie, perhaps because they forgot or misunderstood its original meaning, while some clues possibly remain in the foreign cultures, such as the instance of "Taotie eats its own body".

Finally, since the taotie and greed demon share common features, they play a similar role. The difference is just that the Chinese are accustomed to taking the taotie 饕餮 instead of the greedy demon as a caution instrument. It should be noted that the symbol taotie is used not only to warn

---

[46] About this opinion, cf. R.C. Zaehner, *The Dawn and Twilight of Zoroastrianism*: "(It may be that) the demon Āz is a Buddhist rather than a Zoroastrian idea; there is no trace of it in the Avesta. In Buddhism, on the other hand, the root cause of the chain of conditioned existence is *avidyā*, 'ignorance', and its principal manifestation is trshnā, 'thirst', which means the desire for continued existence in time — intellectual error, then, manifesting itself in concupiscence. The Zoroastrian Āz, too, is both 'ignorance' and 'thirst', both 'wrong-mindedness' and concupiscence; she attacks man both in his body and in his mind." (New York, 1961, p. 229).

against gluttony but also to caution against desiring concupiscence, wealth, etc. *Xuanhebogutu* 宣和博古圖 said that the taotie patterns decorated on the drinking vessel aimed at cautioning against indulging greedy desires.[47] In addition, Huangbosi 黃伯思 of the Song Dynasty believed that the taotie symbol was not only to caution against gluttony and desire for wealth but also to warn against drinking to excess.[48] Apparently, as a symbol, taotie was used to caution against all greedy desires. I think, because the drinking vessels or other food utensils are frequently seen by people, the taotie patterns were generally adorned on these containers so that as many people as possible could accept its teachings.

---

[47] Cf. Wangfu 王黼, *Chongxiuxuanhebogutu* 重修宣和博古圖, fasc. 16.
[48] Cf. Huangbosi 黃伯思, *Dongguanyulun* 東觀餘論, fasc. I.

Chapter 14

On the Origin of the Title Mani

Mani is merely the title of the founder of Manicheism instead of his real name; hence, this term has necessarily strong religious and symbolic meanings. Then, a question is raised: what does it mean? Or, where is the cultural origin of the title *Mani*? A discussion on it is given as follows.

A number of scholars have studied this problem to varying degrees. For example, Maxiaohe 馬小鶴 says the following: "Manicheism likens its doctrine to 如意寶 ruyibao (a gem that can fulfill any wish) and 如意珠 ruyizhu (a pearl that can fulfill any wish), while these terms undoubtedly derive from Buddhism. However, such Buddhist color gradually appears only after Buddhism spread to Central Asia and China, it could be called as *regenerator*, while its origins ought to be found in Gnosticism, Christianism and Judaism in the West."

The corresponding conclusion says the following: "Influenced by *Gospel of Thomas* and other literatures, perhaps in its early period Manicheism already likens its doctrine (*Nous*) to pearl. After it is introduced into Central Asia and China, and frequently communicates with Buddhism, Manicheism adopts the Buddhist metaphor of likening Buddhist doctrine to ruyizhu and ruyibao, called also its own doctrine as ruyizhu and ruyibao. ... In the early period Manicheism is influenced by *Acts of Peter* and *Acts of Peter and Twelve Apostles* etc, named Jesus as *Pearl Stone*. When it spreads over the East, the Manicheans find that the Buddhist term *Pearl*'s pronunciation happen to be similar to the name of their hierarch, so they officially name their hierarch, who claims himself the apostle of Jesus, as Mani Light Buddha. His title is translated into

Chinese 摩尼光佛, 摩尼 or 末尼 for short, meaning 'the precious pearl Mani'."[1]

According to this opinion, the term *Mani* of the Manicheism originated in Christianism and Gnosticism of the West Asia; it was written as 摩尼 moni or 末尼 moni in Chinese literatures because the meaning of the Buddhist term 摩尼 (Sanskrit *maṇi*) happened to be the same as that of the Manichean hierarch's name, thus it was taken as the official title of the Manichean founder. However, this idea is debatable. I think there are many similarities between the Buddhist "Mani Light Buddha" and the founder of Manicheism "Mani"; in addition, the meaning of the Buddhist term "maṇi" is also similar to corresponding ideas of Manicheism. It is unreasonable to regard so many similarities as pure "occasionality". Hence, my opinion is that in the period prior to the founding of Manicheism rather than after it spread eastward, Mani had adopted a lot of cultural factors from Buddhism, including the Sanskrit word "maṇi".

1. The *Maṇi Buddha* in Buddhist Sutras

There are numerous mentions of Maṇi Light Buddha in Chinese sutras; for instance, *Buddha-dhyāna-samādhisāgara-sūtra* 觀佛三昧海經 says that Mañjuśrī told the believers that when the Maṇi Light Buddha appears, he does Buddhist affairs and saves the people from the misery in the world. Thereby, 20000 Buddhas are given the same title "Maṇi Light", all of them teaching the people with their wonderful light embodiments. Another kind of buddha is named "Candana Maṇi Light", numbering as many as ten billion.[2]

According to sutras, these "Maṇi Light" buddhas belonged only to two kinds of buddha among 1500 kinds of buddhas all over the universe. Many other kinds of buddhas include "All Righteousness Buddha 一切正義佛", "Sakyamuni Buddha 釋迦牟尼佛" and "Light Buddha 光明佛", reaching 6.2 million, 3 billion and 6 hundred, respectively.[3]

---

[1] Cf. Maxiaohe 馬小鶴, "A Study on the Mani Light Buddha 摩尼光佛考", in *Shilin* 史林, 1999, No. 1, pp. 14, 82.
[2] Cf. Buddhabhadra (tr.), *Buddha-dhyāna-samādhisāgara-sūtra* 觀佛三昧海經, fasc. 9, in *Dazhengxinxiudazangjing* 大正新修大藏經, Book 15, No. 643, p. 688.
[3] Cf. *1500 Kinds of Buddha Names All over the Universe* 現在十方千五百佛名並雜佛同號, in *Dazhengxinxiudazangjing* 大正新修大藏經, Book 85, No. 2905, pp. 1448–1449.

In addition to "Maṇi Light Buddha" and "Candana Maṇi Light Buddha" being listed in the "1500 buddha names", there are a lot of buddha names consisting of "maṇi" and other words, which were listed in the categories of "Fifty-three Buddhas in the Past" and "Buddhas of all Place". For instance, there are "Maṇi Pennant Buddha 摩尼幢佛" and "Maṇi Pennant Lamp Light Buddha 摩尼幢燈光佛" in the category of "Fifty-three Buddhas in the Past", while "Candana Maṇi Light Buddha of the South 南方栴檀摩尼光佛" is one of the ten Buddhas, located respectively in ten orients.[4] Strictly, "Sun-Moon-Pearl Light Buddha 日月珠光佛" of the "Fifty-three Buddhas in the Past" should also be a name related to "maṇi", because the Sanskrit word *maṇi* means *pearl*.

Besides, there are many other buddha names including the component "maṇi", such as those recorded in *Buddha Names Sutras* 佛名經: Moon Maṇi Light King Buddha 月摩尼光王佛, Maṇi Wheel Buddha 摩尼輪佛, Maṇi Gem Buddha 摩尼寶佛, Maṇi Light Buddha 摩尼光佛, Maṇi Vajra Buddha 摩尼金剛佛, Maṇi Armor Buddha 摩尼鎧佛, Maṇi Fragrant Buddha 摩尼香佛, Maṇi Moon Buddha 摩尼月佛, Maṇi King Buddha 摩尼王佛, Maṇi Pure Buddha 摩尼清淨佛, Maha Maṇi Buddha 大摩尼佛, Southern Maṇi Pure Cloud Buddha 南方摩尼清淨雲佛, Victorious Maṇi Buddha 勝摩尼佛, and so on, numbering over fifty names.[5] After frequently chanting these buddha names, the believers could atone for their sins, and can avoid falling into hell.

In Chinese sutras, the Buddhist founder Sākyamuni was transliterated as 釋迦牟尼 shijiamouni, 牟尼 mouni for short. Though the meaning of *Sākyamuni* or *muni* is quite different from that of *maṇi*, the Chinese Manicheans of later generation often confused 摩尼佛 and 牟尼佛, hence in some writings 摩尼 (Mani) is regarded the same as 牟尼 Mouni.

2. The Meaning of "Maṇi" in Buddhist Sutras

The pearl is an important symbol in Buddhism; it is applied so universally that it has close relations with some essential doctrines of Buddhism. The "pearl" is pronounced as "maṇi" in Sanskrit, so it was transliterated into

---

[4] Cf. Dharma-mitra 曇摩蜜多 (tr.), *Ākāśagarbha sūtra* 觀虛空藏菩薩經, in *Dazhengxinxiudazangjing* 大正新修大藏經, Book 13, No. 409, pp. 678–679.
[5] Cf. Bhodiruci 菩提流支 (tr.), *Buddha Names Sutra* 佛名經, fasc. 1–12, in *Dazhengxinxiudazangjing* 大正新修大藏經, Book 14, No. 440, pp. 114–184.

the Chinese word 摩尼 moni, 末尼 moni, etc. Generally speaking, the Buddhists applied the term "maṇi (pearl)" mainly in two ways: First, they focused on the pearl's physical attributes, praising and even greatly exaggerating its properties, regarding it as a kind of rare jewel possessing wonderful powers. Second, these physical attributes were used to symbolize some ideas, thoughts and spiritual qualities. For instance, it was often used to symbolize the most excellent wisdom of the Buddhism.

In the Chinese Buddhist Sutras, "maṇi" is transliterated as 摩尼 or 末尼, and is sometimes paraphrased as 珠 (pearl) or 寶珠 (precious pearl). According to popular legends, 摩尼 moni had the singular functions of eliminating disasters, curing sickness, cleaning sewage and changing the water color. Furthermore, it is called *cintā maṇi*, and is transliterated into the Chinese words 真陀摩尼 zhentuomoni and 震多末尼 zhenduomoni, while the paraphrased names are 如意寶珠 ruyibaozhu (precious pearl which is able to satisfy all wishes), 如意寶 ruyibao (jewel that is able to satisfy all wishes), 如意珠 ruyizhu (pearl that is able to satisfy all wishes), 如意摩尼 ruyimoni (maṇi which is able to satisfy all wishes), 摩尼寶珠 monibaozhu (precious maṇi pearl), 末尼寶 monibao (the gem maṇi), 無價珠寶 wujiazhubao (priceless precious pearl), etc. Apparently, people believed that this pearl could satisfy all wishes the owner asked for. Exactly for this reason, maṇi (pearl) was regarded as one of the *Seven Treasures*. There are various statements about the composition of *Seven Treasures*, but maṇi/pearl is always listed in every composition, thereby showing its importance in Buddhism. The pearl's characteristic of light and illumination is vividly depicted in the following sutra text:

> Oh, every bhikshu, when the Rotating Wheel King (Cakravarti-rājan) is present, the great maṇi treasure will appears. This maṇi treasure is most beautiful and most wonderful. It is extreme bright, shines everything and has great powers. If there is such gem in the palace, even at dark night and without the lamps, it will shine brightly, just like the sun does in the day. Oh, bhikshus, long ago, when the great Wheel King is present, the big maṇi also appears, shining brightly. The king orders to visit the garden at night together with his army for the sake of testing the maṇi's function. After his officials gather the army, they set off for the garden. The king puts the big maṇi on the banner in front of the procession. Its light is shining over a wide area (far to one yojana), including all his soldiers. Immediately, the night becomes exactly same as the day.

Oh, bhikshus, this is the sixth great maṇi which appears at the same time as the Wheel King (Cakravarti-rājan).[6]

Here, though the light of the pearl (maṇi) is depicted vividly, it is obviously extremely exaggerated. For instance, the ancient Indian length unit *yojana* is roughly equivalent to a dozen kilometers at present. Undoubtedly, no natural pearl can be so bright.

The so-called *maṇi gem* or *maṇi treasure* also has many other peculiar functions, such as exorcising, detoxification, curing, improving eyesight and purifying water. The *Prajñāpāramitā sutra* says the following:

> One who accepts the doctrine of Prajñāpāramitā is like one who gains the priceless maṇi, wherever he goes, no evil forces can hurt him. Regardless of the gender, when one holds a maṇi the ghosts and godlings will run away instantly. If one suffers from internal thermal, he or she can be cured by carrying a maṇi. If one has stroke or catches cold, he is able to restore to health by means of maṇi. It can illuminate in the darkness; it can cool oneself when he is hot, and warm himself when he is cold. It can remove all toxicities. As soon as one who is bitten by a poisonous snake sees the maṇi, the toxicity will be removed immediately. If someone's eyes are in pain, or are dim, as long as the eyes are near the maṇi, the disease can be cured. If the maṇi is put into the water, the color of water will become same as that of the maṇi. If the maṇi is put into the dirty water, the latter will become pure. The wonderful virtues of the maṇi is incomparable.[7]

All these inconceivable peculiarities and functions are only the maṇi's physical attributes. Why do the Buddhists emphasize the characteristics of the maṇi so much, even greatly overstating its advantages? In fact, they just take it as a metaphor, aiming at explaining popularly the teachings and ideas of the Buddhism. Therefore, these *physical properties* of maṇi are merely its outward form; what the Buddhists want to express mostly are the excellent thoughts, qualities and exalted spiritual realm of Buddhism. A passage of *Abhidharmamahāvibhāṣā-śastra* vividly shows this.

---

[6]Cf. Dānapāla 施護 (tr.), *Cakravarti-rājan sapta ratnāni sūtra* 佛說輪王七寶經, in *Dazhengxinxiudazangjing* 大正新修大藏經, Book 1, No. 38, p. 822.

[7]Cf. Lokaṣema 支婁迦讖 (tr.), *Das'āsahasrikā Prajñāpāramitā sūtra* 道行般若波羅蜜經, fasc. 2, in *Dazhengxinxiudazangjing* 大正新修大藏經, Book 8, No. 224, pp. 435–436.

Śāriputra asked Sakyamuni why the *asamaya-vimukta*[8] was symbolized as maṇi treasure. The Buddha gave a detail explanation, displaying various distinguished qualities of the *asamaya-viṁukta*. He said that just like the maṇi is able to dispel darkness and illuminate everything, asamaya-viṁukta can also remove all silly ideas, and so it is named maṇi. In addition, when maṇi is put into the dirty water, the water immediately becomes clean and pure, while the asamaya-viṁukta can also purify one's mind, expelling all desires. The maṇi can attract and gather other treasures, thereby eliminating poverty; the asamaya-viṁukta can also accumulate sacred wealth, namely, the ways to become Buddha, to avoid shortage of merits and virtues. Putting the pearl on the high banner, various jewels will rain down with the will of the people, and save millions of poor from poverty. By the same reason, when the Buddha puts the maṇi of asamaya-viṁukta on the banner of apramāda, various real teachings will rain down as the people wish, so making their merits and virtues be perfect, and be free from the suffering of reincarnation. For the reasons stated above, the asamaya-viṁukta is called maṇi.[9]

In sum, the maṇi or pearl is taken as a symbol here to represent one of the Buddhist doctrines "asamaya-viṁukta", because their characteristics are similar to each other. In addition to this metaphor, maṇi is also used to symbolize the term *prajñā-pāramitā*. It is the greatest wisdom of Buddhism: one who holds this truth or has this wisdom can get rid of samsara, reaching the realm of nirvana.

A related passage was recorded in *Pañcaviṁśati-sāhasrikā-prajñapāramitā*. Śakra Devānām Indra talks about the maṇi and prajñapāramitā in the presence of the Buddha and other gods. He says that where there is maṇi, the amanuṣya (ghosts and goblins) dare not do evil. In a like manner, where there is prajñapāramitā, there is Buddha. Besides, the maṇi can cure various diseases and relieve all pains; it can dispel darkness, illuminate everything; it can make the scorching heat become cool and the severe cold become warm; it can restore health to the blind and deaf; it can eliminate any toxins; it can also purify the dirty water. Because of all these wonderful functions and virtues, where the maṇi exists, there

---

[8] As for the so-called "asamaya-viṁukta", it is a high spiritual realm reached by a Buddhist who practices. When one gets into this state, he is able to freely get rid of all secular desires.

[9] Cf. Xuanzang 玄奘 (tr.), *Abhidharmamahāvibhāṣā-śastra* 阿毗達磨大毗婆沙論, fasc. 102, in *Dazhengxinxiudazangjing* 大正新修大藏經, Book 27, No. 1545, p. 526.

is no any disease and disaster. Just like maṇi, where the prajñapāramitā exists, there is no error idea and desire.[10] Obviously, what the maṇi/pearl symbolizes is the most perfect truth and the highest wisdom of Buddhism.

The examples of using maṇi as a metaphor for the Buddhist wisdom are found in many other sutras, such as a passage in *Sāgaramatiparipṛcchāsūtra* 海意菩薩所問淨印法門經, which gives a considerably detailed explanation and vivid depiction. The Buddha answers the question of Sāgaramati Bodhisattva, finally, and concludes that the real, great maṇi can withstand grinding and hammering, and does good deeds, and seeks happiness for people. Just like the maṇi, *sarva-jñāna* can also withstand all kinds of tests and blows, and eliminates all errors, and benefits the people.[11] That is to say, here, the maṇi symbolizes *sarva-jñāna*, while the so-called *sarva-jñāna* roughly means "all wisdoms" or "supreme intelligences". The *sarva-jñāna* is one of the paramount wisdoms of the Buddha; they are *śuddha-jñāna*, *sarva-jñāna* and *assaṇga-jñāna*. Regardless of the precise definition of *sarva-jñāna*, it is certain that the maṇi symbolizes the most important thoughts and supreme intelligences of Buddhism.

Perhaps owing to the metaphorical relationship between maṇi/pearl and Buddha's supreme wisdom and perfect enlightenment, when Sakyamuni was in the final enlightenment state, maṇi played the leading role in the whole scene, such as the depiction in *Buddhā vataṃsaka mahāvaipulya sūtra* 大方廣佛華嚴經:

> (when Sakyamuni truly awakes and gains the supreme intelligence) the earth of the spot becomes very solid and is made of vajra (diamond); his throne is decorated with precious wheels and other jewels, as well as the pure maṇi (pearls). The maṇi on the banners and pillars shine brightly and sound the wonderful music forever. The great maṇi causes the rain of numerous jewels and various beautiful flowers, spreading over the earth. There are a lot of precious trees, their leaves are flourishing and bright. Owing to the miraculous power of the Buddha, the whole scene appears in this religious spot.

---

[10] Cf. Kumārajīva 鳩摩羅什 (tr.), *Pañcaviṃśati-sāhasrikā-prajñapāramitā* 摩訶般若波羅蜜經, fasc. 10, in *Dazhengxinxiudazangjing* 大正新修大藏經, Book 8, No. 223, pp. 291–292.

[11] Cf. Weijing 惟靜 & others (tr.), *Sāgaramatiparipṛcchāsūtra* 海意菩薩所問淨印法門經, fasc. 2, in *Dazhengxinxiudazangjing* 大正新修大藏經, Book 13, No. 400, pp. 476–477.

> The bodhi druma (bodhi tree) is particular tall and magnificent, its main body is of vajra, the trunk is of vaiḍūrya, the branches are of varied jewels. Its leaves are lush and thick as clouds; the colorful blossom scatter among the branches. Its fruits are of maṇi, glittering together with the blossom. All around the tree is extreme bright, countless maṇi precious stones rain down from the light, and numerous bodhisattvas appear amongst the pearls.
>
> By his miraculous power, Tathāgata makes the bodhi tree to sound wonderful music, and he interprets about various Buddhist teachings. The palaces he stays are very broad, they stretch so widely that are over the whole universe. Large quantity of colorful maṇi are collected there; various jewels and flowers are used as the decoration of these palaces. Bodhisattvas at all levels attend this religious assembly, miraculous light shine brightly.
>
> Applying his supernatural power, Tathāgata makes the net of great maṇi display every scene. All creatures' resident places show their images in this net. By means of their supernatural power, buddhas' ideas contain all things in the world. Tathāgata's throne is lofty and spacious, the pedestal consists of maṇi, being decorated with lotus and pure jewels. Buddha's necklace is made of various flowers. … At the moment Sakyamuni sits on this throne, understands the perfect truth, attains the supreme enlightenment.[12]

Apparently, when the Buddha attained supreme enlightenment, maṇi had the most distinguished role among all propitious signs and miraculous scenes. Various words of praise are given to the maṇi, such as "pure maṇi", "great maṇi", "maṇi fruits", "maṇi precious stones", "maṇi light clouds", "colorful maṇi" and so on.

All these depictions not only display the excellent physical characteristics of maṇi but also reveal the close relationship between maṇi and the perfect intelligences of Buddha and Bodhisattvas, because maṇi frequently appeared at the moment of Sakyamuni attaining supreme enlightenment and being Buddha. Hence, it is believable that maṇi/pearl is a symbol to represent the senior practitioners, such as Buddhas and Bodhisattvas, and their supreme intelligence and enlightenment.

---

[12] Cf. Śikṣānanda 實叉難陀 (tr.), *Buddhā vataṃsaka mahāvaipulya sūtra* 大方廣佛華嚴經, fasc. 1, in *Dazhengxinxiudazangjing* 大正新修大藏經, Book 10, No. 279, pp. 1–2.

3. Manichean Ideas about the "Maṇi" or Pearl

Now, let us discuss the meaning and status of the pearl in Manicheism. First, there is also a considerable close relationship between pearls and Manichean deities. For instance, as the founder of the Manicheism, Mani is often symbolized by the pearl, featuring mainly the light. A Manichean hymn in Turkic shows this clearly:

> Oh, bright Sun-God ... Oh, bright Moon-God! Like the diadem of the God Ohrmizd, like the garland of the God Zurvān. Bright in appearance is my Father, the Buddha Mani. Therefore I praise and worship you so.
>
> Like the cintāmaṇi-jewel are you, worthy to be worn on the crown of the head. Oh, you are worthy! As you shone brightly with the brightness of the commandments, so are you shining ... Radiant to behold is my Father, the Buddha Mani. Therefore I praise and worship you so.
>
> You who have come quite unhindered, remove greed and other passions! As your origin is in good Nivāṇa, you are worthy to be worn on the crown of the heads of the former Buddhas. Therefore I praise and worship you so.[13]

Here, Mani is likened to *cintāmaṇi*, while it is a Sanskrit word and means a miraculous pearl which can give anything its owner wants. In other words, such a pearl is able to satisfy all the wishes of its owner. Significantly, this *Pearl* refers directly to the Buddhist or Indian pearl, namely, maṇi.

Mani (maṇi) is thought to be worthy to be worn on the crown of the former gods (Buddhas); one of the primary gods of Manicheism is Ohrmizd, originally the supreme god of Zoroastrianism, origin of light and creator of the world. In Manicheism, Ohrmizd is an early deity named Primal Man. In this short hymn, Mani is almost completely identified with the pearl. Both of them are "bright", "shine brightly" and "bright in appearance"; furthermore, they have "brightness of commandments" and can "remove greed and other passions", just like the miraculous spiritual functions of the maṇi in India.

Another important Manichean deity is also likened to the pearl; he is Jesus, borrowed from Christianism. In the earlier period of Manicheism,

---

[13] Cf. the file T III D 259 and 260. The English translation is in Hans-Joachim Klimkeit, *Gnosis on the Silk Road: Gnostic texts from Central Asia*, New York, 1993, p. 285.

Mani once claimed himself as the apostle of Jesus; even after the eastward spreading of Manicheism, Jesus was still a deity second only to Mani. The Manichean Coptic *Hymn* says, "A pearl-stone is Jesus in the Gospel."[14] Obviously, the pearl is used as a symbol for Jesus. This metaphor is almost the same as that of Buddhism; that is to say, the pearl/maṇi symbolizes the supreme intelligences or the sages having these intelligences. A passage in the *Psalm-Book* expresses a similar meaning:

> He (Jesus) went to the shores of the sea, seeking pearls. First he found Peter, the foundation of his Church. He found Andrew, the first holy statue. He found John, the flower of virginity. James he found, the spring of the new wisdom. He found Philip, who is great in endurance. He found Bartholomew, the rose of Love. He found the other Thomas, the sweet smell that went to India. The other James he found, the true brother of the Lord. Simon the Cananite he found, full of zeal for life. He found Levi, the throne of faith. He gave the fragment to Judas, he took even the little light.[15]

Here, the so-called *Pearls* that Jesus sought actually referred to the excellent Christians, namely, the later apostles of Jesus. Just like the Buddhas and Bodhisattvas of the Buddhism, Peter, Andrew, John, James, Philip, Bartholomew, Thomas, Simon and Livi were also true and virtuous sages, and so are likened to pearls.

This paragraph doubtlessly derives from the *Bible*, thus it seems to be reasonable to think that the *Pearl Idea* of the Manicheism was influenced considerably by Christianism. However, among these apostles, several persons had been to the oriental regions for mission work. It is said that Philip had been to the foreign countries of Asia to witness the Lord Jesus. Bartholomew had been to Armenia and India, and converted many people to Christianity. According to ancient legend, Thomas had once missioned in Syria, Parthia, Persia, India and even China. He was so zealous in his mission work that it caused the infidels to feel jealousy and hatred, and he was killed by them. The Indian Christians founded a church to commemorate him, which exists in modern times.

We do not know whether these statements are based on facts, but it is possible that the apostles of Jesus indeed missioned in the East.

---

[14] Cf. C.R.C. Allberry, *A Manichaean Psalm-Book (Part II)*, Stuttgart, 1938, p. 192.
[15] Cf. *ibid.*, p. 194.

Therefore, we could reasonably suppose that in its earlier period Christianity had some direct or indirect communications with Buddhism. If so, we cannot deny the opinion that the Manichean *Pearl Idea* derives from Buddhism.

In Manicheism, in addition to symbolizing various deities, the pearl is also likened to souls, namely, the so-called *Light Elements*. For example, in a Manichean Parthian text, the savior says the following to the souls: "I shall deliver thee from all the waves of the sea, and from its deep wherein thou hast gone through these drownings ... which ... through thee ... and I shall ... the anguish. And ... I shall take thee afar from ... thy limbs ... through perfect healing. I shall set thee free from every sickness, and from every distress at which thou hast wept. I shall not wish to leave thee longer in the hands of the Sinner; for thou art my own, in truth, forever. Thou art the buried treasure, the chief of my wealth, the pearl which is the beauty of all the gods."[16]

According to the Manichean teachings, the souls of all creatures, including plants, are light elements which are swallowed by the dark devils in the genesis era, while all the light elements are emitted by the Great Light God, that is to say, they are a part of this supreme God. The essential mission of the Manicheans is to deliver the souls from the imprisonment of the dark devils and lead them back to the light world. Hence, the sentence "thou art my own, in truth, forever" means that all souls are actually light elements. These light elements are the most wonderful beings of Manicheism; they are also symbolized by the pearl, just like in Buddhism.

Another instance likening the soul to the pearl is seen in the Coptic *Kephalaia*. It detailedly depicts the ways and processes of saving souls, and likens this process to gathering pearls. It says that the Enlightener Mani tells his disciples how pearls come about and are formed in the sea. Drops of rainwater fall in the sea, and float on the surface of the waters. At first, the drop is foam, and is accommodated in the shell. They shall be joined with each other, and are shaped and become a great pearl. However, when a drop of rainwater breaks into many droplets and various particles of water, they shall be formed into and be confined into numerous pearls. When the pearls are formed, the pearlers shall bring the pearls up from the depths of the sea. The pearl divers shall give them to the traders, and the traders give them to the kings and nobles.

---

[16] Cf. Mary Boyce, *The Manichaean Hymn-Cycles in Parthian*, Oxford University Press, 1954, p. 147.

"This also what the holy church is like. It shall be gathered in from the living soul, gathered up and brought to the heights, raised from the sea and placed in the flesh of mankind; while the flesh of mankind itself is like the shell and the pearl-shell."

"The booty that shall be seized is the drop of rainwater, while the apostles are like the divers. The traders are the light-givers of the heavens; the kings and nobles are the aeons of greatness. For all the souls that ascend in the flesh of mankind and are freed shall be brought back to the great aeons of light. A place of rest comes about for them, at that place in the aeons of greatness. You too, my beloved ones, struggle in every way so that you will become good pearls and be accounted to heaven by the light diver. He will come to you and bring you back to … the great chief merchant, and you will rest in the life forever. You have … and the light."[17]

Apparently, Mani takes the trouble to talk about the formation and gathering of the pearls, because he wants to more vividly interpret the Manichean teachings, namely, how the soul or light element is imprisoned by the flesh; how it suffers, purifies itself, and how it is saved from the flesh, and returns to the light world. It is a clever metaphor that likens pearls being confined in the shell to the soul being imprisoned in flesh. In addition, the analogy between gathering pearls from shells in the deep sea and relieving souls from the flesh is also very lively. The typical pattern of saving the souls of mankind is embodied in a story of Manichean myth, which describes the rescue of Primal Man by other gods. The important deity Primal Man is often likened to the pearl, such as the description in *Kephalaia*: "Once again the enlightener speaks: The Living Spirit has done seven works with his strength. The first: He brought the First Man up from the contest, the way a pearl is brought up from the sea."[18]

There are numerous cases of analogy between the pearl and the soul in Manichean literatures; Maxiaohe already has a paper that discusses this subject,[19] so I am not going to discuss it in detail here. However, it is worth noting that because there is a close relationship between the "soul" of Manicheism and the "Buddha Nature" 佛性 of Buddhism, possibly the

---

[17] Cf. Iain Gardner (tr.), *The Kephalaia of the Teacher*, Leiden: E. J. Brill, 1995, pp. 211–212.

[18] Cf. *ibid.*, p. 88.

[19] Cf. Maxiaohe 馬小鶴, "A Study on the Manichean Religious Symbol *Pearl* 摩尼教宗教符號明珠研究", in *Academic Collection* 學術集林, Vol. 17, Shanghai Yuandong Publishing House 上海遠東出版社, 2000, pp. 290–301.

Pearl Idea of Manicheism involves some Buddhist factors, as the following discussion shows.

4. Analysis and Deduction

In order to more clearly trace back to the origin of the Manichean *pearl idea*, I will take the maṇi/pearl idea of Buddhism as the standard and compare the corresponding doctrines and opinions of the two religions.

First, in Buddhism, the "pearl/maṇi" has an intimate relation with the "light". On many occasions, the most distinguished feature of the maṇi seems to be "radiating brightly", "Shining over the world" and so on. Furthermore, this "light" usually not only refers to the natural physical light but also signifies the brightness of mind and spiritual enlightenment; sometimes, it also has a certain holy meaning. When the sutra cited above discusses the enlightenment of the Buddha, it uses repeatedly the words "maṇi" and its "light" to depict the scene; this is good evidence. Therefore, based on these Buddhist materials, we may safely assume that the pearl/maṇi is the typical symbol for both physical and spiritual "light". The intimate relationship between "maṇi" and "light" seems to inspire a lot.

Significantly, the essential doctrine of the Manicheism is so-called *dualism*, namely, the view of the Light struggling against the Darkness forever; in other word, "light" is the most admired and worshiped object of Manicheism. Thus, Manicheism is also named as *Light Religion*, while the founder of this religion happens to be called Mani, a word pronounced almost totally the same as maṇi. Some think that it is the Chinese translators of later generations who borrowed 摩尼 (maṇi) as Mani's Chinese name, but I suppose that it is Mani himself who personally borrowed the Sanskrit word *maṇi* as his title, rather than the later people changing his name or title. The reasons are as follows.

First of all, initially, Mani's name was Cubricus or Ubricus; "Mani" is only the title he called himself when he was an adult. "Mani" is written as "Manys" in Greek and "Manes" in Latin. Although the Christians claimed that this name means "lunatic" or "corrupting clothing", it is possibly only an insulting explanation instead of the true definition. Some believe that "Mani" probably derives from the Babylonian Aramaic word "Mānā", who is a light god of the Mandaean sect: *mānā rabba* means *Light King*. In sum, "Mani" is an honorable title adopted by the Manichean founder for himself, which might include the meaning of "light".

Besides, in the period of creating religion, in order to persuade the Persian king Shapur I to accept Manicheism, Mani dedicated his *Šābuhragān* to the king. It was written in Middle Persian and summarized the essential teachings of Manicheism. The king agreed to the request of Mani, and thus Manicheism was allowed to spread freely in Persia. In the beginning of this book, Mani said, "Wisdom and deeds have always from time to time been brought to mankind by the messengers, called Buddha, to India, in another by Zarādusht to Persia, in another by Jesus to the West. Thereupon this revelation has come down, this prophecy in the last age through me, Mani, the messenger of the God of truth to Babylonia."[20] Apparently, from the start, the founder of Manicheism called himself "Mani"; furthermore, at that time, he already knew about the Buddha of India, as he mentioned Buddha in his *Šābuhragān*.

From these reasons, we may infer that Mani borrowed the maṇi idea of Buddhism, taking maṇi as the symbol of light, thereby calling his religion "Manicheism" or "Light Religion", and titling himself "Mani". This inference is at least more logical than the opinion that the name 摩尼 (maṇi) was adopted after this religion spread eastward.

In addition to the proofs above, some other materials also show that a major part of the pearl idea of Manicheism derives from Buddhism. In Buddhist sutras, the maṇi/pearl is often used to liken to "self-existent pure mind 自性清淨心", namely, "Buddha nature 佛性" and "Bhūtatathatā 真如", such as the following depiction:

> The Buddha says to the Oceanic-Wisdom Bodhisattva: For example, the priceless large vaiḍūrya-maṇi even if has been buried in mud for a thousand years, after it being dug out and washed, the maṇi is still bright and pure. Oh, Oceanic-Wisdom, Mahāsattva is just like that. He can see clearly that the "self-existent light pure mind" of every creature is polluted by desires. Thus, these Bodhisattvas think, "I will preach the truth for them, to help these creatures getting rid of the evil desires."[21]

---

[20]Cf. C. Edward Sachau (tr. & ed.), *Al-Biruni, The Chronology of Ancient Nations*, London: William H Allen and Co., 1879, p. 190.

[21]Cf. Ratnamati 勒那摩提 (tr.), *Ratnagotra-vibhāgo Mahāyānottaratantra-śāstra* 究竟一乘寶性論, fasc. 3, in *Dazhengxinxiudazangjing* 大正新修大藏經, Book 31, No. 1611, p. 834.

Here, the "self-existent light pure mind 自性清淨光明淨心" or "self-existent pure mind 自性淨心" is "self-existent nature 自性", which are terms applied by the Hinayana school, corresponding to "Buddha nature 佛性", "Bhūtatathatā 真如" and "Dharmakara 法性" of the Mahayana school. According to Buddhist teachings, the mind is originally pure, but has been polluted by external desires since the beginning. So, the believers must practice hard to eliminate the desires, just like maṇi/pearl, after washing off the mud contaminated over it, can still display its pure nature.

Then, let us compare the Manichean ideas corresponding with the Buddhist ones. As pointed above, the most distinguished feature of the Manichean pearl idea is likening the soul (light element) to the pearl. What is the essence of the *Soul* in Manicheism? The Manicheans believe that, at the beginning of the universe, the light gods were defeated by the dark devils, and their light elements were swallowed by these demons. Later, a considerable part of the light elements were rescued, but a lot of them are still imprisoned in the flesh bodies, especially that of mankind, suffering severely. Therefore, the most important mission of the Manicheans is saving thoroughly all light elements or souls from the material prisons.

Although the soul (light element) is personified in Manicheism, it actually means "real knowledge", "divine insight" and "supreme intelligence", being the key factor for saving humanity. In *The lower Section of the Manichean Hymns* 摩尼教下部讚, the term "soul" is translated into the Chinese word 佛性 (Buddha nature) and 法性 (Religious nature), while this text shows that the "Buddha nature" is "real knowledge (gnosis)".

For instance, "By him have now been opened my Buddha-natured eyes, and thus they can see the four-placed wonderful Law-Body; through him also, my Buddha-natured ears have been enlightened, and can hear the clear and pure voice from the Three Constancies." "Open my Light-eyes of the Law Nature, so that they see, without obstacle, the four-placed Body; That they see, without obstacle, the four-placed Body, I am therefore spared the four kinds of intense hardship. Open my Light-ears of the Law Nature, so that they hear without obstacle the voice of the wonderful Law; that they hear without obstacle the voice of the wonderful Law, I am therefore spared a myriad kinds of fallacious sons. Open my Light-mouth of the Law Nature, to praise the four Law-Bodies of the three Constancies; to praise the four Law-Bodies of the three Constancies,

I am therefore spared from uttering confused, mind-bewildering praises. Open my Light-hands of the Law Nature, to touch thoroughly the four solitary Bodies of reality; to touch thoroughly the four solitary Bodies of reality, I am therefore spared from sinking into the four great calamities."[22] Obviously, all the phrases of "open my Buddha-natured eyes" and "open my ears of the Law Nature" signify that the believer is aware of the true knowledge or attains the *gnosis*.

According to the Buddhist teachings, "Buddha nature" is explained as paramārtha-śūnyatā (the first emptiness), bhūtatathatā (reality), namely, also nirvana, supreme truth and perfect intelligence. Thus, it is proper to define "Buddha nature" as "gnosis, enlightenment" in the dictionary.[23]

Now, a distinct fact is that both Manicheism and Buddhism take the pearl/maṇi as a metaphor of soul/Buddha-nature, while the so-called "soul" or "Buddha-nature" signifies the supreme intelligence and the paramount knowledge, which is the ultimate goal of the believers. It seems to be impossible for this similarity to be only a coincidence instead of the result of cultural communications. Since this pearl symbol appears in Manichean teachings of the early stage, it is unreasonable to think its "pearl idea" was adopted from Buddhism only after Manicheism spread eastward.

Another instance is also helpful to manifest the communications between Manicheism and Buddhism in earlier times. As the above Manichean text shows, the savior promises to rescue the souls from the depths of the ocean, get rid of their sufferings; and claims that the souls are perfect pearls which represent all deities. A passage of the Buddhist sutra expresses a similar meaning: "One cannot get priceless precious pearls if he does not dive into the deep sea. For the same reason, if Tathāgata (i.e., Buddha) does not enter into the ocean of desires, he would

---

[22] Cf. *The Lower Section of the Manichean Hymns* 摩尼教下部讚, tr. by Tsuichi 崔驥, in BSOAS, Vol. 11, No. 1, 1943, pp. 176, 180–181. The Chinese text is as follows: "我今蒙開佛性眼, 得睹四處妙法身。又蒙開發佛性耳, 能听三常清淨音。" "開我法性光明眼, 無礙得睹四處身; 無礙得睹四處身, 遂免四種多辛苦。開我法性光明耳, 無礙得聞妙法音; 無礙得聞妙法音, 遂免萬般虛妄曲。開我法性光明口, 具嘆三常四法身; 具嘆三常四法身, 遂免渾合迷心讚。開我法性光明手, 遍觸如如四寂身; 遍觸如如四寂身, 遂免沉于四大厄。"

[23] Cf. William, E. Soothill and Lewis Hodous, *A Dictionary of Chinese Buddhist Terms*, reprint by Teipei: Ch'eng Wen Publishing Company, 1975, p. 227.

not attain the supreme wisdom preciousness."[24] Evidently, the Buddhists also liken eliminating desires and getting real intelligence to diving into the ocean and gathering pearls. Perhaps, in a rather earlier period, the pearl idea of Manicheism was derived to a considerable extent from Buddhism.

Finally, in Buddhism, a lot of buddhas have the term "maṇi" in their titles, and they nearly unexceptionally feature the "light". Particularly, there is a title "Maṇi Light Buddha 摩尼光佛" in Buddhism, while it is used in Chinese Manichean literature without any change. When Manicheism was founded, Buddhism had already been flourishing in India, Central Asia and China; therefore, it is quite possible that Manicheism has been influenced by Buddhism at the earlier stage of Manicheism.

Significantly, another possibility cannot be excluded completely. The founder of Buddhism is called Śākyamuni, meaning "the saint of the Śākya clan". It is transliterated into Chinese 釋迦牟尼. As for the "muni", it refers to saint, holy man, sage ascetic and monk; in addition, it is also interpreted as benevolent, charitable, kind, seclusion and silence. So, sometimes, *Muni* 牟尼 is the shorter form of Śākyamuni. Obviously, the pronunciation of *Mani* and *Muni* is almost the same. Then, is it possible that the Manichean founder's title "Mani" derives from the Buddhist founder's name "Muni"?

I think the reasons for this possibility might be as follows. The Sanskrit word "muni" means saint, sage, etc., being a noble religious title and suitable especially for a religion's leader, while the Manichean founder has many similar titles, such as "Enlightener" in *Kephalaia*. As for the word "enlightener", it generally means "a person who gives others more knowledge and greater understanding about something." Evidently, it almost equates to the Buddhist term "buddha". The latter means "awake" or "awareness", or "person who has broken through the bondage of sense, perception and self, knows the utter unreality of all phenomena, and is ready to enter Nirvana." Since the meaning of the Manichean "Enlightener" is similar to that of the Buddhist "Buddha", it seems to be possible that the Manichean title "Mani" is also borrowed from the Buddhist founder's name "Muni 牟尼", because the two words are quite similar both in their sense and pronunciation.

---

[24] Cf. Kumārajīva 鳩摩羅什 (tr.), *Vimalakīrti-nirdeśa* 維摩詰所說經, fasc. 2, in *Dazhengxinxiudazangjing* 大正新修大藏經, Book 14, No. 475, p. 549.

However, regardless of the above supposition, I prefer the view that because the Manichean founder was influenced by the "maṇi idea" of Buddhism, he took "Mani" as his title. The reasons can be summarized as follows: First, the Manicheans liken the pearl to the soul/light element or gnosis, while the Buddhists liken muṇi/pearl to Buddha-nature or supreme intelligence. The two views are very alike. Second, the pronunciation of the Manichean founder's title "mani" is very similar to that of the Sanskrit word "maṇi (pearl)", while Mani's Chinese name 摩尼 is even completely identical to the transliteration of "maṇi". Third, so far, people have not found an appropriate etymon of the name "Mani" in western languages. Fourth, when Manicheism was establishing itself, the cultural communications among the Eurasian Continent were flourishing; this circumstance could supply adequate favorable conditions for Manicheans understanding Buddhism. Therefore, the conclusion may be as follows: At the beginning of the religion's establishment, the founder borrowed the Buddhist ideas about "maṇi" (pearl), and used "Mani" properly as his own title, thereby highlighting his relationship with light. Undoubtedly, after Manicheism spread eastward, its Buddhist color became more and more strong, but this phenomenon cannot deny or ignore the fact that in its early period, Manicheism had already been influenced by Buddhism.

Chapter 15

Origins and Variations of the Belief in "Killing Someone in Order to Save Him"

The Silk Roads spread across Eurasia from very early times, and once played a significant role in the developmental processes of human civilization, such as economic trade, cultural exchanges and ethnic integration. Important among these processes is the communication and transformation of religious ideas.

It is well known that Buddhism was founded in ancient India. About 2000 years ago, Buddhism was introduced to China via overland and maritime silk roads. Since then, many religious sects claiming to be Buddhist appeared in various areas and historical periods of China. Some of their beliefs and teachings were quite unusual and seemingly incomprehensible, e.g., the claim that killing persons constitutes the performance of "good works" 善業 shanye. Does this idea, which violates acceptable ethical standards, really come from Buddhism, or does it originate from other belief systems? Is it possibly a misunderstanding and distortion of a particular religious doctrine? Or is it a phenomenon resulting from the exchange of religious conceptions in the ancient world? I attempt to answer these questions in this chapter, and provide some analysis and inferences.

1. The Belief in "Killing Someone in Order to Save Him" in Ancient China

In lunar June of the fourth year of the Yanchang 延昌 reign period (512–515) of Emperor Xiaoming 孝明 in the Northern Wei Dynasty, Faqing 法慶 who claimed to be a Buddhist organized an insurrection in Jizhou 冀州. This rebellion lasted three months and was finally suppressed by an official army numbering a 100000. *History of the Wei* 魏書 records this event as follows:

> Faqing 法慶, the śramaṇa of Jizhou 冀州, tempts the crowd with sorcery and magic. He persuades Liguibo 李歸伯 of the Bohai 渤海 region to join him. The latter follows him with his own family and countrymen; they take Faqing as their leader. Then Faqing designates Liguibo as *The Tenth Grade Bodhisattva* 十住菩薩, *Commander of the Invincible Devil Army* 平魔軍司, and *The King Ruling China* 定漢王; and takes *Mahāyāna* as a title for himself. They believe that if someone kills one person, he would be a first grade Bodhisattva, while kills ten, he would become a tenth grade Bodhisattva. Furthermore, they concoct drugs that induce madness, so that even father and son, elder brother and younger brother would not recognize each other, and one would blindly kill the other. These mobs then kill the administrator of the city, and capture the prefecture of Bohai 勃海, leaving many officials slaughtered. The prefectural governor Xiaobaoyin 蕭寶寅 sends Cuibolin 崔伯驎 to attack them, but he is defeated at Zhuzao City 煮棗城 and is killed in fighting. The mob's power greatly increases; they destroy the temples, slaughter both monks and nuns, and burn Buddhist sutras and images. They allege that the new Buddha has now come into the world, so the old demons must be eliminated. The Emperor appoints Yuanyao 元遙 as a general of northern expedition troops. His force consists of cavalry and infantry, totaling one hundred thousand. Faqing and his men attack Yuanyao, but are defeated. Yuanyao sends Fuguo 輔國 general Zhangqiu 張虯 and others to pursue them with cavalry. Finally, Faqing and his wife, the nun Huihui 惠暉, are captured and put to death. Their heads are sent to the capital. Later, Guibo 歸伯 is also caught, and is executed at the center of the city.[1]

---

[1] Cf. "The Biography of Yuanyao" 元遙傳 in *Weishu* 魏書 (History of the Wei), fasc. 19A, Zhonghua Book Company 中華書局, 1974, pp. 445–446.

From this, it appears that Faqing was an authentic Buddhist, because he took *Mahāyāna*[2] as his title, and people called him a *śramaṇa*.[3] In fact, however, he seriously violated Buddhist commandments concerning sexual activity and killing. For instance, he not only took a wife but the latter was even a nun. Moreover, he killed many persons, and even asserted that the more persons one killed, the easier it was to become a Buddha. Therefore, the faith practiced by Faqing was clearly inconsistent with true Buddhism. In fact, the statements of "they destroy the temples, slaughter both monks and nuns, and burn Buddhist sutras and images" and "the new Buddha has now come into the world, so the old demons must be eliminated" show distinctly that although Faqing adopted Buddhist terminology for the form of his faith, its true doctrine was not Buddhist at all. On the contrary, the Buddhist church even became one of the enemies of Faqing's sect, and became the main object to be destroyed and eliminated by them.

The most peculiar thing was that Faqing believed that "if someone kills one person, he would be a first grade Bodhisattva, while kills ten, he would become a tenth grade Bodhisattva." In other words, the more persons one killed, the easier and quicker it was to be successful in religious practice. This teaching and action puzzled many subsequent scholars. For example, while Lüsimian 呂思勉 discussed historical riots by Buddhist adherents, he expressed an inability to comprehend Faqing's behavior. He wrote, "It is incomprehensible why Faqing takes killing as his main work, even harming Buddhist disciples."[4]

Nevertheless, some scholars attempt to explore the source of this belief. For instance, Tangchangru 唐長儒 pointed out that certain stories in the Taoist scriptures *Xiaobingjing* 消冰經 (*Melting Ice Scripture*) and *Zhaolitiandiji* 造立天地記 (*A Record of the Establishment of the Heaven and Earth*) may have been the origin of Faqing's teachings because *Xiaobingjing* states that Laozi demands Yinxi 尹喜 to kill his own parents

---

[2] *Mahāyāna*, a school of Buddhism, formed by Nāgārdjuna 龍樹. The characteristics of this system are an excess of transcendental speculation tending to abstract nihilism, and the substitution of fanciful degrees of meditation in place of the practical asceticism of the *Hīnayāna* 小乘 School.

[3] *śramaṇa*, Buddhist monks and priests, who have left their families and renounced passions.

[4] Cf. Lüsimian, *Lüsimiandushizhaji* 呂思勉讀史札記 (*Notes on the History, by Lüsimian*), Shanghai Classics Publishing House 上海古籍出版社, 1982, pp. 977–978.

as the condition for learning Taoism, and *Zhaolitiandiji* states that after killing the sons of the barbarian king and many of his people, Laozi forces them to yield and worship Taoism. Tangchangru wrote, "*Xiaobingjing* and *Zhaolitiandiji are* both forged by Taoist followers in the wake of the popularity of Buddhism, when Buddhist doctrines are wildly misinterpreted by Taoist sects. The so-called *Mahāyāna* sect preached heresy in the form of Buddhist sutras; this modus operandi replicates that in the stories in *Xiaobingjing* and *Zhaolitiandiji*. The sect induces people to take drugs inducing madness, causing fathers, sons and brothers to kill each other. This is similar to Yinxi's call to kill one's parents in order to learn Taoism. Moreover, their slaughters resemble the alleged killing of seven princes and a tenth of the population by Laozi."[5]

In fact, this story of *killing one's parents in order to learn Taoism* is derived from the retelling of a story in a Buddhist book. In the fifth year (570) of the Tianhe 天和 reign of Emperor Wudi 武帝 of the Northern Zhou, a treatise *Xiaodaolun* 笑道論 (*Laughing at Taoism*) written by Buddhist Zhenluan 甄鸞 criticized what he regarded as Taoist fallacies. He said the following:

> Laozi writes in his *Xiaodaolun* as follows: Laozi says to Yinxi, "If you want to learn Taoism, you should first get rid of the five affections, namely affection for one's parents, for one's wife, for sexual desire, for wealth and for official ranking. If you have done this, you may travel west with me." Yinxi is very impetuous, so soon kills seven persons and bring their heads to Laozi. Laozi laughs and says to him, "I am just testing your inner ideas; you do not really have to kill anyone. And those killed by you are not your relatives at all, but only birds and beasts." When Yinxi watches carefully, he finds that the seven human heads were actually seven gems, and the seven bodies are only seven birds. Yinxi does not believe his eyes, but he returned home immediately and finds his seven relatives are all alive.
>
> In addition, *Zhaolitiandiji* records: Laozi wants to civilize the barbarians, but the barbarian king does not submit. Then Laozi kills seven sons of the king, as well as a tenth of his population.[6]

---

[5]Cf. Tangchangru 唐長儒, *Baiyitianzishishe* 白衣天子試釋, "An Interpretation of Heaven's son in White Dress", in *Yanjingxuebao* 燕京學報 (*Yenching Journal of Chinese Studies*), Vol. 35, p. 234.

[6]Cf. Shidaoxuan 釋道宣, *Guanghongmingji* 廣弘明集 (*Guang Hongming Collection*), fasc. 9, Shanghai Classics Publishing House 上海古籍出版社, 1991, p. 155.

The text here explains that Laozi just wanted to test Yinxi's inner thoughts, and did not really persuade him to kill anyone, but Zhenluan 甄鸞 still condemned Laozi. He said that at the moment that Yinxi killed persons, he did not know it was only a hallucination, so Yinxi was truly malevolent at that time. Furthermore, those killed by him were his parents and other relatives, so he had already committed a grave crime. As for the saying "half of the population is slaughtered" elsewhere, it was more absurd and ridiculous.[7]

Obviously, Zhenluan tried to belittle Taoism by pointing out absurdities in Taoist scriptures. Since Tangchangru traced Faqing's teaching to "kill a person in order to save him" to the statement by Laozi, the founder of Taoism, that one must "kill one's parents in order to worship Taoism", this belief seemed to have been regarded by him as a Taoist doctrine. However, this might not be the case because in early Taoist scriptures much of the content and teachings were adopted from Buddhist sutras, and other religious beliefs were also referenced. There is academic consensus that Manichaeism is among these sources. See, for instance, the following:

> The process of additional editing of *Huahujing* 化胡經 (*Scripture of Civilizing the Barbarians*) by Taoists is also a process of plagiarizing other ideas and materials. Mr. Luqinli 逯欽立 studies this subject in detail, and points out that it is logical that the Taoists are cribbing Manichean teachings as long as there is an opportunity. In fact, the Manichean ideas adopted by the Taoists are not only drawn from *Huahujing*. In his paper *Traces of Zoroastrian and Manichaean Activities in Pre-Tang China* Professor Liuts'unyan 柳存仁 presents a textual criticism of *Durenjing* 度人經 (*The Scripture of Saving Persons*), which is written in the fifth century by Taoists and given four kinds of annotations. He demonstrates a number of Manichean traces in this scripture.[8]

In his *Xiaodaolun* 笑道論, Zhenluan also frequently cited sentences of *Huahujing* 化胡經 to be criticized and refuted. It is well known that there were obvious Manichean elements in *Huahujing* (*Scripture of Civilizing the Barbarians*), so we cannot exclude the possibility that the

---

[7] *Ibid.*, p. 155.
[8] Cf. Linwushu 林悟殊, *Monijiaojiqidongjian* 摩尼教及其東漸 (*Manicheism and Its Spreading Eastward*), Zhonghua Book Company 中華書局, 1987, pp. 80–81.

other Taoist scriptures cited by Zhenluan also contained some Manichean ideas.

We can, moreover, offer more examples to demonstrate the close relationship between the belief in redemptive killing and the Manichean doctrine. For instance, the religious sect known as the "Vegetarianism and Devil Cult" 吃菜事魔 Chicaishimo held similar views to those of Faqing 法慶, and this sect was generally regarded as a faith containing many important Manichean factors.

A description of Chicaishimo 吃菜事魔 is provided in *Rongzhaiyishi* 容齋逸史 (*The Lost Histories Recorded in Rongzhai*). Some of its features resembled those of Manicheism, and one of the characteristics was in fact redemptive killing! The outline of this text is as follows:

> According to the law of Song Dynasty the faith of *Chicaishimo* is strictly prohibited. Anyone violating this prohibition would be exiled to remote areas, and his property would be confiscated.
>
> The followers of this faith do not take meat and wine; they worship neither Buddha nor ancestors. After their death they are buried without any dress.
>
> If the neophytes are impoverished, they will receive some money and resources contributed by their fellow believers; which is enough to supply their livelihood.
>
> The leader of this religious sect is called King of the Devils 魔王, and his assistant is called Mother of the Devils 魔母. They do not worship the Buddha, but take the sun and moon as the real gods.
>
> They believe that Zhangjiao 張角 (?–184), the leader of rebels at the end of the Later Han Dynasty (25–220), is the founder of their religion. Any followers of this faith dare not to pronounce the name of Zhangjao, even if subjected to the threat of death.
>
> Furthermore, they insist that the life of persons entails their suffering. So, killing persons actually means saving them from suffering; the killer is thus one who conferred salvation. He who kills many persons will become Buddha.[9]

---

[9] Cf. Fangsha 方勺, *Rongzhaiyishi* 容齋逸史 (*The Lost Histories Recorded in Rongzhai*), in Taozongyi 陶宗儀, etc. ed., *Suofusanzhong* 說郛三種 (*Three Versions of Shufu*), pp. 1807–1808, Shanghai Classics Publishing House 上海古籍出版社, 1988. The original Chinese text of the whole paragraph is as follows:

From this, we can see that the belief in redemptive killing was one of the doctrines ascribed to these Vegetarian Servants of the Devil in the Song Dynasty. Their reasoning seems logical: people suffer greatly while they live in this world, so if someone kills a person, the latter will naturally escape from all his pain and misfortune. Therefore, what seems like killing or murder is actually rescue and salvation. In other words, *Killing* is in fact *Beneficence*; correspondingly, the more a man kills, the more *good deeds* he has performed, and the more easily and quickly he will become a Buddha.

Why does such a faith and logic form, or what ideas does it derive from? In discussing this problem, I should point out that the idea does not derive initially from the sect Chicaishimo 吃菜事魔, but probably originated in the teachings of Manicheism.

In fact, the paragraph quoted above already displays a clearly strong Manichean hue. First, the title Chicaishimo has been regarded by many scholars as a Chinese nickname of Manicheism, such as the following passage states: "Emperor Wuzong 武宗 of the Tang Dynasty has banned all religions, and removed the ban soon afterwards, but the ban on

---

契菜事魔, 法禁甚嚴。有犯者, 家人雖不知情, 亦流遠方, 財產半給告人, 餘皆沒官。而近時事者益眾, 始自福建, 流至溫州, 遂及二浙。睦州方臘之亂, 其徒處處相煽而起。

聞其法斷葷酒, 不事神佛、祖先, 不會賓客, 死則裸葬。方斂, 盡飾衣冠, 其徒使二人坐於屍傍。其一問曰: "來時有冠否?" 則答曰: "無。" 遂去其冠。次問衣履, 亦去之, 以至於盡, 乃曰: "來時何有?" 曰: "有包衣。" 則以布囊盛屍焉。云事後致富。小人無知, 不知絕酒肉、燕祭、厚葬自能積財也。

又, 始投其黨, 有甚貧者, 眾率財以助, 積微以至於小康矣。凡出入經過, 不必相識, 黨人皆館穀焉。凡物用之無間, 謂為一家, 故有無礙被之說。以是誘惑其眾。

其魁謂之魔王, 右者謂之魔母, 各有誘化。旦望, 人出四十九錢於魔公處燒香, 魔母則聚所得緡錢, 以時納于魔王, 歲獲不貲云。亦誦《金剛經》, 取以色見我為邪道故, 不事神佛。但拜日月, 以為真佛。其說不經, 如 "是法平等, 無有高下", 則以 "無" 字連上句, 大抵多如此解釋。俗訛以魔為麻, 謂其魁為麻黃, 或云易魔王之名也。

其初授法, 設誓甚重, 然以張角為祖, 雖死于湯鑊, 終不敢言 "角" 字。傳言何執中守官台州, 州獲事魔之人, 勘鞫久不能得。或云: "何處州龍泉人, 其鄉邑多有事者, 必能察其虛實。" 乃委之窮究。何以雜物百數, 問能識其名則非是, 而置一羊角其間。餘皆名之, 至角則不言, 遂決其獄。

如不事祖先、喪葬之類, 已害風俗, 而又謂人生為苦, 若殺之是救其苦也, 謂之度人。度人多者, 則可成佛。故結集既眾, 乘亂而起, 日嗜殺人, 最為大害。尤憎惡釋氏, 蓋以不殺與之為戾耳。但禁令太嚴, 罕有告者。株連既廣, 又當籍沒全家, 流放與死為等, 必協力同心, 以拒官吏, 州縣憚之, 率不敢按, 反致增多也。

Manicheism remained. From then on, there were secret folk religions such as the Devil Sect 魔教, the adherents of which were called Vegetarians of the Devil Cult 事魔吃菜人, as well as the White Lotus Society 白蓮社, White Cloud Sect 白雲宗, and the Light Sovereign Religion 明尊教, all of which were branches of Manicheism."[10]

In a similar vein, we read the following:

> The Religion of Light is Manicheism. ... The Religion of Light does not worship spirits and ghosts. The portraits of Mani and Jesus worshiped by the believers all show features with large noses and deep eyes, demonstrating that they are Persians or Jews. This religion has been abominated by both government and Buddhists. The Buddhists always pronounce the heresies as "devils" 魔, and so they named the Religion of Light as the Religion of the Devil 魔教, and its leader as the King of the Devils 魔王. Thus the entire sect is called the Vegetarianism and Devil Cult 吃菜事魔, because one of its commandments is strict vegetarianism.[11]

In addition, "Manicheism is also named the Religion of Light 明教 and the Vegetarianism and Devil Cult 吃菜事魔. The Persian Mani first founds Manicheism. It is formed by mixing Buddhism, Christianity and Zoroastrianism together."[12] "In the sentence '(During the period of the Northern Song) the faith of Chicaishimo 吃菜事魔 is prevalent in areas of Zhejiang 浙江', the word 'shimo 事魔' means worship the devil, namely Manicheism."[13] "Another secret religious sect spreads in some districts, which is called by the government of the Song as Chicaishimo

---

[10] Cf. Fanwenlan 范文瀾, *Zhonggujindaishi* 中國近代史 (*Modern History of China*), Part I, Book 1, People's Publishing House 人民出版社, 1953, p. 354.

[11] Cf. Wuhan 吳晗, "The Religion of Light and the Great Ming Empire", in his *Dushizhaji* 讀史劄記 (*Notes on the Histories of Records*), Joint Publishing (Peking) Company 北京三聯書店, 1956, pp. 237, 241.

[12] Cf. Fangying 方瑛, "*Bailianjiaodeyuanliujiqiyu monijiaodeguanxi* 白蓮教的源流及其與摩尼教的關係 (*The Origin of the Religion of White Lotus and Its Relationship with Manicheism*)", in *Lishijiaoxuewenti* 歷史教學問題 (*Subjects of History Teaching*), No. 5, 1959, p. 34.

[13] Cf. Yexianen 葉顯恩, "*Yetanchuogengluzhongdefujishi* 也談《輟耕錄》中的扶箕詩 (*Also talk about the sciomancy poem in chuogenglu*)", in *Lishiyanjiu* 歷史研究 (*Historical Research*), No. 9, 1978, p. 94.

吃菜事魔. ... because the features of these believers are vegetarian diets and the Mani cult, and so their faith is named Chicaishimo 吃菜事魔 .... Thenceforth, the term Chicaishimo 吃菜事魔 has been applied unchanged, and become a specialized name for this secret sect."[14]

The descriptions and conclusions cited above all obviously equate the Chicaishimo 吃菜事魔 sect with Manicheism. Of course, there are also some differing opinions in academic circles; one of these views is that the Chicaishimo 吃菜事魔 sect is not exactly the same as Manicheism. For example, Chengaohua 陳高華 said, "To be specific, so-called Chicaishimo is the general name for various heretical sects of that time; Manicheism is just one sect among them. The relationship between them is that of the whole and the part; these two religious schools are neither equivalent nor independent. Apparently, therefore, it is incorrect to regard Chicaishimo as the same with Manicheism. On the other hand, it is also inappropriate to think that Chicaishimo is heretical Manicheism different from orthodox Manicheism. ... Chicaishimo 吃菜事魔 is the general name for all heresies including Manicheism and other Buddhist heretical sects."[15]

Linwushu 林悟殊 said, "It is possible that in the Song Dynasty only some Buddhists exclusively termed Manicheism or the Religion of Light as Chicaishimo 吃菜事魔, while the rulers never specifically denominated the Religion of Light by this name. So among those who are called Vegetarians and Devil Worshipers 吃菜事魔者, some people might be Manichean believers, while others could not be regarded as Manicheans. Hence I think it is inexact and incorrect that some scholars identify a particular leader of a peasant uprising in the Song Dynasty as a Manichean believer, just because this person has been depicted as the Vegetarians and Devil Worshipers 吃菜事魔者."[16]

---

[14] Cf. Zhuruixi 朱瑞熙, "*Lunfanglaqiyiyumonijiaodeguanxi* 論方臘起義與摩尼教的關係 (*On the relations between the rebellion of Fangla and Manicheism*)" in *Lishiyanjiu* 歷史研究 (*Historical Research*), No. 9, 1979, p. 76.

[15] Cf. Chengaohua 陳高華, "*Monijiao yu Chicaishimo* 摩尼教與吃菜事魔 (*Manicheism and Chicaishimo*)", in *Zhongguo nongminzhanzhengshi luncong* 中國農民戰爭史論叢 (*Forum on the History of Chinese Peasant Wars*), Vol. IV, Henan People's Publishing House 河南人民出版社, 1982, pp. 98, 103.

[16] Cf. Linwushu 林悟殊, *Monijiaojiqidongjian* 摩尼教及其東漸 (*Manicheism and Its Spreading Eastward*), Zhonghua Book Company 中華書局, 1987, p. 142.

Although we recognize that there are certain differentiations between the Chicaishimo 吃菜事魔 religious sect and Manicheism, it is also undeniable that there are relations, even close relations, between them. In my opinion, every Chicaishimo group, especially those of the Song Dynasty, probably contained some elements of Manicheism. I once expressed this view in one of my papers:

> The faith of Chicaishimo 吃菜事魔 in regions south of the Yangtze River in the Song Dynasty is a popular faith including multicultural elements, blending Manicheism, Buddhism, Taoism and native traditional beliefs. Generally speaking, the common aspects of all sects of this religious faith are vegetarianism and collective scriptural chanting. But every sect has also its own features; one is more like Manicheism, another is more like Buddhism, and the third might be similar to Taoism, and so on. Therefore, we cannot assert that it is a particular religion just because of its cultural elements similar to that religion, nor can we neglect its close ideological relations with that religion. In a word, every sect called Chicaishimo contains some Manichean factors in the mix.[17]

For this reason, I think the Chicaishimo faith described in *Rongzhaiyishi* 容齋逸史 probably adopted a number of cultural elements from Manicheism. For example, the citation mentions that the leader of the Chicaishimo sect was called a "devil" (魔 *mo*). In fact, in Chinese, the word "devil" is a derogatory name for Mani or Manicheism because *devil* 魔 is pronounced as *mo* in Chinese, and the first syllable of Mani 摩尼 or Manicheism 摩尼教 is also pronounced as *mo*. It is quite possible that in Chinese society, these homophonic words effect the transformation of *Mani* into *devil* 魔, and Manicheism into the "devil religion" 魔教.

Moreover, the preceding passage from *Rongzhaiyishi* 容齋逸史 also mentions that the adherents of Chicaishimo did not worship the Buddha, but regarded the sun and moon as the real gods. These words manifest clearly the Manichean origin of the Chicaishimo sect, because the worship of the sun and moon is the basic doctrine and important ritual of Manicheism. The sun and moon cult is also the distinctive feature of the Chinese Manicheism (the Religion of Light 明教) and Chicaishimo

---

[17] Cf. Ruichuanming 芮傳明, "*Lun songdaijiangnan zhichicaishimoxinyang* 論宋代江南之吃菜事魔信仰 (*On the Faith Chicaishimo in Regions South of the Yangtze River of the Song Dynasty*)", in *Shilin* 史林 (*Historical Review*), No. 3, 1999, pp. 12–13.

sects.[18] Thus, it is reasonable that the Chicaishimo sect discussed in that passage was regarded as a kind of Chinese folk belief including multiple Manichean elements. Hence, the belief in redemptive killing may also derive from Manicheism.

Nevertheless, the instances cited above are only indirect evidence of all this. We need to find more evidence within the fundamental doctrines of Manicheism itself.

2. Teachings Forbidding Killing in Manicheism

It is distinctive that Manicheism never officially advocates killing. On the contrary, like Buddhism does, it also strictly forbids killing, and is renowned for its commandment forbidding killing. So, if we want to look for a concept of redemptive killing related to Manichean doctrines, we must first know and comprehend various Manichean statements about killing or forbidding killing.

Moniguangfojiaofayilüe 摩尼光佛教法儀略 (*The Compendium of the Doctrines and the Styles of the Teaching of Mani, the Buddha of Light*) is one of the three more complete Manichean scriptures in Chinese. This document was written in the Tang Dynasty (618–907). In the paragraph describing rules of the Manichean temple, some strict regulations are listed: All disciples of the temple must chant and live together, and are prohibited from having a private room or kitchen; they must follow a vegetarian diet and entirely rely on alms to get food; if nobody gives them alms, they have to beg for food; they are not permitted to own servants and domestic animals; and, only the worldly adherents, namely, the so-called hearers, can be their helpers.[19] Thus, we know that, according to

---

[18] For a study on the worship of sun and moon, cf. Maxiaohe 馬小鶴, "*Monijiaozhaobairiyebaiyueyanjiu* 摩尼教 '朝拜日夜拜月' 研究" (*A Study on the ritual 'worship sun in the morning and worship moon in the night' of Manicheism*) Part One and Part Two, in *Xueshujilin* 學術集林 (*Academic Collection*), Vol. 15, Jan. 1999 and Vol. 16, Oct. 1999, Shanghai Yuandong Publishing House 上海遠東出版社.

[19] The original text in Chinese of this paragraph is as follows: "右置五堂, 法眾共居, 精修善業, 不得別立私室廚庫。每日齋食, 儼然待施, 若無施者, 乞丐以充。唯使聽人, 勿畜奴婢及六畜等非法之具。" in Rui Chuanming 芮傳明, *Monijiaodunhuangtulufanwenshuyisheyuyanjiu* 摩尼教敦煌吐魯番文書譯釋與研究 (*Translation, Annotation and Study on the Manichean Documents Discovered in Dunhuang and Turpan*), Lanzhou University Press 蘭州大學出版社, 2014, p. 52.

Manichean commandments, the adherents of Manicheism, especially their professional monks, must be vegetarians for life.

In the early 860s, Manicheism was established as the state religion of the Uighur Khanate, a nomadic regime that flourished to the north of the Tang Dynasty. The Chinese inscription titled *Jiuxinghuigupigakehanbei* 九姓回鶻毗伽可汗碑 (*Stele of Bilgä Kagan of the Nine Clan Uighurs*)[20] describes the great achievements of this Uighur Kagan, and the narration about the introduction of Manicheism into Uighur takes up significant space. This inscription also demonstrates distinctively the vegetarian emphasis of Manicheism.

The inscription records that when the Uighur Kagan was going to leave China for home, he invited four Manichean monks to go with him. These four were all distinguished monks. They had mastered all fundamental doctrines of Manicheism, and had read thoroughly all the works written by Mani himself. The Kagan entrusted them to preach Manicheism in the Uighur Khanate, and believed that they would be highly successful. Not long after, Manicheism flourished in the Uighur Khanate, and many people were converted to Manicheism. All the followers of Manicheism were vegetarians, so people who had once killed creatures because they were fond of meat now became vegetarians and doers of good works.[21]

The Uighurs were nomads. It was natural for them to kill animals to sustain their diet of meats, but it would be an exaggeration to say that the Uighur people changed from killers into vegetarians immediately after becoming Manichean believers. However, such a statement shows at least that vegetarianism and the forbidding of killing were among the main features of Manicheism.

---

[20] This stele was erected in 814. There are three versions of inscription on the stele, in Chinese, Sogdian and Turkic. Among them, the Chinese inscription is the most complete. Since it was discovered in Mongolia in 1890, a lot of scholars at home and abroad have studied this stele in depth.

[21] The original text in Chinese of this paragraph is as follows: "可汗乃頓軍東都, 因觀風俗敗民弗師, 將睿息等四僧入國, 闡揚二祀, 洞徹三際。況法師妙達名門, 精通七部, 才高海岳, 辯若懸河。故能開正教於回鶻, 以茹葷屏湩酪為法, 立大功績, 乃曰汝俟悉德。… 曰: 既有志誠, 任即持贊, 應有刻畫魔形, 悉令焚蕉, 祈神拜鬼, 並擯斥而受明教。熏血異俗, 化為蔬飯之鄉; 宰殺邦家, 變為勸善之國。" in Chengsuluo 程溯洛, *Tangsonghuigushilunji* 唐宋回鶻史論集 (*Treatises on the Uighur History in the Tang and Song Dynasties*), People's Publishing House 人民出版社, 1994, p. 104.

When Mani answered a question about entering into Manicheism asked by his adherents, he taught them as follows: "He who would enter the cult must examine his soul. If he finds that he can subdue lust and covetousness, refrain from eating meats, from drinking wine, as well as from marriage, and if he can also avoid causing injury to water, fire, trees, and living things, then let him enter the cult. But if he is unable to do all of these things, he shall not enter the cult."[22]

Indeed, those who would enter Manicheism referred to here by Mani were not meant to be general believers, but the professional and high-grade monks, namely, the so-called Elects. In other words, even the persons eating meats and killing living things could be permitted to be Manichean adherents. They were named Hearers or Auditors, and had to try their best to serve the Elect.

Nevertheless, forbidding meat consumption and killing remained strict commandments of Manicheism. Forbidding killing is listed among the ten fundamental ordinances of Manicheism: (1) renouncing the worship of idols; (2) renouncing the telling of lies; (3) renouncing avarice; (4) renouncing killing; (5) renouncing adultery; (6) renouncing stealing; (7) renouncing the teaching of incantations; (8) renouncing magic; (9) renouncing upholding different opinions about the Manichean faith; (10) renouncing neglect and lassitude in action.[23] Though the lists of ordinances given by various authors are sometimes slightly different, the forbidding of killing is always an important item.

The Manicheans thought that most adherents were apt to commit some sins consciously or unconsciously, so they were required to confess every day. A text of confession was thus provided for the repentance of Manichean followers. At the beginning of the 20th century, some fragments of a Manichean confessional text in Turkic[24] were discovered in the Dunhuang 敦煌 region. It was a confession used by lay believers, namely, *Hearers*. The confessor was required to repent for fifteen items of sins.

---

[22] Cf. Bayard Dodge ed. & tr., *The Fihrist of al-Nadīm--A Tenth-Century Survey of Muslim Culture*, Vol. I, Chapter IX, Columbia University Press, 1970, p. 788.

[23] Cf. *ibid.*, p. 789.

[24] This Manichean document is titled *X^uāstvānīft*. The main part of it was found by Aurel Stein (1862–1943) in the region southeast of Dunhuang, and was eventually brought back to London. In addition, several other fragments of this confessional text are collected in St. Petersburg and Berlin. This document is regarded as a work of the fifth century and is an important document for understand the religious life of ancient Manicheism.

Among them, several items concerned the killing of living things. For instance, the fifth item states the following:

Fifthly. About sins against the five kinds of living beings:

> And that is firstly, against two-legged human beings, secondly, against four-legged living beings, thirdly, against flying living beings, fourthly, against living beings in the water, and fifthly, against living beings creeping on the ground on their belly.
>
> If we ever, my God, somehow should have inspired fear in or scared these five kinds of living beings, from the biggest to the smallest, if we somehow should have beaten or cut them, somehow have pained or tortured them, and indeed, somehow should have killed them, then we to the same degree owe life to these living beings. Therefore, we now, my God, pray that we may be liberated from sin. Forgive my sin.[25]

In the conclusion of *X^uāstvānīft*, it is emphasized once again that killing and injuring the five kinds of living beings are sins, and even hurting vegetation is also a sin:

> My God, we are encumbered with defect and sin, we are great debtors. Because of the insatiable and shameless Āz demon we in thought, word, and deed, likewise looking with its eyes, hearing with its ears, speaking with its tongue, seizing with its hands, and walking with its feet, incur constant and permanent agony on the light of the Fivefold God in the dry and wet earth, the five kinds of living beings and the five kinds of herbs and trees. Likewise, we in other ways are encumbered with defect and sin.[26]

Here, the word "debtor" should mean that the confessor is in debt of life or lives because of his frequent killing of living things. So, it is also referring to the crimes committed by killing living beings. In addition, destroying plants is also regarded as a sin. The reason for this idea is that a lot of Light Elements are said to have been imprisoned within plants, and these Light Elements are thought to be important gods originating from their supreme God.

---

[25] See Jes P. Asmussen, *X^uāstvānīft, Studies in Manichaeism,* Copenhagen, 1965, in *Acta Theologica Danica*, Vol. VII, p. 195.
[26] Cf. *ibid.*, pp. 198–199.

A Pahlavi work titled *Shikand-Gūmānīg Vizhār* (*Doubt-dispelling Explanation*), probably written in the later part of the ninth century, sought to refute certain heretical doctrines held by Mani, and thus afforded a number of teachings of Manicheism including several views on forbidding killing. It states the following:

> Furthermore, about the difference of the nature of life (= soul) and body he states this, that the life (= soul) is bound and imprisoned with the body. Since according to Mani the creator and maintainer of all material beings that have bodily forms is Ahriman, for the same reason it is not proper to occasion birth and arrange for posterity, because he who does so is a co-worker with Ahriman through the maintaining of mankind and cattle and the forcing back of life and light within bodies; — nor even to cultivate plants and grain.
>
> Furthermore, they inconsistently say also this, that the destroyer of creatures is likewise Ahriman; and the same reason it is not proper to kill any creature whatsoever, because killing is the work of Ahriman.[27]

According to the teachings of Mani cited here, it is obvious that the Manicheans insisted on forbidding killing and even disapproved of breeding offspring. Though there are various sayings about such subjects, all of them manifest the concepts of forbidding killing held by Manicheans. Is then the belief in redemptive killing in disagreement with Manichean teachings? In fact, after analyzing carefully Manichean doctrines, we find that the belief in redemptive killing probably did draw on ideas from Manicheism.

3. The Manichean Concept of Light Elements

As a matter of fact, the Manichean views on killing creatures and forbidding killing derives from concepts about Light Elements, and the teachings concerning the latter come from the creation mythology of Manicheism. The creation mythology of Manicheism may be outlined as follows:

In the beginning, the Paradise of Light stretches unbounded upwards (northwards) and to left (east) and right (west). Below, or southward, lay

---

[27] Cf. A.V. Williams Jackson, *Researches in Manichaeism, with Special Reference to the Turfan Fragments*, Columbia University Press, 1932, p. 181.

the Hell of Darkness. The land of Paradise is uncreated and eternal. Its substance is the Five Light Elements: Ether, Air, Light, Water, and Fire. It is ruled over by the Father of Greatness, and is inhabited by countless Aeons.

Hell is divided into five kingdoms, each of the substance of one of the Five Dark Elements. The five infernal kingdoms are inhabited by five kinds of devils, two-legged, four-legged, winged, swimming, and crawling. The Devil, or Prince of Darkness, king over all, combines in himself features of all five species of devil, namely demon, lion, eagle, fish, and dragon. He is treated sometimes as the personification of Matter, sometimes as its chief manifestation. By chance the Devils come to the boundary between hell and heaven, and see, desire, and invade the Light.

To protect his realm, and to preserve its eternal peace, the Father of Greatness evokes by word Emanations of himself, to do battle with the powers of Darkness. These Emanations are the gods of Manicheism. Being essentially the same, they are distinguished from one another mainly by their functions. There are three separate "Creations" of gods.

Those of the First Creation are the Mother of Life (whose Chinese name is Shanmu 善母), who evokes in turn her "son", the First Man (whose Chinese name is Xianyi 先意). And he evokes as his "sons" the Five Light Elements, from the substance of the Paradise of Light. With these the First Man goes forth to do battle with the devils. The Light Elements are also called his "armor" and "bait", but they are overwhelmed by the powers of Darkness. The First Man is forced to throw them to distract them from Paradise. The devils swallow the Light Elements, are appeased, and cease their invasion. By this act a part of the Light has become absorbed in Darkness. This lost Light is smothered by the Matter which has devoured it, suffers, and forgets its divine nature. Matter itself rejoices in the Light it has obtained, and grows to depend upon it.

The First Man, overwhelmed in the depths of hell, remains unconscious on the battlefield. After recovering his senses, he cries out for help; and his Mother, hearing him, pleads with the Father of Greatness, who evokes the Second Creation of gods for his aid: the Friend of Lights, the Great Builder, and the Living Spirit (whose Chinese name is Jingfeng 淨風) with his five "Sons". The Living Spirit goes to the edge of the abyss and utters a call, and the First Man answers from the depth. Call and Answer themselves are made gods, the Sixth Sons of Living Spirit and the First Man respectively. When the First Man awakens from his unconsciousness, he rises up from the pit, and is led back to Paradise by the

Mother of Life and the Living Spirit. The rescue of the First Man is a pattern for the redemption thereafter of all individual souls.

The Living Spirit then attacks and defeats the powers of Darkness. From the bodies of the demons he has killed he makes eight earths, from their skins ten skies. From a portion of the swallowed Light that is still undefiled he makes the sun and moon, and from Light that is slightly defiled, the stars, which are set in an eleventh sky, i.e., the one which is seen from this earth.

The world at this point is motionless and without life, the sun standing still in the sky. The Father of Greatness then evokes the Third Creation, that of the redeeming gods. The first of three is the Third Messenger; he evokes in turn the Maiden of Light, who sometimes also appears as the Twelve Maidens, and the Chinese name is Dianguangfo 電光佛。The two divinities show themselves naked to the Archons chained in the sky. Beholding them, the males ejaculate, and their seed which falls into the water becomes a huge sea-monster, which is overcome by the Adamas of Light. Part falls on land and forms the trees and plants. The female devils, pregnant from unions in hell, miscarry, and their abortions, containing less Light than the male semen, fall to earth and people it with the five kinds of living creatures, which correspond with the five species of demons.

Then the Great Builder evoked in the Second Creation makes the New Paradise or New Aeon; its ruler is the First Man. The third god of the redeeming Creation is the Column of Glory, who is both a god and the path by which the redeemed Light ascends to the sky. By this path the souls pass to the moon at its time of waxing, and thence to the sun, from which they go to the New Paradise.

To defeat this process of redemption, the Demon of Greed prompts two great demon-animals to devour the offspring of the other animals, and thus to absorb into their own two bodies all the Light which they possess. The pair then mate, and produce Adam and Eve, whose appearances are the same as that of the Third Messenger and the Maiden of Light seen by their parent-devils in the sky. The accumulated Light in their bodies is transmitted to the first human pair, and forms their souls. Thus, the souls or Light elements are imprisoned by the material bodies; and relieving the souls (Light Elements) of their captivity will be a durable and arduous task for the Manicheans.[28]

---

[28] Cf. Mary Boyce, *A Reader in Manichaean Middle Persian and Parthian*, Brill, Leiden, 1975, pp. 4–7.

When the dark devils invade Light Paradise, the saving of the Light Elements begins; this mission continues until the secular world is destroyed. In other words, as long as humans and creatures still exist on the earth, the process of redeeming Light Elements will not stop. So, the redeeming task is a durable one. On the contrary, the Light Elements are imprisoned not only in all persons and animals but also in various plants, so the thorough redeeming of Light Elements is also a very difficult task. Thus, liberating Light Elements from the material substance becomes the most important and fundamental mission of the Manicheans. Accordingly, for the Manicheans, all good or evil and right or wrong are judged by the standard of whether favorable for saving Light Elements.

There are numerous examples of liberating Light Elements from their imprisonment, especially from human bodies, in Manichean literature in Chinese and other languages. For instance, *The Fragmentary Manichean Treatise* (*Monijiaocanjing* 摩尼教殘經) states, "All the saints appeared in the world, to free the light natures 明性 from their multitude of sufferings by means of appropriate methods, and to make them calm and happy." "The great sage Light Nous (*huiming* 惠明) saves Light natures from carnal bodies by excellent methods, thus liberating them."

The Second Section of the Manichean Hymns (*Xiabuzan* 下部讚) reads, "He comforts and heals all those who uphold filial piety, and reanimates all light natures." "Please bestow great opportunity and compassionate power, and reanimate the universally suffering light natures." "Who can deliver my nature from tortures and calamity, and who can make the pure body always joyful and happy." "Each of you, please pity and remember the compassionate strength, and please save the universally suffering light natures, enabling them to leave the great waves and billows of the fiery sea. We, all the members, eternally wish it may be so." "Laud and praise the real and true Master, the herculean Mani, the venerable Lord, who can enliven the Body of Pure Law, and can rescue the light natures." "Pray, the two Lights, the five-fold Law-Body, clean and pure Teacher-Priests, the great compassionate power! Rescue and lift that nature, free it from transmigration, the rough and hard bodies, the various hells, boiling water in caldrons and burning charcoal in furnaces. Pray may all Buddhas have pity on that nature, beget great compassion, and give it emancipation; conduct it themselves into the world of Light."

The terms "Buddha Nature" 佛性, "Light Nature" 明性 and "Natures" 性 in Chinese Manichean literature all refer to Light Elements or the souls, especially human souls.[29] These passages quoted above show clearly that the strongest wish of the Manichean adherent is his own soul ridding of the incarceration of carnal bodies, and returning to his original homeland, the World of Light. Similar concepts are seen in the literatures of non-Chinese languages. For example, a Coptic hymn states the following:

> Save me, O blessed Christ, the Savior of the holy souls.
>   I will pass up into the skies and leave this body upon the earth. The trumpet sounds, I hear, they are calling me up to the immortals.
>   I will cast away my body upon the earth from which it was assembled. Since I was in my childhood I have learned to walk in the way of God.
>   Let no man weep for me, neither my brethren nor them that begot me. My true Fathers, they that are from on high, they love my soul, they seek after it.
>   The enemy of my soul is the world, its riches and its deceit. All life hates godliness: what am I doing in the place of my enemies?
>   … in the flesh of death that burns
>   … my Savior has not deserted me, he has sated me from his fountain that is full of lives.
>   I have known the way of the holy ones, these ministers of God who are in the church, the place wherein the Paraclete planted the tree of knowledge.
>   I have cast away from my eyes this sleep of death which is full of Error …[30]

It is clearly shown here that the Manichean followers are very eager to be saved, and extremely despise their own flesh bodies, while they most respect souls, namely, the Light Elements. Even the real world wherein their flesh bodies live is regarded as the enemy, and all creatures living in this world are considered to be hostile to godliness. Thus, the Manichean feature of hating earthliness and looking forward to *liberation* is displayed

---

[29] About the so-called Buddha Nature in Chinese Manicheism, please refer to Rui Chuanming 芮傳明, "*Monijiao foxingtantao*" 摩尼教佛性探討 (*A Discussion on the Buddha Nature of Manicheism*), in *Journal of Chinese Literature and History* 中華文史論叢, Vol. 59, Sept. 1999, pp. 186–216.

[30] See C.R.C. Allberry, *A Manichaean Psalm-Book II*, CCLXI, Stuttgart, 1938, pp. 75–76.

vividly. In other words, the departing of the soul from the body is regarded as the final aim and the best prospect by Manicheans; or we may say, in their eyes, the death of a creature is actually lucky and fortunate.

Accordingly, the life of a creature is thought by them to be great pain, for it is a condition of the soul or Light Element being imprisoned and suffering. *The Fragmentary Manichean Treatise* 摩尼教殘經 says the following:

> When the Demon realizes this fact, he comes up with a lustful and venomous idea, and imprisons the five light natures in the small universe consisting of flesh bodies. He incarcerates the five light natures with thirteen kinds of dark powers, and does not permit them to be free. …
>
> When the five light bodies endure such sufferings of imprisonment and binding, they forget their original consciences, as though being mad and drunken. Or just like that someone is hung upside down in a cage filled with many poisonous snakes, and because of the venom squirted by these snakes he is confused in his mind, no longer considering his father, his mother, his relatives, as well as his original happiness. Now the five light natures have been bound by the devils in the flesh bodies, suffering day and night, the situation is the same.[31]

Now, I will cite another Manichean hymn in the Parthian dialect wherein the Living Soul recounts the great sufferings while he is imprisoned:

> I hail from the Light and from the gods,
> Yet I have become as one banished, separated from them.
> The foes assembled above me
> And took me to the realm of death.
> --- Blessed be he who rescues my soul from distress, so that it may be saved. ---
> A god am I, born of the gods,
> A bright, radiant, and shining,

---

[31] The corresponding Chinese text is as follows: "魔見是已, 起貪毒心, 以五明性, 禁於肉身, 為小世界。亦以十三無明暗力, 囚固束縛, 不令自在。… 其五明身, 既被如是苦切禁縛, 廢忘本心, 如狂如醉。猶如有人以眾毒蛇, 編之為籠, 頭皆在內, 吐毒縱橫; 復取一人, 倒懸於內, 其人爾時為毒所逼, 及以倒懸, 心意迷錯, 無暇思惟父母親戚及本歡樂。今五明性在肉身中, 為魔束縛, 晝夜受苦, 亦復如是。" Lines 29–30, 43–48; cf. Rui Chuanming 芮傳明, *Monijiaodunhuangtulufanwenshuyisheyuyanjiu* 摩尼教敦煌吐魯番文書譯釋與研究, 2014, pp. 6–7.

Beaming, fragrant, and beautiful god.
But now I have fallen into misery.
Countless demons seized me,
Loathsome ones captured me.
My soul has been subjugated by them,
I am torn to pieces and devoured.
Demons, *yakshas*[32] and *peris*[33],
Black, hideous, stinking dragons
That I could hardly repulse;
I experienced much pain and death at their hands.
They all roar and attack me,
They pursue me and rise up against me,
…[34]

In addition to the hymns cited above, there are other examples that express the infinite pains which the imprisoned souls or light elements suffer in flesh bodies. See, for instance, the following:

Who has transformed you into so many different forms? And who has cast you into male and female bodies, putting you to shame?

Oh god of Light, dear soul! Who took away the Light from your eyes?

… And then you did writhe in pain;

And you are afflicted ever anew, and you yourself are not aware of it.

Oh god of Light, dear soul!

…

And who led you from your wonderful divine land into banishment, and who fettered you?

And who jailed you in this dark prison, this incarceration, this place with no refuge, which constituted this body of flesh?

---

[32] *Yakshas* is a Sanskrit word used frequently in Buddhist sutras, which means demon in most cases.
[33] *Peris* is a Parthian or Middle-Persian word meaning she-devil or witch.
[34] About the Parthian text and German translation of this hymn see F.C. Andreas and A. Henning, *Mittel-iranische Manichaica aus Chinesisch-Turkestan*, III (SPAW, 1934), pp. 874–875. The English translation of it is in Hans-J. Klimkeit, *Gnosis on the Silk Road: Gnostic Texts from Central Asia*, Harper Collins Publishers, New York, 1993, p. 46.

Oh god of Light, dear soul!
Who trapped you in this satanic creation, that oozes sweet poison, and why did he do so?
And who gave you over as a slave to the Devil who nourishes himself in this body in which a great snake (greed) resides?
And who has made you a servant of this dark, shameless, unquenchable, vile fire?
Oh god of Light, dear soul!
Who has sundered you from eternal life?
...[35]

Obviously, it was extremely abhorrent to Manicheans that their souls were imprisoned in flesh bodies; they regarded human bodies as dark prisons filled with poison, greed and evil fire. For this very reason, it was not impossible that they took the initiative in separating the soul from the flesh body, in other words, ending another person's life. In this sense, there is little difference between *liberating souls* and *killing persons*.

Some Manichean writings actually contain ideas of encouraging the soul to detach itself from the body. In other words, they encourage death in the general sense. This idea even evolves into a strong appeal, as expressed in the following hymn:

Come, oh spirit! Fear no more!
Death has fallen, and sickness has fled away.
The time of troubled days has ended,
Its terror has departed amid clouds of fire.
Come, spirit, step forth!
Let there be no desire for the house of affliction,
Which is mere destruction and the anguish of death,
Truly you were cast out of your native abode.
And all the pangs you have suffered in Hell at the outset
You have undergone for the sake of this joy.
Come yet nearer, in gladness, without regret;

---

[35] For the original text, see the Sogdian fragments M131, M395 and T II D138. The Sogdian text and its German translation are in W.B. Henning, *Ein manichäiches Bet und Berichtbuch*, pp. 44–45, in *W.B. Henning Selected Papers*, I, Leiden, 1977. For the English translation of it, see also Hans-J. Klimkeit, *Gnosis on the Silk Road: Gnostic Texts from Central Asia*, Harper Collins Publishers, New York, 1993, pp. 149–150.

Lie not content in the dwelling of death.
Turn not back, nor regard the ugly forms of the bodies,
Which lie there in wretchedness, they and their followers.
See, they return to earth with every rebirth,
Through every agony and every choking prison.
See, they are reborn among all kinds of creatures,
And their voice is heard in burning sighs.
Come yet nearer, and do not dote on this worldly beauty
That perishes in all its variety.
It falls and melts as snow in the sunshine,
For no fair form survives.
It withers and fades as a dying flower,
Whose grace is destroyed, and it wilts in the sun.
Yet come, you spirit, and be not fond
Of the passing of the hours or the fleeting days.
Turn not back to every outward show.
Sensual desire is death, and leads to destruction.
Hence, spirit, come! ...
I shall lead you to the heights, to your native abode.
I shall show you your home,
The hope you have yearned for ...
Remember, oh spirit! Look on this anguish
That you have born through the fury of all your enemies.
Behold the world and the prison of creation;
For all desires will be destroyed quickly.
Terror, fire, and destruction
Will overcome all those who dwell therein.
...[36]

Quite obviously, on the one hand, the secular world and all its creatures are depicted as terrible and abominable. On the other hand, the souls are urged to detach from the bodies, and return to their native land, the Paradise of Light; the souls are warned also not to come back into flesh bodies again. Being influenced by such an idea, ordinary followers of the

---

[36] This quotation is a part of the long hymn cycle *Angad Rōšnān*, which is probably composed in the middle of the third century A.D., and by Mani's disciple Mār Ammō. See Hans-J. Klimkeit, *Gnosis on the Silk Road: Gnostic Texts from Central Asia*, Harper Collins Publishers, New York, 1993, pp. 114–115.

religion would inevitably have the impression that "life is troublesome and death is fortuitous." This could naturally give rise to a belief that "killing someone means helping him be free from suffering."

In addition to the reasons shown above, the fundamental doctrines of Manicheism probably also afforded a theoretical basis for the belief in redemptive killing because of the insistence on the idea that eternal fighting exists between the principle of Light (goodness) and the principle of Darkness (evil), and this purely ideological "eliminating of devils" might transform into the real killing of persons.

Some descriptions of the creation myth of Manicheism are given in *The Fragmentary Manichean Treatise* 摩尼教殘經, which discusses many aspects of the fighting between the principles of Light and Darkness. For instance, Living Spirit 淨風 incarcerates five kinds of devils with thirteen kinds of Pure Light Bodies. The Demon also imprisons five Light Elements in the flesh bodies with thirteen kinds of dark powers. The Greed Demon plants five kinds of poisonous and dead trees to confuse the Light Natures. The Light Messenger jails the venomous snakes and evil beasts, and cuts down poisonous trees with his intelligent axe.[37]

Moreover, *The Second Section of the Manichean Hymns* 下部讚 records how all male and female devils are derived from flesh bodies. The souls imprisoned in them suffer greatly, and are eager to be rescued from this poisonous sea of fire. All stupid carnal bodies are sons in the deep pits. These devilish natures damage the pure souls constantly, just like fierce beasts and venomous snakes. The real judges and divine gods can conquer all the dark devils and destroy all the devilish teachings.[38]

---

[37] Cf. the original texts in Chinese: "其彼淨風, 取五類魔, 於十三種光明淨體, 囚禁束縛, 不令自在。魔見是已, 起貪毒心, 以五明性, 禁於肉身, 為小世界, 亦以十三無明暗力, 囚固束縛, 不令自在。" "貪魔以此五毒死樹, 栽於五種破壞地中, 每令惑亂光明本性, 抽彼客性, 變成毒果。" "若有明使, 出興於世。… 禁眾毒蛇及諸惡獸, 不令自在; 復賚智斧, 斬伐毒樹, 除去株杌, 並餘穢草。" lines 28–30, 34–36, 52–55, see Rui Chuanming 芮傳明, *Monijiaodunhuangtulufanwenshu yisheyuyanjiu* 摩尼教敦煌吐魯番文書譯釋與研究, pp. 6–7.

[38] Cf. the original texts in Chinese: "一切魔男及魔女, 皆從肉身生緣現。又是三界五趣門, 復是十方諸魔口。… 聽我如斯若痛言, 引我離斯毒火海。" "無知肉身諸眷屬, 並是幽邃坑中子。內外堙塞諸魔性, 常時害我清淨體。一切惡獸無能比, 一切毒蛇何能類。" "真斷事者神聖者, 遊諸世間最自在, 能降黑暗諸魔類, 能滅一切諸魔法。" verses 23, 29, 49–50, 187, see *ibid.*, pp. 69–71, 81.

Now, we have to admit that although the Manicheans formulated the commandment forbidding killing, basic Manichean doctrines imply a hatred of life, and even a quest for death. Apparently, once these ideas were slightly misunderstood or distorted, the belief in redemptive killing was apt to form. A short analysis of this follows.

4. A Brief Conclusion

In conclusion I would like to provide a summary of a number of points:

First, it must be understood that the reasons for forbidding killing in Buddhism are greatly different from those in Manicheism. The Buddhists pity all living beings of the world, so they prohibit killing; in other words, their forbidding of killing is motivated by compassion. On the contrary, the Manicheans prohibit killing only in order to avoid injuring the so-called light elements or souls imprisoned in animals or plants; what they care about is only the imaginary light elements or souls; whether or not the real creatures or plants are hurt is not within their consideration.

Since the most fundamental and important mission of Manicheism is "liberating light elements/souls from living beings", anything can be done so long as it is thought to be beneficial to achieve this aim. According to this logic, it does not seem illogical to kill a person in order to help his "soul" or "light element" to free itself from the "evil flesh body". In any case, we might draw an inference that the belief in redemptive killing held by Faqing 法慶 of the Northern Wei Dynasty probably derived from Manichean doctrines rather than Buddhist teachings.

Second, the religious ideas of Manicheism are virtually hostile to all creatures of the secular world. For instance, the scripture titled *Doubt-dispelling Explanation,* which is cited in the foregoing text, says that according to Mani's ideas, since the creator and maintainer of all material beings that have bodily form is the Dark Demon, it is not proper for humans to give birth and arrange for posterity. He who does so is actually a co-worker of the Dark Demon; a person forces the light elements back into the prison of flesh bodies through maintaining mankind and cattle. For the same reason, even cultivating plants and grain is considered a sin. This opinion is expressed distinctly in a large number of Manichean works; the souls or light elements always lament their suffering within flesh bodies.

For this reason, St. Augustine leveled the following accusations against Manichean teachings: "Fearing lest a member of your God should be bound in flesh, you do not give bread to the hungry. From fear of a fancied homicide you commit a real one. So when you come across a hungry man, who may die if you do not give him food, you are certain to be reckoned a murderer, either by the Law of God if you don't give, or by the Law of Mani if you do!"

Indeed, these words of Augustine are somewhat inaccurate and extreme, because the Manicheans also gave alms to the poor, but bread, fruits and water were given exclusively to their high-grade monks, the so-called Elects. Many scholars have long been aware of the peculiarity of this Manichean concept. Discussing the difference between Christian and Manichean ethics, F. C. Burkitt, for example, said the following: "it can be expressed in a single sentence: Christianity is concerned with persons, Manicheism with things. Christian sympathy goes out to men and women, who are even in a fallen state regarded as in the image of God and for whom Christ has died, and this sympathy has been in modern times, by a natural transition, extended to other animals. The sympathy of the Manicheans was directed not towards men, but towards the Light imprisoned in men. Men were, to some extent, and at second hand, in the image of God, but they were only a sort of pirated copy, made by the evil, dark Archons to imitate the messenger of the Light who had appeared to them."[39]

This conclusion of "valuing the material and disregarding the human" is inferred from Manichean ideas and concepts, which is helpful for us to speculate that the belief in redemptive killing of the ancient Vegetarians was probably formed by blending in cultural elements of Manicheism.

Third, Manichaeism always regards the secular world as an evil place, and insists that the flesh bodies are jails imprisoning light elements. Thus, it emphasizes particularly the pains of human life. In fact, this saying is in accord with the real situation of the lower classes, so it is easy for the masses to accept Manichean teachings. Owing to their inferior educational level, these people are apt to misinterpret Manichean doctrines, and hence not impossible for them to form certain faiths like the belief in redemptive killing.

Finally, what must be emphasized is that though there is much evidence to support the speculation that the belief in redemptive killing is influenced by Manichean teachings, it does not mean this belief

---

[39] The quotations from St. Augustine are also included in F. C. Burkitt, *The Religion of the Manichees*, Cambridge University Press, 1925, pp. 59–60.

inherited Manichean doctrines. Perhaps this belief is simply the result of a misunderstanding or misinterpretation of Manichean teachings, for in terms of form, the Manicheans after all asserted the forbidding of killing. Of course, even if we understand this subject in such a way, it cannot be denied that Manicheism exerted great influence on Chinese religious beliefs and social life. It is an issue deserving of more attention among modern scholars.

To be sure, the adherents of certain religious sects are ruthless and inhuman when they kill persons for the purpose of saving them. However, there is still an obvious distinction between them and autocratic tyrants, because the former kill others out of a belief in redemption, while the latter slaughter people to benefit themselves.

Chapter 16

A Speculation on the Possible Manichean Influence on Wuzetian and Baijuyi

Manicheism was founded in West Asia in the 3rd century AD and spread immediately toward the east and west. It spread eastward to Central Asia and even China roughly along the so-called Silk Road, and thus the oriental Manicheism was named the "Religion of Silk Road" by modern scholars. This phenomenon shows that the ancient Silk Road has played an important role in the communications of religious thoughts.

Formally, the Chinese ruling class disliked this religion and did not actively support it. So, the flourishing period of Manicheism in mainland China only lasted several decades. However, some concepts and ideas of Manicheism influenced various classes of Chinese society more or less, which included intellectual elites and even the monarch. Here, I will instance two distinguished characters of the Tang Dynasty, and inquire into the possibility of Manicheism exerting influence on them.

1. About the Religious Ideas of Wuzetian 武則天

Wuzetian was the only female monarch of Chinese authoritarian regimes in thousands of years. Generally, her religious belief is regarded as Buddhism. For example, "The Queen Wuzetian has the closest relationship with Buddhism. In the second year of the reign Tianshou 天授, she promulgates *Great Cloud Sutra* 大雲經. Using the cover of Buddhist legends, she covertly promotes the preaching of her revolutionary ideas.

Furthermore, she stipulates that the status of Buddhism is above that of Taoism."[1]

Besides, "Meanwhile, the patronage of Buddhism passed into the hands of the empress. She came from a very pious Buddhist family, and was clearly seen as patron and protector by the Buddhists wishing to approach the emperor. She was also a major patron of religious building, and responsible for great numbers of images carved at the great cave temples of Lung-men during her period as empress." "It is only recently that historical scholarship has come to realize how deeply the beliefs and practices of Manāyāna Buddhism permeated the lives of the ordinary people of the T'ang. Conveniently, there existed at that time two translations of a minor sutra called Mahāmegha, or *Great Cloud* 大雲. This sutra contained a prophecy of the imminent incarnation of Maitreya as a female deity, monarch of all the world."

"The empress professed surprise, but was naturally gratified, and immediately took steps to promulgate the teaching. In a staggering act of patronage to the Buddhist clergy, she founded state-maintained Great Cloud Temples 大雲寺 in every prefecture of the empire, some of them new foundations, others existing temples which were brought under imperial patronage." "At court, though, the empress showed little awareness of serious administrative problems, and busied herself with literary compilation, the creation of new posts to fill and overfill, and her Buddhism. To her title, she added 'Maitreya the Peerless, Golden Wheel'; she reversed the T'ang precedence of Taoism over Buddhism, and even forbade the butchering of animals."[2]

In addition to such general descriptions instanced above, there were also dissertations inquiring into the Buddhist belief of Wuzetian; a famous paper among them was *Wuzhao and the Buddhism* 武曌與佛教 written by Chenyinke 陳寅恪. That thesis discussed in detail the background of the pious Buddhist belief of the Sui royal family, and thought that Wuzetian was deeply influenced by her mother, a royal family member of the Sui. Thus, Wuzetian had been a Buddhist nun since her childhood, "She has a long relationship with Buddhism", concluded Chenyinke. Furthermore,

---

[1] Cf. Cenzhongmian 岑仲勉, *History of the Sui and Tang Dynasties* 隋唐史, Znonghua Book Company 中華書局, 1982, p. 167.
[2] Cf. Denis Twichett & John K. Fairbank (Gen. ed.), *The Cambridge History of China*, Vol. 3, *Sui and T'ang China*, Cambridge University Press, 2008, pp. 265, 305, 311.

because the Buddhist teachings and its prophecies were propitious to Wuzetian's political revolution, she was zealous in preaching Buddhism.[3]

Formally, many teachings, ideas and measures adopted by Wuzetian were much like that of Buddhism, but they were not actually the *pure* or *orthodox* Buddhist ones. On the contrary, Wuzetian appeared to have pursued a new religion, for the sake of benefiting her political revolution. This new belief combined the factors of both Buddhism and Manicheism intentionally or accidentally, while the latter is also an important aspect. A corresponding detailed discussion is given as follows.

(1) About the *Great Cloud Sutra*

It is said that the *Great Cloud Sutra* 大雲經 is a pseudograph made up at Wuzetian's command, being used as the theory foundation for her empress throne.[4] *Jiutangshu* 舊唐書 says, "Xuehuaiyi 薛懷義, Faming 法明 and others compose *Great Cloud Sutra*, offer the heavenly commission, claim that Wuzetian is the reincarnation of Maitreya. She will rule Jambu-dvipa (the existing world); while the Tang Dynasty is declining. Later, Wuzetian leads a revolution, sets up the Zhou 周 regime. ... The fabricated *Great Cloud Sutra* is issued over the country. Every temple must collect at least one book, and preach this sutra frequently."[5] Obviously, according to this *Sutra*, Wuzetian was regarded as the incarnation of Maitreya Buddha, and was appointed by the supreme god as the monarch of this world, to replace the emperors of the Tang. Thus, *Great Cloud Sutra* became the main evidence to prove Wuzetian possessed the "divine right of kings", and also an important document of Wuzetian's revolution. Now let us analyze the content of *Great Cloud Sutra* as follows.

If Wuzetian's *Great Cloud Sutra* was a revision of the earlier edition, the *Mahāmegha-sūtra* 大方等無想經/大方等大雲經, which was translated by Dharma-rakṣa 曇無讖 of the Northern Liang Dynasty (397–439),

---

[3] Cf. Chenyinke 陳寅恪, "Wuzhao and Buddhism" 武曌與佛教, in *Jinmingguan Symposium, Part II* 金明舘叢稿二編, Shanghai Classics Publishing House, 1980, pp. 137–155.

[4] Whether *Great Cloud Sutra* is a complete pseudograph or is merely a doctored writing? This problem has arisen since the Song Dynasty, and there are still different opinions in modern ages. Because it is not relevant to this topic, I am not going to talk about it in detail here.

[5] Cf. *Jiutangshu* 舊唐書, fasc. 183, Zhonghua Book Company 中華書局, 1975, p. 4742.

it can possibly provide significant enlightenment. It depicts a devakanyā (goddess) in detail and states the following:

At that time, a goddess Pure-Light 淨光 respectfully offers flowers, streamers and music to the Buddha, and asks the Buddha to talk about the achievements of some outstanding Buddhist practitioners. Then the Buddha interprets the *Great Cloud Sutra*. He says, once upon a time, the king, queen and his prime minister were all piously devoted to Buddhism. The queen once prayed: "When the Sakya Tathāgata appears, I could eliminate all error ideas." Both in the present and the future, these persons insist on Buddhist teachings, and protect them. When the goddess wants to know more about these pious Buddhists, Buddha will tell her first the story of herself.

The Buddha goes on with his speech: That queen was actually the present Pure-Light. At that time, she listened to the Buddha's preaching on *Mahā-parinirvāna-sūtra* 大涅槃經, so becoming the goddess after her rebirth. "Now, when I appear on this world, you listen to my preach once again. Therefore, you will be an empress instead of goddess, ruling over a quarter of the territory dominated by Cakra-varti-rājan 轉輪王; and as an upāsikā 優婆夷 (female devotee), you will civilize all the people living in your country, including those of male, female, old and young. You must defend our righteous doctrine, destroy all heretical beliefs. You are in fact a Boddhisattva, and for the sake of saving all creatures, you will reincarnate into a female."[6]

In another passage, the Buddha predicts the future about this goddess: Seven hundred years after nirvana of the Buddha, there is a small kingdom called Avidyā 無明 (unwise/ignorant). There is a river in this country, named Darkness 黑暗. The king and queen have a daughter, who is named Increase 增長, and is an elegant and cultivated girl, so is loved by everyone. She deeply believes in Buddhism, and practices it hard. Since she was born, this country has had always good harvests; the population increases constantly; people enjoy their happy life, without poverty, sickness, disaster and any other sufferings. Hence, many neighboring kingdoms are willing to be subordinated to this regime. Later, after the king died, the daughter succeeds on the throne, and rules over the world.

This empress actively promulgates Buddhism and severely criticizes heretical ideas. She sets up a lot of Buddhist stūpas all over the world;

---

[6] Cf. Dharma-rakṣa 昙無讖, *Mahāmegha-sūtra* 大方等無想經, fasc. 4, in *Tripitaka Edited in Taisho Era*, Book 12, No. 387, pp. 1097–1098.

provides for every pious adherent, and punishes anyone who hurts Buddhism. She preaches *Great Cloud Sutra*, to teach all creatures. Finally, the Buddha asserts, "In the future, after countless millennia, this empress will become Buddha."[7]

The *Great Cloud Sutra* describes Buddha's interpretations on various questions inquired about by the conventioneers; apparently, the description about the devakanyā 天女 (goddess) Pure-Light is a significative part of it, indicating that this female being is an important role. Therefore, also being a female, Wuzetian taking *Great Cloud Sutra* as the theoretical grounds of her sovereignty was quite reasonable. However, it does not mean that these ideas all derive from Buddhist teachings; interestingly, there seems to be palpable Manichean factors in the description about goddess Pure-Light.

First, "Light" is the most important element of Manichean teachings, while the name of the goddess is exactly Pure-Light. Besides, this *Sutra* mentions that one of the conventioneers coming to listen to Buddha's preach was a Bodhisattva, whose name was Boundless-Light 無邊光. To welcome this Bodhisattva, Buddha "emits infinite light from his face. The colorful light illuminates over the boundless world, up to the Brahmalōka (Heavens of Brahma), after winding around his body for three times, entering into his mouth." At the same time as Buddha's speech about goddess Pure-Light, another bright light also appears; this phenomenon shows that this future empress or female Bodhisattva has a close relationship with *Light*.

Second, some place names are also noteworthy. For example, the queen's country was called Avidyā 無明, literally "without light" and meaning unwise, ignorant and lack of intelligence. In addition, the river of their kingdom was named Darkness 黑暗; the homeland of the Bodhisattva Boundless-Light was called 安樂 (peace and happiness).

The core doctrine of Manicheism is "Two Principles" and "Three Times". The former refers to the two elements of Light and Darkness, which fight against each other forever. The latter refers to three eras of the past, the present and the future. That is to say, the Manicheans regard the Light and Darkness as two principles of the cosmos, and the two principles are embodied in two adjoining kingdoms: Light country located in the North, East and West, while the Darkness occupying the South.

---

[7] Cf. *ibid.*, pp. 1106–1107.

Admittedly, the so-called "Southern India", "Without-Light Kingdom" and "Darkness River" mentioned in *Great Cloud Sutra* are very similar to the terms frequently used in Manichean myths. Especially in Chinese literatures of Manicheism, some terms are exactly the same as that in *Great Cloud Sutra*. For instance, "enter into the dark pit, the world without light"; "such terrible dark night that without light"; "transform into devils from the lightless mind"; "the lightless and dark power falls into the hell"; and "expel the lightless dark mind".

Another term often used in both *Great Cloud Sutra* and Chinese Manichean literatures is Anleguo 安樂國 (Peace and Happiness Country). The Buddha says in fascicle 6 of *Great Cloud Sutra*, "There is a world in the West. Its name is Anle 安樂 (Peace and Happiness). The Buddha who resides there is called Amitāyus/Amitābha (Boundless Age or Boundless Light)." On the contrary, the Bodhisattva Boundless-Light is sent by the Amitābha Buddha of the Peace and Happiness Country to attend the preaching of Tathāgata. Obviously, the Anleguo 安樂國, i.e., the Western Pure Land, also has a close relationship with the *Light*.

According to Manichean teachings, when someone dies, the destiny of his soul might be in three forms: *Living Soul* comes to the New Paradise; the Mixed soul has to return to the earthly world; and the Dead one falls into the hell. All the righteous souls go to the New Paradise; led by the angels, they ascend through Light Column, Moon and Sun successively, finally reaching the New Paradise.[8] This "New Paradise" is the Anleguo 安樂國 in Chinese Manichean literatures, and is also the same term in the Chinese version of *Great Cloud Sutra* 大雲經.

It is rather puzzling that the goddess Pure-Light, a righteous and kind sacred being, lives in a country named *Lightless*; furthermore, there is a river named *Darkness* in her homeland. These ideas are very different from the general Manichean concepts. Besides, even if the same terms, such as lightless 無明, darkness 黑暗 and Anleguo 安樂國, are used in both *Great Cloud Sutra* and Chinese Manichean literatures, it is not necessary that there has been cultural communication between the two kinds of writings. Indeed, we cannot deny these reasons. However, Wuzetian and especially her monks took the *Great Cloud Sutra* as a "theoretical weapon", possibly not only because they were interested in its story of goddess Pure-Light but also because some of its teachings were similar to

---

[8] Cf. Mary Boyce, *A Reader in Manichaean Middle Persian and Parthian*, Leiden, 1975, pp. 7–8.

that of Manicheism. Perhaps, the *Great Cloud Sutra* is more revolutionary than orthodox Buddhist sutras, hence was more suitable for Wuzetian's political needs.

(2) Worship of the Sun and Moon
The core of Manichean doctrine is light, and the sun and moon are the most typical symbols of the light. According to the Manichean myths, after the creation of heavens and earths, Living Spirit, one of the major deities, divides the light elements, which have been swallowed by the dark devils, into three categories: the unpolluted light-elements are used to make the sun and moon; the slightly polluted ones are used to make stars; and the severely polluted light-elements, namely, the souls of mankind, are liberated and purified through three wheels operated by The Third Ambassador, then ascend along the Light Column, pass the moon, to the sun, and reach the New Paradise finally. Evidently, during the course of the light-elements journey returning to their homeland, the sun and moon play a very important role; this process is the most significant mission and ultimate aim of Manicheism.

For this reason, the words to praise the sun and moon are frequently seen in Manichean literatures, such as the following: "With you lives the Mother of the Righteous; near you is also the Living Spirit; near you are the mighty Fathers who gather pearls, the light leaders of the two great Lamps. There is a spring of peace where the gods dwell. They move the world and shine out splendor. Entirely full of joy are the divine dwelling places, the noble ships, the spiritual vessels."[9]

Here, the "two great lamps", "noble ships" and "spiritual vessels" all refer to the sun and moon, so the lofty status of the sun and moon is distinctly shown. Correspondingly, any disrespect to the sun and moon is a sin, such as described in *Xuāstvānīft*:

> Secondly, also the sins against the God of the Sun and Moon, against the gods sitting in the two palaces of light. If one goes to the land of gods, the origin, root, and rallying-ground of all prophets, the pure doctrine, the souls provided with good action and the light belonging to the earth, the God of the Sun and Moon is its front door. In order to free the

---

[9] Cf. Jes. P. Asmussen, *Manichaean Literature: Representative Texts Chiefly from Middle Persians and Parthian Writings*, New York, 1975, p. 140.

Fivefold God and separate Light and Darkness, they revolve in a circle and irradiate the four quarters of the heavens.

My God, if we ever, unwittingly, should somehow have sinned against the God of the Sun and Moon, the gods who sit in the two palaces of light, and if we should not have believed: "True, mighty, and powerful is the God of the Sun and Moon," if we should have somehow have used much evil blasphemous speech, if we should have said: "The Sun and the Moon will die," if we should have said: "Without their own power they rise and set. If their own absolute power is present, then make them stop rising!" and if we should have said: "Our self is different from the Sun and the Moon," then we pray, when as we unwittingly have committed this other sin, to be forgiven. Forgive my sin![10]

It is exactly because of such importance and lofty status of the sun and the moon that a misunderstanding was caused later among the Chinese that the Manicheans specifically worshiped the sun and moon. For instance, a writing of the Song Dynasty says that, at that time, there were a lot of believers of "Vegetarianism and Devil Cult" 吃菜事魔 in Fujian 福建 and Zhejiang 浙江 Provinces. Although they also recited *Vajrachedikā-prajñāpāramitā-sūtra*, they worshiped only the sun and moon instead of the Buddha and Bodhisattvas.[11] Generally speaking, the so-called "Vegetarianism and Devil Cult" in ancient times, especially in the Song Dynasty, was regarded as an eastern branch of Manicheism, or "Sinicized Manicheism", at least a belief which merged many Manichean factors. Therefore, "Worship of the Sun and Moon" could be thought to be a belief deriving from Manicheism.

Apparently, Wuzetian also adored the sun and moon. A typical instance was that she created a new word for her name. In 689, she designed twelve Chinese characters, among them 曌 zhao was taken as her name.[12] Interestingly, this pictograph 曌 consists of three Chinese characters: 日 (sun), 月 (moon) and 空 (sky). Thus, in terms of the shape of 曌, it can be understood as the meaning of "the sun and moon in the

---

[10] Cf. Jes. P. Asmussen, *Xᵘāstvānīft: Studies in Manichaeism*, Copenhagen: Prostant Apud Munksgarrd, 1965, p. 194.
[11] Cf. Fangsha 方勺, *Rongzhaiyishi* 容齋逸史 (*The Lost Histories Recorded in Rongzhai*), in Taozongyi 陶宗儀, etc. ed., *Suofusanzhong* 說郛三種 (*Three Versions of Shufu*), Shanghai Classics Publishing House 上海古籍出版社, 1988, pp. 1807–1808,
[12] Cf. *Xintangshu* 新唐書, fasc. 76, Zhonghua Book Company 中華書局, 1975, p. 3481.

sky", and actually, its meaning is precisely "shine" or "the sun and moon shine on the sky". The pronunciation of 瞾 is also the same as that of the common word 照, the latter meaning "shine". In addition, 日 (sun) and 月 (moon) are two components of 瞾, and they can combine into a new character, namely 明, meaning "light". So, the new name 瞾 seems to indicate Wuzetian's adoration of the sun, moon and light, the major features of Manicheism.

Another example is seen in *Ratnamēgha Sūtra* 寶雨經. Dharmarutchi 達摩流支 retranslated the former version of *Ratnamēgha Sūtra*, and dedicated it to Wuzetian four years after *Great Cloud Sutra* was respectfully presented. Significantly, a story about an empress ruling Mahācīna (Great China) of the East is added into the new version of *Ratnamēgha Sūtra*.

It says that there is a god in the East, named Light of Sun and Moon 日月光. He takes colorful clouds as the vehicle, comes to listen Buddha's sermon. The Buddha says to this god: "Your light is very rare. Because you once had respectably provided for Amitābha with various flowers, jewels, decorations, dresses, beds, foods and medicines, thereby laid the foundation for good. Therefore, thousand years after my Nirvana, as a female Bodhisattva, you will be the monarch of kingdom Mahācīna northeast of this country. In numerous years you will promote Buddhist teachings and civilize the people. … The Mahācīna (Great China) is very peaceful and wealthy, its populace is flourishing and happy." Then, the god Moon Light gives thanks for Buddha's prediction, and salutes him respectably.[13]

It should be emphasized that this passage is not seen in the old version of *Ratnamēgha Sūtra* 寶雨經, which was translated in the Liang Dynasty (502–557), thus is possibly a fabrication of the translator in the Tang Dynasty. Even if the resemblance of "Pure-Light Goddess" and "Empress" in *Great Cloud Sutra* to Manichean factors is purely a coincidence, it is unreasonable to regard "light of Sun and moon", "pure light of moon" and "moonlight" in *Ratnamēgha Sūtra* as also a coincidence. More possibly, the translator intentionally borrowed the Manichean cultural factors, such as the sun, moon and light, to meet the needs of politics.

Both *Great Cloud Sutra* and *Ratnamēgha Sūtra* involve a goddess or empress, who has a close relationship with the sun, moon and light, and happens to be the ruler of China. Wuzetian actually took the two sutras as

---

[13] Cf. Dharmarutchi 達摩流支 (tr.), *Ratnamēgha Sūtra* 寶雨經, fasc. 1, in *Tripitaka Edited in Taisho Era*, Book 16, No. 660, p. 284.

the proof that the Gods chose her to be the sovereign of China. For example, she claims in the preface of the translation of *Buddhāvataṃsakamahāvaipulya sutra* that because she does good and accumulates virtue in her previous incarnations, Buddhas commission her as the ruler of China, and predict it in both *Great Cloud Sutra* and *Ratnamēgha Sūtra*.[14] So, the sun, moon and light seem to be a considerably important role in Wuzetian's religious ideas, and they were also the major features of Manichean teachings.

(3) About the Light Hall
The construction of the Light Hall 明堂 has a long history. It is said that since the era of the Yellow Emperor 黄帝, the Light Hall had been set up, though there were various designations and structures for it.[15] The Light Hall is also the so-called "the Hall of Monarch"; it was usually a building where the state grand ceremonies were held, such as official assembly, state sacrifice, medal presentation, and choice of elites and education. That is to say, it was roughly a place for the monarchs to moralize and civilize the people.

According to the explanations of the ancients, the structure of the Light Hall imitated the celestial bodies and natural phenomena, hence it was usually the pattern of "round above and square below". In addition, holding z ceremony in Light Hall had a certain meaning of "communicating with the deities and ghosts". Since there was a close relationship between the Light Hall and the heavens or celestial bodies, the factors of sun, moon and light certainly were clearly reflected in Light Hall. The fact that it was called the Sun House 陽舘 during the Shang Dynasty and the Light Hall 明堂 during the Zhou Dynasty proves it evidently.

Wuzetian paid special attention to the Light Hall. She did not completely follow the ancient ways to build the Light Hall; she seemed to merge some other beliefs into the Confucian thought and etiquette.

Precisely prior to formally ascending the throne, Wuzetian finished the building of the Light Hall. It was square, 294 feet tall, 300 feet long on each side, and had three floors. She made a number of changes to its

---

[14] Cf. "Preface for New Translation of Buddhāvataṃsakamahāvaipulya sutra in Great Zhou 大周新譯大方廣佛華嚴經序, in *Complete Prose Literature of the Tang* 全唐文, fasc. 97, Zhonghua Book Company 中華書局, 1983, p. 1002.

[15] Cf. *Jiutangshu* 舊唐書, fasc. 22, Zhonghua Book Company 中華書局, 1975, p. 851. The Chinese text is as follows: "始之黃帝,降及有虞,彌歷夏殷,迄于周代,各立名號,別創規模。"

structure and pattern, even doing some innovations. These anti-traditional designs caused much criticism. The distinctiveness of this Light Hall was roughly as follows.

First, after demolishing the Qianyuan Palace 乾元殿, Wuzetian built the new Light Hall, while this palace was the place where the former emperors disposed political affairs. This practice provoked resentment among the officials, and it was regarded as a great disrespect for the previous emperors. Even so, Wuzetian still stuck to her own plan, and constructed the Light Hall on the original site of the Qianyuan Palace. One of the main reasons for this practice was probably that she believed the Light Hall must be built on "the place with straight sunlight", while the Qianyuan Palace was located exactly on that land parcel. Wuzetian attached much importance to sunlight; it seems to hint at her Manichean ideas.

Second, a giant pearl was set on the top of the Light Hall. According to the historical records, this giant pearl was made of copper and decorated with gold. It seemed to irradiate during both the day and night. Cuishu 崔曙 of the Tang Dynasty had a poem titled *Pearl of the Light Hall*, vividly depicting this giant pearl. It said that this giant pearl stands high in the air. In the night, there seem to be two full moons; after dawn, only a single star left. If it is sunny, the pearl gives off a faint light; if the cloud covers, it almost disappears.[16]

Here, this giant pearl is likened to the bright moon, star, and is compared to the sun; it appears that there is little difference between the pearl and other celestial bodies. The fact that the pearl is so prominent reminds us to pay attention once again to the significance of maṇi/pearl in Manicheism. In other words, the giant and prominent pearl of the Light Hall seems to indicate some Manichean ideas of Wuzetian.

Third, Wuzetian violated the traditional principle of "painting on the wall and sculpturing the beam" fir the Light Hall. Wangqiuli 王求禮 presented an expostulation to Wuzetian, criticizing the Light Hall, saying that it has "weird sculptures and decorations, and is much luxurious and

---

[16] Cf. Cuishu 崔曙, "Pearl of the Light Hall", in *Quantangshi* 全唐詩 (*The General Anthology of Tang Poetry*), fasc. 155, Zhonghua Book Company 中華書局, 1960, p. 1600. The Chinese text is as follows: "正位開重屋, 凌空出火珠。夜來雙月滿, 曙後一星孤。天淨光難 (微) 滅, 雲 (煙) 生望卻 (若) 無。遙知太平代, 國寶在名都。"

lack of simplicity."¹⁷ So, he suggested that the empress correct these shortcomings.

Naturally, Wuzetian did not accept his suggestion, as she was obviously very fond of these innovative designs. Among them, some religious factors were merged except for that of Buddhism. A number of points of evidence indicate that what Wuzetian believed in was not pure Buddhism, rather a belief merging some factors of other religions, especially that of Manicheism.

(4) The Possibility that Wuzetian was Influenced by Manicheism

In addition to the points mentioned above, there are also some other clues to prove that some Manichean ideas were probably adopted by Wuzetian. For instance, the *Great Cloud Sutra* 大雲經 claims that Wuzetian was the reincarnation of Maitreya; it shows that she embraced the Maitreyan belief. On the contrary, in the Manichean documents in Central Asia, some designations and titles appear, such as "Master Maitreya", "Lord Maitreya", "Maitreya Buddha" and "Maitreya". Although the origin of the Maitreyan faith of Central Asia and China differs from each other[18], there is still a possibility of indirect or partial communications between the two faiths. That is to say, it is not absolutely impossible that Wuzetian once had been exposed to Manichean culture and borrowed some of its ideas.

Another piece of evidence is that Manicheism was introduced into China in the reign of Wuzetian (694). Furthermore, about twenty years prior to this year, Manicheism was already popular in inland Chinese in fact.[19] Therefore, Wuzetian could obviously have learnt much about Manicheism. In order to conveniently spread their religion, the Chinese Manicheans usually pretended to be Buddhists. Thus, it was natural that Wuzetian possibly wittingly or unwittingly borrowed some so-called "Buddhist factors", merging them into her innovative religion.

Many materials show that what Wuzetian believed in was not the real or orthodox Buddhism. For instance, after the Light Hall was built, Wuzetian often summoned a number of learned men to preach, give

---

[17] Cf. *Xintangshu* 新唐書, fasc. 112, p. 4172.

[18] About this opinion, cf. my paper "A Study on the Relations between Maitreyan Faith and Manicheism" 彌勒信仰与摩尼教關係考辨考辨, in *Journal of Historical China Studies* 傳統中國研究集刊, Vol. I, Shanghai People Publishing House 上海人民出版社, 2006.

[19] About the correlative materials, cf. *Minshu* 閩書 (*Book on Fujian*), fasc. 7; and W. Bang & A. von Gabain, *Turfan Texte II*, APAW, 1929, pp. 425–426.

lectures and discussions in Light Hall; the attendees included believers both of Buddhism and Taoism, as well as Confucians and other religious adherents. She seemed to be tolerant of religious beliefs.

On the orders of Wuzetian, the Buddhist monk Xuehuaiyi 薛懷義 built the Merit Hall 功德堂 north of the Light Hall, and it was finished in 695. In appearance, this Merit Hall was used for Buddhist worships, but this *Buddhism* was probably not the orthodox one, just as the following description shows:

> To the north of the Light Hall, monk Xuehuaiyi builds the Merit Hall, one thousand feet high. The giant statue of it is nine hundred feet tall; his nose is like a big ship, can hold dozens of persons sitting together. In the 15th day of lunar January, the Great Quinquennial Assembly (Pañca-vārṣika paricad 無遮大會) is held in Light Hall. A large pit is dug, about fifty feet deep; a palace made of colorful silks is built over it. A giant Vajra statue is put in this pit, and is lifted gradually during the course of ceremony, pretending the deity is ascending from the underground. Furthermore, they paint a large image of deity head of 200 feet tall with the bull's blood, and pretend that the blood comes from Xuehuaiyi's knees. Thus, people rush to watch, and are crowded very much.[20]

The Merit Hall 功德堂 mentioned here was also called Heaven Hall 天堂, seeming to symbolize the Tuṣita Palace, where Maitreya Buddha resides, because Wuzetian was regarded as the reincarnation of Maitreya. However, as mentioned above, the oriental Manicheism was merged also with the Maitreyan faith, so this "Heaven Hall" might also reflect the Manichean factor. As for the Great Quinquennial Assembly, it was undoubtedly the traditional Buddhist assembly, namely, almsgiving assembly which took in anybody regardless of their being rich, poor, noble or humble. But, the rites about the giant Vajra statue and bull's blood were obviously not the real Buddhist ceremony, especially the latter; it is more like the folk witchcraft.

Another case shows more clearly that Wuzetian deeply believed in some pretended "Buddhist faiths": There was an old nun in Henei 河內, residing in Linzhi Temple 麟趾寺. She colluded with Weishifang 韋什方 and others to cheat and mislead the public with magic and sorcery.

---

[20] Cf. Zhangzhuo 張鷟, *Chaoyeqianzai* 朝野僉載, fasc. 5, in *Sikuquanshu* 四庫全書, Taibei: Commercial Press, pp. 1035–269.

She called herself Pure Light Tathāgata 淨光如來, claiming that she could predict the future. Weishifang said that he was born 250 years ago; another foreigner also claimed that he was already 500 years old and that he was acquainted with Xuehuaiyi 薛懷義 200 years ago. Wuzetian trusted him deeply, even endowing him the surname Wu 武; later she promoted him as a high official.[21] Apparently, Wuzetian was very interested in and trusted in these religious believers in pseudo Buddhism.

Three aspects of this passage are worthy of attention. First, the old nun is titled "Pure Light Tathāgata", which is the same as "Goddess Pure Light" in *Great Cloud Sutra* and "Pure Light Moon" in *Ratnamēgha Sūtra*; all of them indicate the significance of light in their religious faiths.

Second, the so-called "old foreigner" is apparently a close friend of Xuehuaiyi, while the latter is trusted much by the empress. Therefore, they possibly impact greatly Wuzetian's faith; that is to say, what Wuzetian believes in perhaps is not real Buddhism.

Third, in the period of the Sui and Tang Dynasties, the so-called Hu 胡 (foreigner) usually referred to the Iranians from Central Asia or West Asia, who were also the major groups involved in the spread of Manicheism in the East. So, it could be inferred that a number of Chinese or foreign "Buddhist" monks and nuns were trusted deeply by Wuzetian, and they might have communicated some Manichean ideas to Wuzetian under the cover of Buddhism.

To sum up, a brief conclusion may be given as follows. In the era of Taizong 太宗 and Gaozong 高宗 of the Tang Dynasty, the cultural exchanges were very frequent and flourished between the East and West. Manicheism, which had established a solid foundation in Central Asia for several centuries, spread further eastward and disseminated gradually into the Chinese populace. When Wuzetian was in politics, she was possibly already influenced by Manichean ideas directly or indirectly. Later, when she was anxious to search theories for her monarchical power, some Manichean factors, such as Light, Sun, Moon and Maitreya, were adopted by her and merged into her religious system. Whether or not it is out of coincidence, the revolutionary thoughts of "reincarnation of Maitreya" and "light defeats darkness" happened to meet her political needs. Thus, she skillfully utilized these Manichean teachings and hid them in the form of Buddhism. Possibly, while Wuzetian took advantage of Manichean ideas, Manicheism also spread secretly by the help of her active promotion.

---

[21] Cf. *Zizhitongjian* 資治通鑑, fasc. 205, Zhonghua Book Company, 1956, pp. 6494–6495.

2. The Poem on Manicheism Said to be Written by Baijuyi 白居易

In his *Fuzutongji* 佛祖統紀, Zhipan 志磐 of the Southern Song Dynasty mentions the heresy "Vegetarianism and Devil Cult 吃菜事魔" being popular at that time. He says the following:

> According to *Yijianzhi* 夷堅志, the faith "Vegetarianism and Devil Cult" is popular in the region of Three Mountains. It is called Light Religion 明教; its leader wears purple hat and loose coat, the women wear black hats and white clothing. The God they worship dresses white, deriving from so-called "White Buddha" in Buddhist sutras. They claim their God is the Fifth Buddha mentioned by *Vajracchdikā- Prajñāpāramitā-Sūtra* 金剛般若波羅蜜經, and is also named Mar Mani 末摩尼. According to *Civilizing the Foreigners Scripture* 化胡經, initially, Mar Mani drives the natural light air, flies to Suristan Kingdom, and is born in the palace, as a son of the king and queen. When the religion is founded, he titles himself Mar Mani. Their Scripture is titled *Two Principles and Three Times*. "Two Principles" means the Light and Darkness; "Three Times" means three ages of the Past, Present and Future.
>
> In the reign of Dazhongxiangfu 大中祥符 (1008–1016), the government attaches great importance to the compilation of *Collected Taoist Scriptures*. A man of wealth Linshichang 林世長 bribes the chief manager to add the *Two Principles and Three Times* into the *Collected Taoist Scriptures*. Furthermore, the adherents write a poem in Baijuyi's name: "As the *Story of Suristan* shows, Manichean doctrine is wonderful. The two principles are always fighting, the Fifth Buddha inherits the light. The sun and moon must be revered, the whole universe is created. As for keeping the fasts, they are similar to that of the Buddhism." This poem is placed at the beginning of the *Scripture*. The followers of this faith take food only at the noon; after death, they are buried nakedly. I once checked the *Changqingji* 長慶集 of Baijuyi, but did not find this poem. In fact, Baijuyi believes in Buddhism, he would not have written such ridiculous poem.[22]

Roughly speaking, the "heresy" mentioned here is Manicheism, or *Sinicized* Manicheism. Apparently, this faith disgusted Zhipan greatly, for

---

[22] Cf. Zhipan 志磐, *Fuzutongji* 佛祖統紀, fasc. 48, in *Tripitaka Edited in Taisho Era* 大正新修大藏經, Book 49, No. 2035, p. 431.

he was a Buddhist disciple, and was unwilling to admit that the respectable poet Baijuyi had once been interested in such a "heretical faith".

Generally, most people thought that Baijuyi was a devotional Buddhist, so the opinion of Zhipan was acceptable. However, after a detailed inquiry, perhaps we could find that Baijuyi really had written a poem to depict the foreign religion Manicheism. The related reasons and grounds are given as follows.

(1) The Multiple Beliefs of Baijuyi

Zhipan asserted that Baijuyi could not write this Manichean poem, because he thought that Baijuyi only believed in Buddhism. If Baijuyi's belief diversity was proved, then he was more likely to have written this poem. Actually, a number of materials showed that Baijuyi was rather tolerant of religious beliefs, and he was interested in both different Buddhist sects and various other so-called heresies.

First, even for Buddhism, Baijuyi was not very attentive and pious. He was regarded as an outstanding adherent of the Dhyana sect, and he had learnt Buddhism from many masters of the Dhyana sect. On the basis of *Eight Key Words* written by Master Ning 凝禪師, he wrote *Eight Gathas*, a famous writing for practicing Dhyana.

Besides, Baijuyi was also famous as a believer of the Pure Land Sect of Buddhism, especially in his later years. For the Chinese Buddhists, the Pure Land Sect could be divided into two branches: one is the Maitreya Faith, another is the Amitābha Faith; the former pursues life in Tuṣita (Joyful Heaven) after death, while the latter pursues life in the Western Paradise. Baijuyi believed in both faiths. In his *A Laud to the Painting of Maitreya's Ascent* 畫彌勒上生幀讚, Baijuyi clearly expressed his Maitreya faith:

> In the summer of the eighth year (834) of Taihe 太和 Era, the grand bhikṣu Daosong 道嵩, Cunyi 存一 and Huigong 惠恭 etc, a total of 60 persons, and upāsaka Shiliang 士良, Weijian 惟儉 etc, a total of 80 persons, assemble in the Changshou Monastery 長壽寺 of the Eastern Capital, they keep vegetarian fast, hold ceremony, donate money and draw a picture to depict the scene that Maitreya's reincarnation in the palace of Tuṣita; the people are crowded, but the atmosphere is solemn. Daosong and others burn incense respectfully, and take the oath that they want to live in Tuṣita, enshrining and worshipping Maitreya forever. As a Maitreyan disciple, I, Bailetian 白樂天 (Baijuyi),

have the same wish, may I serve Maitreya Buddha in the afterlife, with unlimited respect to Your Majesty. Let's recite the hymns together: "140 persons have the same hope, 140 mouths say the same words. Look at Maitreyan appearance, and repeat Maitreyan name. May we reincarnate in Tuṣita in the afterlife."[23]

The same belief is also expressed in *A Note on the Painting of Maitreya's Ascent* 畫彌勒上生幀記, and is even firmer than before:

I am Bailetian 白樂天 (Baijuyi), my hometown is Taiyuan 太原 of the Great Tang Empire in Jambu dvipa 南贍部洲. Now, I am old and fall ill, suffering much. I pray to be delivered from misery and attain happiness together with all creatures of this world. Therefore, I draw this picture of Maitreya according to the depiction in sutras. I am fancying the scene of Palaces in Tuṣita, imagining the appearances of Maitreya and other devas; I respectfully consecrate this picture with incense, flowers and fruits. I hope my courtesy and praise could accumulate enough merits to remove my pains and fulfill my wish.

My wish is as follows: Initially, I converted to Buddhism. For many years, I have kept dietary fast and observed commandments. Everyday I burn incense in front of the Buddha, pray afterlife to be born in Tuṣita, and then descend to the earth with Maitreya. I wish to follow Maitreya forever, exempting from the samsara, reaching the state of nirvana. Now, I am old and ill, I pray and swear once again, never forget the original wish, never give up until reaching the goal. Oh, Maitreya, please hear what I say. Salute again, and write this note. In lunar March of the fifth year (840) of Kaicheng 開成 Era.[24]

Interestingly, in the same month of the year 840, Baijuyi expressed his Amitābha Faith, saying in his *A Note on the Painting of the Western Paradise* 畫西方幀記 that he held the Amitābha Faith. Its brief content is as following:

There is the most joyful world in the distant West, where is called Pure Land, and the Buddha is Amitābha. I, Baijuyi, being old and falling in ill, now spend a lot of money to draw a picture of the Western

---

[23] Cf. *The Corpus of Baijuyi* 白居易集, fasc. 70, proofread and punctuated by Guxuejie 顧學頡, Zhonghua Book Company 中華書局, 1979, pp. 1475–1476.
[24] Cf. *The Corpus of Baijuyi* 白居易集, fasc. 71, pp. 1497–1498.

Paradise. The picture was nine feet long and three feet wide; the Amitābha Buddha is sitting in the center, while the entourages Avalokiteśvara 觀音 and Mahasthāma 勢至 are standing on both sides. They are surrounded by many devas. Pavilions, trees, waters, flowers and birds also appear in the scene. Baijuyi burned incense and worshiped in front of the picture, swearing to dedicate this merit to all sentient beings, wishing all oldies and patients like him to separate from misery and live in the Western Paradise. Finally, Baijuyi recited a hymn: "The Western Paradise is a pure land, there is no evil teachings and sufferings. Wish all oldies and Patients like me, to live together in the country of Amitābha Buddha."[25]

In the same month, Baijuyi prayed for afterlife to live in both Tuṣita Heaven and Western Paradise. Apparently, the two intentions were contradictory, thus indicating that he seemed to have a rather tolerant attitude toward religious beliefs; at least he was not a stickler for form.

People often cite a story to show that Baijuyi only believed in Buddhism, but was not interested in Taoism at all. It is recorded in *Taipingguangji* 太平廣記 (*Wide Gleanings Made in the Taiping Era*); the brief content is as follows:

During the Huichang 會昌 Era (841–846), a merchant ship was drifting for a month because of the fierce wind, eventually reaching a mountain, a wonderful place similar to the fairyland. The shipowner was warmly welcome by the local residents. He was led to meet a senior Taoist. The master told him that the place was named Penglai Mountain 蓬萊山, the abode of immortals. He invited the merchant to visit their residence, including dozens of buildings. One of the mansions was locked, but was cleaned carefully. The guide said, "This the mansion for Baijuyi. He is now still staying in China, so is absent here."

After a voyage of dozen days, the merchant returned to Zhejiang. He immediately reported this experience to Baijuyi. The latter wrote two poems to explain his religious belief: "Recently someone comes back from the Island, tells me that there are various buildings in the sea. One of the wonderful mansions, is said to prepare for me." The other poem is as follows: "I believe in Buddhism instead of Taoism, please do not misunderstand me. The residence I always pursue, is the Tuṣita Heaven rather than oceanic fairyland."[26]

---

[25] Cf. *ibid.*, pp. 1496–1497.
[26] Cf. *Taipingguangji* 太平廣記, fasc. 48, in *Sikuquanshu* 四庫全書, pp. 1043–243—1043–244.

Although whether this merchant had been to so-called Penglai Mountain is doubtful, the fact that Baijuyi wrote two poems about this story can be affirmed, for he compiled these poems into his collection of writings.[27] Nevertheless, it could not prove that Baijuyi only believed in Buddhism and was not interested in Taoism at all.

For example, his poem *Appreciation of Religious Practice* 味道 states that the major feature of his daily religious practice was as follows: "Seven chapters of *Immortals' Precepts* 真誥 discuss the celestial beings; while one volume of *Altar Sutra* 壇經 interprets the Buddhist truth" (七篇《真誥》論仙事, 一卷《壇經》說佛心).[28] The *Immortals' Precepts* was written by Taohongjing 陶弘景, a Taoist disciple living in the 5th–6th century. It consists of seven chapters, and is one of the important scriptures of Taoism, so it was used to represent all Taoist writings. As for the *Altar Sutra*, it is a record on the sermon preached by Huineng 慧能 on the Altar of Grand Brahmā Monastery 大梵寺 of Shaozhou 韶州. Huineng was the sixth generation master of the Zen Sect, so this *Altar Sutra* was likened to all Buddhist sutras, especially writings of the Zen Sect. Apparently, Baijuyi was interested in both Buddhism and Taoism.

Besides, Baijuyi once made an attempt on alchemy. His poem *Fail in Alchemy, Drunken alone* talked about his failure on alchemy, and mentioned alchemy terms Dansha 丹砂 (cinnabar) and Chanü 姹女 (girl); naturally, after his failure, he had to "dispel melancholy by drinks".[29] Alchemy is one of the main characteristics of Taoism, thus this poem shows Baijuyi's Taoist belief to some extent, though he possibly only did it out of curiosity. Nonetheless, it could be certain that Baijuyi believed in Buddhism, but did not reject other faiths.

For instance, Baijuyi often attended ceremonies which worshiped various deities of popular faiths. In autumn of 823, as the governor of Hangzhou 杭州, he offered up a sacrifice to a local deity Qiuwang 仇王, appealing to this deity to eliminate the scourge of tigers attacking people in recent years.[30] A month earlier, as the representative of the local government, Baijuyi sacrificed to the god of the Gaoting Temple 皋亭廟, praying for rain to mitigate drought. However, there was still no rain. The next month, he was forced to pray again to "the Northern Black Dragon"

---

[27] Cf. *The Corpus of Baijuyi* 白居易集, fasc. 36, p. 840.
[28] Cf. *ibid.*, fasc. 23, p. 517.
[29] Cf. *ibid.*, fasc. 33, p. 761.
[30] Cf. *ibid.*, fasc. 40, p. 900.

for rain.[31] Obviously, Baijuyi often held ceremonies to worship folk deities, this fact indicating the variety of his faiths.

Since Baijuyi did not believe only in Buddhism, there is not enough reason to deny the possibility of him writing a poem to talk about Manicheism.

(2) Baijuyi Lived in the Period when Manicheism Prevailed

The period Bajuyi lived in was exactly the so-called "Golden Age" of Manicheism. In this period, Manicheism was sheltered by the government, and was allowed to missionize openly. In addition, Baijuyi had written for the emperor letters to the Uighur Qaghan, mentioning the affairs involving the Manicheans, so it was impossible for him to be unaware of Manicheism. Such a circumstance shows, first, that Baijuyi ought to have been familiar with Manicheism; second, he had no any reason to be hostile to Manicheism, thereby it was impossible for him to refuse to write something about this religion.

In the middle of the third century, the Persian Mani founded the dualism religion of Manicheism, which borrowed many factors from Zoroastrianism, Christianity, Buddhism and folk beliefs of ancient Babylonia. Soon after, however, it was persecuted by Vahram I (r. 274–277), the Sasanian king; numerous followers fled from Persia, moving toward the West and East. Later, Manicheism prevailed eastward in Central Asia, and spread further to Siberia, Mongolia, Northeastern India and China. Roughly at the end of the seventh century, the reign of Wuzetian, Manicheism was officially introduced into China proper.

At the end of the reign of Xuanzong 玄宗, the so-called "Rebellion of An and Shi" 安史之亂 broke out. In order to regain the territory occupied by the rebels, Suzong 肅宗, the successor of Xuanzong, was forced to seek the support of the Uighur army; in return, the Tang government had to give them a lot of wealth and young girls. Finally, the Tang regime recovered the lost territory with the help of the Uighur forces; hence, the latter became the benefactor of China. Therefore, as the *State Religion* of the Uighur Khanate, Manicheism was preached freely in China; a number of Manichean monasteries were successively built interiorly.

Husanxing 胡三省 recorded, "According to *Tanghuiyao* 唐會要, fasc. 19, the Uighur Qaghan orders the Manicheans to preach in China. In lunar June 29 of the 3rd year (768) of Dali 大歷 Era, the Emperor built a

---

[31] Cf. *ibid.*, fasc. 40, pp. 901–902.

monastery for the Manicheans of Uighur, the inscription of the plaque is *Grand Cloud Light*. In lunar January of the 6th year (771) of Dali Era, the Emperor orders to build *Grand Cloud Light Monasteries* in Jinzhou 荊州, Hongzhou 洪州 and Yuezhou 越州 etc, one monastery per city."[32] Jingzhou, Yangzhou, Hongzhou and Yuezhou lie respectively in present provinces of Hubei, Jiangsu, Jiangxi and Zhejiang. Obviously, at that time Manicheism already spreads to the vast areas south of the Yangtze River. Naturally, there are also many Manichean monasteries in North China, for example, "In lunar January of the 2nd year (807) of Yuanhe 元和 Era, the Uighur envoy requests that build three Manichean monasteries in Henan Prefecture and Taiyuan Prefecture respectively. He is granted the permission."[33]

The Manicheans of the Uighur Khanate always maintained a close relationship with the ruling class; they were not only the adherents and preachers of Manicheism but also politicians in the Uighur regime. When *New History of the Tang* 新唐書 mentioned these Manicheans, it was asserted that "Qaghan governs the regime together with them."[34] Besides, *Old History of the Tang* 舊唐書 said that, in lunar December of the 8th year (813) of the Yuanhe Era, eight Manicheans of the Uighur Khanate were entertained by the government, and the prime ministers granted an interview to them. They discussed the affairs involved in the intermarriage between China and the Uighur Khanate. In lunar May of the 1st year (821) of the Changqing 長慶 Era, the prime minister, governors, princesses and Manicheans of the Uighur Khanate, totaling 573 persons, came to China to welcome and receive the Chinese princess, who was to marry the Uighur Qaghan. They were entertained warmly.[35]

Exactly because of the close relationship between the Manicheans and Uighur rulers, the former's fate changed along with that of the latter. A letter of the Chinese Emperor to the Uighur Qaghan displayed this fact clearly: "Before the Tianbao 天寶 Era (742–755), Manicheism is banned in China. Later, because Uighur Qaghans believe in it, the government allows it to circulate in China. Manicheans can preach freely in the basins of Yangtze River and Huai River 淮河. Recently, the alms provided by

---

[32] Cf. *Zizhitongjian* 資治通鑑, fasc. 237, p. 7638.
[33] Cf. *Cefuyuangui* 冊府元龜, fasc. 999, Zhonghua Book Company 中華書局, 1960, p. 11724.
[34] Cf. *Xintangshu* 新唐書, fasc. 217A, p. 6126.
[35] Cf. *Jiutangshu* 舊唐書, fasc. 195, pp. 5210–5211.

Chinese adherents are less than before because of the decline of Uighur regime, so the foreign Manicheans live arduously. Since the natives no more piously believe in this faith, you need not to stay there reluctantly. In order to keep your good livelihood, I allow you to continue missionary work in the two capitals and Taiyuan Prefecture, but stop staying around the areas south of Yangtze River. After your own country being peaceful, you may return here again."[36]

Apparently, in about one hundred years from the middle of the 8th century to the middle of the 9th century, taking advantage of the Uighur power, Manicheism developed rapidly in the mainland of China; this period was also the age when Baijuyi lived. That is to say, during that period, believing in Manicheism was not only legitimate but also "fashionable" and "glorious". The Uighur rulers were "benefactors" of the Tang regime; a majority of the Manicheans were "Western foreigners" or Sogdians, playing an important role in the Uighur government. As compared with the Manicheans in the Song Dynasty, the status of the Manichean believers of the Uighur era was much higher than the latter. Therefore, there was a good reason to speculate that Baijuyi possibly observed Manicheism objectively and scientifically, rather than discriminated against it.

(3) The White Dress and Religious Fast of Baijuyi
One of the features of Baijuyi's religious faiths was that he set Vimalakīrti as a model, and even likened himself to Vimalakīrti. The name "Vimalakīrti" literally means "undefiled reputation" or "good fame". He was a wealthy senior of Vaiśāli City in Middle India, and also a secular Buddhist, but a distinguished practitioner. It was said that his wisdom was superior, almost the same as that of Buddha, even beyond Bodhisattva. He lived in the secular world for the sake of saving all creatures from suffering.

When Baijuyi retired from the post of the minister of the ministry of justice, he wrote a poem, claiming himself as "Minister Bai, the senior of Vaiśāli City" (毗耶長者白尚書).[37] A similar instance was in his poem *Humming for Self* 自詠, which depicted the daily life of Baijuyi, and

---

[36] Cf. Lideyu 李德裕, *Huichangyipinji* 會昌一品集, fasc. 5, in *New Edition of Series Integration* 叢書集成新編, Book 59, Taibei: Xinwenfeng Book Company 新文豐出版公司, 1985, p. 31.

[37] Cf. *The Corpus of Baijuyi* 白居易集, fasc. 37, p. 844.

embodied his enjoyment of *Lay Buddhist*. He claimed that he was "a lay Buddhist in white dress, an intellectual immortal"; he "sometimes drinks, sometimes sings and sometimes sits in meditation." Just like Vimalakīrti, he did not abstain from drinking while practicing Buddhism.[38]

According to the Buddhist convention, the monks or nuns dressed in black, while the secular Buddhists dressed in white. Thus, "white dress" was generally used to refer to the lay Buddhists, and Vimalakīrti became a typical representative of "one who dresses in white". *Vimalakīrti Nirdeśa Sūtra* praised Vimalakīrti for dressing in white, but practicing like a monk; although he had a wife and children, and enjoyed secular life, he thoroughly comprehended the Buddhist doctrine.[39]

Though we may speculate that because of his worship of Vimalakīrti, Baijuyi gave himself an imitation of the title "Lay Buddhist Dresses in White" 白衣居士, the other reasons also ought to be noticed. For example, whether there was some relation between the white dress of Manicheism and that of Buddhism. I will discuss this topic in another paper.

Another feature of Baijuyi's faiths was "keeping fast frequently". As a Buddhist, even a lay believer, Baijuyi ought to have fasted on certain dates. However, his fast seemed to be too frequent, and the fast duration was unusually long. For example, his poem *Tranquil Life in the Month of Fast* 齋月靜居 said, "I always abstain from meat in the month of fast, and burn incense when sit in meditation" (葷腥每斷齋居月, 香火常親宴坐時).[40] Furthermore, his poem *The Long Month of Fast is Over* 長齋月滿 said, "I have kept fast already for thirty days, I can open the wine crock for drinking today" (齋宮前日滿三旬, 酒榼今朝一拂塵).[41] Evidently, these two poems show that the fast duration was as long as a month.

Interestingly, it seems that there were several lengthy fast months every year or at least two times in the first half of the year. According to the depiction of Baijuyi's poem, there was a lengthy fast in lunar May: "I have great entertainment in Spring, while practice Buddhism earnestly

---

[38] Cf. ibid., fasc. 31, pp. 701–702. The Chinese text is as follows: "白衣居士紫芝仙, 半醉半歌半坐禪。今日維摩兼飲酒, 當時綺季不請錢。等閒池上留賓客, 隨事燈前有管弦。但問此身銷得否? 分司氣味不論年。"
[39] Cf. Zhiqian 支謙, *Vimalakīrti Nirdeśa Sūtra* 佛說維摩詰經, fasc. A, *Tripitaka Edited in Taisho Era* 大正新修大藏經, Book 14, No. 474, p. 521.
[40] Cf. *The Corpus of Baijuyi* 白居易集, fasc. 26, p. 582.
[41] Cf. ibid., fasc. 33, p. 750.

in May …. After the meditation, my mind becomes purer; owing to the dietary fast, I lost my weight. I not only forget the taste of meat, but is also forced to abstain from intercourse with woman" (三春多放逸，五月暫修行。… 禪后心彌寂，齋來體更輕。不唯忘肉味，兼擬滅風情).[42] In the long title of this poem, "Lengthy Fast of the May" is mentioned.

Obviously, this lengthy fast was set in lunar May. For the duration of the fast, one had to be vegetarian, sit in meditation, abstain from sexual life and even avoid meeting guests. Such a lengthy fast seemed to be also set in lunar February to March. Another poem of Baijuyi states in the title that "the fast ends in the 5th of March"; the verse says, "The fast begins at last month and the ceremony finishes yesterday" (前月事齋戒，昨日散道場).[43] So, the duration of the fast was probably from the beginning of lunar February to the beginning of lunar March.

Indeed, there were rules of three "Lengthy Fast Month" in Buddhist regulations, namely, lunar January, lunar May and lunar September. According to Buddhist legend, accompanied by the Devas, the Lord of Dēvas inspected whole world with a large precious mirror, recording all good works and evil deeds done by the people. By the mirror, he shone the Southern Continent in the first month each year, and he took turns shining the Eastern, Northern and Western Continents, respectively, in the 2nd, 3rd and 4th month; in the 5th and 9th month, he shone the Southern Continent again. China is located on the Southern Continent, namely, the so-called "Jambu dvipa", so the people there endeavored to do more good works in lunar January, lunar May and lunar September.

In the light of these regulations, the fast kept by Baijuyi seemed to not be a completely Buddhist one, because he kept "lengthy fast" in lunar May, but kept another "lengthy fast" in lunar February and lunar March instead of lunar January. Besides, in addition to the "lengthy fast 長齋", Baijuyi also kept "ten fasts 十齋", just as he claimed in his *A Note on the Painting of Maitreya's Ascent* 畫彌勒上生幀記 that he had "kept ten fasts and observed eight precepts 八戒 for many years." "Ten Fasts" meant keeping fast on ten single days of every month, namely, keeping fast on the 1st, 8th, 14th, 15th, 18th, 23rd, 24th, 28th, 29th and 30th day. If people kept fast on these dates, recited sutras in front of the Buddhas, Bodhisattvas and other deities, they would be rich in food and clothing, and escape all suffering and disasters.

---

[42] Cf. *ibid.*, fasc. 34, p. 772.
[43] Cf. *ibid.*, fasc. 36, p. 825.

Thus, the writings of Baijuyi showed that he seemed to be very keen on keeping fast. He kept both "lengthy fast" and "ten fasts", spending at least half a year in keeping fasts annually. Baijuyi was a high official and a famous poet, and was fond of wine, so such a long duration of fast keeping was not an easy life for him. Many of his poems reflected his great joy at the ending of a fast; it appeared to hint at a certain *formism* of his fast. Nevertheless, keeping a vegetarian fast was a main feature of Baijuyi's faiths, while it was also the characteristic of Manicheism. Therefore, it was possible that owing to the similar vegetarian fast, Baijuyi became interested in Manicheism, thereby writing a poem on this foreign religion.

(4) A Speculation on *the Poem on Manicheism*
In order to judge whether this poem was possibly written by Baijuyi, we will examine its content first.

This poem is rather short, consisting of forty Chinese characters and being divided into eight lines of verse, but it truly and vividly depicts the essential doctrines and the features of Manicheism. The first and second lines say the following: "As the *Story of Suristan* shows, Manichean doctrine is wonderful 靜覽蘇鄰傳, 摩尼道可敬." They clearly indicate the locality where the religion was founded, and the name of this religion and its founder. In its earlier period, Taoism once borrowed teachings and ideas from Manicheism, thereby leaving some records about Manicheism in Taoist scriptures. For instance, the *Laozi Civilizes the Barbarians Scripture* mentions that Mani 摩尼 was born in Sulin 蘇鄰 Country (Suristan), and founded Manicheism 摩尼教 later, and so on. Therefore, in Chinese literatures, "Sulin Country 蘇鄰國" usually refers to the hometown of Mani or the place where Manicheism was initially founded. The word 摩尼 may refer to both *Manicheism* and its founder's name *Mani*.

From the 3rd line to the 6th line, the essential teachings of Manicheism are briefly described. According to the Manichean creation myth, two principles of Light and Darkness have existed from the beginning and are always opposite each other. Later, the dark devils invade the Light Kingdom. Though the light forces once failed, numerous light elements are devoured by the dark devils; they defeat the enemy soon afterward, and create the sun, moon, heavens, earths and other celestial bodies made from the corpses of the dark devils and light elements devoured by them. In addition, Mani often claimed to be the "messenger of God". He is the fifth messenger after other four distinguished religion leaders, such as Buddha, Zaradusht, Jesus[44] and Brahmā.

Naturally, the word 五佛 in this poem is regarded by others as "five Buddhas" instead of "the fifth Buddha". The former refers to the light elements emitted by the supreme Light God; they fight against the dark devils in the form of five sons of the Primary Man, and are devoured by the devils. They are the five elements of the Light, and are air, wind, light, water and fire; thus, they are usually called "five light elements 五明子", "five light Buddhas 五明佛" and "five Buddhas 五佛".

Nevertheless, either "the fifth Buddha" or "five Buddhas" was the important Manichean term, so these four lines of verse correctly phrase the fundamental doctrines of Manicheism: "The two principles are always fighting, the Fifth Buddha inherits the light. The sun and moon must be revered, they are created by the universe 二宗陳寂默, 五佛繼光明。日月爲資敬, 乾坤認所生."

The 7th and 8th lines of verse are rather significant: "As for keeping the fasts, they are similar to that of the Buddhism 若論齋潔志, 釋子好齊名." Apparently, the poet noticed the strict fast regulation of the Manicheism, thinking it could be comparable to the fast precept of Buddhism. The vegetarian fast is indeed an important feature of Manicheism, especially the Sinicized Manicheism "Light Religion 明教". Coincidentally, Baijuyi was also a pious fast keeper, so it was not unnatural for him to pay attention to the Manichean fast precept, though the two faiths had different reasons for their own fasts.

As mentioned above, Zhipan 志磐 asserted that it was impossible for Baijuyi to write the poem about the heresy Manicheism, because he only believed in Buddhism. It is actually an erroneous opinion. First, Baijuyi did not evidently "only believe in Buddhism", but had interest in many religious faiths, as I have noted above. Second, in the period when Baijuyi lived, Manicheism was sheltered by the Chinese government, rather than being accused as an illegal heresy, just like the "Light Religion" in the

---

[44] About the composition of "Five Buddhas", there were several statements. Based on the Chinese materials discovered recently, Maxiaohe thinks the combination of Nārāyaṇa, Zardrušt, Śākyamuni, Jesus and Mani is comparatively correct. Nārāyaṇa is also called Brahmā, the creator god of Brahmanism. Cf. Maxiaohe 馬小鶴, *Studies on Xiapu Documents* 霞浦文書研究, Lanzhou University Press 蘭州大學出版社, 2014, pp. 196–219.

Song Dynasty. In other words, at that time, anyone could observe and worship Manicheism without any danger.

Finally, if this poem was really written by Manicheans in the name of Baijuyi, it would greatly praise Manicheism and even claim Baijuyi to believe in this faith. However, the truth is that the poem just briefly summarized the main teachings and features of Manicheism; it had neither laudatory words about Manicheism nor any hint of Baijuyi believing in this religion. Therefore, a logical conjecture may be that under the circumstance of Manicheism being popular, Baijuyi wrote a poem about it, but had not then collected it in his *Corpus*, because he did not really value this faith.

In summary, we can give the following conclusion. The period when Baijuyi lived was exactly the only "Golden Age" for oriental Manicheism. At that time, Manicheism was sheltered and supported by the Chinese government, and did not suffer from discrimination. Besides, in order to preach more easily, Manicheans intentionally emphasized their Buddhist color, and thus were usually regarded as a sect of Buddhism.

Since Baijuyi had the characteristic of being "multi-faith", generally speaking, it was impossible for him to absolutely refuse to be acquainted with a new faith, especially when it was similar to Buddhism. In addition, Baijuyi worshiped Maitreya, adored Vimalakīrti and kept fast strictly, which are characteristics somewhat similar to that of Manicheism in form. This made Baijuyi more willing to understand Manicheism.

Hence, it was quite natural that Baijuyi occasionally wrote a short poem to outline objectively the teachings and features of Manicheism, but did not claim to believe in this faith. Perhaps the later generations ought to appreciate *Fozutongji* 佛祖統紀 for preserving a valuable piece of information. This poem was indeed written by Baijuyi, and displays the influence of Manicheism on the intellectual class of the Tang Dynasty.

Index of Chinese Literatures
漢語文獻拼音索引

Anlushanshiji
   安祿山事跡, *Story of Anlushan*, written by Yaorunen 姚汝能, punctuated and proofread by Zengyifen 曾貽芬, in *Collection of Historical Records of the Tang and Song* 唐宋史料筆記叢刊, Zhonghua Book Company 中華書局, 2006.

Baijuyiji
   白居易集, *The Corpus of Baijuyi*, proofread and punctuated by Guxuexie 顧學頡, Zhonghua Book Company 中華書局, 1979.

Beishi
   北史, *History of the Northern Dynasties*, Zhonghua Book Company 中華書局, 1974.

Cefuyuangui
   冊府元龜, *Outstanding models from the storehouse literature*, Zhonghua Book Company 中華書局, 1960.

Chaoyeqianzai
   朝野僉載, *Draft Notes from the Court and the Country*, proofread and punctuated by Henghe 恆鶴, in *Tangwudaibijixiaoshuodaguan* 唐五代筆記小說大觀, Shanghai Classics Publishing House 上海古籍出版社, 2000.

Congshujichengchubian
　　叢書集成初編, *Preliminary Edition of Series Integration*, Xinwenfeng Publishing Company 新文豐出版公司, 1985.

Congshujichengxinbian
　　叢書集成新編, *New Edition of Series Integration*, Xinwenfeng Publishing Company 新文豐出版公司, 1985.

Datangchuanyeqijuzhu
　　大唐創業起居注, *Records of the Tang Dynastic Founder's Daily Activities*, written by Wendaya 溫大雅, punctuated and proofread by Lijiping 李季平 and Lixihou 李錫厚, Shanghai Classics Publishing House 上海古籍出版社, 1983.

Datangxinyu
　　大唐新語, *A New Narration of the Great Tang*, written by Liusu 劉肅, punctuated and proofread by Xudenan 許德楠 and Lidingxia 李鼎霞, Zhonghua Book Company 中華書局, 1984.

Datangxiyueji
　　大唐西域記, *Great Tang Records on the Western Regions*, in Ruichuanming 芮傳明, *Datangxiyuejiyizhu* 大唐西域記譯注 (*Translation and Annotation on Great Tang Records on the Western Regions*, Zhonghua Book Company 中華書局, 2019.

Dazhengxinxiudazangjing
　　大正新修大藏經, *Taisho Revised Tripitaka*, edited by Takakusu Junjiro 高楠順次郎 and others, Tokyo, 1934.

Dongjingmenghualu
　　東京夢華錄, *The Records of the Former Eastern Capital*, in Yiyongwen 伊永文, *Dongjingmenghualujianzhu* 東京夢華錄箋注 (*Comments on The Records of the Former Eastern Capital*), Zhonghua Book Company 中華書局, 2006.

Fengshiwenjianji
　　封氏聞見記, *Records of the Hearsays by Mr. Feng*, in Zhaozhenxin 趙貞信.

Fengshiwenjianjijiaozhu 封氏聞見記校註 (*Corrections and Comments on Fengshiwenjianji*), Zhonghua Book Company 中華書局, 2005.

Foguangdacidian
佛光大辭典, *Foguang Dictionary of Buddhism*, Taibei: Foguang Publishing House 佛光出版社, 1989.

Hanshu
漢書, *History of the Former Han*, Zhonghua Book Company 中華書局, 1962.

Houhanshu
後漢書, *History of the Later Han*, Zhonghua Book Company 中華書局, 1965.

Jingkangxiangsuzaji
靖康緗素雜記, *Miscellanies of the Classical Literatures*, written by Huangchaoying 黃朝英, punctuated and proofread by Wuqiming 吳企明, Shanghai Classics Publishing House 上海古籍出版社, 1986.

Jinshi
金史, *History of the Jin*, Zhonghua Book Company 中華書局, 1975.

Jinshu
晉書, *History of the Jin*, Zhonghua Book Company 中華書局, 1974.

Jiutangshu
舊唐書, *Old History of the Tang*, Zhonghua Book Company 中華書局, 1975.

Jiuwudaishi
舊五代史, *Old History of the Five Dynasties*, Zhonghua Book Company 中華書局, 1976.

Lüshichunqiu
呂氏春秋, *The Spring and Autumn of Lübuwei*, commentated by Gaoyou 高誘, in *Zhuzijicheng* 諸子集成 (*Philosophers Integration*), Book VI, Shanghai Book-shop Press 上海書店, 1986.

Mengxibitan

夢溪筆談, *Brush Talks from Dream Brook*, written by Shenkuo 沈括, tr. by Wanghong 王宏 and Zhaozheng 趙崢, in *Library of Chinese Classics* 大中華文庫, Sichuan People Publishing House 四川人民出版社, 2008.

Minghuangzalu

明皇雜錄, *A Miscellaneous Record of the Emperor Ming*, in *Tangwudaibijixiaoshuodaguan* 唐五代筆記小說大觀, Shanghai Classics Publishing House 上海古籍出版社, 2000.

Monijiaodunhuangtulufanwenshuyisheyuyanjiu

摩尼教敦煌吐魯番文書譯釋與研究, *Translation, Annotation and Study on the Manichean Documents Discovered in Dunhuang and Turpan*, written by Ruichuanming 芮傳明, Lanzhou University Press 蘭州大學出版社, 2014.

Monijiaojiqidongjian

摩尼教及其東漸, *Manicheism and Its Spreading Eastward*, written by Linwushu 林悟殊, Zhonghua Book Company 中華書局, 1987.

Mutianzizhuan

穆天子傳, *Tale of King Mu, Son of Heaven*, in *Sikuquanshu* 四庫全書, Book 1042, Taibei: Commercial Press 商務印書館, 1983.

Qingsuogaoyi

青瑣高議, *Comment on the Various Historical Records*, written by Liufu 劉斧, Shanghai Classics Publishing House 上海古籍出版社, 1983.

Quantangshi

全唐詩, *The General Anthology of Tang Poetry*, Zhonghua Book Company 中華書局, 1960.

Sanguozhi

三國志, *The Record of the History of the Three Kingdoms*, Zhonghua Book Company 中華書局, 1959.

Shanhaijing
    山海經, *Stories of Mountains and Seas*, commentated by Guopu 郭璞, in *Sikuquanshu* 四庫全書, Book 1042, Taibei 臺北: The Commercial Press 商务印书馆, 1983.

Shenyijing
    神異經, *Miraculous Stories*, in *Sikuquanshu* 四庫全書, Book 1042, Taibei 臺北: The Commercial Press 商务印书馆, 1983.

Shiji
    史記, *The Records of the Grand Historian*, Zhonghua Book Company 中華書局, 1959.

Shiyiji
    拾遺記, *Supplementary Notes*, collated and annotated by Qizhiping 齊志平, Zhonghua Book Company 中華書局, 1981.

Sikuquanshu
    四庫全書, *Complete Library of the Four Branches*, Taibei 臺北: Commercial Press 商務印書舘, 1983.

Songshi
    宋史, *History of the Song*, Zhonghua Book Company 中華書局, 1975.

Suishu
    隋書, *History of the Sui*, Zhonghua Book Company 中華書局, 1973.

Tangguoshibu
    唐國史補, *A Supplement of the History of the Tang*, written by Lizhao 李肇, Shanghai Classics Publishing House 上海古籍出版社, 1979.

Tanghuiyao
    唐會要, *Important Documents of the Tang*, Shanghai Classics Publishing House 上海古籍出版社, 1991.

Tangwudaibijixiaoshuodaguan
    唐五代筆記小說大觀, *Collection of the Notes and Novels in the Tang and the Five Dynasties*, Shanghai Classics Publishing House 上海古籍出版社, 2000.

Tangyulin
唐語林, *A Collection Narrating the Tang*, in Zhouxunchu 周勛初, *Tangyulinjiaozheng* 唐語林校證 (*A Correction and Study on A Collection Narrating the Tang*), Zhonghua Book Company 中華書局, 1987.

Tongdian
通典, *Encyclopaedic History of Institutions*, Zhejiang Classics Publishing House 浙江古籍出版社, 2000.

Tujuejishi
突厥集史, *A Comprehensive History of the Turks*, written by Cenzhongmian 岑仲勉, Zhonghua Book Company 中華書局, 1958.

Weishu
魏書, *History of the Wei*, Zhonghua Book Company, 1974.

Xiapuwenshuyanjiu
霞浦文書研究, *Studies on Xiapu Documents*, written by Maxiaohe 馬小鶴, Lanzhou University Press 蘭州大學出版社, 2014.

Xintangshu
新唐書, *New History of the Tang*, Zhonghua Book Company 中華書局, 1975.

Xinwudaishi
新五代史, *New History of the Five Dynasties*, Zhonghua Book Company 中華書局, 1974.

Yiqiejingyinyi
一切經音義, *Notes on Buddhist Sutras*, in *Zhengxuyiqiejingyinyi* 正續一切經音義 (*Notes on Buddhist Sutras and the Continuation of the Notes on Buddhist Sutras*), Shanghai Classics Publishing House 上海古籍出版社, 1986.

Yiwenleiju
藝文類聚, *Collection of Literature Arranged by Categories*, punctuated and proofread by Wangshaoying 汪紹楹, Shanghai Classics Publishing House 上海古籍出版社, 1982.

Youyangzazu
酉陽雜俎, *A miscellany of Ancient History*, written by Duanchengshi 段成式, punctuated and proofread by Fangnansheng 方南生, Zhonghua Book Company 中華書局, 1981.

Zhanguoce
戰國策, *Stratagems of the Warring States*, recorded by Liuxiang 劉向, Shanghai Classics Publishing House, 1985.

Zhenguanzhengyao
貞觀政要 *A Digest on the Governance of Zhenguan*, written by 吳兢 Wujing, Shanghai Classics Publishing House 上海古籍出版社, 1975.

Zhongxijiaotongshiliaohuibian
中西交通史料彙編, *A Compilation of Historical Materials on the Intercourses between China and the Occident*, written by Zhangxinglang 張星烺, proofread by Zhujieqin 朱傑勤, Zhonghua Book Company 中華書局, 1977.

Zhongxiwenshebijiao
中西紋飾比較, *The Comparison of Symbols between China and the Occident*, written by Ruichuanming 芮傳明 & Yutaishan 余太山, Shanghai Classics Publishing House 上海古籍出版社, 1995.

Zhoushu
周書, *History of the Zhou*, Zhonghua Book Company 中華書局, 1971.

Zhushujinian
竹書紀年, *Bamboo Annals*, in Fangshiming & Wangxiuling 方诗铭、王修齡, *Gubenzhushujinianjizheng* 古本竹書紀年輯証 (*A Collection and Research on Bamboo Annals of the Ancient Edition*), Shanghai Classics Publishing House 上海古籍出版社, 1981.

Zixiaji
资暇集, *Materials for Chat*, written by Likuangai 李匡乂, in *Sikuquanshu* 四庫全書, Book 850, Taibei: The Commercial Press 商務印書館, 1986.

Zizhitongjian
資治通鑑, *Comprehensive Mirror for Aid in Governance*, Zhonghua Book Company 中華書局, 1956.

Zuozhuan
左傳, *Commentary on Spring and Autumn Annals by Zuoqiuming*, in *Interpretation on the Thirteen Classics* 十三經注疏, Book II, Zhonghua Book Company 中華書局, 1980.

Index

A

Ahriman, 291, 337
Ahura Mazda, 290–291, 297
Alani, 130–131
Amu Darya, 58–59, 64, 113, 154, 163
Amu River, 156–157, 160–161, 164–165, 171–172, 254
Anagui 阿那瓌, 88–89
Anchonghui 安重誨, 233–234, 240
Anchongrong 安重榮, 232
Ancongjin 安從進, 230–231, 233
Anjinquan 安金全, 236–238
Anleguo 安樂國, 356
Anlushan 安祿山, 65, 85–86, 95, 189, 198, 200, 221, 242–243, 245, 247, 249–252, 258
Annuopantuo 安諾槃陁, 206–207
Anqing 安慶, 227, 230
An-Shi Rebellion, 65–66, 250
arani, 275–276
Asena, 128
Asmussen, Jes. P., 149–150
Āz, 289–294, 296–301, 303, 336

B

Baiyi 白義, 4–6
Beihu 北胡, 1–2, 30, 69
blacksmiths, 133–134

Blood Sweat Horse 汗血馬, 5, 8, 12–13, 15, 17–18, 30
bodhi tree, 312
Bögü Khan, 214–215
Bögü Qaghan, 218
Bögü Qayan, 216–217, 219
Buddha nature, 318–320, 322
Bukhara, 152, 158, 163–164
Bumin Qaghan, 58, 134
Byzantines, 57–58, 62, 121, 135

C

Caomiaoda 曹妙達, 192–194
Caspian Sea, 60, 63–64, 128, 130–134, 138–139, 144–145, 156–158, 177–178
Chicaishimo 吃菜事魔, 328–333
Chiyou 蚩尤, 286
cintāmaṇi, 313

D

Dahan 大漢, 115–120, 122, 125
Dajia 大家, 122–125
Daoli 盜驪, 4–5
Darouzhi 大月氏, 81, 160, 167–168, 172, 175
Donghu 東胡, 1, 19, 21

E

El Qaghan, 211, 251
Ephthalites, 161, 208

F

Faqing 法慶, 324–325, 327–328, 347
fast, 372–377
fire pattern, 278–279
forbidding killing, 333, 335, 337, 347
foreignization 胡化, 189, 197–200
foreign music, 190–192, 196–197, 199
foreign tribes 胡部, 233, 241
foster son, 251–254, 256

G

Genghis Khan, 111, 164
gnosis, 320
Grand Cloud Light, 222
grape wine, 182
Great Cloud Sutra, 353–357, 359–360, 362
Great Cloud Temples, 352
greedy demon, 281, 289, 293–300, 303

H

Hephthalites, 40, 58–59, 160
horse dance, 35–36, 185
Huahujing 化胡經, 327
Hualiu 華騮, 4, 6
hufu 胡服, 22–24, 26–30
hufuqishe 胡服騎射, 19–20, 22–23
Huhanye 呼韓邪, 46, 51–52, 56, 69, 77–79, 94, 96, 191
Huilin 慧琳, 272
huji 胡姬, 184–185
huma 胡馬, 23, 29, 35
Humbaba, 287, 302
huntuo 渾脫, 99, 101–106, 109
huntuo dance, 106–109
huntuo hat, 106–109
hutengwu 胡騰舞, 201
huxuanwu 胡旋舞, 200–201

I

intermarriage policy, 72, 75–76, 95
Išbara Qaghan, 54, 137
Issyk-Kul, 155
Istami Qaghan, 58–65, 208–209

J

janissary, 255–257
Jesus, 313–314
Jiehu 羯胡, 248
Jieyou 解憂, 81
jimi 羈縻, 45–46
jiuhuzi 酒胡子, 186–188
jiujiahu 酒家胡, 180–182, 184–185, 188–189

K

Kang 康, 179, 198, 251
Kangju 康居, 17, 165–166, 170–172, 175–176, 179, 288
Kangkunlun 康昆侖, 195–196
Kangshaoli 康鞘利, 44, 210
Kangsumi 康蘇密, 212
Kangyuanzi 康願子, 242
Karakhan, 163–164
Khazars, 64, 131, 135–140, 173–174, 178
Khosrow, 58–59, 63–64
Khwarizm, 164
King Mu of Zhou 周穆王, 3–4, 6–7, 11, 19
King Wuling of Zhao 趙武靈王, 19, 22, 24, 26
Kula, 6–7
Kullar, 255–256
kumyss, 102
kutur, 105–106
Kuwabara Jitsuzo, 114

L

Land Silk Road, 156
light element, 315–316, 319, 336–343, 346–347, 357, 376
light hall 明堂, 360–363
light nature, 340, 342, 346
lightning, 275
Liguangli 李廣利, 13–17, 172
Loujing 婁敬, 46–47, 70–72, 93, 95
Lüshichunqiu 呂氏春秋, 282–285, 288, 296, 299

M

Mahān Qaghan, 41–42, 90
Maitreya, 352–353, 362, 364, 366–367, 377
Mani, 305–306, 312–318, 321–322, 332, 334–335, 337, 365, 370, 375
Maniakh, 59–62, 208–209
Maṇi Light Buddha, 306–307, 321
Maritime Silk Road, 157–158
Maxiaohe 馬小鶴, 305
Mesembria, 276–277
Modu 冒頓, 25, 46, 71–73, 91, 93, 119
Možag, 218, 221

N

Nine Clans of Zhaowu 九姓昭武, 179, 192, 227–229, 232, 234, 239
Ningguo 寧國, 86–87, 96

O

Oasis Silk Road, 156–158
Old Turkic, 142–144, 259

P

pearl, 307–310, 312–317, 319–320, 322, 361
Peiju 裴矩, 53, 80, 83, 157–158, 210
pipa, 190–191, 194–196
polo, 30–35
Pushao 蒲捎, 6, 18

Q

Qaghan, 61
Qianjin Princess 千金公主, 90
Qimin Qaghan, 54–55, 83

R

reciprocal trade, 45, 48
redemptive killing, 329, 347–348
Rouran 柔然, 58, 88–90, 92, 134, 139, 146, 161, 205

S

sa:g, 259–260
Sage 薩葛, 227, 230
Saluzi 颯露紫, 7–8
Samarkand, 152–158, 162–164
Sanmiao 三苗, 283, 288–289
Sanskrit, 270
sauwastika, 270
Shadpit Qaghan, 43–45, 85, 210
Shanhaijing 山海經, 283, 286–288
Shapur I, 160, 318
Shatuo 沙陀, 225–228, 230, 235–236
she-wolf, 129, 146
Shijiantang 史建瑭, 238–240
Shijingtang 石敬塘, 228–229, 231–232, 234–236, 238, 240
Shiratori Kurakichi, 1, 114, 129, 135, 246
silk exportation, 39–40, 56, 65
silk–horse trade, 65, 68, 95
Simocatta, Theophylactus, 112–113, 121, 139
Sinor, Denis, 206
Six Foreign Prefectures, 212
Soghd, 151–153, 165, 168, 171–172, 174–175, 178, 231

solak, 259–260
Son Generals 子將, 253
Śrivatsa, 264, 272–273, 280
Steppe Silk Road, 60–61, 63, 156–158
sun and moon, 357–359, 376
Sunzuoyun 孫作雲, 284–286
Suristan, 375
Suyi 粟弋, 151, 165–178, 182
swastika, 263–264, 266–269, 271–280
Syr Darya, 59, 177
Syr River, 153, 155, 157, 160, 162, 165, 171

T
Tabγač, 112–113, 115–116, 120–122, 125
Taohuashi 桃花石, 111, 114, 122
Taoism, 326–327, 332, 352, 368
Taotie 饕餮, 281–289, 295–304
Tardu Qaghan, 63, 65
Tarqan, 140
Taspar Qaghan, 41, 94
Telebiao 特勒驃, 9, 11
Tenth Grade Bodhisattva, 324–325
The Blood Sweat Horse, 11
Tibetans, 87
Tong Yabγu, 140, 142
triskèles, 276, 278
Tujue 突厥, 121, 127
Turxanthus, 63

V
vegetarians, 330–331, 334, 348
Vimalakīrti, 372–373, 377

W
Wangzhaojun 王昭君, 77–79, 94, 96, 191
Wencheng Princess, 97

Western Barbarians, 149–150, 179, 183
Western Foreigners, 192, 222
Western Liao, 164
Western Paradise, 367–368
Western Sea, 40, 128–130, 145–146
white dress, 373
wonton, 99, 101, 105, 109
Wusun 烏孫, 15, 51, 80–81, 92–93, 96, 173, 175, 191, 226
Wuzetian 武則天, 123, 199, 264–265, 277, 352–353, 355, 357–363

X
Xihu 西胡, 1, 29–30, 179
Xijun 細君, 50–51, 81, 96, 191
Xuehuaiyi 薛懷義, 353, 363–364

Y
Yancai 奄蔡, 131, 166–171, 173, 176–178, 288
Yangdi 煬帝, 52–56, 79–80, 83, 123, 198, 210
Yangximei 楊希枚, 284–285, 288, 302
yeluohe 曳落河, 245–246, 248–254, 258–260
Yili River, 81, 176
Yinxi 尹喜, 325–327
Yueku 月窟, 37

Z
Zarafshan River, 152, 154–155, 158–159, 161, 177
Zemarchus, 61–62, 135, 144, 158, 209
Zhangqian 張騫, 11, 50, 55, 80–81, 117, 129, 160, 171, 196
Zhangxinglang 張星烺, 115, 251
Zhangxun 章巽, 115, 120

Zhao 罌, 358
Zhaowu 昭武, 153, 200
Zhejie 柘羯, 245–251, 253–254, 258–260
Zhizhi 郅支, 78–79, 175

Zoroastrianism, 165, 289–291, 296–297, 300, 303, 313, 330, 370
Zuozhuan 左傳, 281, 283–284, 288, 295, 299

www.ingramcontent.com/pod-product-compliance
Lightning Source LLC
Chambersburg PA
CBHW050526300426
44113CB00012B/1967